IMPERIALISM, POWER, AND IDENTITY

MIRIAM S. BALMUTH LECTURES IN ANCIENT HISTORY AND ARCHAEOLOGY

The Miriam S. Balmuth lectures are delivered annually at Tufts University through generous funding provided by the family and friends of Miriam S. Balmuth, professor of classics and art history at Tufts for more than forty years. The lectures are intended to explore the continuing relationship between antiquity and the contemporary world.

IMPERIALISM, POWER, AND IDENTITY

Experiencing the Roman Empire

David J. Mattingly

PRINCETON UNIVERSITY PRESS

PRINCETON AND OXFORD

Copyright © 2011 Princeton University Press

Published by Princeton University Press, 41 William Street, Princeton,
New Jersey 08540
In the United Kingdom: Princeton University Press, 6 Oxford Street,
Woodstock, Oxfordshire OX20 1TW

press.princeton.edu

Second printing, and first paperback printing, with a new preface by the author, 2014
Paperback ISBN 978-0-691-16017-7

The Library of Congress has cataloged the cloth edition of this book as follows

Mattingly, D. J.
   Imperialism, power, and identity : experiencing the Roman empire / David J. Mattingly.
     p. cm. — (Miriam S. Balmuth lectures in ancient history and archaeology)
   Includes bibliographical references and index.
   ISBN 978-0-691-14605-8 (cloth)
1. Rome—History—Empire, 30 B.C.-476 A.D. 2. Rome—Foreign relations—
30 B.C.–476 A.D. 3. Roman provinces—Administration. 4. Rome—Ethnic relations.
5. Romans—Ethnic identity. 6. Acculturation—Rome. 7. Imperialism. 8. Power (Social
sciences) I. Title.
   DG271.M183 2011
   937'.06—dc22   20102467

British Library Cataloging-in-Publication Data is available

This book has been composed in Sabon and Penumbra

10 9 8 7 6 5 4 3 2

In loving memory of Erica Mattingly
21 April 1929–31 July 2008

CONTENTS

LIST OF ILLUSTRATIONS

Illustration credits are noted in the captions where individuals or organizations have kindly granted copyright permission. Other illustrations are either my own photographs, were specially drawn for this book, or were originally produced for projects in which I have played a leading role—the Fazzan Project (FP), the UNESCO Libyan Valley Survey (ULVS), and the Wadi Faynan Landscape Survey (WFLS). In this regard, I would like to pay particular thanks to the following for permissions to reproduce various figures: Graeme Barker (figs. 6.3, 7.4–7.6, 7.8–7.11), Hella Eckardt (fig. 8.9), Susan Gilmour (figs. 2.3–2.4); John Grattan (figs. 7.10–7.12), Muftah Hdad (fig. 2.7), Simon James (fig. 1.6), Mary Harrsch (fig. 4.7), Chris Riddell (fig. 8.1), and Roger Tomlin (fig. 8.8). Thanks are also due to the following artists who produced maps and plans from my roughs: Debbie Miles Williams (figs. 1.1, 1.3–1.4, 2.1, 6.1, 6.4, 7.1, 8.5–8.6, 9.1–9.2, 9.10), Joe Skinner (figs. 1.2 and 3.2), Mike Hawkes (figs. 2.5 and 7.8), Paul Newson (figs. 7.6 and 7.9), Dora Kemp (figs. 7.4 and 7.6), and Alison Wilkins (fig. 6.5). Mark Kurtz kindly helped me source and obtain copyright permissions for a number of other illustrations.

LIST OF TABLES

FOREWORD

The Miriam S. Balmuth Lectureship in the Department of Classics at Tufts University was established in 2005 through the vision, generosity, and support of the family and friends of Miriam S. Balmuth, professor of classics, archaeology, and art history at Tufts from 1962 to 2004. Its purpose is to explore the continuing relevance of the study of antiquity to the modern world. Professor David Mattingly's inaugural lectures, Experiencing Empire: Power and Identity in the Roman World, delivered in April 2006 and published here in expanded form, affirms the merit of a lectureship dedicated to this purpose. Issues of power and identity lie at the core of our interest in the Roman Empire. From the late nineteenth century until the end of the Second World War, Roman rule and the role it played in influencing the identity of the peoples of the empire was viewed in positive terms, reflecting the mostly favorable views of imperialism and colonialism held by classical scholars throughout this period. But with the breakup of the European empires after World War II, assessments of Roman imperialism began to shift, albeit rather cautiously. Indeed, as Mattingly demonstrates in these lectures, classical historians and archaeologists have remained surprisingly hesitant to abandon entirely visions of the Roman Empire from the age of imperialism. His call, for example, to replace the outdated imperial-age concept of Romanization in favor of an approach emphasizing the insights provided by postcolonial studies is a bold attempt to transform the terms of the debate on the meaning of the Roman Empire in the contemporary world.

Mattingly backs up his call for a new vocabulary for interpreting the Roman imperial experience by applying a powerful postcolonial perspective to a diverse array of topics in the history of the empire—the exploitation of landscapes and resources, sexual relations, art, family values, native societies—to create a new and challenging vision of Roman power and imperialism. The empire evoked in these lectures is populated by people whose lives are severely challenged and exploited but also enhanced through their encounters with Roman power, and whose "Roman" identity, as a consequence, is as diverse and localized as we might have every reason to expect from an empire that stretched from the North Sea to the Sahara and the Atlantic to Mesopotamia.

It is with great pleasure, therefore, that I thank David Mattingly for his courage and conviction in preparing the first Miriam S. Balmuth

Lectures. They represent an exemplary template on which to build a tradition of scholarship at Tufts that will strengthen the intellectual, cultural, and moral bonds that continue to link antiquity with the contemporary world.

R. Bruce Hitchner
Professor and Chair
Department of Classics
Tufts University

My Roman Empire

THE GENESIS OF THIS BOOK

This book has evolved from a series of lectures given at Tufts University in April 2006 that provided an excuse for me to reflect on an interconnected series of issues that had been individually engaging my attention for some time. My title to this introduction may seem somewhat presumptuous, but it is *perspective on*—not *ownership of*—that is at issue here.[1] After studying the Roman Empire for over thirty years, this has been a great opportunity for me to take stock of where my own understanding has reached. The 1990s and the early years of this new century have seen some very significant developments in the study of the Roman Empire, in part at least occasioned by contemporary political changes in the wake of the end of the Cold War and the emergence of the United States as a solitary superpower.[2] Archaeological theory has started to have an impact, though the impact has been constrained to some extent by different national traditions in the study of classical antiquity.[3] My own views of the Roman Empire have been transformed almost out of recognition during these years and this book will chart some of that personal intellectual journey. The geographical emphases of the essays, of course, reflect my physical travels and fieldwork, drawing in particular on evidence from Britain, Jordan, and Africa. At the outset, I must acknowledge that perceptions of the Roman Empire (indeed any empire) are profoundly situational, and someone who has spent all their life researching a corner of, say, Asia Minor or a particular field, such as sculpture, will likely construct a very different set of perceptions of Rome. For this reason I emphasize the personal nature of the view offered in these pages, though I hope that many readers will recognize common ground with their own knowledge and experience of the Roman Empire. However, it also needs to be stated at the outset that this is a book about Roman imperialism, not civilization, and some readers with interests in, say, classical literature

---

[1] I take my inspiration here from Richard Reece's provocative and brilliant essay *My Roman Britain* (1988).

[2] In a broad survey, Peachin 26 specifically identifies the Rome of the High Empire as a "superpower."

[3] For a series of varied reviews of the developments in Roman archaeology in this period, see Alcock and Osborne 2007; Dyson 1993, 2006; Gardner 2003, 2006; James 2003; Laurence 1999, 2001; 2006; Scott 2006; Woolf 2004c.

or artistic connoisseurship may be disconcerted by the critical analyses offered of the operation of power and its effects on subject peoples.[4]

The invitation to deliver the inaugural series of Tufts lectures in memory of Miriam S. Balmuth induced in me equal feelings of pride and panic. I was very conscious of the honor bestowed, but equally aware of the obligation to measure up to the high standards of scholarship that she embodied. I never met Miriam but from what I know of her personality and her published work (especially her work on Sardinia and Iberia) I suspect she would have been interested in the theme of the lectures and this book. I would like to thank the family and friends of Miriam S. Balmuth for making possible the lecture series and this publication arising from it. Bruce and Becky Hitchner must take huge credit for creating the event at Tufts in April 2006, and I am particularly grateful to them for their hard work, hospitality, and friendship.[5]

I am not a classicist nor a Roman historian per se, but an archaeologist with particular interests in the Roman Empire and more generally in the nature of imperialism and its material effects on colonial societies. The suggestion that the theme should link between antiquity and modernity was a positive encouragement in that much of my work over the past decade on the theme of Roman imperialism had been exploiting the space between the historiography of classical archaeology and postcolonial studies.

The lectures on which the core of this book is based were offered as a series of reflections on the theme of *Experiencing Empire*, with a leaning toward archaeological and comparative approaches rather than purely historical ones.[6] In the course of the four lectures I explored a number of themes that have interested me in recent years and I must reiterate that this is very much a personal perspective and one that takes a relatively pessimistic view of the impact of the Roman Empire on its subjects at large. This book is structured around four lectures: "From Imperium to Imperialism: Writing the Roman Empire"; "Power, Sex and Empire"; "Ruling Regions, Exploiting Resources"; and "Identity and Discrepancy." These are picked up by the four main sections of the book: "Imperialisms and Colonialisms"; "Power"; "Resources"; and "Identity."

---

[4] This has been an emerging theme of reviews of my 2006 book, in which my characterization of Britain as an "imperial possession" has confounded the preconceptions of some readers—a point I will return to in the afterword to this volume.

[5] Many others within the classics department at Tufts contributed to the event in practical terms, but I would like to single out for special mention David Proctor, the departmental administrator, for all his help with practical arrangements.

[6] While Huskinson 2000 has a somewhat similar title (and is a book I admire and use a lot with students), the intent and content of the present book of essays is rather different.

Though foreshadowed by my previous work in this general area, my hope for the lectures was that they would be thought-provoking and insightful not only in terms of how we think about the Roman Empire but also how we understand imperialism and colonialism in other historical periods, including the contemporary world. In preparing these essays for publication, and in consultation with Bruce Hitchner, I have added a number of other studies that link to these same themes. These additions comprise this introduction and a brief afterword to conclude the volume, plus reworked versions of three previously published articles and a couple more unpublished papers, that are brought together here to give the reader easy reference to what I see as my key work to date on the theme of Roman imperialism. The resulting book thus has the character of a set of linked essays, with a certain amount of repetition of argument and bibliography among them, rather than of a coherent monograph written at a single moment in time. The bibliographical references reflect what I have been reading in the last decade and what has influenced, informed, or challenged my own thinking. I very much hope that the notes and extensive bibliography will provide a valuable resource for interested readers and students to pursue in more depth particular aspects of debate or to explore contrary views to those promoted here.

Part 1 of the book, "Imperialisms and Colonialisms," comprises two essays. In the first lecture (chapter 1), which set the scene for the series, I reviewed traditional understandings of the Roman Empire and reflected on how recent developments in the study of imperialism more generally could influence the future of Roman studies.[7] Problems with the orthodox paradigm of Romanization were explored and the need for alternative interpretative frameworks highlighted.

Chapter 2 was one of my first forays in the mid-1990s into postcolonial analysis of the prevailing discourse in Roman provincial archaeology and history.[8] In deconstructing the underlying attitudes and the process of formation of the modern (Western) view of Roman Africa, I addressed what I believed to be some of the flaws of the modern consensus model. Since that article appeared ten years ago, there have been further studies in French and Italian following this critical line of approach.[9] With a view to making the article more accessible to readers who do not read French or Italian, I have translated the original passages quoted in those

---

[7] The original order of the lectures as delivered followed the sequence chapter 1, chapter 5, chapter 4, chapter 8, but in preparing the text for publication I have reversed the middle two.

[8] Mattingly 1996b.

[9] Dondin-Payre 2003 and Munzi 2001, 2004.

languages into English and have further enlivened the bare text by the addition of a series of illustrations.

Part 2, "Power," begins with chapter 3, which introduces the theme of power in relation to a still expansionist Rome in the first century AD. It concerns a specific example of the way in which imperial policy was enacted through the use of client kings in advance of directly controlled territory. The larger purpose of this previously unpublished essay is to illustrate the flagrant way in which Rome devised policy (and reinvented history) to suit its own interests. Loyal and trusted imperial clients in Britain found themselves suddenly personae non gratae at the accession of a new emperor, with the established alliances cynically sacrificed for what was seen as easily attainable military kudos. The second Balmuth lecture (chapter 4) presented a no-holds-barred approach to Roman sex and sexuality and advanced some novel ideas about how this can be related to a discourse on colonial power. Certain characteristics of Roman sexuality seem to have been created or accentuated by the drastic social inequalities that imperial rule created between people (free versus slave, ruler versus ruled, soldier versus civilian). Some comments are also offered here on the broader implications of the socialization of sexual violence and humiliation in an imperial context and how this represents one aspect of wider patterns of exploitative behavior.

Part 3, "Resources," brings together three linked essays dealing with the Roman economy, landscape archaeology, and Roman mining. This section opens with the third Balmuth lecture (chapter 5), which focused on the interrelationship between the administration and garrisoning of the empire and the requirement placed on provinces to deliver up the resources to pay for this.

Chapter 6 (on African landscapes) was originally published in a 1997 *Journal of Roman Archaeology* supplementary volume that I edited, where it formed one half of a dialogue, alongside an essay by Susan Alcock on Roman landscapes of Greece.[10] My key argument was that there was considerable variation in the African landscapes, but that fundamentally all of them are to be viewed as landscapes of imperialism—that is, as direct products of the colonizing experience of empire. Although I have subsequently published other papers on similar themes,[11] I think that this essay set out my position in a particularly clear way and intersects well with the themes of chapter 5.

Chapter 7 is developed from a previously unpublished paper (presented at various conferences and seminars in recent years), relating to

---

[10] Alcock 1997; Mattingly 1997a and c.
[11] Mattingly 1998; Matttingly and Barker 2005.

fieldwork in Jordan between 1996 and 2000. The Wadi Faynan Survey explored a pre-desert landscape from the palaeolithic age to its present occupation by pastoral bedouin. A major focus of exploitation was the abundant copper sources of the region. In the Roman period this was a large-scale imperial mining operation, and the results provide a particularly graphic illustration of a key theme of this book: the economic imperatives of empire and the human consequences. While the main archaeological results of the Faynan study have recently been published in detail, the sociohistorical and economic analysis offered here takes the study somewhat further.[12]

Part 4, "Identity," comprises a pair of essays. In the final Balmuth lecture (chapter 8) I returned to the search for an alternative interpretative framework to apply to culture change within the Roman Empire. I present new approaches to identity and discrepant experience within Roman society, using examples from a number of provincial regions. The origins of this chapter lie in a 2004 article published in the *Journal of Roman Archaeology*,[13] but I have taken the opportunity to expand the scope and argument considerably in the present volume. A particular development here is my exploration of the concept of discrepant identity in the context of both Britain and Africa.

Chapter 9 is one of a pair of previously published papers in which I have addressed the theme of provincial art using the tombs at Ghirza in Libya as an example.[14] The chapter exposes the limitations of conventional Romanization readings of the iconography—which underestimate the significance of more local identity issues. A brief afterword rounds out the book, by drawing together some of the key conclusions and summarizing my research agenda for further investigation of the phenomenon of Roman imperialism.

Different Stories, Different Memories

But there is no story to tell, no one story anyway, not since that day in 1505 when Don Laurenco de Almeida ... landed on our shores and broke us from our history. No one story, with a beginning and an end, no story that picks up from where the past left off—only bits and shards of stories, and those of the people I knew ... or heard tell of. ... And no story of the country—or if of the country, not our story but

---

[12] Barker, Gilbertson, and Mattingly 2007.
[13] Mattingly 2004a.
[14] Mattingly 1999; 2003b.

theirs. . . . Except that we all have the imprint of that history . . . internalized it even, made it our own, against our will, calling to memory the while to lose it by losing memory itself.[15]

Memory and the loss of it is a consequence of colonialism ancient and modern.[16] Much of this book concerns how we might seek to recover different stories from the historical and material record of the Roman Empire, including the lost social memories of subject peoples. The conventional metanarrative of Rome emphasizes its grandeur, its relative uniformity, its longevity, and its positive impacts in bringing to new areas (or taking to new levels) the entity called classical civilization. I have tried to demonstrate that this model, while true to an extent, does not help us in our attempt to understand the impact of the Roman Empire on subject people; rather, it limits us to a rather one-dimensional picture. For this reason also, the essays in this book are predominantly concerned with the periphery of the Roman Empire rather than its core. This is a view from the frontier lands, where the fruits of Roman civilization were somewhat less self-evident. Although in general it might be argued that the benefits and opportunities of empire for provincial subjects were more tangible in the core Mediterranean provinces, I would argue that even these areas were in their turn peripheral to the expanding empire at some stage and the sort of issues and processes discussed here have relevance to all territory within the empire, even Italy itself.

The key themes and arguments of the various essays herein can be briefly summarized: Roman imperialism is presented as something much more complex than is generally accepted today; I combine elements from several modern models of empire and colonialism. In particular, the extent to which the center (senate or emperors) was always the driver is questioned, with reference to pericentric and systemic aspects of other instances of imperialism (see chapter 1). The demographic, economic, and social impacts of empire—and in particular the ugly side of Roman imperialism—require much closer attention. It needs to be recognized that these impacts were much less homogeneous than commonly presented under the Romanization model—which I have now utterly rejected. Future studies need to explore the heterogeneity and regionality of the data more fully. Power and identity (especially the notion of discrepant identity) are offered as useful analytical concepts in place of Romanization.

---

[15] Sivanandan 1997, 5. This novel provides an insightful take on Sri Lankan colonial and postcolonial history.
[16] Alcock 2001.

REFLECTIONS AND ACKNOWLEDGMENTS

One final point of introduction. The first of my Balmuth lectures was de-livered at Tufts University on 18 April 2006—a date of considerable local resonance. This was "Paul Revere night"—the anniversary of his famous ride of 18–19 April 1775, signaling the start of a war of liberation against imperial overlords.[17] In that ride he passed through Medford, now site of the Tufts campus, on his way to Lexington and Concord. Members of the Tufts family were also much involved in the events of that night and the battles of the following day. It seemed all the more appropriate then that I should have brought before an audience at Tufts University my skepti-cal view of the supposed universal benefits of the Roman Empire and my appraisal of the differing levels of engagement with it and resistance to it.

Looking into the true story behind the mythic tale of Paul Revere's ride and the rising of Massachusetts against the British imperial army, I was very struck by the fundamental importance of the fact that his ride was not, in fact, a solitary act. Knocking on the doors of many houses along the way, Revere called out a whole posse of other riders, who by morn-ing had spread the news of the fateful British march to all points of the compass and had raised the whole of Middlesex, not just a narrow tract along the anticipated line of advance the column took.[18] Like Revere, I am equally determined to rouse support for a cause, and I hope that this book that has arisen from the lecture series will serve as a rallying call for other riders to add their own voices to my appeal against the consensus view of a wholly benign Roman Empire.[19] There are, of course, other riders already on the trail—I think particularly of Richard Hingley, Nico Roymans, Jane Webster and Peter Wells—and I hope the significance of those other contributions are sufficiently clear from the footnotes and bibliography.

[17] Fischer 1994 (with thanks to Bruce and Becky Hitchner for this inspired Christmas present ahead of my delivering the Balmuth lectures).

[18] Ibid., 139–48.

[19] In the UK, the Theoretical Roman Archaeology Conference has already sent many outriders in advance—Baker et al. 1999; Bruhn, Croxford, and Grigoropoulos 2005; Carr, Swift, and Weekes 2003; Carruthers et al. 2002; Cottam et al. 1995; Croxford et al. 2004, 2006, 2007; Davies, Gardner, and Lockyear 2001; Fincham et al. 2000; Forcey, Hawthorne, and Witcher 1997; Leslie 1999; Meadows, Lemke, and Heron 1997; Rush 1995; Scott 1993b. Of the editors of these volumes, at least eleven are in academic posts, and others hold established positions in professional archaeology. The inaugural meeting of the Criti-cal Roman Archaeology Conference at Stanford University in March 28 represents a wel-come introduction of similar theoretical approaches to Roman archaeology in the United States. A volume of papers is currently in preparation.

I must finally record my extreme gratitude to Bruce Hitchner, who refused to take no for an answer and eventually persuaded me to overcome my initial qualms about whether I had something worth saying or the time to prepare the lectures.[20] In the long run it proved an exhilarating (if rather frenetic) experience researching and writing these linked papers on a tight timetable.[21] I have in the process redefined or clarified my own image of the Roman Empire in many ways. Bruce's own work has been a constant inspiration, just as much as his profound friendship has been a huge support at every moment of doubt. Final revisions of the text were made during the 2008–2009 academic year, in the breathing space provided by University of Leicester Study Leave, which is gratefully acknowledged here. I was also much assisted by the generous encouragement and wise advice of two anonymous reviewers and the Princeton University Press production staff.[22] As ever, I owe a huge debt of gratitude to the many colleagues and postgraduate students in the large and stimulating Iron Age and Roman research group at the University of Leicester, who have engaged with and debated many of the issues explored here. Similarly, my family has been a constant and patient support of my long hours working on the book.

The book is dedicated to my mother, Erica Mattingly, who has been an inspiration throughout my life and whose personal take on Roman triumphalism adorns my living room wall and the cover of this book. Sadly, she did not live to see the finished book in her honor.

---

[20] I must also acknowledge the fantastic contribution he made to shaping the book. In addition to providing me with numerous marginal comments and questions on the first draft of the manuscript, his suggestions have helped determine the running order of the sections and chapters.

[21] Final revision for publication has been delayed longer than I had hoped by the intrusion of other projects, though this has allowed me to engage with many additional publications that have appeared in the last two years.

[22] At Princeton University Press, special thanks are due to acquisition editor Rob Tempio, production editor Beth Clevenger, and Brian Bendlin for his excellent and painstaking copyediting.

It can be a daunting prospect for an academic to hold up a new idea for critical scrutiny (or savaging). However, what most authors fear more than bad notices are no reviews and limited sales—essentially finding one's work ignored. Fortunately, *Imperialism, Power, and Identity* has sparked an intense and interesting debate. The mainly favorable reviews and numerous unsolicited emails suggest that it strikes a chord with many readers. That is very satisfying as the book is a deliberately argumentative one and my hope was always that it would engage people in a process of reflection on the state of Roman archaeology and of the discipline of Classical Studies.

Since the publication of the hardback edition, I have given lectures on its themes in Britain, the U.S., and Australia, but also in non-Anglophone countries (Rome, Leuven, Amsterdam, Bayreuth). The issues I raise evoke strong passions in some readers, both pro- and anti-, but the discussions that the book sets in motion have proved lively and illuminating. My experience debating this book with these varied groups, representing very different intellectual traditions, have confirmed my belief that these are important issues for study of the ancient world, not just a British intellectual side-show. As acknowledged in the original preface, many of the ideas in this set of essays are not original or unique to me, but rather represent the first fruits of a group of scholars who have engaged with post-colonial theory and thought about how the discipline of Classical Studies (and Roman archaeology in particular) can profit from joining in such debates. This book may thus serve as a useful waymarker on a collaborative intellectual journey that seeks to re-position Roman archaeology in the 21st century. However, it is far from being the end point of the itinerary.

Some of the (minority of) less positive reviews have attacked my methods and approaches, without seeming to comprehend what the book is really about. My book is above all an exploration of different perspectives on the nature of Roman imperialism, on the operation of power networks, on identity presentation and on the inter-relationships between these three aspects of Roman societies. Following a trend established in reviews of my earlier book on *Britain in the Roman Empire*, there have been further suggestions that I am anti-Roman because I seek to offer a more balanced critique of negative and positive aspects of Roman imperialism. The most serious charges levelled at my work have been that I have no method as such, but simply pull random incidents and bits of evidence to support a predetermined case. That I refute most strongly and I suggest that such challenges would have more weight if the reviewers who have disliked my approach had also offered a point by point rebuttal or alternative reading of my analytical conclusions.

One reviewer took me to task for reiterating my view that Romanization is a broken paradigm and that Roman archaeology needs to find new tools of the trade. Apparently, this is 'old news,' though my experience in debating the book with different audiences suggest that this is still not as widely acknowledged as that reviewer seems to think. For a more acute reading of my objectives and methods, the interested reader is referred to *The Classical Review* 62.1 (April 2012), 249–251.

I am sometimes asked if I consider myself a post-colonial theorist and tend these days to deny this, though admitting that I have been profoundly influenced by post-colonial theory. What I have tried to do is to integrate some of the key post-colonial ideas about imperialism in my thinking about the Roman world, while at the same time contextualizing these new approaches with the vast dossier of more top-down data that has been accumulated in Roman studies over the past centuries of research. My overall goal is to promote the study of Roman societies from multiple perspectives: top-down, bottom-up and sidewards-in.

The present book was in many ways my attempt to broaden out an intellectual debate that had been running for some time in the British and Dutch research community, expressed in terms that would open up its relevance to a broader Classical Studies community. I have major concerns about an agenda of study of the ancient world that, in relation to some fundamental characteristics, has not been seriously updated in the past century and that is still very off-putting for the bulk of the modern population occupying the southern and eastern half of the area of the Roman Empire. An approach that focuses above all on elite culture, on a benign view of colonialism and that strongly correlates the Roman Empire with Western Civilization does look curiously old-fashioned and ill-suited to the world we live in. In the aftermath of the Arab Spring, these issues seem even more urgent to address. The lack of a sophisticated theory of Roman imperialism generated from within Classical Studies has also relinquished the field to modern specialists and politicians who all too readily misrepresent the nature of the Roman Empire in modern debate about imperialism more broadly. The Roman Empire has great potential, it seems to me, to contribute in more dynamic ways to the comparative study of imperialism.

Another question that is often raised in discussion about the book is whether I can explain further how I define and employ the term 'identity.'

I hope the answer to that will be clear from a careful reading of the book, but feel it worth clarifying some important characteristics here. The first point to stress is that I believe that individuals did not frame their identity in terms of a singular affiliation, but rather than for many people there were multiple identities that they adopted according to social context, life-stage, social status, employment and so on. Regional and local identities remained strong in most parts of the empire, with behavior in certain key areas of life revealing strong continuities with pre-Roman cultures (notably in things like religion and burial). These plural identities of individuals were also accompanied by a multiplicity of group identities, more or less formalized within society. The Roman military community or early Christian communities would be two examples of such identity groups. The archaeological identification and analysis of this multiplicity of identities requires a sophisticated understanding of a range of factors that promote and constrain displays of identity in ancient society, especially relating to elements of the population less represented in traditional epigraphic and artistic displays of status and culture. A key point here is that identifying an element of material culture in the archaeological record is not the same as diagnosing a display of identity. We also need to define and analyze the patterns of behavior associated with the use of that material culture. In addition, we need to frame that knowledge within a broader understanding of how the structures of imperial power and colonial exploitation operated in the Roman Empire and how these constrained and directed human agency. So my formulation of 'identity' aims to bring together a consideration of material culture and behavioral practices in relation to an analysis of structure and agency. My initial analyses of this sort have provided confirmation that there are distinctive patterns in the archaeological record that serve (and served) to differentiate self-identifying groups and individuals from each other.

Some people struggle with the use of the term 'discrepant' in my particular reading of multiple identities in the Roman world. Indeed, my ideas might have enjoyed wider acceptance had I simply opted for the expression 'Different Identities' or 'Plural Identities' in place of 'Discrepant Identities'. However, I am unrepentant on this point. Discrepancy is strongly linked in my work to the networks of power and my response to criticism of the term is that it reminds us that power operated through both hard and soft channels in the Roman Empire. We are confronted with a very broad spectrum of experiences of empire and reactions to colonial power—spanning from strong promotion of cosmopolitan elite norms to outright resistance and rebellion. The word discrepant encompasses all of that range, though I would emphasize that by its use I am not claiming that the negative reactions to empire always and everywhere outweighed the positive engagement. Nonetheless, in studying a colonial encounter such as Rome, it seems to me that our default reading should err on the side of caution, rather than assuming strong approbation and engagement on the basis of the material traces left behind by the elite and the most privileged groups in society (the stuff we tend to find in our museums and published in most detail).

In Britain, the long-running Theoretical Roman Archaeology Conference has facilitated an open debate on the agendas and driving paradigms of the discipline, as well as test-driving a range of theoretical models. Classical archaeology in the U.S., in comparison, has for long been seen as a more conservative and under-theorized discipline, but there are positive signs of change. A 'Critical Roman Archaeology Conference', held at Stanford, has now been published and a 'Theory in Greek Archaeology Conference' has recently been held (http://sitemaker.umich.edu/tiga/home). We need more of this sort of critical reflection. It will increase the relevance of Classics to the world in which we live, which cannot be a bad thing in terms of the long-term health of the discipline and student recruitment.

In Spring 2013, I delivered the Jerome Lectures at the American Academy in Rome and the University of Michigan, Ann Arbor, using the occasion to amplify the themes of this book in relation to the specific example of North Africa. The responses of the audiences were very positive and many stimulating conversations ensued with graduate students, early career, and more established researchers and practitioners from many different branches of Classical Studies. This experience has reassured me that this sort of critique has a real value. I very much hope that the appearance of the paperback edition will facilitate the extension of those discussions even further in the teaching of Classical Studies.

David Mattingly
Leicester, May 2013

PART ONE

Imperialisms and Colonialisms

CHAPTER ONE

From *Imperium* to Imperialism

WRITING THE ROMAN EMPIRE

> The rise and fall of a great empire cannot fail to fascinate us,
> for we can all see in such a story something of our own times.
> But of all the empires that have come and gone, none has a
> more immediate appeal that the Empire of Rome. It pervades
> our lives today: its legacy is everywhere to be seen.
> —Barry W. Cunliffe, *Rome and Her Empire*

> The endurance of the Roman Empire is one of the success
> stories of history. That it survived so long is a sign of its prin-
> cipal achievement, whereby a heterogeneous mixture of races
> and creeds were induced to settle down together in a more or
> less peaceful way under the *Pax Romana*.
> —J.S. Wacher, *The Roman World*

DEFINITIONS OF EMPIRE AND IMPERIALISM

It is generally agreed that the Roman Empire was one of the most successful and enduring empires in world history.[1] Its reputation was suc-
cessively foretold, celebrated and mourned in classical antiquity.[2] There
has been a long afterlife, creating a linear link between Western society
today and the Roman state, reflected in religion, law, political structures,
philosophy, art, and architecture.[3] Perhaps partly in consequence, many

---

An early version of this chapter was delivered as the 2005 Ronald Syme Lecture at Wolf-
son College, Oxford, on 20 October 2005. It was substantially developed for delivery as
my opening lecture in the Miriam S. Balmuth Lectures in Ancient History and Archaeology
series at Tufts University on 18 April 2006 and has been further revised and expanded for
publication here.

[1] Empires seem to be fashionable these days. Visitors to the British Museum in recent
years have been presented with a series of blockbuster exhibitions showcasing an array
of ancient empires, from Babylon (Finkel and Seymour 2008), to China (Portal 2007), to
Persia (Curtis and Tallis 2005) and Hadrian and Rome (Opper 2008). Note also the Royal
Academy Byzantium show (Cormack and Vassilaki 2008). Rome certainly stands up to this
sort of scrutiny as an extraordinary example of a preindustrial superstate.

[2] Dalby 2000, 8–20, provides a good introduction to some of the key sources.

[3] See Goodman 1997, 3, for an example of this sentiment.

people in the United States and Europe are curiously nostalgic about the Roman Empire in a way that has become deeply unfashionable in studies of modern empires.[4]

There have even been attempts to imagine a world in which the Roman Empire never ended. Some readers may be familiar with the wonderful conceit of Robert Silverberg's novel *Roma Eterna*, and his imagined episodes of later Roman history, including the conquest of the Americas and extending to an attempted "space shot" in the year 2723 AUC (*ab urbe condita*). The global scope and extreme longevity of Silverberg's Rome—still a resolutely pagan state at the end, having averted the rise of both Christianity and Islam—emphasizes the unedifying aspects of military dictatorship.[5] Like bald narrative accounts of Roman history, these modern reimaginings blur into a catalog of wars, coups, attempted revolts, persecutions, assassinations, and murders.[6] Here, of course, is the great paradox of the Roman Empire. Lauded in many modern accounts as an exemplary and beneficent power,[7] it was also a bloody and dangerous autocracy.[8] Of course, Rome was not the only human society prone to war and violence—much debate has been prompted by Lawrence Keeley's *War before Civilization* concerning humanity's predilection for intercommunal conflict from prehistory onward.[9] However, the scale, frequency and length of wars in Roman society were undeniably unusual in a preindustrial age. Despite interesting differences from modern colonial regimes in the manner in which local elites were integrated into the imperial project, the facade of civil government was underpinned by violence, both real and latent.[10]

[4] Notwithstanding Ferguson's recent efforts to rehabilitate the British Empire (2004), the strongly expressed proempire sentiments of Wells 1996 are less self-evidently correct to a postcolonial generation.

[5] Silverberg 2003. McDougall 2005 represents another attempt to imagine the Roman Empire in the modern world, complete with high-tech crucifixion on steel crosses. For all its imagination (and pretension) neither book depicts the Roman world and power structures as well as Harris (2006).

[6] Potter 2009 is a fine modern example of the grand narrative history, with the wars and power struggles predominating. Wells 1992 and Woolf 2004a are more rounded accounts of wars, politics, social institutions, and much more, but presented in an almost entirely positive manner.

[7] A recent example is the work of British politician Boris Johnson (whose 2006 *Dream of Rome* is actually more of a fantasy than a dream).

[8] See, most recently, Faulkner 2008 for a blow-by-blow description of Rome's history as "a system of robbery with violence" (p. xii).

[9] Keeley 1996. See Parker Pearson and Thorpe 2005, and Thorpe 2003, for some of the ensuing debate.

[10] Potter 1999 strikes a good balance between lauding the positives of Roman rule and acknowledging the effects of the state's "monopolization of extreme force."

Cinematic visions of Rome have changed over the years, but in general there is a mismatch between these depictions and the rosier scholarly consensus on the Roman Empire—typically what has been highlighted in "sword and sandal epics" has been sex and violence, with the empire more often than not representing the "dark side."[11] Occasional ruminations on Rome's decline and fall, of course, have had as much to tell us about contemporary unease about the future of the American empire.[12] It remains a paradox to me that cinema has done more to challenge our preconceptions of Rome than academic study. For instance, I can think of no darker depiction of life at the sharp end of Roman power than the scourging scene in Mel Gibson's *The Passion of the Christ.*[13]

Definitions of imperialism and of empire are varied and controversial, so I need to make my position clear at the outset. Some commentators have argued that the *imperium Romanum* was quite distinct from the modern term *imperialism* and, in comparison with modern empires, the Roman Empire was a product of very different political and economic forces.[14] A recent study has suggested that Roman expansionism fits more readily into an analytical frame of state building rather than an anachronistic back-projection of imperialism.[15] Yet that seems to ignore much about Rome that was exceptional in relation to other states of classical antiquity—the nature of Rome as a cosmopolis or metropolis fits more readily into analysis of imperial systems than of other ancient cities.[16]

[11] On Rome as the "dark side," see, e.g., the films *Ben Hur* (1959, dir. William Wyler), *Spartacus* (1960, dir. Stanley Kubrick), the TV miniseries *Masada* (1981, dir. Boris Sagal), or many a biblical epic. Even in the fabulous comedy of *Monty Python's Life of Brian* (1979, dir. Terry Jones) there is much spot-on critical comment on Roman oppression and cruel punishments. The salacious sexuality of Rome is notably shown off in Federico Fellini's *Satyricon* (1968) and Bob Guccione's dreadful (what was Helen Mirren thinking?) *Caligula* (1979). The highly compulsive HBO TV series *Rome* (2005–2007) pulled off the neat trick of combining graphic sex and violence with soap opera characters to present Rome as a truly cruel and decadent society from top to bottom.

[12] See Anthony Mann's *The Fall of the Roman Empire* (1964) and Ridley Scott's *Gladiator* (2000).

[13] Almost unwatchable for its graphic detail and cruelty, the scourging in Mel Gibson's *The Passion of the Christ* (2004) is nonetheless a compelling depiction of the mundane violence of the Roman Empire.

[14] Hobson 1902.

[15] Eich and Eich 2005; the definitional problem is, however, acknowledged on page 5: "The word imperialism seems to defy any easy definition." Their linkage between violence/warfare and state-building seems reasonable for the early stages of Roman expansionism, but their analysis seems to elide the transformative effect on Roman society of the "extraordinary success in war" (which they admit distinguishes Rome from contemporary societies). I would argue that Rome's success did transform its social, economic, and political structures in ways that have more in common with other empires than with other nascent states.

[16] See various chapters in Edwards and Woolf 2003; also Morley 1996.

Similarly, the detail of extant Roman treaties with subject and allied peoples emphasize the extraordinary and unequal nature of these relations and the mechanisms that Rome adopted to control or to exert influence on far-flung territories.[17] Furthermore, I believe that there are issues relating to the exercise of power and the responses that power evokes, where it is legitimate to draw comparisons as well as contrasts between ancient and modern. Current attempts to situate the modern United States among past empires recognize the relevance of the Roman world.[18]

So, let us move on to some key definitions. An *empire* is the geopolitical manifestation of relationships of control imposed by a state on the sovereignty of others.[19] Empires generally combine a core, often metropolitan-controlled territory, with peripheral territories and have multiethnic or multinational dimensions. *Empire* can thus be defined as rule over very wide territories and many peoples largely without their consent. While ancient societies did not have as developed a sense of self-determination as modern states, the fact that incorporation was often fiercely contested militarily is symptomatic of the fundamentally nonconsensual nature of imperialism.

Imperialism refers to both the process and attitudes by which an empire is established and maintained. Some have argued that imperialism is essentially a modern phenomenon, though I would counter that the process existed in antiquity even if less explicitly developed in conceptual terms.[20] However, just as empires evolve over time, imperialism need not be static or uniform. When we look at the dynamics of the Roman Empire, we perhaps need to look beyond the rather monolithic definitions of most accounts and to consider several distinctive phases of imperialism. We also need to beware of the tendency of both modern and ancient commentators to explain earlier phases in the light of institutions and ideologies that developed only in later phases. Imperialism should be seen as a dynamic and shape-shifting process.

[17] See Mitchell 2005 for a detailed study of a recently recognized treaty of 46 BC between Rome and Lycia, with accompanying discussion of other treaties. Mitchell notes (2005, 185) that there were "fundamental instruments of Roman policy. Countless bilateral agreements with nominally independent partners created a complex network of reciprocal legal relationships which underpinned Rome's imperial authority."

[18] Hardt and Negri 2000; James 2006; Maier 2006. Vidal 1989 is perceptive on the influence of Rome on the formative years of American imperialism, with the first chapter alone containing numerous allusions by the protagonists to classical mythology and specific references to Julius Caesar (twice), Augustus, and Cicero.

[19] For a range of definitions see Doyle 1986; Hardt and Negri 2000; Kieran 1995; Lieven 2000; Said 1993; and Webster 1996b.

[20] For a variety of views on imperialism, see Doyle 1986, 19; Howe 2002, 30; Lichtheim 1971, 4; Reynolds 1981, vii; and Said 1993, 8.

Colonialism is a more restricted term that defines the system of rule of one people over another, in which sovereignty is operated over the colonized at a distance, often through the installation of settlements of colonists in the related process of *colonization*.[21] Both words, of course, derive from the Roman term *colonia*, initially definable as a settlement of citizens in conquered territory.[22] In recent years there has been increasing interest in the diverse nature of colonialism and colonization through the ages and the archaeological manifestations of these processes.[23] We shall look in more detail at colonialism later on.

Explaining empire is much more tricky than defining it, but I think the key approach must be to explore the networks of power that sustain it. What unites all types and ages of empires is the combination of the "will to power" and the large scale at which it is expressed. The domination of others is a characteristic of human societies, but empires very often achieve the step change of effecting rule over vast areas and huge populations by comparatively small numbers of imperial servants.[24] For this reason alone, I do not accept that the ancient land empires can have nothing in common with the capitalist sea empires of the nineteenth and early twentieth centuries or the American airstrip and aircraft carrier empire of the later twentieth and twenty-first centuries.[25] Even a modern account attempting to rehabilitate the reputation of the British Empire reveals telling structural similarities with the themes of this book—the changing realities of any specific empire as it went through phases of (d)evolution, globalization, the shrinking of the world though improved communications and infrastructure, the construction of power around the acquisition of knowledge, resource exploitation as driver or consequence of expansion, and the smoke-and-mirrors realities of minute provincial administrations ruling huge territories and millions of subjects.[26]

[21] Ashcroft, Griffiths, and Tiffin 1998, 45–51; Howe 2002, 30; Maier 2006, 44.

[22] Gosden 2004, 1.

[23] Given 2004; Gosden 2004; Hodos 2006; Hurst and Owen 2005; Lyons and Papadopoulos 2002; Stein 2005; Van Dommelen 1997; 1998; Van Dommelen and Terrenato 2007a.

[24] See Mitchell 2004 for a brilliant literary exploration of the Nietzschean view of power. For summary accounts of the relative economy of imperial rule in British India, see James 1997; Morris 1979.

[25] For similar arguments, see Webster 1997a. The work of international relations specialists such as Fitzpatrick (1992, 2005) reflects a similar preference for broad-based comparative study of empires.

[26] Ferguson 2004, xi–xxviii. While I disagree with many of his conclusions about the positive balance sheet of the British Empire (characterized on xxvii as the triumph of capitalism, the Anglicization of North America and Australasia, the predominance of Protestantism and the survival of parliamentary institutions), the analysis does not duck the issue of the negative impacts as well.

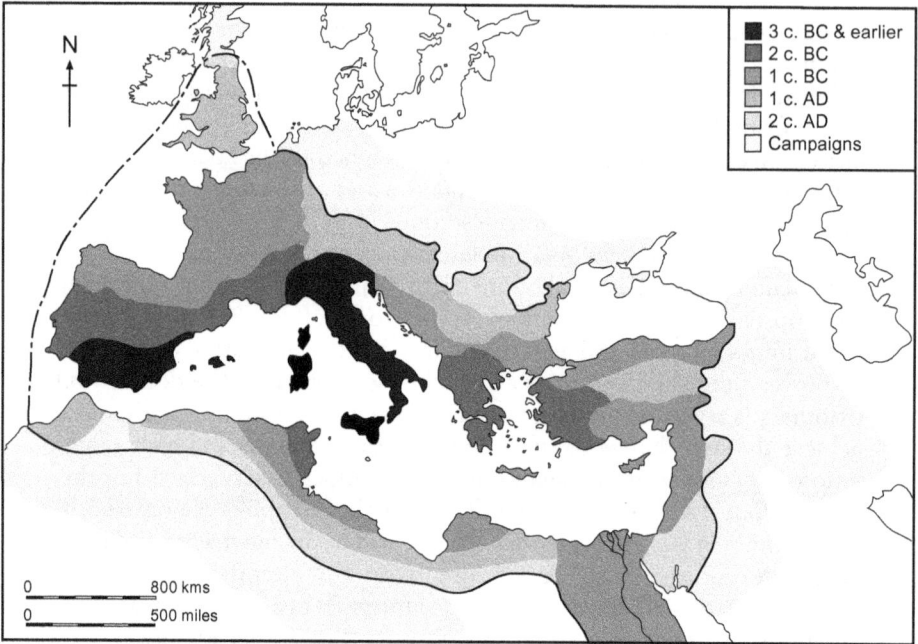

Figure 1.1 Map showing phases of expansion of the Roman Empire.

If we consider the extent and chronology of the Roman Empire, along with the manner in which it was acquired and governed, it is apparent that it shares many common characteristics with political and military entities that have been described as empires in world history.[27] But it is equally obvious in surveying historical "snapshot" maps of the growth and decline of the Roman territorial empire that this was a dynamic process, with structural breaks and discontinuities, more than a manifest destiny (see figs 1.1–1.2). The scale and formal processes of empires differ over time, but certain states—by their size, complexity, expanding borders, and populations—can be recognized as belonging to a family of empires. The Roman Empire at its height in the mid-second century encompassed an area of about 4 million square kilometers, with an ethnically diverse and polyglot population probably in excess of 60 million. The same area today is occupied by more than 40 modern nation states. Although Rome does not share all the characteristics of modern empires, the scale of the Roman Empire (especially in relation to preindustrial communications and infrastructure) is particularly striking and would suggest that Rome has as at least as much in common with megastates

[27] See Alcock et al. 2001 for a comparative perspective.

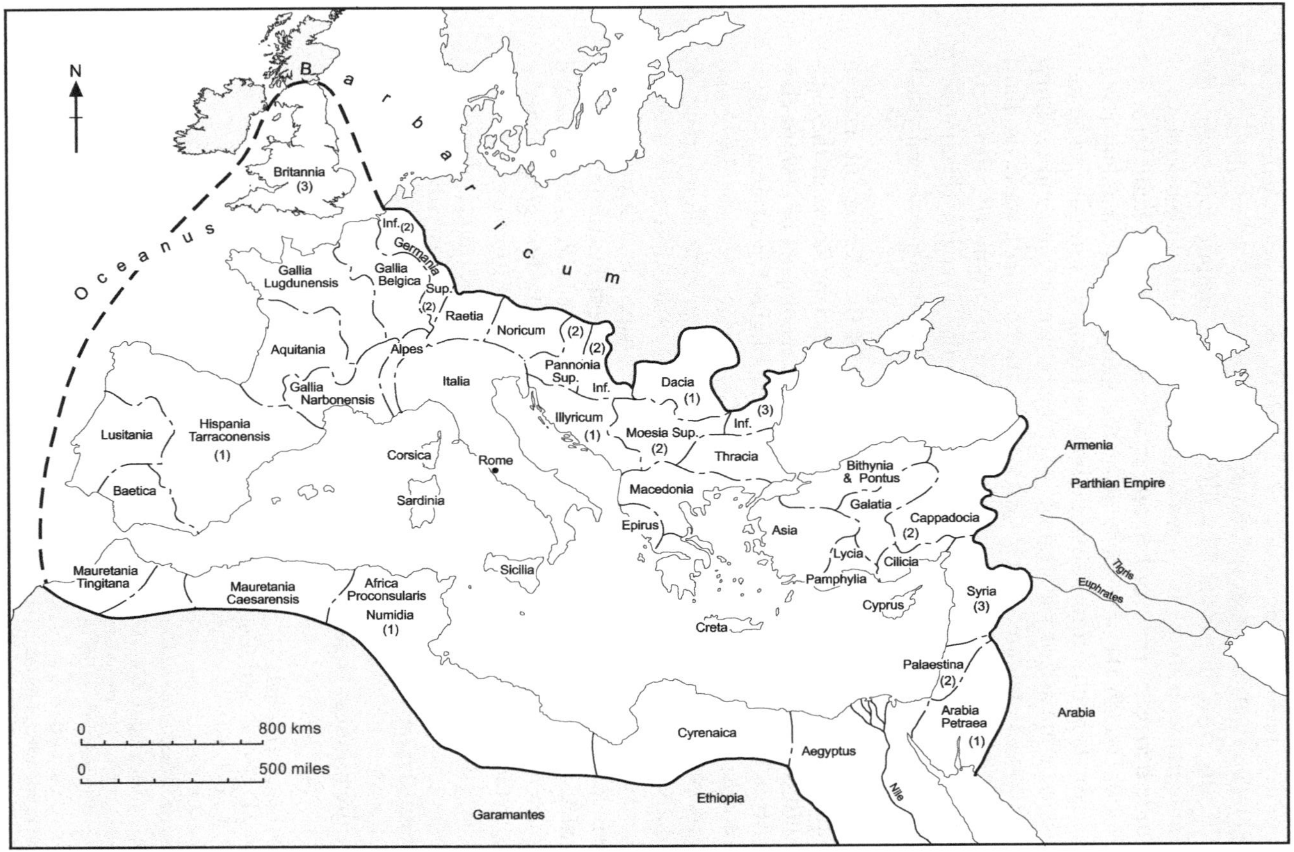

FIGURE 1.2 Map of the Roman Empire in the mid-second century AD, with an indication of the distribution of the legions (numbers in parentheses).

from the same or later eras as it does with the process of state formation and lesser rivals in classical antiquity.[28]

In any case, historiographically the Roman Empire has been "the paradigmatic example from which many traditional understandings of empire derive."[29] The word *empire* itself comes from the Latin term *imperium*, though the development of the modern understanding represents the fusion of three semantic lines in European thought.[30] The first of these emphasized the idea of sovereignty over people and territory; the second assimilated empire with any nonsubordinate state; the third focused attention on expansionist states that incorporated other states and territories, with a resulting level of internal diversity. This, in part, explains the difficulties of coming up with a universally accepted definition today.

We must also note the interconnectedness of the ideology of modern empire and the development of the study of ancient Rome in the eighteenth to twentieth centuries.[31] For example, the impact of Oxford classicists in the Indian Civil Service has been highlighted by Oswyn Murray and others: Oxford provided half the ICS entrants between 1892 and 1914, and in 1938 no less than six out of eight provincial governors in India were Greats men (that is, had Oxford classics degrees).[32] Knowledge and admiration of the Roman Empire shaped British policy in its own colonies,[33] while at the same time the modern British imperial experience reinforced a particular view of the Roman world; as Edward Fiddes noted in 1906, "The Roman Empire was the first great imperial experiment which rose above the methods of brute force or mere well-devised bureaucracy. Rome made a genuine effort to unite liberty and Empire ... she offered, if not political lessons ... at least a highly interesting analogy to similar modern experiments. In particular the English historian is irresistably reminded of the British Empire, and especially of the great Indian Dependency."[34]

---

[28] Contra Eich and Eich 2005.

[29] Alcock et al. 2001, xviii.

[30] Lintott 1981; cf. Kallett-Marx 1995, 18–29; Richardson 1991; Woolf 2001. See Morrison 2001 for the discussion on the development of the concept of empire in European thought. MacCormack 2007 is a fascinating study of the ways in which the example of the Roman Empire informed Spain's understanding of the Inca empire that it conquered in the sixteenth century, provided models for Spain's own emerging imperial structures, and ultimately was influential in helping the conquered Andean population to understand the new world order.

[31] Brunt 1965; Freeman 2007; Hingley 2000, 2008.

[32] Murray 2000; Vasunia 2003, 94.

[33] Chakravarty 1989, 5–12.

[34] Fiddes, in the introduction to Arnold 1906, 5–6; cf. Brunt 1990, 110–11, who notes that modern imperialism "influenced the interpretation of Roman history with false analo-

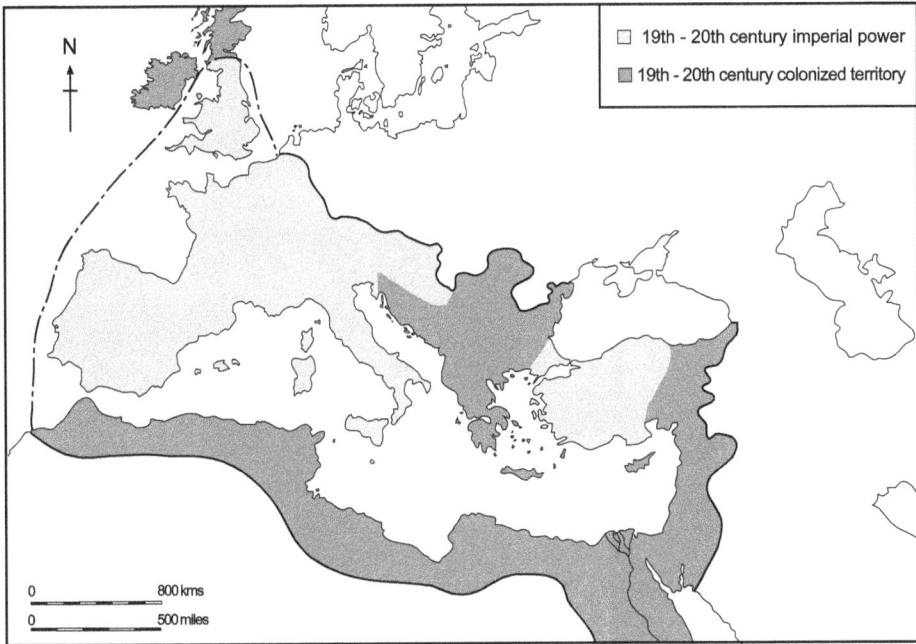

FIGURE 1.3 Map of the Roman Empire showing division of area between nineteenth- and twentieth-century imperial powers and colonized territories.

Modern empires have made extensive use of images of Rome to shape popular perceptions.[35] They have also exploited architecture that evokes past empires and have amassed knowledge and collections in support of their claims to be successor states. As Charles Meier notes, "The Louvre, the Pergamon Museum, the British Museum collected the tribute of ancient civilizations, sometimes merely taken, occasionally bestowed by the current rulers of despoliated sites. Empire meant to conquer and to collect, to appropriate the testimony of civilizations as tribute, and to build the capacious structures that would befit the acquisition."[36]

The European and American enthusiastic adoption of classical antiquity as the birthright of Western civilization is an intellectual proposition that is based as much on modern colonial history as on direct cultural inheritance. Consider the spatial relationship between the Roman Empire and modern colonial powers and colonized peoples (fig. 1.3). The

gies." See Hingley 2008, 228–325, for an extended analysis of the impact of Romans in Britain on the British in India (and vice versa).

[35] Hingley 2001.

[36] Maier 2006, 47; cf. Dyson 2006. See also the important collection of essays in Hingley 2001.

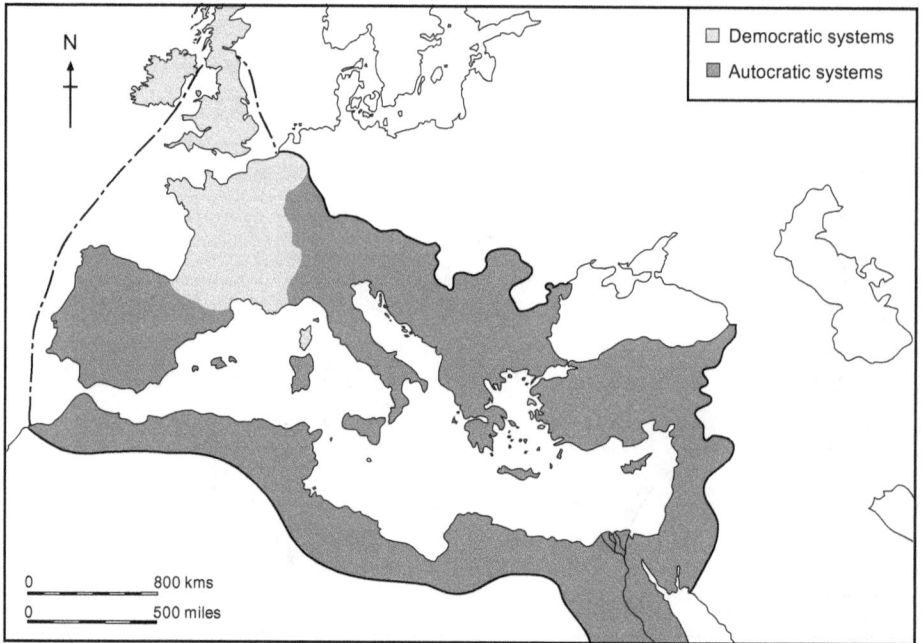

FIGURE 1.4 Map of the Roman Empire showing twentieth-century territories that were predominantly under democratic government and those that endured significant periods of nondemocratic rule.

strongest proponents of Western civilization have been the modern imperial powers of Western Europe (plus the United States), while the roots of opposition to this ideology are in part to be found in territories that were placed under the colonial authority of Western "great powers" who claimed to be successors of Rome.[37] It is also striking that of the countries that have done most to promote the idea of Rome as an exemplary empire, many have enjoyed the luxury of long-term democratic systems of government (Britain, France, the United States), while a large part of the territory of Rome's empire has been and in some instances continues to be governed by nondemocratic systems of various hues (see fig. 1.4).

Three European states enshrined an extreme reverence of Rome in their own fascist ideology and iconography, further discrediting the reputation of Rome for many of the people within its former territories. The Western European/North American positive attitude to all things Roman is thus far from universally shared by people now living in, for instance, the countries corresponding to Rome's African and Eastern territories.

---

[37] This theme is developed further in chapter 2.

The discipline of classics in general (and Roman archaeology in particular) needs to address the fact that its foundations are built on a modern imperial discourse and that this has major implications for its current practice.[38]

APPROACHES TO ROMAN IMPERIALISM

A dominant theme in studies of the Roman Empire—drawing on the late classical tradition—has concerned explanations of decline and fall. This remains as true today as in the time of Edward Gibbon, notwithstanding a tendency in late antique studies to stress the positives and continuities of what followed after.[39] I do not wish to add to the literature on this subject and my focus will be much more concerned with the operation of the empire than with its failure and collapse. However, a recurrent feature in studies of Rome's decline is a sense of wonder that something so emblematic of civilization and order should have been brought down by "barbarians." In the Western tradition, the fall of Rome is felt keenly because we have internalized Roman civilization as our own heritage without pausing to reflect on the real links between ourselves and ancient Rome.

This observation links with another aspect of eighteenth-, nineteenth- and early-twentieth-century views of the Roman Empire that stressed the positive appraisal of its effects. "Seldom has the government of the world been conducted for so long in an orderly sequence," notes Theodor Mommsen. "In its sphere, which those who belonged to it were not far wrong in regarding as the world, it fostered the peace and prosperity of the many nations united under its sway longer and more completely than any other leading power has ever done."[40] Gibbon posits, "If a man were called upon to fix the period in the history of the world during which the condition of the human race was most happy and prosperous, he would, without hesitation name that which elapsed from the death of Domitian to the accession of Commodus."[41]

---

[38] Goff 2003 represents a first step in exploring the relationship between classics and colonialism, though as Fletcher 2008 observes (with some exceptions—notably, Vasunia and Goff), "colonialism, rather than responsible postcolonial dialogue, is a ghostly presence . . . [the book] offers a . . . start to the difficult process of decolonization within the discipline of classics itself" (296–97).

[39] See the extraordinary cluster of recent overviews by Heather 2005; McCormick 2001; Ward-Perkins 2005; Wickham 2005. On Gibbon and the evolution of Roman studies, see Hingley 2008.

[40] Mommsen 1968, 4.

[41] Gibbon 1896, 78.

These views have had a long afterlife and expressions of uncritical adulation of all things Roman can still be found in many popular books and TV series like *What the Romans Did for Us* or *The Dream of Rome*.[42] Much analysis still rests on the belief that Rome's rule was based principally on loyalty and consensus among its subjects, or at least those who were rich and powerful enough to matter.[43] The recent Hadrian exhibition at the British Museum ostensibly provided an up-to-date picture of the man and his empire, though the title *Hadrian: Empire and Conflict* rather overstated the extent to which this show got beyond art and image.[44] Another tendency in some modern scholarship is to sidestep the awkward associations of the word *empire* in favor of the more laudable term *civilization*: "Roman civilization has survived through the centuries as a tangible living tradition, manifesting itself in every aspect of the modern world, from language and legal systems, to roads and buildings ... this magnificent survey of the astonishing achievements of one of the greatest and most influential of all civilizations."[45]

Important though they are, the specific political and constitutional aspects of the Roman Empire are of lesser relevance to my thesis than the nature and effects of imperial power.[46] I am interested, above all, in how subject peoples experienced empire and how this affected their behavior and material culture. The realities of power at the center were complex and changed over time. It requires a different sort of study to deconstruct, for example, the accounts of Polybius (*Histories*) on the Republic or of Dio on the changes under Augustus.[47] Polybius extolled the Roman state as the ideal form of government, comprising the best aspects of the three main political systems (monarchy, oligarchy, and democracy). There is much work still to be done in this area, of course, as demonstrated by Fergus Millar's recent reevaluation of the democratic

---

[42] Wilkinson 2000; Johnson 2006.

[43] Ando 2000, 66–67, attacks attempts (including my own) to compare past and present experiences of imperialism as leading to "profound errors in understanding the past." But the question could also be asked whether we are equally compromised by avoiding the existence of a distinct discourse of imperialism in our ancient sources and in accepting at face value the view of the empire offered us by the elite testimonies that survive.

[44] "Conflict" as a theme in the book of the exhibition is largely restricted to the presentation of a few exquisite photographs of well-preserved finds from the Bar Kokhba revolt (see Opper 2008, 89–97). This strikes me as an opportunity missed, as some reviewers have noted (see Beard 2008). This is the problem with much traditional scholarship on the Roman Empire: it may on the surface appear to promise an equal emphasis on assimilation and on resistance, but in reality tends to concentrate on the former (Pippidi 1976).

[45] Book jacket blurb, Liberati and Bourbon 2001.

[46] See Lintott 1993 for these traditional emphases.

[47] See, for example, Dio, *Roman History*, 52; cf. Swan 2004 for an up to date commentary.

credentials of the Late Republic and the Republic's afterlife in later political thought.[48]

A significant development in modern studies of imperialism, much influenced by contemporary world developments, is the linkage to be made between imperialism and globalization.[49] One definition of globalization presents it as a "a social process in which constraints of geography on social and cultural arrangements recede and in which people become increasingly aware that they are receding."[50] It is readily apparent that empires create and maintain conditions that will tend to favor such processes. The collapse of the Soviet Union and the perceived aspiration of U.S. foreign policy toward universal world order have focused interest on earlier imperial powers with similar claims to "world" dominance. The Roman case is seen by some as an important example of the phenomenon. An interesting aspect of Michael Hardt and Antonio Negri's's view is that empire is a theoretical concept "characterized fundamentally by a lack of boundaries: Empire's rule has no limits."[51] The idea of an empire without limits had a strong Roman pedigree, of course, encapsulated in Virgil's "*imperium sine fine*" that Jupiter ordained was to be without physical or temporal constraints (*Aeneid* 1.278–79).[52]

Michael Doyle has identified three main models of imperial expansion (see table 1.1).[53] The metrocentric model emphasizes the attitudes and aspirations of those at the center. The pericentric model gives greater emphasis to events on the periphery determining the actions of an imperial state. Finally, the systemic or realist view seeks to explain empire in relation to theories about the nature of power and power disparities: war is a natural outcome of inherent instability in situations where the security of states is not guaranteed by international law. Security in such situations is often only achievable through a state acquiring power and influence at the expense of others. Modern studies of the nature of power in society are thus of potential interest to ancient historians.[54]

In terms of the Roman Empire, there has been considerable interest in Joseph Schumpeter's ideas about metrocentric militaristic societies creating "war machines" dedicated to imperial expansion.[55] William

---

[48] See, among others, Millar 2002.

[49] Hardt and Negri 2000; Hingley 2005; Hitchner 2008; Osterhammel and Petersson 2003; Pitts 2008; Sweetman 2007; Witcher 2000.

[50] Waters 2000, 5; cf. Sweetman 2007, 65–67.

[51] Hardt and Negri 2000, xiv; Howe 2002, 117.

[52] On the late Republican genesis of the Roman "vocation" for Mediterranean empire, see Gruen 1984a, 273–84.

[53] Doyle 1986, 11–47.

[54] See, for example, Foucault 1979, 1980; Said 1986.

[55] Schumpeter 1955, 88–89; see also the good summary in Champion 2004, 1–8.

Table 1.1

Different models of imperialism

	Metrocentric	Pericentric	Systemic
SCENARIO	Metropolitan state expands at expense of neighbors	Reaction or resistance of periphery to a state leads to expansion of state	Expansion of states conditioned by the balance of power relations among them
CAUSAL FACTORS	Disposition for conquest and domination at center	Action of officers of state at periphery or external factors override policies of center	Power asymmetries among states/territories create opportunities for expansion
PRIME MOTIVATION	Greed (profit), ideology, militarism, political capital (prestige, glory)	Personal greed/ambition, external pressure	Fear, competition

Source: Doyle 1986.

Harris has been the most influential exponent of this view of an atavistic and aggressive Roman state, though scholarly opinions vary on what motivated expansionism. Put bluntly, the main modern explanations of Rome's aggressive expansionism are fear, greed, glory, or a combination of all three.[56] There are crucial differences, for instance, between those that highlight economic motivation, as opposed to a simple lust for glory and prestige, underlying Roman behavior.[57] Moreover, some scholars have mixed a metrocentric approach that focuses on imperialism as a central element of Roman politics and society, with a more pericentric view.[58] The view that Roman expansion was sometimes undertaken with great reluctance in the face of external threats and severe provocation rests in part on the post facto justifications offered by the Roman sources for the frequent wars of conquest.[59] There have been rather fewer theoretical explorations of the systemic operation of power in Roman imperialism, though Edward N. Luttwak's analysis of the rationale behind Roman frontiers in these terms remains a valuable and underrated attempt.[60]

[56] Harris 1971, 1978, 1984. See also Dyson 1985; North 1981; Rich 1995 (an excellent summary of the three main theories regarding motivations). The recent monographs by Eckstein (2006, 2008) on the rise of Rome and its relations with the Hellenistic world will be both controversial and influential for their engagement with modern political science.

[57] See Gruen 1984b; Harris 1971; Rich 1995 (all reprinted in Champion 2004). See also Cornell 1995 on early Roman expansionism.

[58] See, for example, Champion 2004, 5.

[59] Badian 1968; Frank 1914 famously named this "defensive imperialism" and the theme is common in so-called gradualist appraisals of the acquisition of Rome's empire.

[60] Luttwak 1976; cf., among others, Drummond and Nelson 1994; Frontières 1993; Hanson 1989; Isaac 1990; Mattern 1999; Whittaker 1994, 2004a.

TABLE 1.2
Bartel's model of Roman colonialism and imperialism

Strategy	Imperialism	Colonialism
ERADICATION OR RESETTLEMENT	Regional "empty cell"	Abrupt culture change
ACCULTURATION	Slow indigenous culture change	Slow indigenous culture change
EQUILIBRIUM	Indigenous cultural maintenance	Settlement enclaves

Source: Bartel 1989.

An alternative approach to the Roman Empire (and indeed perhaps to many other empires) is to see its territorial and political development as the ad hoc amalgam of metrocentric, pericentric, and systemic impulses, which varied in relative intensity over time. The logical conclusion from this is that there was no such thing as one Roman imperialism; we must talk of Roman imperialisms and recognize that the empire's shape-shifting nature was outside the control of any one person or body of people.

This proposition that Roman imperialism was a dynamic phenomenon, affected by change at center and periphery as well as through systemic factors, has important implications and helps to resolve some of the problems with prior attempts to model the impacts of Roman imperialism and colonialism. For example, one 1980s model presented variation primarily in terms of binary social groupings (Romans and natives) and envisaged three alternative strategies for political and economic control in colonial situations, with a matrix of six possible outcomes (see table 1.2).[61] The categories appear now perhaps to be rather crude and static either/or choices.

The Romans themselves tried to rationalize their understanding of their imperial power and, though a somewhat retrospective process, this ideological element gave the Roman Empire a distinctive character.[62] The Roman upper classes devoted considerable energy to legitimizing and justifying their empire. Some of the greatest works of classical literature, such as Virgil's *Aeneid*, were thinly veiled apologias for Roman dominance, evoking its predestination for the role and the universality of its Empire: "You, Roman, remember by your empire to rule the world's peoples, for these will be your arts, to impose the practice of peace, to be sparing to the subjected, and to beat down the defiant."[63]

---

[61] See Bartel 1989, esp. 174–76; cf. Jordan 2003, 26–30, for a discussion of the problems with the model.

[62] Champion 2004, 162–213; Woolf 1995.

[63] Virgil, *Aeneid*, 6.851–53.

Throughout Livy's *History* a principal theme was that of the glory and justice of Rome's territorial and political expansion. A particular point of scruple was the notion of the just war, which governed and ostensibly limited the circumstances under which Rome could declare war on prospective opponents.[64] However, the claims made by our ancient sources about the insistence on *iusta causa* in the fetial procedure clearly misrepresented the reality. Rome had very broad definitions of its "hemispherical interests" and a low threshold of how these might be threatened by others.[65] Moreover, there was no independent body to sit in judgment on Rome's claims that it had done everything to avoid war and that ultimate responsibility for the outbreak of hostilities always lay with its neighbors and opponents. This goes beyond mere self-justification, particularly when coupled with consideration of Roman writings on the clemency and justice shown to defeated enemies and new subjects. Taken together these reveal the creation of a complex ideology of empire that distorted reality and allowed the Roman elite to believe in the justice and divine approval of its colonial role.[66]

The expansion of the Roman citizen elite and the integration of provincials into the fabric of government are generally recognized as characteristic aspects of Roman imperialism.[67] They certainly provide significant contrasts with the behaviors of modern empires and help to explain the extent and the durability of the Roman Empire.[68] The imperial rhetoric of the Late Republic and the early empire built up concepts of honor and moral reputation, but we must be careful not to take this self-image of the Roman elite entirely at face value.[69] In any case, the empire was not a level playing field; some provincial elites were noticeably more advantaged than others in the competition for posts and stipends. Behind the rhetoric of universal benefits there was fierce infighting within and between provincial elites to secure advantage for themselves and their communities. The elite class was always small—for every winner in the provinces there were a hundred other people whose exploitation supported the social position of the elite.

It is no surprise that juridical justifications of later empires have often sought and found support in the workings and values of the Roman

---

[64] Cicero, *De officiis*, 1.34–36; Dionysius of Halicarnassus, *Roman Antiquities*, 2.72.

[65] Webster 1995b, 1996b.

[66] See Brunt 1978 for an excellent discussion.

[67] See, for example, Dench 1995 for the transformation of the central Apennine peoples.

[68] Ando 2000 provides a recent (but traditionally framed) analysis of how colonial government involved local elites. Note, however, the critical view of Ando's political naïveté expressed by Rose 2006. See also De Blois 2001; Hanson 1988; Levick 1985.

[69] Cf. Lenden 1997.

Empire.[70] The concept of imperial right and the emphasis on the maintenance of peace through the waging of aggressive "just wars" are especially strong in comparative situations.[71] It is, in fact, a common feature of imperial systems to create elaborate facades that at one and the same time disguise the true nature and motivation of imperial government and provide imperial servants with an apparently moral backdrop for their actions; colonization "could be (re)presented as a virtuous and necessary 'civilizing' task involving education and paternalistic nurture. An example of this is Kipling's famous admonition to America in 1899 to 'Take up the White Man's Burden' . . . colonialism developed an ideology rooted in obfuscatory justification, and its violent and essentially unjust processes became increasingly difficult to perceive behind a liberal smokescreen of civilizing 'task' and paternalistic 'development' and 'aid.'"[72]

Whatever people made of such ideological posturing in the nineteenth and early twentieth centuries, the demise of the modern colonial empires has led to a significant shift in opinion. In popular British culture, the idea of empire was transformed during the later twentieth century from a normative power for good to an archetype of evil—think *Star Wars* and *The Lord of the Rings* as the successors to Rudyard Kipling or Rider Haggard.[73] The effect of this on scholarly work on the Roman Empire has not been as profound as might have been expected.

There are several reasons for this. While Oxford classicists influenced the running of the British Empire, the British Empire also profoundly affected the nature of the study and teaching of ancient history in the early twentieth century.[74] The situation was paralleled in other European countries with nineteenth-century imperial ambitions and classical pretensions. Some classicists have been quick to cry "anachronism" when contemporary reflections have impacted negatively on the orthodox presentation of the ancient world. Ronald Syme's writing of *The Roman Revolution* was, of course, influenced by his concerns about the rise of fascism and Stalinism, a point some used in criticism of his depiction of

---

[70] The links between past and present in the formative years of the British Empire are quite explicit, for instance, in "The Heirs of Rome," the first chapter in Jan Morris's marvelous *Pax Britannica* (1979). See also the debate between Freeman 1991, 1996 and Hingley 1991, 1993, 1995.

[71] Hardt and Negri 2000, 10.

[72] Howe 2002, 47; cf. Champion 2004, 162–63.

[73] Fox 1929, v, provides an excellent example of the self-delusional aspects of the early-twentieth-century view of the British Empire as a "theory of world policy which is essentially the creation of the British mind: that of co-operation, without compulsion, of communities with common interests and common affections." Rather prematurely, Fox dismissed French and German claims that the British Empire was on the wane (vi–viii).

[74] Freeman 2007; Hingley 2000, 2008; Vasunia 2003, 2005.

Augustus as a cynical and cold-blooded manipulator.[75] In a somewhat different manner, Marcel Benabou's book on African resistance to Romanization caused a storm of protest in French academic circles by explicitly drawing parallels between resistance to French and Roman colonization of the Maghreb; this despite the fact that the entire direction of French research on Roman Africa had been thoroughly compromised by its links with the modern imperial project.[76] The implications of this have to be faced: it is not just the postcolonial scholars who need to beware of anachronism; all modern literature on Roman imperialism is in effect part of an imperialist discourse of considerable longevity.

I shall return to the place of postcolonial perspectives later on. For the moment let me just say that recent approaches to the study of imperialism in the modern period lay greater stress on evaluating both the positive and negative impacts of imperialism on subject peoples than has habitually been the case in Roman studies. There is still too much of a tendency in writing on the Roman Empire to ignore the sinister side of its power and to assume that the best motivations lay behind its operation. Overall, both Roman history and Roman archaeology remain relatively undertheorized disciplines.[77] For instance, the twenty-first-century reception of the messages of power and majesty from Roman times is still handled somewhat uncritically.[78] There have also been disappointingly few attempts in the modern period to write wide-ranging accounts of the nature of the Roman Empire from an archaeological perspective.[79]

The traditional approaches to the study of the Roman army and the frontiers of the empire, for instance, illustrate a chronic lack of intellectual engagement with bigger issues in favor of a piling up of descriptive detail of forts, equipment, inscriptions, military careers, and so on (see fig. 1.5).[80] There are some important initiatives to create a more dynamic agenda for the study of the impacts of the military community or of the complex interactions of the frontier zones.[81] Ultimately, our understanding of the demise of the Roman Empire must focus on the long-term

[75] Syme 1939; Millar 1981.

[76] Benabou 1976; Fentress 2006, 3–4; see also chapter 2 of the resent volume.

[77] See, among others, Dyson 1993; James 2003; Woolf 1990, 2004b.

[78] Zanker 1988 is the most notable exception, but two recent volumes reveal continuing mixed success at engaging with critical issues: De Blois et al. 2003; and Hingley 2001.

[79] Among the plethora of recent companion volumes on all aspects of classical antiquity, there is a continuing lack of a volume devoted to the archaeology of the Roman Empire. Earlier attempts at synthesis include Johnson 1989; Wacher 1987a, 1987b.

[80] See James 2002 for a detailed critique of the current state of Roman army studies. For a different view of the status quo, see Le Bohec 1994.

[81] Goldsworthy and Haynes 1999; James 1999b; Whittaker 1994, 2004a.

FIGURE 1.5 A remarkable modern monument erected at Wallsend near Newcastle upon Tyne, commemorating by name Roman soldiers known to have been involved in the construction of Hadrian's Wall. This celebration of imperial overlordship is a striking example of a tendency in Britain to regard the Roman Empire with uncritical adulation.

impacts of the frontier armies and changes in power relations across the frontier zones.[82]

Vulgar and Ugly: The Other Face of Roman Imperialism?

> In modern text books the term "Romanization" is put to frequent employment. It is vulgar and ugly, worse than that, anachronistic and misleading. "Romanization" implies the execution of a deliberate policy. That is to misconceive the behaviour of Rome.[83]

The quotation above is a characteristic Syme insight—he had both a good eye for spotting the questionable concept and a certain bluntness in exposing it. The use of "vulgar and ugly" catch the eye here, though Syme was, of course, fundamentally expressing his dislike of the use of the term *Romanization* in academic debate, not commenting on the nature of the Roman regime. One is reminded of a famous aphorism, "Imperialism is not a word for scholars."[84] However, Syme's words also recall to my mind some similarly trenchant comments by another Oxford scholar, R. G. Collingwood, on the Romanization of art in Roman Britain: "The conquest forced artists 'into the mould of Roman life, with its vulgar efficiency and lack of taste, destroyed that gift and reduced their arts to the level of mere manufactures' and Romano-British art was 'dull, mechanical imitation . . . third rate artistic achievement . . . an ugliness which pervades the place like a London fog: not merely the common vulgar ugliness of the Roman Empire, but a blundering, stupid ugliness that cannot even rise to the level of that vulgarity.'"[85]

This is not the place to engage in a broader debate about the aesthetics of Roman art and rchitecture. But I think it is noncontroversial to aver that its products were not always subtle and, just as in Victorian England, for instance, this is in part a reflection of grandiosity overcoming good taste. The vulgarity of absolute rulers has often been remarked on, with plenty of examples in the modern world of lavish but monstrous palaces.[86]

Sadly, Syme's demolition job on the use of the term Romanization was not widely picked up on first publication, with the consequence that the false paradigm of Romanization still haunts us today.[87] I shall return to

---

[82] Pohl, Wood, and Reimitiz, 2001. Cf. Heather 2005; Ward-Perkins 2005.

[83] Syme 1988b, 64.

[84] Lord Hailey, quoted in Doyle 1986, 11.

[85] Collingwood 1936, 247, 250.

[86] York 2005 is an engaging study of modern dictators' palaces.

[87] For a range of views, see Keay and Terrenato 2001; Mattingly 2002; Millett 1990a, 1990b; and Woolf 1992b.

the issue of Romanization near the end of this chapter; for the moment, though, I want to develop the theme of vulgarity and ugliness in another way, by moving beyond the meanings intended by Syme and Collingwood and considering whether the terms could be applied also to aspects of Roman imperialism itself.[88]

The ugly side of Roman imperialism is represented most obviously by the record of warfare and destruction left in its wake.[89] Surely, we must question the benign view of Roman warfare as illustrated by Cicero, who wrote, "rather than inflicting harm, our wars were waged on behalf of allies or to uphold our *imperium* and their conclusion was either moderate or no harsher than necessary."[90]

We need to consider losses to Rome and its enemies not only in terms of battlefield deaths but also the "collateral damage" inflicted in war on civilian communities, settlements, farmland, and other economic resources.[91] The enslaving of enemies was another routine element of ancient warfare, as was the levying of troops from defeated enemies and allies under treaty terms. The pillaging of wealth from conquered peoples to offset the costs of campaigns and to fund extravagant offerings of thanks to the gods who had supported Rome's victories had severe regional impacts. In the same way, initial confiscation and potential large-scale redistribution of land served equally as a tool of retribution, coercion, and persuasion.

Of course, Rome was not a unique instance of an ancient state that resolved problems of security with extreme violence against its neighbors. As Craige Champion notes, "The world of the ancient Mediterranean states, the world in which Rome existed, seems to fulfil the grimmest paradigms of state behaviour proposed by international systems theoreticians."[92] However, while we can debate the exactitude of figures given in the ancient sources, it is arguable that the scale of Rome's martial effort and colonial violence was unprecedented in antiquity.[93] For instance, more than three hundred triumphs are recorded from the sequence of wars between 509 and 519 BC and a "triumph" was only awarded for a victory in a battle that ended a declared war and killed at least 5,000 of the enemy.[94]

---

[88] MacMullen (1966, 1988) is a rare example of a modern scholar who has turned the spotlight on the deficiencies of Roman imperialism and its servants; there is much interesting material also in Bauman 2000; and Isaac 2004.

[89] Faulkner 2008, 46–176 presents the bloody narrative of the key period of the mid-fourth century BC down to Actium in 30 BC.

[90] Cicero, *De officiis* 2.26–27.

[91] "Collateral damage" is a modern expression for a phenomenon that is as old as war.

[92] Champion 2004, 6.

[93] See Campbell 2002, 1–21 for a general review of the process by which Rome went to war.

[94] *Inscriptiones Italiae* 13.1. For a fascinating new sociohistorical study of the Roman triumph, see Beard 2007.

The total casualties in these wars must have far exceeded the implied minimum of 1,500,000. As an example, Caesar's decade of campaigning in Gaul alone is alleged to have cost a million Gaulish lives.[95]

Damage was not all one-sided, and Roman casualties in certain wars were high, with at least 90 severe defeats in battle suffered during the Republican era alone, with total casualties measured in hundreds of thousands.[96] In their darkest hour, confronting Hannibal, more than 50,000 Roman and allied troops perished in the years 218–215 BC alone. The ambush and destruction of three legions in the Teutoburg Forest in AD 9 was the single greatest catastrophe of the Early Principate.[97] But there were plenty of other setbacks, reflecting the ability of Rome's enemies to learn its weaknesses and to develop the tactics to inflict major defeats. This was an occupational hazard for the frontier armies of the principate.[98] They were the dominant force, but their dominance was neither unchallengeable nor unchallenged.

For a power that espoused civilization, justice, and law, the Roman way of war was not always gentle—particularly against those perceived as intransigent or guilty of humiliating Roman armies in the past. The fire and sword devastation meted out by Germanicus on the villages of the Marsi, Chatti, and Cherusci to avenge the Varian disaster is typical of the sort of conduct that could border on attempted genocide.[99] Some of the most graphic depictions of the sort of treatment that might be inflicted on civilian communities after military victories over conventional forces concerned occasions when civil war resulted in the sacking of Roman cities, as at Cremona in AD 69.[100] Although Roman writings are often tempered with talk of "sparing the vanquished," it is equally clear that Rome had no compunction about employing the tactics of

[95] Plutarch, *Caesar* 15.5. There are difficulties with all such figures, of course, and Caesar was notable for his exaggerations and inventions. Nonetheless, the cumulative picture from a wide array of figures recorded in the Roman sources is that casualties in Roman wars were extraordinarily high overall in comparison to many other preindustrial societies and pre-gunpowder, unmechanized warfare. The demographic issues surrounding Rome's wars have been recently reviewed in Rosenstein 2004.

[96] Champion 2004, 7. It was of course an axiom of Roman history that "Romans have been beaten, they have lost battles, but never a war, and only wars matter" (Lucilius 613, quoted in Dalby 2000, 8).

[97] For a good evocation of the events and background to the Varian disaster, see Wells 2003.

[98] See Burns 2003 and Williams 1999 for the historical consequences of this.

[99] Tacitus, *Annals*, 1.51.1, 1.56.3–4, 2.16.1, 2.21.2.

[100] Tacitus, *Histories*, 3.33–34; I disagree with Whittaker 2004b, 131–32 that this breakdown of discipline may reflect the particularly high temperature of civil war. The Roman army was not an easily controlled machine; it was made up of lots of individual soldiers (James 2001b). On mass murder as a recurrent option in Roman warfare, see Isaac 2004, 215–24.

extermination where it was felt inadvisable to offer a safe pardon to defeated enemies.[101]

The human impact went much deeper, due to the practice of enslaving certain categories of prisoners taken in war. For example, in a single five-year period of the Third Samnite War (297–293 BC), figures from Livy indicate that over 66,000 captives were enslaved from a variety of defeated enemies.[102] The capacity of the slave market increased over time; in 167 BC over 150,000 slaves from Epirus were disposed of, and Caesar allegedly took over 1 million in the conquest of Gaul.[103] The analysis by Keith Hopkins of the potential numbers of slaves transported into the heartlands of the empire by the first century BC may still be debated, but the argument is about the relative balance between the freeborn and slaves in Italy; the massive scale of the enslaved population, numbering in the millions, is not seriously disputed.[104] The demographic impact of such relentless and ruthless warfare was thus profound, though in time the subjugated peoples were allowed to participate in the next round of expansion and in the foundation of colonies on captured lands. Latin colonies established between 334 and 263 BC are estimated to have required the seizure and reallocation of over 7,000 square kilometers of prime farming lands to over 70,000 settlers.[105] In chapter 4, I shall explore the darker aspects of the operation of Roman colonial power, using sexuality as a main focus.

Paradoxically, the long-term maintenance of Rome's empire required far larger standing armies than had been levied to conquer most of its constituent territory. In the early second century BC the average number of legions in service was less than nine, with eleven the highest number attested; from 167 to 91 BC the annual average is estimated to have been slightly lower.[106] Under the Principate the average number of legions was generally twenty-eight to thirty, though expansionist wars became rare (see fig. 1.2). This seems to me to represent a fundamental change in the nature of the Roman Empire—perhaps of similar magnitude to the moment when the British Empire took over from the East India Company the commitment to garrison a huge land territory in India. The corollary of higher recurrent military spending was a need to exploit the various overseas territories more effectively in order to pay for it all. The

---

[101] Augustus, *Res Gestae*, 3, is explicit on this point.

[102] Cornell 1989, 389.

[103] See Livy 45.34.4–6; Hammond 1967, 634–35, on Epirus; Plutarch, *Caesar*, 15.5; and Faulkner 2008, 159 on Gaul.

[104] Hopkins 1978, 99–132. See also Dal Lago and Katsari 2008; Webster 2005, 2008; and the range of studies on slavery in *Journal of Roman Archaeology* 18 (2005).

[105] Cornell 1989, 405.

[106] Rich 1995, 44–47.

extremely ad hoc provincial arrangements for levying tribute of the second and early first centuries BC, often remarked on by the "gradualists," were supplemented or replaced by more complex bureaucracies and far-reaching changes in land ownership and taxation. The initial stages of this were already evident by the time of Caesar, but took more concrete form with the establishment of the Principate. Chapter 5 will focus on the mechanisms that the state developed for exploiting the land, portable wealth, people, and natural resources of subjected territories.

Postcolonial Approaches: Giving Voice to the Subaltern

What these instances remind us of is the powerful and disruptive impact of imperialism where the power inequalities were particularly large. The problem is that we have little extant writing from the Roman world that explicitly explored the feelings of provincials about the process of incorporation into the empire.[107] There is one prime exception to this general rule—the Jews. While there is a substantial ancient and modern literature on their relations with the empire, there is also perhaps a tendency to overstress the atypicality of the Jews.[108] They are seen as something special in the empire, and their voices thus are used to give life to ancient Judaism rather than to form a basis for understanding the experience of other provincials under Roman rule.

For other provincial societies, the voices that made themselves heard were primarily those of elite people who had closely aligned themselves with Rome and had taken their place in delivering local government and justice. Men like Aelius Aristides or Dio Chrysostom expended great efforts to extol the benefits of the empire for their fellow citizens, but the existence of such eulogies in some ways reinforces the sense that they did not contain universally self-evident truths.[109] The complicity of high status men in the government of Empire and as conspicuous consumers of its globalized culture must be recognized.

The Roman armies were another group who were vocal in registering their loyalty to the empire and who used its material culture to shape their identity in distinctive ways and to give themselves a sense of commonality.[110] In some provinces, such as Britain, the community of soldiers had a hugely distorting impact on the provincewide pattern of evidence

---

[107] McCarthy 2006.

[108] Goodman 1998 and Schwartz 2001 are good points of introduction to the impact of imperial domination on Jewish society.

[109] Cf. the analysis of Nutton 1978.

[110] James 1999b, 2001.

of literacy and the use of certain types of material culture.[111] Discoveries like the Vindolanda tablets open an extraordinary window on life in the Roman Empire and are rightly celebrated as one of the major discoveries of recent decades.[112] However, they do not cast much light outside the close society of the community of soldiers. Nor is it just the exceptional discoveries like the Vindolanda tablets that distort our picture; the archaeological record of Roman Britain is dominated by the material culture of the Roman garrison. To a considerable extent, the army used its literacy and material culture to differentiate and to distance itself from civilians in the provinces.[113]

A good example of the pervasive influence of soldiers in the frontier zones comes from a remote region in southeast Jordan—the Hisma. A Greek graffito was carved on a rock here: "The Romans always win. I, Lauricius, wrote 'Hail Zenon.'"[114] However, this is neither indicative of "barbarian" defeatism nor acknowledgment of Roman superiority by civilian subjects. Lauricius and Zenon were almost certainly Roman soldiers (Zenon an Arab tribune in a Roman auxiliary unit), and in these frontier lands this was a standard (if superstitious) mantra of the garrison troops.[115]

Leaving aside the provincial elites and the army, then, what of the rest of the subject people in the provinces? What do we really know about their lives in and experiences of the Roman Empire? This is the area where postcolonialism can serve as a particularly valuable tool to aid our understanding of the Roman situation.[116] Postcolonialism concerns the study of the cultural effects of colonialism and colonization.[117] One of the major achievements of postcolonial studies has been to identify alternative narratives—to give voice to the subaltern.[118] For instance, the rare accounts

[111] De la Bédoyère 2001, 11 notes, "The army monopolizes the historical and epigraphic record. . . . Even when cities do yield inscriptions, more often than not they record soldiers passing through, on detachment. . . . The army influenced the goods brought in, and new goods manufactured, while army pay fuelled the liquid economy, and the need to pay the army fuelled the need to conquer."

[112] Bowman and Thomas 1994, 2003; cf. Birley 2003; Bowman 1994.

[113] The argument is developed in some detail in Mattingly 2006c, 199–224; 520–28, and in chapter 8 of the present volume.

[114] Sartre 1993, 165–82, no. 138.

[115] Isaac 1998, 341.

[116] Though not all have welcomed the emergence of the new agenda; see Branigan 1994.

[117] Excellent introductions to postcolonial studies are Ashcroft, Griffiths, and Tiffin 1995; Ashcroft et al. 1998, esp. 186–92; Schwarz and Ray 2000; and Williams and Chrisman 1993.

[118] Spivak 1995. Chakrabarty 2000, 27, notes that there still remains a problem in constructing postcolonial or subaltern history "insofar as the academic discourse of history . . . is concerned, 'Europe' remains the sovereign, theoretical subject of all histories, including the ones we call 'Indian', 'Chinese', 'Kenyan', and so on." A key aspect of modern postco-

that present the indigenous side of what happened during the Spanish conquest of South America are particularly illuminating specifically because they can be set alongside Spanish accounts that provide a radically different version of events and behaviors.[119] The issue of resistance was a key motif of much early research, with some interesting insights on how material evidence could be subjected to different readings.[120]

As John Moreland has illustrated, it is too simplistic to equate people without history to a lack of texts. Equally it can be unhelpful to try to promote archaeological evidence as a complete proxy for the written word in writing these hidden lives.[121] Nonetheless, writing is just one "technology of power" and a broad-based study of texts and objects has much to recommend it. "The reality," notes Moreland, "is that people in the past . . . made and manipulated objects (and texts) as projections of their views about themselves and their place in the world . . . [objects] were actively used in the production and transformation of identities, they were used in the projection of, and resistance to, power, and they were used to create meaning in, and to structure, the routines of daily life."[122]

I shall return in chapter 8 to explore in detail the theme of identity and the way a variety of different forms of material culture can be assimilated with the literary and epigraphic evidence.

Though initially disdained by some historians, postcolonial studies have come to influence the mainstream agenda of historical research.[123] For example, historical studies of more recent periods of imperialism have shown an increasing interest in exploring the relations between colonizer and colonized, following the lead set by a number of ex–colonial subjects.[124] A key element of this new wave of research is the emphasis on the forging of multiple new identities, both in the peripheral territories and at the core of colonial worlds.[125]

The achievements of postcolonial scholarship in relation to imperialism in the modern world are considerable and present both a challenge to and an opportunity for scholars of antiquity to address similar issues.

---

lonial studies thus concerns the decentering of this discourse, and I can see how similar approaches to the Roman Empire might produce interesting results.

[119] See De las Casas 1992; and MacCormack 2007, esp. 66–100.

[120] Ferguson and Whitehead 1992; Miller, Rowlands, and Tilley 1989; Scott 1990.

[121] See Moreland 2001, 9–32, esp. 19.

[122] Moreland 2001, 80–84.

[123] Colley 2002 is a useful way into this debate, albeit with a modern British focus. Mignolo 2000 is a good example of the convergence of postcolonial studies with globalization, with an emphasis on subaltern identities, colonial difference, border thinking, and occidentalism.

[124] Daunton and Halpern 1999; cf. Fanon 1986 and Memmi 1965.

[125] Bailey 1999, Morgan 1999.

The methodologies and exemplars are available. To date, it seems to me that archaeologists have shown more interest than ancient historians in applying postcolonial thinking to the study of the Roman Empire.[126] It is important that such studies look beyond evidence of direct resistance to Roman power if we are to avoid simply creating a binary opposition with traditional assimilative models.[127]

My own interest in these issues was greatly stimulated by the writing of Edward Said, from whom I adopted the concept of discrepant experience.[128] The notion of discrepant experience demands that modern scholars explore different narratives of colonial pasts, not just the historical account of the victors. Said saw this primarily as a dichotomy between ruler and ruled, where "each had a set of interpretations of their common history with its own perspectives, historical sense, emotions and traditions."[129] Indeed, the term *discrepancy* has sometimes been employed in postcolonial studies to denote only indigenous resistance to the imperial power, though I think the true potential of discrepant experience is realized when it encapsulates *all* the varied impacts of and reactions to colonialism. We need to break free from the tendency to see the colonial world as one of rulers and ruled (Romans and natives) and explore the full spectrum of discrepancy between these binary oppositions.[130]

An immediate objection in relation to the ancient world is that unlike with more recent imperialisms we have little surviving written testimony of subject people. The twenty-first-century narrative of Roman history will thus always struggle to break free of the influence of the historical winners who penned it. However, the absence of evidence is not the same as evidence of absence. The deliberate burning of the library of Carthage or the setting aside of Etruscan accounts bearing on the early history of Rome indicate clearly that there were once alternative narratives. The critical point here is that we must be aware that imperial systems elicit a range of reactions in those who become subjects, from self-interested collaboration to resistance unto death, and all manner of intermediate positions. Postcolonial and postmodern literature provide plenty of examples of imaginative ways to explore the existence of discrepant experiences of empire and its subthemes of culture, identity, memory, and systemic injustice.[131]

---

[126] See Mattingly 1997a; Scott and Webster 2003; Webster and Cooper 1996; Wells 1999, 2001.

[127] On resistance and rebellion in the Roman world, see Bowersock 1987; Burnham and Johnson 1979; and Dyson 1975.

[128] Said 1978, 1993; Mattingly 1997a, 1997b.

[129] Said 1993, 11.

[130] Woolf 1997.

[131] See, e.g., Brenton 1989; Kunzru 2003; Sivanandan 1997; and Soueif 1999.

Fundamentally, we need to move away from interpretational models that stress only the advantages and "self-evident" attractions of being subject to Roman dominion. An awareness of discrepant experience allows a different sort of analysis of colonial discourse that works top down *and* bottom up. It also points out the changeability of attitudes and experiences across a spectrum of response, not just between dichotomous extremes. We should expect significant shifts in the nature of the Roman Empire (and its reception by its subjects) over time.[132] It would be surprising indeed if attitudes to Roman rule had not changed—for instance, becoming more generally positive with successive generations in provincial areas that enjoyed peaceful and prosperous conditions. But it is also clear that the Roman state did not offer the same opportunities and inducements to all in society (or to all provincial territories alike) and that some regions underwent little material change in their basic condition of exploitation and dependence across centuries of Roman military occupation.

COLONIALISM AND COLONIZATION

With these postcolonial approaches in mind, it is time to return to the definitions of colonialism and colonization.[133] Chris Gosden's work on colonialism is of particular importance in that he has proposed a series of important theoretical models to encompass a wide array of "colonial" situations in world history.[134] It is interesting to note that he draws his net wide and not all his colonial societies might meet the criteria that historians would require of an imperial power (for example, Vikings, Tongans). What is particularly attractive about Gosden's analysis is that he focuses his comparative study of colonialism on the nature and relationships of power, with particular emphasis on the interplay of people and material culture rather than on political structures.[135] He defines three main types of manifestation of colonial power, ranging in impact from extreme violence, to creative experimentation, to dominance achieved in a common cultural network (see table 1.3).

[132] An interesting sidelight on the Roman Empire is the fact that it made increasing use of exemplary violence in its judicial systems over time (Garnsey 1968). What does this tell us about the level of acceptance of the regime across society?

[133] Two important recent essays on the changing debate about what Roman colonization was and was not are Purcell 2005b and Terrenato 2005.

[134] See Gosden 2004, 24–40, for the presentation of the models.

[135] Ibid., 24.

TABLE 1.3
Gosden's models of colonialism

Gosden's models	Characteristics	Examples	Gosden reference
COLONIALISM WITHIN A SHARED CULTURAL MILIEU	Colonial situation arises within/among societies that share cultural values. Power operates within understood norms of behavior and limited by area of shared culture	Early forms from Mesopotamia to Greek colonies, Aztecs, Incas, early Chinese, Vikings, Tongans	2004, 41–81
MIDDLE-GROUND COLONIALISM	Based on high level of accommodation between colonizer and colonized. Cultural change is multilateral, not unilateral	Roman Empire, peripheries of Greek colonization, early modern colonial contacts in America, Africa, India, etc.	2004, 82–113
TERRA NULLIUS	Nonrecognition of preexisting culture opening way for massive land appropriation and destruction of indigenous societies. Colonial violence aided by impacts of disease	Spanish South America, later colonization of North America, Australia, New Zealand, Africa	2004, 114–52

Source: Gosden 2004.

Before looking at his typology and considering the implications of this for our understanding of the Roman Empire, I want to highlight Gosden's own qualifications about the use of his typology:

> The typology ... should not be seen as stable and fixed. Nor should [it] be seen as anything other than an attempt to simplify a large and confusing reality for initial heuristic purposes: it is something to be put at risk and modified through an encounter with different cases, rather than an adequate description of them all. The last qualification ... is that the typology should not be seen as a linear progression from one form to another: within one colonial formation all three types can exist simultaneously; there can be movement from one to another, or one form can be found alone.[136]

The earliest form defined by Gosden is colonialism within a shared cultural milieu, and it is also the one that seems farthest from modern expectations of imperial power.[137] Some of these cases can be presented

[136] Ibid., 25.
[137] Ibid., 32–33, 41–81.

as "colonialism without colonies."[138] The operation of power within societies sharing many cultural values in common has sometimes been perceived as a process of imposition of colonies by a colonizing power, as in the case of early Greek colonization. What Gosden argues is that the appearance of these colonies may have been due more to cultural and mercantile forces than military or political will. The formation of common points of identity created strong links between widely separated and initially independent states or polities. To some extent, this may be seen as a necessary initial stage in some colonial situations, bringing societies into cultural proximity and facilitating subsequent attempts by one to impose its dominance on others.

The middle ground is defined by Gosden as a more probable outcome of colonial contact than either destruction or acculturation of a subservient culture by a dominant power.[139] This gives active agency to the colonized as well as the colonizer in the cultural interaction consequent on the political domination of the one by the other.[140] Culture change here is seen as a two-way street in which the preexisting culture and values of the dominant power do not necessarily supplant those of the colonized society. Rather, what is likely to emerge in many colonial situations is a new set of cultural forms that are unique to the colonial situation, and which can in some cases be transmitted back to enact change at the empire's metropolitan core. On the other hand, it is important to remember that the power asymmetries in such situations can profoundly influence and constrain social behavior.[141] While native agency was clearly a significant factor in many colonial situations, we should not lose sight of the distorting effect of imperial power.

The third model defined by Gosden is that of *terra nullius*.[142] The violent dispossession of native peoples of their lands, accompanied by mass killing and eviction or deportation, has often been justified by the colonial fiction of creating something from a virgin landscape. The denial of the meaningful relationship of the existing population to their land was an important element in asserting the colonizers' right to take it over. Gosden argues that the terra nullius approach was unique to modern imperialism and lists its extreme impacts on indigenous societies in Australia, New Zealand, North America, and South Africa, among other notorious cases. There is no doubt that the combination of capitalism,

---

[138] Ibid. 2004, 41.

[139] Ibid, 2004, 30–32, 82–113.

[140] This trend in recent work on colonialism is well reflected in the work of Hodos 2006; Van Dommelen 1997, 1998, 2002, 2005; and Van Dommelen and Terrenato 2007a, 2007b.

[141] Mattingly 1997b; Webster 2001, 218.

[142] Gosden 2004, 25–30, 114–52.

technological advantages, racism and notions of social superiority, religious convictions, and the unintended weapon of disease have all given modern imperialism a particularly brutal aspect in some of its manifestations.

However, there are aspects of this catalog of acts of inhumanity that raise important questions, it seems to me, about the extent to which colonial domination creates conditions in which people transgress normal rules of behavior. Sven Lindquist's meditation on European colonialism in Africa, *"Exterminate All the Brutes"*, draws out the important conclusion that the Nazi concentration camps simply brought home to a European base the evils perpetrated in the name of empire elsewhere.[143] The atrocities committed by European powers in Africa encompassed not just the Germans, of course, but Belgians, French, British, Dutch, Spanish, Italian, and Portugese. I am struck not so much by the magnitude of the crimes against humanity carried out in the name of empire (shocking though they are); rather, it is their generality that registers.[144]

Yet it is clear that this slaughter was not a planned and coordinated action from the start, but something that evolved in the peripheral zones. The Roman colonial elites, like those of these more recent ages, were generally perturbed by the signs of moral degeneration in their societies as a side effect of imperial power.[145] The scientific and scholarly energy put into imperial justification was largely a post facto attempt by the imperial society at large to come to terms with what had happened in certain colonies. It seems entirely plausible that excesses that were similar in kind if not in scale have occurred in earlier colonial situations where there have been significant power imbalances and wide cultural difference between colonizer and colonized.

The potentially corrosive effects of colonial power are readily documented both by the celebrated villains (Verres in Sicily) and by real or claimed exemplars of the "good governor" (Agricola and Cato the Younger). The power dynamics of empires create the potential for brutality, injustice, and corruption even if the central authority strives to check this by creating channels for the legal recourse of aggrieved provincials and by exerting moral pressure on colonial servants to behave honorably. Many colonial officials/servants comply with the rules, but those that do not can have a disproportionate effect. The gap between aspiration and achievement is starkly illustrated by the conduct of U.S. troops in Iraq, responsible for both the moral action of removing the odious regime

---

[143] Lindquist 2002.

[144] See Pakenham 1991 and Newsinger 2006 for a detailed catalog of the horrors perpetrated in the name of modern imperial regimes.

[145] Lintott 1972.

of Saddam Hussein and for replicating some of its notorious behavior through the torture of civilians and the recently documented "war pornography" websites. I think that here we see, perhaps, an important systemic contributor to the evolution of imperialism, whether of the ancient or modern period.[146]

Gosden places the Roman Empire in his second category of colonialism, the middle ground, reflecting the modern consensus view of the integration of local elites and their contributions to the hybrid cultural pattern that was characteristic of the principate. That seems a fair enough judgment of the long-term impact of the Roman Empire, but I think there is certainly scope for Roman historians and archaeologists to explore the possible existence of Gosden's other types of colonial power at certain times and places. For instance, in many ways the earliest stages of Roman expansion within Italy could be presented as a good example of colonialism within a shared cultural milieu, especially since Rome's role as leader does not seem to have been as apparent initially as the later annalistic accounts painted it. There are also indications in Rome's dealings with "barbarians" and peoples on the extreme fringes of the empire that the colonial contact could pass through a phase akin to the *terra nullius* approach of the most extreme modern situations.

A necessary condition of the *terra nullius* was the dehumanizing of the "other," something we can find plenty of evidence for at the outer edge of empire. For example, Roman writers regularly portrayed peoples they came in contact with as falling into a series of bands of progressively more degenerate character. Brent Shaw has noted that the main cause of the inability of Roman writers to provide a true picture of peoples outside the empire was the "ideological necessity for a negative image of the barbarian."[147]

The parallelism of descriptions of the peoples of Britain and of Libya, for instance, suggests that we are looking at topoi (purposive stereotypes) designed to present conceptual prejudices rather than actual reality (see table 1.4). The main people of the Libyan Sahara were the Garamantes, commonly presented in Greco-Roman sources as the archetypes of warlike nomads, living in tents or scattered huts, lacking in laws or civilized structures. The investigation of the archaeology of their heartlands has revealed a radically different perspective of a sedentary agricultural people, exhibiting a highly sophisticated level of social and cultural

---

[146] The systemic transformation of righteous power into transgressive power in colonial situations is, of course, famously illustrated by Joseph Conrad's *Heart of Darkness* (2002) and its Vietnam and Cambodia–framed modern update in Francis Ford Coppola's *Apocalypse Now* (1979).

[147] Shaw 2000, 374–75.

TABLE 1.4
"Progressive Barbarization" in Britain and Africa

	Britain	*Libya*
COAST	Agricultural people, semicivilized, towns	Agricultural people, semicivilized, towns
INTERIOR	Pastoral peoples, no towns, scattered settlements	Pastoral peoples, no towns, scattered settlements, huts and tents
DEEPER INTERIOR	Warlike and lawless bands, sexually promiscuous, living in temporary shelters	Warlike and lawless bands, nomadic pastoralist, sexually promiscuous, living in huts and tents
DEEPEST INTERIOR	Naked savages, hunting and gathering part of lifestyle, can live like animals deep in bogs, eat bark	Naked savages, unintelligible batlike language, live in caves or sleep in open air, still further beyond are inhuman creatures with no heads, eyes in chests, etc.

evolution.[148] A similar trend emerges in Britain, where the sources paint a particularly bleak picture of the people of northern Scotland:

[The northern tribes] inhabit wild and waterless mountains and desolate and marshy plains; they have neither walls nor cities nor tilled fields, but live on their flocks and by hunting and on certain fruits ... They live in tents, naked and without shoes, possess their women in common, and rear all offspring in common. They have a democratic system for the most part and are very fond of plundering. For this reason they choose their boldest men as rulers ... They can endure hunger and cold and every hardship. For they plunge into the marshes and exist there for many days, only keeping their heads above the water, and in the forests they support themselves on bark and roots.[149]

The archaeological data on the Iron Age peoples of the region reveal aspects of social and economic sophistication that are unheralded in the literary sources, such as the existence of substantial timber and stone-built roundhouses and the development of agriculture in the suitable parts of the landscape in Fife and Moray.[150]

How much easier it must have been to deal with these enemies at the point of the sword if they were first relegated to subhuman status. It is clear that Rome sometimes acted against "barbarian" opponents with

---

[148] Mattingly 2003a, 76–90; 2004a, 47–52; 2006d.
[149] Dio, *Roman History*, 76[77].12.1–5.
[150] Hingley 1992; Mattingly 2006c, 47–54, 122–27, 428–39.

extreme and prejudicial violence, as when the Caledones and Maeatae revolted against Septimius Severus, immediately after their initial subjugation by his army.

> But when those in the island revolted again, he summoned the soldiers and ordered them to invade their country again and to kill everyone they met, quoting this:
> *Let no one escape sheer destruction*
> *At our hands, not even the child that the mother*
> *Bears in her womb, if a male, let him not escape sheer destruction.*[151]

There were other occasions when our Roman sources indicate that attempts were made to exterminate rebellious subjects or intractable opponents on the frontiers, such as the Silures of southeast Wales under Claudius or the Nasamones of Libya under Domitian.[152] It is irrelevant to my argument that there is no evidence that these people were fully exterminated; attempted genocides are rarely completed. However, what these instances do suggest is that license was granted from time to time to Roman armies to act against native groups with extreme prejudice. This situation seems to be at least partly comparable to the excesses of modern imperialism. An interesting aspect of imperial armies is that they very often made use of large native levies—whether Batavians in Britain or Sikhs in British India. The complicity of these troops in acts of violence against provincials and enemies of the empire highlights their psychological separation from civil society.[153]

It also illustrates once again the potential for transgressive behaviors. What occurred at the periphery was often not intended, foreseen, or indeed condoned at the center. The reasons for misbehavior and abuse are to some extent bound up with the realities of the power asymmetries between imperial servants and subjects. Sexual exploitation and judicial and administrative corruption are common symptoms of this.[154] In part they are due to the distances and slowness of communication between core and periphery, which require delegation of considerable authority to those on the ground while imposing problems of oversight and control.

---

[151] Dio, *Roman History*, 76[77].15.1–4, quoting Homer, *Iliad*, 6.57–59. The translation is taken from Birley 2005, where good discussion is also to be found.

[152] See Tacitus, *Annals*, 12.39, for the Silures; and Dio, *Roman History* [Epitome] 77.3.5, for the Nasamones.

[153] Again, this is not to deny that transgressive behavior in war was absent in pre-Roman society in Gaul or Britain, but it is arguable that the severity, extent, and periodicity of such actions was greater under Rome for the simple reasons that warfare and power differentials between soldiers and civilians were more pronounced.

[154] Hyam 1990; Young 1995.

Another driver of warfare against and repression of indigenous peoples at the margins of empires is that the representatives of the colonial power are often few in number and, though supported by the perception of imperial power, they are often more acutely aware of their own weakness than are their potential enemies. "Colonial weakness" can thus be an important catalyst in the segregation and reinforcement of difference between ruler and ruled in imperial settings. This fear factor also perhaps contributed in important ways to unpalatable behaviors by those in authority in colonial territories.[155]

To conclude this section, it seems clear to me that Roman colonialism went through different stages of development. We can contrast Rome's early struggle to establish position within Latium and central Italy with the more assured conquest and incorporation of other Italian peoples—involving significant land confiscations from the fourth century onward. A peculiarity of the Late Republican Empire was its initial reluctance to establish colonies in overseas territories, when there had been no such scruples about Italy, where land allocations and colonial settlements that started in the fourth century were largely completed by 170 BC. The first successful and large-scale overseas colonies were not established until the dictatorship of Julius Caesar, gaining even greater momentum under Augustus.[156] Although these colonies increasingly drew on citizen troops recruited outside Italy, the creation of such citizen communities in provincial territories was a significant development.[157] As has already been noted, this period appears to mark a distinctive new phase of Roman imperialism that was different to what had gone before in important ways. These changes broadly correlate with the institution of the principate, which demanded new ground rules for the exploitation of empire and the command of armies. The empire had largely ceased to expand by the second century AD, with few new colonies thereafter and an increasing focus on the maintenance of established territory and frontiers. By the third and fourth centuries the empire had metamorphosed again in order to preserve the security of the emperor in the face of internal rivals and a shift in the balance of power with neighboring peoples.

What I have just described in outline is a series of fundamental variations of Roman imperialism and colonialism. The same dynamism can be detected in studying the cultural impact of empire and it is to the question of Romanization that I want to return for the final section of this chapter.

---

[155] See Fincham 2001 for an interesting discussion of "colonial weakness."
[156] Kallett-Marx 1995; Rich 1995, 48–49.
[157] Mann 1983.

Romanization and Identity

Although according to the *Oxford English Dictionary* the first attestation of the verb *to romanize* is 1607, we cannot ignore the extent to which the meaning and use of the term Romanization was extended during the most intensive phase of modern imperial expansion, notably through the work of Francis Haverfield.[158] The traditional view of Romanization has been that it was a deliberate policy on the part of the empire to reconcile subjects to colonial rule and to reward their compliance with the fruits of civilization. There is precious little in ancient literature to back up this view, apart from a few pronouncements by upper-class Romans on the benefits of imperial rule that ring no more true than the claims of later imperial servants to have always prioritized the well-being of subject peoples. Yet many histories of Rome use the paradigm of Romanization as the bedrock of interpretation; for example: "Virgil's exhortations regarding the use of Rome's military might were set in a broader context—that of a 'civilising mission.' Indeed, military conquest was not, except perhaps in the minds of a few traditionalists, an end in itself; its purpose was to establish the conditions in which a culture of Romanization could flourish. . . .Only thus could prosperity be realised in the provinces and (eventually) the empire at large. Romanization was, therefore, a crucial part of the process of empire building."[159]

While it is still possible to find plenty of people who maintain the older belief in a systematic and standardized acculturation process that was initiated by the state, Martin Millett, Greg Woolf, and others have reinterpreted Romanization as primarily a manifestation of elite negotiation and native agency.[160] It is easy to overlook the fact that not everyone in society had the same negotiating capital as the native elites and the approach of the agents of the state could also be heavy booted (see fig. 1.6). The problems with the Romanization paradigm have been well aired in recent years. Principal among these is the fact that the term Romanization has lost whatever precision it may once have had due to the multiple and often contradictory understandings of what it means.

To sum up some of the principal objections, Romanization

- has multiple meanings/understandings and these make it a flawed paradigm
- is a very unhelpful term—it implies that cultural change was unilateral and unilinear (with the flow from advanced civilization to less advanced communities)

---

[158] Haverfield 1915; cf. Freeman 2007, 1–42; and Hingley 2000.
[159] Shotter 2003, 230–32.
[160] Millett 1990a; Woolf 1997; cf. Blagg and Millett 1990; and Metzler et al. 1995.

FIGURE 1.6 Negotiation with an imperial power can be a tricky and asymmetric business. An alternative view of what incorporation into the Roman Empire meant on the ground. (Cartoon by Simon James; reproduced with permission.)

- is part of a modern colonial discourse on the nature of empire
- places great emphasis on elite sites, Roman state monuments, and elite culture
- leads scholars to take a fundamentally pro-Roman and top-down view
- de-emphasizes elements suggesting continuing traditions of indigenous society.
- reinforces an interpretation of material culture change that is simplistic and narrow (acculturation, emulation, etc.)
- focuses attention on the degree of sameness across provinces, rather than the degree of difference/divergence.

I am not aware of other areas of the study of imperialism that cling so tenaciously to interpretative models designed in the jingoistic empire days of the late nineteenth and early twentieth centuries. Increasingly the term is put in inverted commas or qualified.[161] A paradigm with so many different definitions is no paradigm at all.

---

[161] Keay and Terrenato 2001, ix: "weak Romanization." See also Millett 2004.

Some scholars have objected to the unilateral or unilinear flow of culture change implied by Romanization, when empirical studies show that what took place was not a uniform process of acculturation of provinces by the dominant civilization.[162] The impact of the diverse civilizations of the eastern empire on the cultural mix that emerged there has been highlighted by both archaeological and historical studies.[163] In the provinces of central and northern Europe, the "Germanization" of society could be seen as a significant long-term trend, while in North Africa the long-term influence of Punic culture was widely recognized.[164] In fact, in every province of the empire, and even in Italy itself, there is increasing evidence of local influence on the cultural pattern that emerged, alongside elements of Roman metropolitan or imported provincial culture.[165] It is certainly not the case that we can identify a pure Roman culture emanating from Italy; Roman culture was an artifact of the provinces as much as it was of the metropolitan center.[166] Archaeological studies increasingly emphasize the degree of regional diversity and nonconformity. On the other hand, we can identify a few specific moments when the coherence and potency of cultural renaissance at the center was disproportionately influential on the periphery, as in the age of Augustus.[167]

Nonetheless, there is still an assumption in many studies of individual provinces that there was a specific Roman cultural identity and that it was relatively homogenous across society. Studies of provincial art or religion, for instance, frequently present the subject as unproblematic and relating to provincewide trends and patterns of behavior. However, far from being a standard cultural package, what is called Romanization appears to have been a manifestation of regional and social heterogeneity within a "global" system.[168]

I am convinced that the best way forward is to discard the term Romanization and to employ other interpretative frameworks to explore the cultural diversity of the empire. For example, Jane Webster has advanced a strong case for applying the concept of creolization to the Roman Empire, despite its connotations primarily with the New World and slave society.[169] Creole language and creole material culture are built up by the

---

[162] See, e.g., those referred to in Gosden 2004.

[163] Ball 2000; Butcher 2004; Millar 1993.

[164] See Wells 1999, 2001 on "Germanization"; and Mattingly 1995, 160–70 on Punic cultural continuities.

[165] See Terrenato 1998 on Italy.

[166] Keay and Terrenato 2001, 113.

[167] Galinsky 1996, 2005; Habinek and Schiesaro 1997; MacMullen 2000; Wallace-Hadrill 1989b, 2008; Whittaker 1997; Zanker 1988.

[168] See the discussion in Slofstra 2002 and Woolf 2002b.

[169] Webster 2001.

integration of the language and traditions of the underclass with elements of language and culture of the dominant colonial society, resulting in a "highly ambiguous material culture, in the sense that it is imbued with different meanings in different contexts."[170] In principle these approaches adopted in North American historical archaeology to understand the material culture and social behavior of the slaves and underprivileged classes can also be applied to the archaeological record of the Roman world. The most important aspect of the creolization model is that it does not ascribe the adoption of new linguistic practices, of new forms of pottery or of cooking equipment to a simple desire of the underprivileged or less civilized to emulate. Indeed it is clear that the social meaning of things is heavily contingent on social context and can be subverted in the creolized use. On the other hand, there is a danger that in seeking to apply the model to the Roman world we could create readings of resistance in the use of material culture at every level of society. A large part of the archaeological evidence of change in material culture in provincial society was in fact generated by people belonging to advantaged groups in society—specifically, foreigners, the local elites, and the army, whose motivations can by no means be assumed to have been the same as the poorest groups in society. Other approaches are thus needed in combination with the creolization model. I shall return to this issue in chapter 8 by exploring the themes of identity and discrepancy in Roman society. For the moment, though, understand that throughout this book I have explicitly rejected Romanization as an interpretative tool. I hope you will not miss or mourn its absence from the scene!

CONCLUSION

Writing this chapter has reminded me forcefully that the study of the Roman Empire is a very large academic subject, with a huge bibliographical backlist. Yet it seems to me that there are still many basic issues about the nature of Roman imperialism and its impacts that remain poorly understood or, simply, little explored. Developments in archaeology, in comparative history, and in the field of postcolonial studies offer a range of avenues that ancient historians, classicists, and specialists in Roman material culture should give further consideration to in the years ahead. In my recent reading I have been struck by how new developments in the study of the Roman world are paralleled in many instances by studies of the frontier societies of modern empires—the transformation of the

---

[170] Ibid., 217–20.

study of the American frontier is particularly pertinent.[171] In place of a traditional model of a uniform white settler society pushing the frontier ever westward, there is now a growing emphasis on the fact that cultural encounters at every stage were far more complex, involving great heterogeneity among communities of both natives and settlers. Roman studies could benefit from a similar sweeping revision of the consensus model.

I am aware that some of what I present in this book is unorthodox and gives more prominence to the lives of the lower orders than ancient historians tend to allow. As Syme once wrote, "The lower classes had no voice in government, no place in history."[172] That, I think, can be changed by seeking to trace something of the lived experience of the empire that they found themselves part of. While some readers will (as some in the audience at the original lectures did) find these ideas challenging, I hope that I will also find some supporters for my skepticism about the supposed universal benefits of Roman rule, my rejection of the Romanization paradigm, and my attempt to put something new in its place.

[171] Axtell 2001; Calloway 1997; Cronon, Miles, and Gitlin 1992; Lamar and Thompson 1981; Nobles 1997; White 1991.
[172] Syme 1979, 476.

CHAPTER TWO

From One Colonialism to Another

IMPERIALISM AND THE MAGHREB

INTRODUCTION

The postcolonial study of Roman Africa is notable for the persistence of the colonialist framework of analysis of Maghrebian (North African) archaeology and history. Modern and ancient colonialism have become so interwoven that this state of affairs is perceived in certain quarters as a natural order of things. However, there are serious distortions in the view of Roman imperialism that was fostered by the self-justifying perspective of nineteenth- and early-twentieth-century colonial antiquarians. Both French and Italians in North Africa presented themselves as the direct and natural inheritors of the Romans and actively sought to ape and emulate the achievements of the earlier imperial regime. The role of indigenous people was relegated to one of being passive receptors of the fruits of civilization or characterized as anarchic barbarians, incapable of proper self-government or socioeconomic advancement without outside (European) intervention. The contrast between French scholarship on Roman Gaul and Roman Africa could not be more marked in this respect. Insofar as there has been a postcolonial backlash to these crude stereotypes it has focused on arguing that the attested revolts were not simply due to native belligerence, but part of concerted and unremitting military and cultural resistance to Rome, akin to the liberation and nationalist movements of the twentieth century.

This chapter thus aims to demonstrate how theories of modern and ancient colonialism have become interwoven and how this has affected

This chapter was originally published in Webster and Cooper 1996; see Mattingly 1996b, 49–69. The research and writing of this essay was a breakthrough moment in my own understanding of the nature of the modern colonial discourse as a distorting mirror on the past. It is reprinted here with minimal changes—in translating Harvard-style references to footnotes I have added a few extra references where recent work or further reading on my part lends weight to the argument. I have also taken the opportunity to provide translations of the French and Italian accounts quoted in the original paper. Thanks in this regard go to Phil Perkins, who allowed me to check my translations against the textual glosses he had prepared when using the article as an assigned text at the Open University.

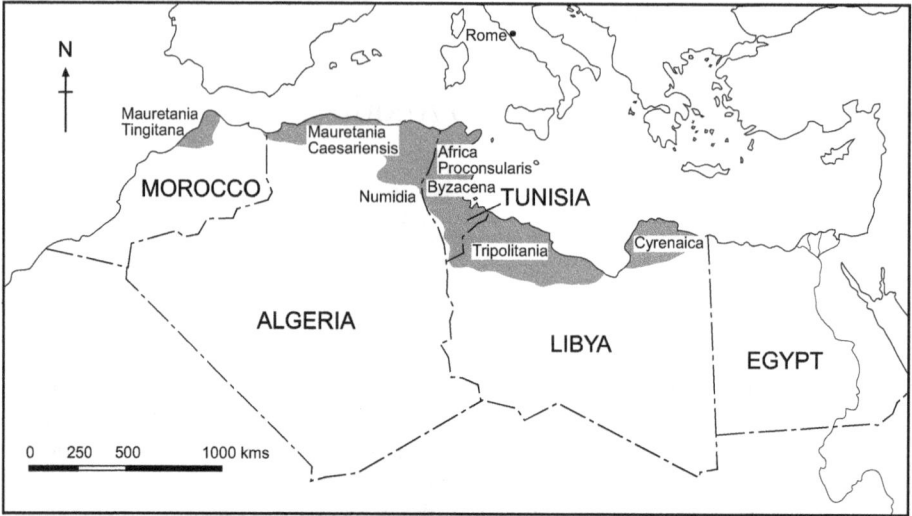

FIGURE 2.1 Map of North Africa, showing modern and ancient political
divisions.

the development of Roman archaeology in the independent countries of
the Maghreb (see fig. 2.1). Morocco (1956), Algeria (1963) and Tunisia
(1957) gained their independence from France—in Algeria's case, following one the bloodiest colonial wars and there were moments of strong
resistance in Morocco and Tunisia.[1] The Italians held Libya (or parts of
it) from 1911 until 1942, when the country fell under the British Military
Administration until independence was achieved in 1951.[2] Resistance to
Italian colonization by the Libyans was concerted, the country being considered not fully pacified until 1932, and the British army received support from the Senussi Arabs of Cyrenaica during the desert war.[3] There
are inevitably "discrepant experiences" of imperialism and colonialism in
the modern context, far from positive for the indigenous people (though
nationalist movements grew out of resistance), while some of the old co-
lons still peddle the myth about a lost golden age.[4] It is inevitable in these
circumstances that the modern experience should have an impact on the
debate about the more remote past. The essential point that I make in this

[1] Algeria: Horne 1977; Morocco, against France and Spain: Woolman 1969; Tunisia,
against the French: Abun-Nasr 1975, 282, 352–53.

[2] Abun-Nasr 1975, 307–12, 377–92.

[3] Peniakoff 1950, received much Libyan aid, but on the other hand found the southern
Tunisian tribes far more sympathetic to the Axis powers because the war offered an opportunity to them for resistance to France.

[4] See Said 1993, 35–50, on the notion of discrepant experiences. See also Mattingly
1997b.

chapter is that *all* these different viewpoints must be understood in their modern as well as ancient contexts and that however wrongheaded some theories now appear we should not exclude them from debate. The overly negative prognosis on Rome by Maghrebi historians is a useful balance to the generally indulgent and uncritical European view of the benefits of Roman civilization. Each of these models for the study of Roman Africa transposes polarized views of recent history into the more distant past, and both tendencies in isolation represent serious threats to the future of classical archaeology in the Maghreb. Although there have been important developments in the study of Roman Africa in recent decades, these have yet to be fully assimilated into a new postcolonial perspective of Africa in the Roman Empire.[5] Many scholars would no doubt claim that no one seriously accepts the more extreme theories of archaeologists and historians working in the colonial heyday, but it is equally clear that there has not been enough explicit rejection of these models. Nor has there been deconstruction of the theoretical positions underlying the consensus vision of Roman Africa. An understanding of the historiography of Roman Africa is thus an essential starting point.[6]

COLONIAL ATTITUDES

The Inheritors of Rome

There are serious distortions in the view of Roman imperialism that was fostered by the self-justifying perspective of the nineteenth- and early-twentieth-century colonial antiquarians. Both French and Italians in North Africa presented themselves as the direct and natural inheritors of the Romans. This theme was a persistent one in the literature of the time and was used as a justification for their presence in the region. This is particularly true of the Italians, who came late onto the scene, fearful of French or German moves against the declining Turkish power in Libya. In the buildup to the 1911 invasion the Italian press was predominantly in favor of such an action and the arguments about Italy's "legal-historical right—as a successor to the Roman Empire—to Libya" were very much to the fore.[7] Giovanni Pascoli, the national poet, typified this attitude in describing Libya as a country made rich by Romans and ruined by the "inertia of the nomads. . . . We were there already, we left signs

---

[5] As is clear in chapter 1, I now advocate the abandonment of the outmoded Romanization concept, and have edited out some references to the term from the text as originally written in 1994, with occasional glosses on the development of my own views.

[6] See Shaw 1980 for a perceptive summary; see Mattingly and Hitchner 1995, esp. 165–76, for an overview of the state of the subject.

[7] Segrè 1974, 20–32.

that not even the Berbers, the Bedouins and the Turks could erase."[8] The same basic sentiment is echoed in many other Italian and French writers, stressing the desolation and emptiness of the modern landscape punctuated by Roman ruins at almost every step:

> Su questa terra che receve di nuovo ... la civiltà Italiana, su questa terra che non si puo smuoverere e scalfine senza incontrare ad ogni passo una rovina o un ricordo del passato romano.
> *On this land that again receives ... Italian civilization, on this land that one cannot turn the soil or scratch the surface without meeting at every step a ruin or a reminder of the Roman past.*[9]

> Tutto ciò significa che la regione era in passato molto abitanta e coltivata ... provato da ruderi ... che di quando in quando s'incontrano attreverso la vasta zona, e che altro non sono che le tracce indelibili di Roma Imperiale.
> *All this signifies that the region was in the past densely settled and cultivated ... proven by ruins ... which from time to time one encounters across the vast spaces, and these are none other than the indelible traces of Imperial Rome.*[10]

> Frappés sinon reconciliés par la ressemblance de notre ouevre civilatrice avec l'ouevre romaine ... dont surtout ils retrouvent à chaque pas des traces, ces hommes [les indigènes] ... se résignent à subir en vous les légataires de Rome.
> *Struck by, if not reconciled to, the resemblance between our civilizing work and the Roman civilizing work, of which they encounter traces at every step, these natives ... resign themselves to submission to you, the heirs of Rome.*[11]

> Lorsque les colonnes françaises s'avancèrent dans la vallé du Chélif, elle trouvèrent maintes traces de l'occupation romaine ... le sol portait partout l'empreinte ineffacable de nos devanciers.
> *When the French military columns advanced into the Chelif Valley, they continually found traces of Roman occupation ... the ground bore the inerasable trace of our predecessors.*[12]

The use to which this claim to be the direct descendants of the Romans could be put is well illustrated by an anecdote concerning Louis Renier, one of the first generation of French epigraphists to descend on Algeria.

---

[8] Pascali, quoted in Segrè 1974, 22.
[9] Piccioli 1931, 194.
[10] Coro 1928, 23.
[11] Boissière 1883, xv.
[12] Yacono 1955, 175.

While copying a Latin text, he was approached by a local sheikh who enquired whether he could read the writing. Renier replied,

> Oui, je la comprends et je l'écris: car c'est la miene aussi. Regards ce sont nos lettres, c'est notre langue
> *Yes, I understand it and I can write it, because it is my language also. Look, these are our letters, this is our language*

after which the sheikh turned to the crowd with him and (allegedly) said,

> Les Roumis sont vraiment les fils des Roumâns, et, lorsqu'ils ont pris ce pays, ils ont fait que reprendere le bien de leurs pères
> *The Roumis [Europeans] are truly the descendants of the Romans, and in seizing this land, they have only reclaimed the property of their forefathers.*[13]

Epigraphy has been the key tool employed in the setting of the academic agenda for Romano-African studies and, indeed, the importance of French North Africa in the development of Latin epigraphy as a discipline cannot be overemphasized.[14] The pacification of Algeria and the French takeover in Tunisia after 1881 opened up undreamed-of opportunities for French epigraphists from the École Française de Rome (up to then greatly overshadowed by their compatriots at Athens). While Roman inscriptions on stone in Britain number about 2,500, the former French territories in the Maghreb have yielded over 60,000 Latin texts. On a single epigraphic mission in 1852–53, Renier reported on around 4,000 texts. Unlike in Italy, here the French had extraordinary freedom to organize the collection, preservation and publication of the inscriptions and built up a formidable power base in international scholarship by training successive generations in the field (see fig. 2.2). The greatest French scholars in Latin epigraphy all passed through North Africa. As Monique Dondin-Payre notes, they were inspired not only by scientific curiosity but by the desire to prove European cultural superiority.[15] Until Maghrebi scholars themselves learned Latin, they were effectively locked out of the study of Roman Africa. By controlling the study of the written sources the French were able to exacerbate the cultural distance from the Romans felt by the Berber and Arab populations.

If the European claim to be the rightful inheritors of North Africa was to carry weight it was necessary to disinherit the native peoples. An important corollary, then, to making a close identification between the

[13] Renier, quoted in Boissière 1883, xv–xvi.
[14] For a clear overview, see Dondin-Payre 1988. Additional material, including further important papers by Dondin-Payre, can be found in Bourguet et al. 1998, 1999.
[15] Notes Dondin-Payre 1988, 33, "par la curiosité scientifique, mais aussi par le désir de prouver la superiorité de la culture européene."

FIGURE 2.2 Latin inscription from Timgad in central Algeria, recording the career of an ex-Roman centurion. The wealth of epigraphic evidence in general, and such testimonies of past imperial servants in particular, formed a strong bond between ancient and modern colonialisms in Africa.

modern imperial power and Rome was to reinforce the feeling of infe-riority and separateness of the indigenous population. Drawing on the orientalist tradition, a crude stereotype of the Berber populations thus emerged: they were barbarians, savages, incapable of living at peace or of organizing themselves at polity level. It was their lot to be raised up peri-odically by indulgent colonizing powers—Carthage, Rome, the Vandals, Byzantium, the Arabs, the Ottomans:

> La tragedia della storia del popolo berbero è rappresentata da questi due estremi: essi non sono mai riusciti a costituirsi a nazione e non hanno mai voluto subire il dominio dello stranieri.
> *The tragedy of the history of the Berber people is represented by these two extremes: they have never succeeded in creating their own nation and they have never submitted willingly to the rule of the foreigner.*[16]

The notion that the North Africans did not act independently of out-side stimuli is strongly echoed by many writers:

> La déconcertante sterilité de leur nature, incapable, lorsqu'elle n'est pas contrainte par une autorité exterieure, de depasser les formes les plus primitives.
> *The disconcerting sterility of their nature, incapable, unless compelled by an external authority, of surpassing the most primitive models.*[17]

> Ces une terre de survivances ... son manque d'originalité est donc un titre particulier ... elle est un terrain privilégé pour l'analyse des influences.
> *It is a land of survivals ... its lack of originality is thus a particu-lar quality ... it is a privileged territory in which to study (external) influences.*[18]

Following standard European orientalist thinking,[19] it was the mission of the colonizer to educate the Africans about their own cultural heritage:

> La France a révelé pleinment l'Afrique à elle-même, en lui apportant le trésor se sa civilisation, héritière des civilisations antiques de la Médi-terranéene.
> *France has fully revealed Africa to itself by taking there the trea-sure of (French) civilization, the heir of the ancient Mediterranean civilizations.*[20]

---

[16] Piccioli 1931, 261.
[17] Picard 1954, 37.
[18] Benoit 1931, 3; Laroui 1970, 53–58, gives many further examples.
[19] Cf. Said 1978.
[20] Benoit 1931, 4.

The problem, of course, was that the history "revealed" by French and Italians was bogus, particularly in the emphasis it laid on the respective roles of immigrant colonists and native Africans in the making of Roman Africa:

> C'est par milliers que les familles romaines viennent dans le pays. Cependent l'agitation [des indigenes] continue, et c'est au milieu des insurrections ... l'épée d'une main et la charrue de l'autre, que Rome porsuit ... son travail colonial et civilisateur sur la terre d'Afrique.
>
> *It was in thousands that Roman families came into this country. However, the (indigenous) unrest continued, and it was in the midst of insurrections ... the sword in one hand and the plough in the other that Rome pursued ... her colonial and civilizing work on the land of Africa.*[21]

The writing of this period spoke almost invariably of Romans and Berbers as opposites, and even in subsequent scholarship the terms Romano-African or Romano-Libyan have been rarely used. Similarly, much greater emphasis was placed on the study of immigrant groups than their actual numbers warranted. For example, as late as 1962, a book (albeit a slim one) appeared titled *Les Gaulois en Afrique*—and this was not a reference to cigarettes.[22]

This double process of cultural annexation and alienation could also be achieved through visual narratives, a classic example being provided by the symbolism ("lo speciale carattere ... il significato simbolico e augurale ..." [the special character ... the symbolic and prophetic significance]) of the Roman gallery in the museum installed by the Italians in the old Turkish castle in Tripoli. The approach staircase was dominated by a colossal statue of Roma, flanked by two large imperial dedicatory inscriptions; in the vestibule stood a magnificent representation of Victory, flanked in turn by inscriptions from the Roman fort at Bu Njem recording "la conquista romana ai limiti del deserto" (Roman conquest at the desert limits].[23] In case the subtlety of this display was missed by anyone, the room next to the Roman gallery preserved the office of the first Italian governor of Libya as he had left it; the wall between the two rooms "non significarse separazione, ma intima unione spirituale fra il passato e il presente" [does not signify separation but an intimate spiritual union between past and present].[24]

The motivation behind the great excavations of the Italian era was questioned by Mortimer Wheeler, who played a vital role in preserving

---

[21] Guides 1906, 288.
[22] Leglay 1962.
[23] Piccioli 1931, 109.
[24] Piccioli 1931, 110.

the monuments when they fell under British jurisdiction during the war: "The Italians had cleared and partially restored considerable and imposing groups of buildings [at Cyrene, Lepcis Magna and Sabratha] ... in no small measure they were political whether the intentions were to advertise the splendour that had been Rome's and was now reincarnated in fascist Italy, or whether to lure tourists and to advertise Italian colonization."[25]

The reconstructed ruins were thus placed on the same footing as the fascist architecture of Tripoli and Benghazi; depending on your perspective they were either wonderful symbols of European civilization or they were propagandist monuments of an alien and authoritarian government (see figs 2.3–2.4). Nor did the situation change rapidly after independence as Anthony Thwaite's memory of National Service in Libya during the 1950s makes clear. The maintenance of foreign military bases in Libya was mirrored by continuing Italian and British excavations at the classical cities, while little effort seems to have been made to expunge the evidence of Italy's colonial vision:

> [Tripoli] still quite clearly bore the remains of the Fascist penchant ... for grandiose slogans, or—more interestingly—passages from d'Annunzio's poems, full of references to Roman Eagles and Roman Legions. I realised later, during my 1965–67 stay in Libya, one reason why most Libyans take no interest in the Roman monuments: to them they are just another manifestation of Fascism—as Graziani never ceased to remind his troops, "Remember that you are Italians, Romans, and remember that your forebears were once in this country."[26]

The long-term legacy of such visual narratives has had profound implications.

A further criticism of colonial analyses concerns the common use of "binary oppositions" for rhetorical purposes: thus nomad and sedentarist, desert and sown, Sahara and Tell, African and Roman are recurrent themes in the historiography.[27] The explicit dichotomies are questionable as generalizations, but were widely adopted as explanations of a supposed historical reality, such as nomadic raiding.[28] Once again, this has the effect of segregating "us" (the colonizers or latterly European scholars) from "them" (the "unruly" African people) and ignores all possible gradations (social, spatial, and temporal) between, for instance, nomad and sedentarist.

---

[25] Wheeler 1955, 152.
[26] Thwaite 1969, 4.
[27] Gsell 1933; Lawless 1972; Leschi 1942.
[28] Benabou 1980, 15–22; Février 1981, 40. The use of such oppositions and prejudicial generalizations is one of the most insidious traits of orientalism; see Said 1978.

FIGURE 2.3 (a) and (b) The wolf of Rome stands atop a pillar alongside the national museum in Tripoli castle in these 1943 images. (Photographs by Major William Robinson; used with permission of Susan Gilmour.)

FIGURE 2.4 (a) Commemorating Mussolini's renewed Roman Empire in Africa, this great arch was erected on the new coast road around the Gulf of Sirte close to the border between Cyrenaica and Tripolitania. (b) Its relief sculptures evoke traditional Roman themes from their own monumental billboards. (Photographs by Major William Robinson; used with permission of Susan Gilmour.)

Emulating Rome

Current discussions on imperialism as a historical phenomenon show that there are fundamental differences in the intrinsic nature of modern European imperialism and that of ancient Rome.[29] The Roman Empire was used by the colonial powers not simply as a precedent and justification for their own activities but also as a reference point for the measurement of achievement. Ostensibly the object of such comparisons was to enable the past to shed light on problems of the modern colonies, though commonly the prime function seems to have been to show the superiority of the modern experience over the ancient:

> Ce serait un ... bien profitable sujet d'étude que de demander à l'histoire de l'Afrique romaine les leçons et l'expérience du peuple ... il ne serait pas inopportun sans doute de revoir ces romaines que nous proposons volontier, pour modeles ... en face de ces graves questions de politique coloniale, de ces difficiles problèmes de rapprochment de races, d'assimilation progressive, de réconciliation des vaincus ... de nous les représenter organisant leur conquête africaine dans des conditions qui étaient non pas identiques ... mais assurément analogues.

> *It was a ... highly profitable subject of enquiry to ask of the history of Roman Africa what were the lesssons and experiences of the people ... it was not at all inopportune to look willingly at these Romans as models: ... faced with serious questions of colonial policy, of difficult problems of racial rapprochement, of progressive assimilation, of the reconciliation of the defeated ... we can present them organizing their African conquest in conditions that if not identical to ours ... were surely analogous.*[30]

> Nous pouvons donc ... comparer notre occupation de l'Algérie et de la Tunisie à celle des mêmes provinces africaines par les romaines: comme eux, nous avons glorieusement conquis le pays, comme eux, nous avons assuré l'occupation, comme eux, nous essayons de le trans-

---

[29] On modern imperialism, see, among others, Curtin 1971; Etherington 1984; Hobson 1938; Lichtheim 1971; Reynolds 1981; and Wesson 1967. On Roman imperialism there is much good sense in Brunt 1965, 1990; see also Hanson 1994. In the heyday of European imperialism the opposite tendency was dominant (Haverfield 1915; Hingley 1991) and many aspects of modern colonial government aped Roman titles or institutions (such as the use—whether formal or informal—of the title *proconsul* for many governors; see Douglas-Home 1978; Gann and Duignan 1978.

[30] Boissière 1883, xvi–xvii.

former à notre image et de gagner à la civilisation ... La seule difference c'est que nous avons fait en 50 ans ce qu'ils n'avaient accompli
en trois siècles.
*We can then ... compare our occupation of Algeria and Tunisia with
that of the same provinces by the Romans: like them, we have glori-
ously conquered the country, like them, we have secured our occupation, like them, we are trying to transform (Africa) in our image and
to bring civilization ... The only difference is that we have done in 50
years what they could not do in three centuries.*[31]

Lo sforza dell'archeologo e quello del colono procedono insieme e si
completano: le lezioni dell'esperienza antica oriente l'attivita moderna.
*The efforts of the archaeologist and the colonist proceed together and
complement each other: the lessons of the ancient experience inform
modern activity.*[32]

The "otherness" of North Africa (in terms of the Arabs and Berbers,
with their Islamic culture and tribal and nomadic societies) was countered by the conscious association of the colonizer with the Roman presence. It was comforting for the French and Italian armies on campaign
to the remote desert and mountain margins to find traces of the earlier
penetration of the Roman legion into the same spaces. Victorious French
generals were compared to legendary Roman commanders, defeated rebels with the great African leaders Jugurtha, Tacfarinas, Firmus, and the
like. French commemorative monuments imitated Roman ones, and inscriptions recording the road building and construction activity of the
foreign legion were self-consciously copying the formulas of earlier Latin
texts.[33] The French army was particularly active in the archaeological
exploration of Algeria and Tunisia, partly through the activities of the
special mapping units (the *brigades topographiques*), but also through
the individual efforts of many soldiers and officers.[34] Their zeal for and
admiration of the Roman past led many soldiers to give up their free
time to carry out excavations and record inscriptions. In what I believe
the most extraordinary case on record, Colonel Carbuccia, the French
commander at Batna in central Algeria and himself an amateur epigra-
phist, had his soldiers restore the mausoleum of a prefect of the Legio III
Augusta close to the Roman fortress at Lambaesis. The rededication of
the tomb in 1849, complete with a new inscription paying homage to the

[31] Cagnat 1913, 776–78.
[32] Piccioli 1931, 194.
[33] Dondin-Payre 1991, 145–46.
[34] See, for example, Baradez 1949.

Roman officer on behalf of the French foreign legion, was carried out with the entire garrison parading before the monument to the accompaniment of a military salute.[35]

There have been several unfortunate consequences of this too close association between the armies of occupation and the exploration of Roman settlement. First there has been an undoubted tendency to overemphasize the military nature of rural sites (*fortin* and *construction militaire* were used as blanket terms by some investigators) and ex-military personnel came to dominate many of the regional archaeological societies ensuring the continued predominance of this perspective.[36] The Roman garrison could not have manned more than a small fraction of these sites, but the military connotations originally attached to them were perpetuated by the development of a body of theory about supposed soldier farmers and frontier militias colonizing the frontier zone (the Roman *limes*).[37] The second and far more damaging consequence in a postcolonial age of its too-close association with the actual agents of modern imperialism has been the stigma attached to Roman archaeology as a result.

Another point of contact between past and present concerned the land. The perceived environmental degradation and dereliction of a region once wealthy required explanation, and although climatic change had its advocates, blame was attached to a far greater extent to the indigenous people (the Berbers) and to later invaders (Vandals and Arabs). Acceptance of this interpretation of the environmental decline being due to human action led to goals then being set for the reestablishment of agriculture and prosperity through strong government, European immigration, technology, and expertise. The *need* for French or Italian farmers to emulate the success of their supposed Roman forebears emerges strongly in much colonial writing.[38] The management of water resources was critical, and the colonial governments all took an interest in the evidence for Roman hydraulic systems (wells, cisterns, canals, aqueducts, wadi walls, etc. In Algeria and Tunisia major surveys were carried out of these *travaux hydrauliques* with a view to renovate cisterns, wells, and other features for modern use.[39] A Latin inscription, placed on a Roman dam that was reconstructed in Libya in 1930,

---

[35] Dondin-Payre 1991, 148–49. Cf. the anachronistic attitudes of the Wallsend monument erected recently to Roman troops in Britain (see fig. 2.5).

[36] Malarkey 1984.

[37] Garrison size: Février 1986, 87–93; Frémeaux 1984. Soldier farmers: Goodchild 1949, 1950, 1976; cf. Mattingly 1995, 194–209.

[38] Février 1986; Frémeaux 1984.

[39] Gauckler 1897–1912; Gsell 1903.

combines the practical with the symbolic aspects of archaeology in the service of colonialism:

Antiquum Romanorum aggerem/aquas continentem vetustate collapsum/coloniae Libycae praeses/Petrus Badoglio/ad agrorum fertilitatem/maiore mole restitui voluit/Camillo Ferrario architecto curante/anno mcmxxx

Ancient Roman dam, for holding back water, having collapsed through age, by order of Pietro Badoglio, governor of the colony of Libya, restored as a larger dam for the fertility of the fields. Overseen by Camillo Ferrario, architect, in the year 1930.[40]

The evident success of farming in Roman Africa was not so easily emulated as it turned out, though this may in part be due to the fact that, as J. A. Hobson has put it, "history devises reasons why the lessons of past empires do not apply to our own."[41] The work on Roman hydraulic systems, for example, is notable more for its "thick description" than for its insights into their functioning.[42] For all the bombastic self-celebration of their similarity with Rome, it is clear that this was more a mechanism for the French and Italians to avoid some unpleasant realities about the late nineteenth- and early twentieth-century situations than an objective intellectual inquiry; it enabled them to moderate these experiences by transposing similar problems back into the Roman period.[43] In effect it was modern imperialism that shaped the interpretation of the past rather than the other way around.[44] This was particularly true of the degree of military resistance encountered and the ugly and repressive measures the colonial regimes were drawn into taking as a result.

Understanding Native Resistance

Within metropolitan France, French archaeologists and historians had no difficulty in understanding the relationship between Roman conqueror and subjugated Gauls. Once the initial trauma of conquest was passed, life under Roman rule was viewed as overall a positive experience, bringing a higher degree of civilization to the region but also allowing native talents to flourish within the Roman system. The concept of Gallo-Roman archaeology was embedded in scholarly thinking at an early stage,

[40] Piccioli 1931, 194.
[41] Hobson 1938, 221.
[42] Shaw 1984.
[43] Frémeaux 1984.
[44] Brunt 1965, 268.

laying great stress on the Gallic contribution to Rome and its empire. Similar tendencies have underpinned Romano-British studies also.[45] As has already been noted, however, the role of indigenous people in Roman Africa was relegated to one of being passive recipients of the fruits of civilization, or such people were characterized as anarchic barbarians, incapable of proper self-government or socioeconomic advancement without outside (that is, European) intervention. The contrast between French scholarship on Roman Gaul and Roman Africa could not be more marked in this respect.[46] This fact more than anything should warn us of the severe distortions of a colonial discourse in which the subject population are allowed no voice.

Nor for that matter was the pacification and reconciliation of the Maghrebian peoples as finally resolved as the military authorities, and scholars such as René Cagnat, kept claiming. The history of Algeria is punctuated by revolts and acts of armed resistance. In Italian-held Libya, the 1911–32 rebellion resulted in well over 50 percent of the native population being killed, locked up in internment camps or exiled.[47] Such resistance, paralleled in its ferocity in Algeria, is unsurprising given the transparent inequalities and injustices of the colonial societies that were emerging. Stephane Gsell, one of the foremost archaeologists and scholars of Roman Algeria, had more enlightened views than most about what could be learned from the past and stressed the need for modern colonialism to follow Rome in equalizing the status of the indigenous population with that of immigrants. His views were largely unheeded because of the strength of the settler lobby in Algeria who resisted any moves to improve the position of the indigenous population.[48]

Already noted is how the colonial discourse strove to disinherit the North African peoples of their cultural history by ascribing to immigrants all the positive achievements of Roman Africa and by portraying the Africans either as passive receptors of superior culture or as nomadic and lawless people incapable of self-government. The latter characteristic is a projection into the past of the difficulties of tribal control encountered by the French and the Italians, who comforted themselves with the thought that Rome had faced similar problems with little more success.[49] Despite the fact that this can now be identified as having more to do with colonialist ideology than with history, it is still accepted by some

[45] Freeman 1991, 1993; Hingley 1991.

[46] This is noted by, among others, Dondin-Payre 1991, 149; and Février 1986, 102.

[47] See Peniakoff 1950, 55–157, esp. 84.

[48] Lengrand 1991; Abun-Nasr 1975, 316–22, describes the defeat by the settler lobby of legislation aiming to give equal rights and status to at least some members of the Algerian elite.

[49] Capot-Rey 1953; Gautier 1952; Gsell 1933; Guey 1939; Leschi 1942.

scholars that Rome's African provinces, especially the mountain and desert frontier zones, were subjected to frequent unprovoked and supposedly irrational attacks by Berber tribes.[50] The debate is particularly controversial for the Mauretanian provinces, where opinion is now divided on the question of whether raiding was endemic or highly episodic.[51] As in Roman Britain, the question may be insoluble, since the extant source data are inadequate for a proper assessment of the seriousness of many attested moments of unrest. But an alternative line of enquiry can also be suggested: that of examining the mechanisms by which the state and indigenous tribal groups may have tried, on a unilateral or multilateral basis, to avoid warfare and for which the well-known altars of peace at Volubilis are the classic example.[52]

POSTCOLONIAL ATTITUDES

Resistance and Nationalism

Insofar as there has been a postcolonial backlash to these crude stereotypes it has focused on arguing that the attested revolts were not simply due to native belligerence but part of concerted and unremitting military and cultural resistance to Rome, akin to the liberation and nationalist movements of the twentieth century. A key moment was the publication in 1970 of Abdullah Laroui's *L'histoire du Maghreb*, a sustained and brilliant deconstruction of colonialist history of the region. His view of Punic and Roman dominance in the region recognized the potential links between past and present,[53] but he also warned of the tendency for such rhetorical comparisons to become historical explanations.[54] Above all he was concerned with demonstrating the way in which the history of the ancient Maghreb had been hijacked by European interests.[55] He also criticized the academic agenda that had been set by Romanists, with its emphasis on Roman military antiquities, on the monuments of towns and on aspects of elite culture (none of which receive more than cursory mention in his book). The potential of archaeology as a source for the history of ordinary Africans in antiquity was immense, he observed, but

---

[50] Rachet 1970.

[51] Euzennat 1984; Février 1981; Frezouls 1981; Lawless 1978; Leveau 1986; Modéran 1989; Salama 1991. See also the extended discussion of such issues in Modéran 2003.

[52] Frezouls 1980; Mattingly 1992; Shaw 1987.

[53] Laroui 1970, 32–65, "d'une colonialisation à l'autre"—hence my title.

[54] Ibid., 52.

[55] Ibid., 25: "la science des antiquités maghrébines fut la science de l'administration colonial" [the science of Maghrebian antiquities was the science of colonial administration].

unexploited.[56] In reply to the colonialist vision of the glorious Roman interlude, he chose to emphasize the importance of resistance to Rome. This resistance was not to be interpreted as an inherent tendency toward lawlessness or to a perverse rejection of the benefits of civilization; rather it was concerted and continuing opposition to alien conquest and culture. Astonishingly, Laroui's book was omitted from the two main bibliographical listings on Roman Africa for 1970,[57] and is still rarely referenced by Roman historians and archaeologists, but its impact has been profound, especially on the approach taken by other Maghrebi historians who have developed the theme of nationalist resistance:

> En pays berbère, l'histoire de la domination romaine est celle de cinq siècles de guerres acharnées pour la liberté et l'indépendance.
> *In Berber lands, the history of Roman domination is that of five centuries of relentless wars for liberty and independence.*

> Pressurées par les fonctionnaires romaine, les tribus attendaient le moment proprice pour s'insurger.
> *Pressurized by Roman functionaries the tribes awaited the right moment to rise up in revolt.*[58]

An essential point to note here though is that the dominant theme of the postcolonial model concerns the rationalization of what I believe to be a suspect element of the colonial discourse. European scholars maintained the thesis that the Africans were rebellious, ungovernable troublemakers; the antithesis was to make them into freedom fighters and partisans, seeking to throw off the burden of alien rule.[59] Both views it must be admitted seem to represent extremes and both perpetuate a crude "us and them" stereotype of Roman Africa.

Civilization and Imperialism

The most sophisticated exponent of the resistance thesis has been Marcel Benabou, whose revisionist scope extended also to the idea of cultural resistance.[60] Essentially he took the view that in their religious preferences, in their maintenance of Punic and Libyan/African languages, even in their selection of names on acquisition of Roman citizenship, Romano-Africans chose to demonstrate their Africanness and thus their passive resistance to the alien power. The controversy that arose over this book

---

[56] Ibid., 41, 59.
[57] Archéologie de l'Afrique Antique 1970; Bibliographie Afrique Antique IV 1970.
[58] Kaddache 1971, 111 and 189.
[59] Benabou 1977 is a good example of the marketability of the idea.
[60] Benabou 1976.

was predictable, it being almost universally hailed as a masterpiece by Maghrebian scholars and condemned as a clever but distorting vision of Romanization by European scholars.[61] Two main tactics have been used to deflect the Benabou thesis: first, arguing that what Benabou called resistance was simply the natural variation that scholars have identified in Romanization, with each province of the empire revealing the assimilation of much local culture alongside "Roman" elements; second, it has been argued that the resistance theme is based on an anachronism:

En ce qui concerne M. Benabou, l'opposition est plus apparente que réelle: il appelle résistances à la romanité ce que nous considérons plutôt commes les modalités de la romanité.
As far as M. Benabou is concerned the opposition is more apparent than real: he calls resistance to Romanization that which we consider as the modalities of Romanization.[62]

[L]a vision d'un protonationalisme maghrébin issu de la rencontre de Jugurtha et de l'analogie. Toute une partie de l'historiographie de l'ancienne Afrique à été ainsi oblitérée depuis pluisers années par la projection dans son passé d'idées et d'évènements récents sans rapport avec lui.
[T]he vision of a Maghrebian proto-nationalism [is] born from the story of Jugurtha and analogy. All of one part of the historiography of ancient Africa has been obliterated by the projection into the past of recent ideas and events that bear no relation to it.[63]

There is a splendid irony in these complaints about the historicity of the postcolonial perspective that refuse implicitly to question the underlying basis of the orthodox view. Sadly, after the flurry of reviews, there has been less willingness to engage in a proper discussion. The scope for disagreement was brilliantly demonstrated by a three-cornered debate.[64] A somewhat acerbic exchange between Lisa Fentress and Brent Shaw on the impact of the army in central Numidia also raised important questions about the extent to which regional development might depend on outsiders.[65] Now comes the revelation from Pierre Morizot, working in

[61] But note the generally sympathetic Anglo-American reviews and responses in, among others, Fentress 1982, 108–9; and Whittaker 1978b.

[62] Picard 1990, 12.

[63] Euzennat 1986, 576.

[64] See Benabou 1978b; Leveau 1978; and Thébert 1978. Benabou insists that Africans needed to be accorded an active role in their relations with Rome, while Leveau supports the view of native Africans resisting a nasty imperial power; Thébert holds the traditional view that Africans were willing participants in empire.

[65] Fentress 1983; Shaw 1983b. Cf. Fentress 2006, where there is an attempt to redefine Romanization as a fundamentally economic process.

two areas of the Aures Mountains (the same region discussed by Shaw and Fentress), that the apparently less Romanized of the two (that with no trace of veterans and far fewer Latin inscriptions) appears to have undergone the more dramatic development, with bigger oileries, larger-scale irrigation works, and splendid mausolea.[66] Similar spectacular development in highly marginal areas is attested in Tripolitania.[67] Only through extending the debate about the meaning of Roman rule can we hope to start to interpret such phenomena. Benabou himself has published an impressive series of papers, modifying and broadening his approach.[68] Some European scholars clearly believe that the argument with Benabou is won, but in cutting it short and in refusing to examine the colonial discourse that still underlies much Western scholarship on the Maghreb, even more extreme views will undoubtedly flourish:

> L'Afrique berbère a eté pour Rome une colonie d'exploitation. . . . Elle a signifié aussi épuissement du sol et deforestation. . . . La grande masse des berbères a vu son niveau de vie diminué, son cadre tribal et communautaire disloqué. La prosperité romaine n'était le fait que d'une minorité; la masse berbère n'a connu que l'exploitation, le dur labeur et la miseure.
> *Berber Africa was for Rome a colony for exploitation. . . . [Rome] also heralded the exhaustion of the soil and deforestation. . . . The great majority of Berbers saw their standard of life fall, and their tribal and community structure was dislocated. Roman prosperity was only a reality for a minority, the mass of Berbers knew only exploitation, hard labor, and misery.*[69]

> Les luttes des berbères contre les impérialismes antiques. . . . Les accaparements de l'Empire romain sur les terres de plaine et la réduction de nombreuses populations en esclavage, pour cultiver les grandes domaines, suscitent de grands révoltes des royaummes berbères.
> *The struggles of the Berbers against ancient imperialisms. . . . The monopolization by the Roman Empire of the plain lands and the reduction to slavery of numerous populations to cultivate large estates aroused the Berber kingdoms to great revolts.*[70]

There are clearly dangers here that we shall replace one distorted view of ancient colonialism with another equally doubtful formulation, in much the same way the reception of Martin Bernal's *Black Athena* on

---

[66] Morizot 1991, 441.
[67] Mattingly 1995, 144–53, 162–70.
[68] Benabou 1978a, 1978b, 1980, 1981, 1982.
[69] Kaddache 1971, 140.
[70] Lacoste and Lacoste 1991, 38.

American college campuses generated passionate debate and extraordinary revisions to popular history.[71]

ARCHAEOLOGY AND HISTORY IN THE POSTCOLONIAL AGE

The progress of scholarship has caused the progressive abandonment or amelioration of many bigoted attitudes. Prosopographical work on the vast corpus of inscriptions, especially the study of personal names, has established conclusively that the vast bulk of the Roman population (both civil and in the army) was in fact of African origin.[72] Studies of ancient religion have likewise demonstrated that the hugely popular Saturn cult was a continuation of pre-Roman Baal-Hammon and that numerous other Punic and African deities enjoyed a long afterlife in Roman guises.[73] Private and public architecture also reveal clear-cut Punic influences continuing under Rome.[74] Even the hydraulic technology that was for long held to be a Roman introduction can now be seen as belonging in part at least to a far older indigenous tradition.[75] Studies of Romanization have moved on considerably.[76] Attention has started to focus on the pattern of rural settlement and its development over time and on the economic success of the African provinces as exporters to Mediterranean markets.[77]

The Garamantian people of the Libyan Sahara has been the subject of intensive investigation, overturning many assumptions about a supposedly nomadic tribe. The Garamantes are now known to have lived in large nucleated settlements (towns and villages), to have had an intensive

[71] Bernal 1987/1991; the campus debate I witnessed firsthand at the University of Michigan in January 1990, following a lecture by Ali Mazrui, nearly degenerated into a full-scale riot.

[72] Lassère 1977; Le Bohec 1989a, 1989b; M'Charek 1986.

[73] Saturn/Baal-Hammon: Leglay 1961/1966; 1966. Other Punic and African deities: Benabou 1986; Brouquier-Reddé 1992a, 1992b; Leglay 1975.

[74] Horn and Ruger 1979; Pensabene 1990; cf. Barresi 1991, 1992 on the continued use of the Punic cubit in public building projects in Roman Africa.

[75] Shaw 1982b, 1984. See also Barker et al. 1996a, 1996b.

[76] In an African context, one may trace the development in the use of the term *Romanization* in such works as Barton 1972; Benabou 1982, 1986; Février 1989/1990; Garnsey 1978; Kotula 1976; Lamirande 1976; Pflaum 1973; Picard 1990 (comparing the 1959 edition); Shaw 1980; Sheldon 1982; and Whittaker 1978a. My take on Romanization in relation to Libyan Tripolitania (Mattingly 1995) recognized significant hybridity among Roman, African, and Punic cultures and also major variability among patterns of cultural makeup in the towns, the countryside, and the army—points that presaged my reconceptualizing of this pattern of cultural change as discrepant identity; see chapter 8 of the present volume.

[77] Hitchner 1988, 1990; Leveau 1984; Leveau, Sillières, and Vallat 1993; Mattingly 1988a, 1988b.

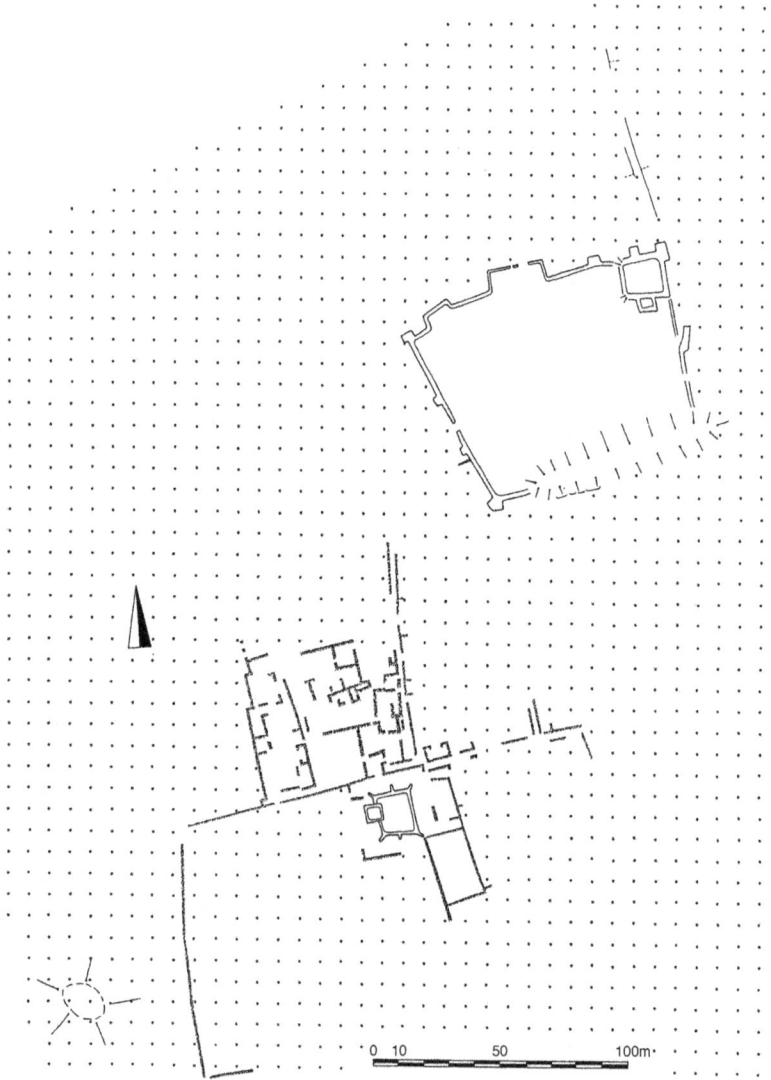

FIGURE 2.5 The Garamantian urban settlement at Qasr ash-Sharaba. Only part of the densely built-up site (stippled area) has been surveyed in detail.

irrigated agricultural economy (including cultivation of cereals, grape-vines, and date palms in the first half of the first millennium BC), to have possessed significant social stratification and a highly developed material culture (see fig. 2.5).[78] Indeed, an altogether more sympathetic vision of

[78] Daniels 1970, 1989. See also Mattingly 2003a, 2006d, 2007.

pastoralists in North Africa has started to emerge.[79] Some of the materials are at hand, therefore, for a radical reappraisal of the history and archaeology of Roman Africa. That the pace of change in conceptual thinking has not been quicker or more profound in its impact is thus disappointing. As we have seen, the postcolonial perspective has polarized the subject and restricted debate to a narrow range of issues. There has also been little formal repudiation of previous views, with many studies continuing to refer to *Romans* when *Romano-Africans* is meant. A partial evolution of sensibilities can be traced in the changing emphasis of British work at the Libyan pre-desert site of Ghirza in the 1950s: from its initial depiction as a frontier settlement of soldier-farmers ("home guard") to the recognition that it was Romano-Libyan farming center.[80] But if anyone doubts that the colonial discourse continues, then consider the following passage that concludes what appears to be a reasonably balanced summary of what Romanization may have meant in Africa:

> It would be pleasant to be able to report, too, that Romanization took place without confrontation, but the fact is that the Berbers, however self-denying and enduring they were, were backward and uninnovative, with no gift for politics or urbanization. They also proved themselves, on occasion, faithless, murderous and (in Jugurtha's case) manic-depressive. To idealize them is to do them a disservice, for to present a falsified picture of a people's past is to betray them. Historical truth, however harsh and cruel, never fails to give to those who know how to receive it—who can grasp the past with human understanding—the consistent clarity of vision that alone makes it possible to plan for the future.[81]

Overall, the recent history of Roman archaeology in North Africa has been one of mixed fortunes. Prehistoric, Punic, and Islamic archaeology have all benefited by the change in intellectual climate.[82] In contrast, and for a variety of reasons, Roman archaeology seems struck in a groove. In the transitional phases, foreign archaeologists from the excolonial powers continued to play a large role in dictating policy in the antiquities services.[83] Subsequently, the archaeological inheritance of the colonial

---

[79] Shaw 1982a, 1983a; Trousset 1980a, 1908b, 1982.

[80] Brogan 1955; Brogan and Smith 1957, 1984). Similarly, two conferences a decade apart sum up the shift: "Cirene e la Grecia" (Stucchi 1976) and "Cirene e i Libyci" (Stucchi and Luni 1987). See also chapter 9 of the present volume.

[81] Mackendrick 1980, 330.

[82] Prehistoric: see, e.g., Camps 1987; Horn and Ruger 1979. Punic: see, e.g., Fantar 1993. Islamic: see Golvin 1970; Mohamedi et al. 1991.

[83] This was notably the case in Libya, where the controllers of the Department of Antiquities remained British or Italian for over fifteen years after independence; see Goodchild 1976.

age has constrained their actions.[84] The conservation problems and/or the tourist potential of the colonial period excavations of Roman city sites in particular continue to dictate spending patterns. New excavations of Roman sites by outsiders are generally not encouraged, though there have been some notable and spectacular exceptions (such as the huge UNESCO Save Carthage project), and some of the oldest established French and Italian teams have continued to work at sites such as Bulla Regia, Mactar and Cyrene. This, of course, has the effect of leaving the shape of the subject much as it was in the colonial age, with the bulk of the excavated sites comprising towns, villas, and forts. The most prestigious academic qualifications for antiquities department staff are still considered to be higher degrees at European universities and, through the influence of research supervisors on the selection of thesis topics, this has also tended to perpetuate the academic agenda of the earlier era. The number of Maghrebian experts in well-established fields such as Latin or Greek epigraphy, church archaeology, architecture, Roman mosaics, Roman cities, the army, and so on, has risen dramatically in recent years.[85] Sadly, there are far fewer with expertise in less traditional aspects such as rural archaeology or the ancient economy.[86] As such, it does not appear that Roman archaeology is being refocused on a new agenda.

However, by keeping within this very traditionalist framework of classical archaeology, the Roman archaeologists are out of line with the views of the Maghrebi historians and have exposed themselves to attacks on the value of their work to the modern state. A good example concerns the UNESCO Libyan Valleys Survey project, which was launched in 1979 following a public reprimand for his antiquities department by Libyan leader Muammar al-Ghaddafi in a major policy speech. He criticized the archaeologists for concentrating on the classical cities and argued that they should instead be using their resources to further Islamic archaeology or to carry out work relevant to the modern needs of Libya. In particular, he suggested that a new investigation be carried out on the ancient farming systems of the Libyan pre-desert, in order that the farming technology be better understood and that the possibility of reintroducing farming to these regions be explored (see fig. 2.6).[87]

[84] See Picard 1985 for the colonial legacy in Tunisia.

[85] Latin or Greek epigraphy: see, e.g., Ben Abdullah 1986; Ben Abdullah and Ladjimi-Sebaï 1983; Beschaouch 1974; Mohamed and Reynolds 1994. Church archaeology: see, e.g., Bejaoui 1988. Architecture: see, e.g., Ferchiou 1989a. Roman mosaics: see, e.g., Ben Abed 1987; Khanoussi 1988; Mahjub 1988. Roman cities: see, e.g., Bouchenaki 1988; Ennabli 1992; Mahjoubi 1978; Slim 1983. The army: see, e.g., Benseddik 1982; Khanoussi 1991.

[86] Also note Ben Baaziz 1991a.

[87] Jones and Barker 1980. See also Barker et al. 1996a, 1–4.

FIGURE 2.6 Roman-period farming system from the Libyan pre-desert. Epigraphic evidence shows that the people who farmed these landscapes were of native Libyan or Libyphoenician origin.

The existence of a plurality of culture in ancient Africa (Berber/Libyan/African/Moorish, Roman, Greek/Hellenistic, Punic/Phoenician etc.) has long been recognized,[88] though the independent states of the Maghreb have tended to be nervous of and unsympathetic toward such diversity in their attempts to unite contemporary society. The recent trends toward Islamic fundamentalism, toward emphasizing Arab culture and the active repression of Berber culture in some regions, have left Maghrebian archaeologists even more exposed in their work on pre-Islamic cultures.[89] In present-day Algeria the civil war between the government and Islamic fundamentalist groups makes archaeological fieldwork impossible to carry out, while at least one archaeologist has been dismissed from her post, and publications have been impounded in warehouses as government policy vacillates between conciliation toward Islamist groups at large and repression of its critics—armed or otherwise. Furthermore, the collapse of tourism as a result of the fundamentalist offensive weakens the case for the custodial role of the major Roman sites absorbing a large part of the budget. Algeria is an extreme and alarming case, but it illus-

[88] Millar 1968.
[89] Lacoste and Lacoste 1991, 131–34.

trates the real dangers of allowing the theoretical basis of Roman Africa to drift in a postcolonial limbo. Unless Roman Africa is adopted (or re-inherited) by North Africans as part of their own history and culture, it seems to me that there is little hope for the long-term health of the subject.

The languages of scholarship, and thus the language of debate, at first sight also suggest continuing academic inequalities of the postcolonial world. A classic case is a conference on Roman Africa held in Senegal in the 1970s, where the organizing committee decreed that Latin should be the lingua franca, thereby excluding all but a handful of African scholars and making the published proceedings a very exclusive item indeed.[90] Among Maghrebian Roman specialists, publication in Arabic remains rare; most Tunisians, Algerians, and Moroccans publish in French, and Libyans in Italian or English. However, in the literary field, at least, it is now recognized that the role of bilingual colonial subjects (whom the French called optimistically *les evolués*) was vital in the subversion of the colonial discourse and in the discovery of a postcolonial perspective.[91] There are potentially interesting subtexts here, as comparison with the ambiguous position of African writers in the Roman period may suggest.[92] In the long term, though, what is needed is both discussion of the new perspectives in the languages of international scholarship (English, French, Italian, German, and Spanish) but also dissemination of those ideas to a wider Arabic reading audience. Yet in the short term, the lack of publication of any sort is a critical problem to overcome, with the details on many excavations of both colonial and postcolonial times still unpublished and the major journals of the antiquities services appearing with ever increasing time lags on their nominal cover dates.

NEW PERSPECTIVES?

This is not intended to be an entirely gloomy prognosis. But it seems to me that there are three fundamental conditions to be met if Roman archaeology in North Africa is to regain some of the momentum lost. First, it is essential that the colonial discourse is more thoroughly deconstructed and repudiated by European scholars. The Roman phase needs to be reestablished as an important part of the cultural heritage of the Maghreb, not simply as a leitmotif for nationalist resistance. Second, more thought should be given to the creation of a new agenda for classical

---

[90] *Africa et Roma* 1979.
[91] Mehrez 1992.
[92] Metty 1983.

archaeology in the region, one that will serve the needs of tourism where that is desired but that will also address concerns of more relevance to the history and current aspirations of the Maghreb. Some new methodological or theoretical ideas will not go amiss.[93] More work is urgently needed on pre-Roman native settlements and on African and Punic influences in Roman period Africa.[94] Recently published lists of all attested Punic and Libyan names and work on Punic and Libyan inscriptions mark fundamental advances in this context.[95] The study of rural settlement, farming technology, crop and husbandry regimes, and economy can also be highlighted as areas that will produce more positive images of Africa in the Roman period. Roman period olive oil factories (oileries), for instance, would be worthy monuments and symbols of national heritage in all the North African countries, but we lack a modern excavation of a large-scale example (see fig. 2.7). This brings me to the third and most vital point: changes in scholarship will only create the right circumstances for postcolonial perspectives to come to the fore; in the end it is the degree to which the ordinary people of the Maghrebian countries overcome their prejudices against Romans as foreign oppressors that will determine whether Romano-Africans are welcome in the national consciousness.

When I first visited Lepcis Magna in 1979, the site was virtually deserted; one could wander around it for hours, hardly meeting anyone apart from the occasional East European or Asian construction worker or oil industry employee. The Libyans, apart from those who worked there, seemed to have turned their backs on the site and the Roman past. This despite the fact that the first North African emperor, Septimius Severus, was born there into a Libyphoenician family. He was educated tri-lingually in Latin, Greek and Punic, the latter of which remained the local vernacular. There is a huge volume of epigraphic evidence from the town, its hinterland and the desert beyond attesting to the local predominance of Libyphoenicians and Libyans.[96] For all the false claims of the Italians in the early part of the twentieth century, there is very little evidence for Roman state-sponsored colonization or immigration in Libya. There were clearly moments of resistance, notably in the late first century BC and early first century AD, but thereafter the region as a whole seems to have participated with great success in the Roman Empire, selling its olive oil on a Mediterranean market, enriching its towns and transforming the countryside. In its heyday, Tripolitania sent numerous men to the senate at Rome, or for imperial service as equestrians, all this culminating

---

[93] See, for example, Alcock 1993; Dyson 1993; Millett 1990a.
[94] See for example, Ferchiou 1990.
[95] Camps 1993; Vattioni 1979, 1980.
[96] Mattingly 1987a, 1987b.

FIGURE 2.7 Monumental Roman olive press in the hinterland of Lepcis Magna, where Libyan student Muftah Hdad is currently researching a PhD on ancient oil and pottery production. (Photograph by Muftah Hdad; used with permission.)

in the extraordinary success of Septimius Severus. This ought to be one of the proudest moments in Libyan history, when a Romano-Libyan was dictating to the rest of the world.[97]

Recent visits suggest that there is hope for the future in this regard. School parties of Libyan children have started to reappear in force at Lepcis Magna, and there are magnificent new museums at Tripoli and Lepcis that give suitable emphasis and context for the Roman phase within the overall history of Libya. Outside the new museum at Lepcis stands a large statue of Septimius Severus, hailed as the African emperor (see fig. 2.8). The vestibule beyond is dominated by a vast photograph of Libya's current leader, arms raised in acclamation or embrace. Visual narratives are

[97] Birley 1988b.

FIGURE 2.8 Italian colonial-era statue of Septimius Severus, now rehabilitated as a monument of Libyan national pride outside the Lepcis Magna museum.

still very much alive in the postcolonial age (though one should note that the design team was Italian). This does not mean, of course, that Roman period archaeology is being prioritized in any way, but that it is no longer "out in the cold" is encouraging.

My final thought returns to the desirability of arriving at a single post-colonial perspective on Roman Africa. Here again the contrast with traditional Gallo-Roman and Romano-British archaeology comes to mind. Could we in Britain not benefit from a little of the skepticism of the North Africans when we consider the impact of Roman conquest and rule on British and Celtic societies? Roman imperialism involved both the iron fist and the velvet glove and provoked varying responses, including compliance, cooperation, resistance, and rebellion.[98] Discrepant experiences of Roman imperialism there certainly were, then—whether synchronous or successive—and the situation was neither static nor uniform. Too often, perhaps, scholarship creates dichotomies in which there are in fact a range of possible actions, reactions, and perceptions in between the extremes of the argument. By debating divergent perceptions of Roman imperialism we may enrich our vision of its workings in a specific time or place. Let us not then simply discard existing flawed models for another monolithic vision of what Roman Africa was about. The achievements, ambiguities, and defects of ancient imperialism can be teased out most effectively through the interrogation of a series of contrasting perspectives.

---

[98] Mattingly 2006c and the present volume represent the culmination of my response to this rhetorical challenge.

PART TWO

Power

CHAPTER THREE

Regime Change, Resistance, and Reconstruction

IMPERIALISM ANCIENT AND MODERN

THE NATURE OF ROMAN IMPERIALISM

This chapter addresses problems arising from the presentation of the Roman Empire in much modern literature as a largely benign power. Recent world events remind us of the potential messiness of imperial adventures designed to bring about regime change.[1] The events of the conquest period in Britain will be reassessed, with a particular focus on the dismantling of the client kingdom that lay at the heart of the Roman decision to invade.

A simple definition of *empire* is "rule over very large territory and many peoples without their consent" (see the introduction to the present volume). The Roman Empire was just such a system of territorial domination, social power, and economic exploitation, and in these respects it shares common characteristics with other empires. Power is the key concept for understanding what empires share in common and in moving beyond observations about the obvious differences between ancient land empires and modern capitalistic and maritime empires.[2] While recognizing that there are profound differences in the scale and operation of modern imperialism, my starting point is that all empires share a common basis in the enforced domination of lands, seas, and peoples. This nonconsensual nature of imperial rule is of the highest importance, because the existence of an empire predetermines the emergence of resistance to its power.[3]

The origins of this chapter lie in an unpublished paper presented at the 2005 Roman Archaeology Conference held in Birmingham, England. I am grateful to Richard Hingley for the invitation to participate in his session on imperialism, and for his comments on the paper that have enabled me to develop and expand on it for publication here.

[1] This chapter was drafted in the direct aftermath of the U.S.-led "regime change" in Iraq.

[2] Power has been a key concept in the attempts of international relations specialists to make sense of the Roman world; see Fitzpatrick 2005; and James 2006, 141–49.

[3] Said 1986, 151; Sarup 1993.

CLIENT RULERS IN THE ROMAN WORLD

> Of the entire area which is subject to the Romans, some is ruled by
> kings, some they rule under the designation 'provincial' territory, ap-
> pointing governors and tax collectors to the inhabitants. There are also
> free cities, some of which attached themselves to the Romans as friends
> from the outset, while to others the Romans themselves granted free-
> dom as a mark of honour. Some dynasts, tribal chieftains and religious
> rulers are also subject to the Romans; these people regulate their lives
> along traditional lines.[4]

Alongside the territorial domination of areas formally annexed, the
Roman Empire made considerable use of hegemonic methods of control.[5]
The recognition of individual client rulers and the formal assignation
of territories to their control was a standard element of imperial rule in
the Late Republic and the Early Principate.[6] The technical title of these
rulers was *rex sociusque et amicus populi Romani*, often abbreviated as
"friendly kings," a status that enshrined a mass of ambiguities of power.[7]
Although these kingdoms differed in their scale and their specific relations with (and obligations to) Rome, there was a sense in which they
were seen as somewhat equivalent to provinces with military forces.[8] Witness also the notion that the principalities were "limbs and parts of the
empire."[9] The British Empire in India was later to accomplish a similar
semantic trick in integrating the numerous minor principalities within the
loose embrace of the Raj.[10]

Regulated by treaties, such friendly kings were an economical way to
rule territory and to extract tribute. However, they were not designed (or
destined) to last, and the story of imperial expansion in the last century
BC and first century AD is in large measure that of a sequence of client
kingdoms being annexed by the Roman state when they had served their
purpose or outlived their utility to Rome—notably, in the early Augustan and Flavian periods.[11] The moment of annexation often coincided
with the death of a friendly king and the decision of the Romans not to
recognize a local successor. A number of friendly kings bequeathed their

---

[4] Strabo, *Geography* 17.3.24.
[5] Luttwak 1976, 13–40, remains an interesting and strategic slant on hegemonic rule.
[6] Braund 1984 is still the standard study; see also Braund 1988.
[7] Braund 1984, 23–37.
[8] Tacitus, *Annals*, 4.5; Luttwak 1976, 30.
[9] Suetonius, *Augustus*, 48, *membra partesque imperii*; Braund 1996, 88.
[10] See Ferguson 2004, 172–73, for a map of British India and the native princely states,
and 208–12 on their exploitation by British imperial administration.
[11] Braund 1984, 165–80.

possessions to Rome in the event of dying without an heir, or sought Roman guardianship for their heirs.[12] This was often linked to Roman protection against rivals or neighboring states, but it was also a tacit recognition of the realities of their treaties with Rome. From the Augustan age onward the position of heirs to a client kingdom was increasingly subject to explicit approval by the emperor.[13] Many client rulers in waiting spent periods within the Roman Empire for education, and those who were ousted by internal coup or as a result of being forcibly retired by Rome could generally count on a pension and lands within the provincial territory.[14] The relationships between Rome and friendly kings were thus essentially individual ones similar to the patron/client links between individual members of Rome's elite classes.[15]

From this perspective the client kingdom existed primarily as a personal gift between the Roman state (or *princeps*) and an individual; it did not necessarily involve Roman recognition of the autonomous or semiautonomous existence of a particular people. The pragmatic nature of these relationships is well summed up by Edward Luttwak: "The client states needed constant management: unsatisfactory rulers had to be replaced . . . and successors had to be found for rulers who died."[16]

However, the "economy of force" achieved by Rome in governing territory by proxy was often revealed to be a false economy in the medium term. Routine deployment of troops may have been avoided, but often at the cost of large-scale crisis management later. A recent analysis of the background to the Jewish revolt under Nero has highlighted the fact that the lengthy series of changing arrangements for the rule of Judaea under the Julio-Claudian emperors—varying from client kingdom to direct rule and back again—prevented consistency of "authority of power." The arbitrary comings and goings of Roman nominated kings and imperial officials exacerbated fault lines in Jewish society, undermining traditional hierarchies and elites. Rome's "long hesitation" about how best to govern the region thus contributed to the horrific savagery of revolt when it came.[17]

Recognition of individuals as client kings was not necessarily restricted to members of the local ruling group of families.[18] A prince whose father's kingdom had been annexed might be accorded a neighboring kingdom to rule—as in the case of Juba II, son of the last king of independent

[12] Ibid., 129–64.
[13] Braund 1996, 85–89; Creighton 2000, 169–70.
[14] Allen 2006; Braund 1984, 9–21, 165–74; Creighton 2000, 89–94.
[15] Wallace-Hadrill 1989a.
[16] Luttwak 1976, 39.
[17] Curran 2005.
[18] Jacobson 2001.

FIGURE 3.1 Gold coin of Augustus, featuring a (Germanic) barbarian chief offering up his child to the emperor. (RIC 1, 201a: Werner Forman / Art Resource.)

Numidia, who became king of Mauretania under Augustus in 25 BC.[19] Forging marriage alliances with clients was also good politics for the empire, as the union of Juba II and Cleopatra, daughter of the last queen of Egypt, indicates.[20]

Figure 3.1 illustrates the theme of the offering of native princes as "hostages" for education in the Roman army and at the imperial

---

[19] Plutarch, *Caesar*, 55.2.
[20] Dio, *Roman History*, 51.15.6; Jacobson 2001, 25.

court.[21] This gold coin of Augustus encapsulates both the *importance* and the *effect* of power in an imperial society. A (German) barbarian leader offers up his own child as a hostage to the emperor. This presents an idealized image of the friendly king and the sacrifices expected of him in his relations with the imperial power.[22] Here we see that power is not simply about dominance—though that is, of course, part of the significance of the scene. We are also witness to the quality of power to change behavior in both predictable and in less tangible ways. Roman power in this situation did not simply control; it acted as a creative force in the societies in contact with Rome, creating dynamic new possibilities for native princes and rulers. Yet, as we shall see, in encouraging expectations and ambitions among clients, there were also dangers to imperial stability.

The basic ground rules of client kingship as far as we can reconstruct them were:

1. Clients were formally bound to the empire by treaties and provided hostages and other sureties of good behavior.
2. All things being equal, Rome favored heirs of client kingdoms who were known quantities (often those who had spent time at Rome as hostages) and who had already espoused Roman values and culture to some degree.
3. The appointment of a client king required his formal acceptance at Rome; a fait accompli of a local strongman seizing power would result in conflict unless he could obtain the explicit authority of a Roman client.
4. Some client kings were able to secure the succession of their heirs, and this appears to have been most straightforward to achieve in periods when territorial expansion was limited (as late in the reign of Augustus or under Tiberius).
5. Client kingdoms were expected to make a financial and military contribution to the empire, as well as covering their own costs of governance.
6. Failure to abide by the terms of their treaties, unauthorized military actions against third parties or other resistance to Rome could result in the renunciation of a client and Roman annexation or replacement with another more pliable client ruler.

Above all, we need to recognize that friendly kings could require a high level of input from the empire. Despite its sometime tendency toward tak-

---

[21] I must thank Bruce Hitchner for suggesting this wonderful image for all the publicity for the lecture series. It is also illustrated and discussed in Roymans 2004, 243.

[22] Braund 1984.

ing ad hoc decisions and to being reactive to events, the Roman Empire required a more proactive basis to the relationship with its clients.

REGIME CHANGE AND THE ROMAN EMPIRE

> Does an invasion need to be hostile to the inhabitants of a country being invaded? Modern experience of United Nations actions, for example, should tell us that such actions can have an altruistic aim.[23]

The reasons for regime change were no doubt varied, but we need to be particularly skeptical of a model that sees the Roman Empire as analogous to the United Nations. There has been something of a revival of views in recent years about the altruistic or disinterested aims of the Roman Empire, as exemplified by Martin Henig's comment above, and a prime goal of this paper is to argue that this is largely the result of uncritical reasoning.

Unsurprisingly, the historical winner (that is, Rome) tended to present a negative image of any client rulers that it deposed. There is no doubt that Roman history features many major 'rebels' who had previously enjoyed a close relationship with Rome (Jugurtha of Numidia, Arminius the German, Boudica the Briton).[24] It is easy to get carried along by the imperial rhetoric concerning the character flaws of these individuals, and so to conclude that their resistance was due to deep-seated anti-Roman sentiment. Yet many of the greatest rebels against Rome had a previous history of close relations and their resistance thus needs explaining in the context of changing relations with the imperial power. In several cases one can see that military conflict resulted from Rome's decision to annex client states or to effect regime change rather than being due to initial disloyalty by the client.

Just as the British and American justifications of their pursuit of regime change in Iraq have been shown to be based on shallow and "sexed up" claims,[25] so our ancient sources on similar Roman interventions are also presumptively suspect. There is, of course, no doubt that Saddam Hussein was a monster, but it was as a client of the West that he became so. For example, the main period of Iraqi use of weapons of mass destruction, in the war with Iran and against the Kurds, occurred at the time of Saddam's closest rapprochement with the United States. The moral paradox here simply emphasizes the political contingency of empires.

[23] Henig 2002, 38.
[24] See Wells 2003, 105–24; Hingley and Unwin 2005, 41–61.
[25] See Runciman 2004 on the Hutton and Butler reports.

In the same way, we need to look at Rome's relations with clients and native rulers on the periphery of its empire with a more critical eye. Threats to the security of empire could on occasion be ascribed to anti-Roman sentiment, but in a number of important cases we should consider the crises to have arisen as a result of sudden breakdowns in what had formerly been close rapprochment with client rulers. Personalities aside, it is possible that complications arising out of the processes of regime change and power transfer represent a systemic weakness of empires.

THE KINGDOMS OF CUNOBELIN AND VERICA AND THE ROMAN INVASION OF BRITAIN

The political history of Britain between the campaigns of Caesar in 55–54 BC and the Claudian invasion of AD 43 is shadowy in the extreme.[26] Many accounts of the period start with disclaimers about the extent to which it is possible to construct conventional narrative.[27] Yet out of the diaphanous factual fabric much has been manufactured. From the coin series issued by late Iron Age peoples, numismatists have endeavored to trace dynastic links between named individuals, constructing plausible but unprovable genealogies for some of the major peoples.[28] That has not stopped historians and archaeologists from attempting to flesh out the biographies of these ghostly individuals.[29] In reality the factual basis of many conventional accounts is illusory and rests heavily on some basic but untested assumptions.[30] Roman and Iron Age experts alike have a habit of adopting without question the idiom of the classical sources (and modern colonial regimes) in talking of "tribes," "civilization," "barbarians," and so on.[31] Most modern accounts are punctuated by such stereotypes—for instance, a repeated insistence on "Catuvellaunian aggression" against neighbors and Romans.[32]

[26] See Mattingly 2006c, 47–84, for my overview of the period.

[27] Braund 1996, 67–69.

[28] Van Arsdell 1989 is a good example of this tendency to push genealogy and chronology to the limits. For changing views on the significance of so-called Celtic coinage, see Aarts 2005; Cunliffe 1981; Haselgrove 1987; Haselgrove and Wigg-Wolf 2005.

[29] Peddie 1987, 15–22, is typical of many.

[30] Todd 1999, 17–54, and Wacher 1998, 13–18, make the best of the material, but the approach seems flawed to me.

[31] See the discussion in Mattingly 2006c, 26–38.

[32] Wacher 1998, 14. The axiom is dubious on two counts: first, the "aggression" may be simply Rome's post facto justification for invading rather than a reality, and second, the conceptualization of a "Catuvellaunian tribe" is at odds with the impression that power in preconquest southern Britain was vested more in individuals with whom Rome had a special relationship than in peoples per se. It is reasonable to infer that there were people called

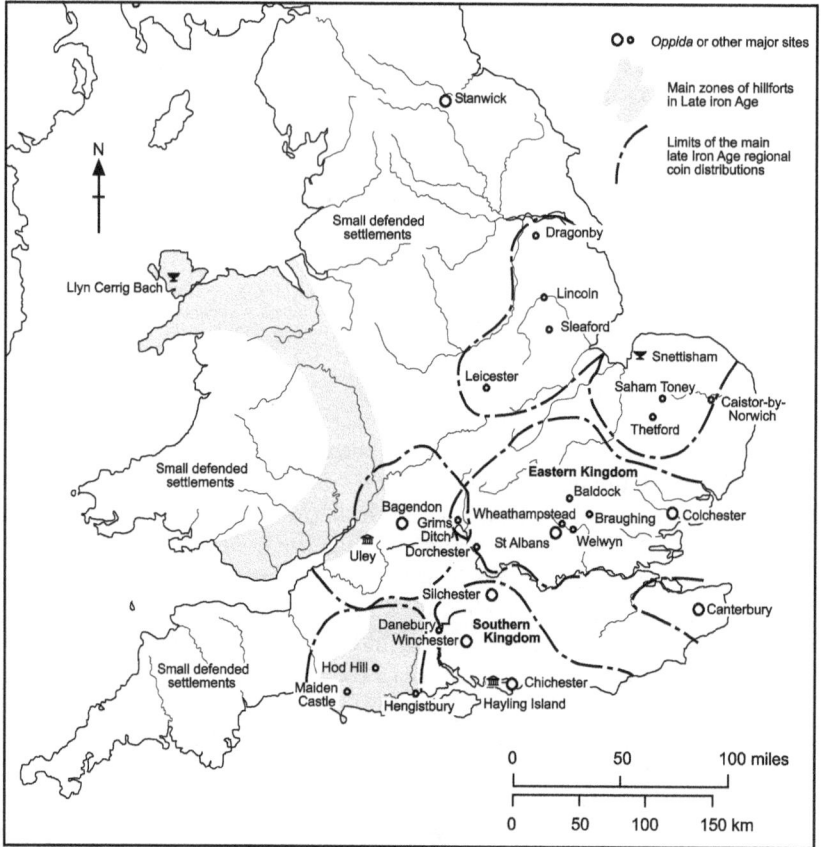

FIGURE 3.2 Map of Britain on the eve of the Claudian invasion of AD 43, showing approximate territories of the eastern and southern kingdoms.

Iron Age specialists tend to take a more archaeological approach but are themselves somewhat wedded to the small scraps of information provided by the ancient literary sources and coin series.[33] Much recent work on late Iron Age Britain has focused on the delineation of significant differences between southeast England and the rest of the British

Catuvellauni who were under the rule of Cunobelin, but they were one of several regional populations associated with his kingdom and it is by no means certain even that they were a dominant group within the kingdom, as is often assumed.

[33] See Cunliffe 2005, 149–77, for a recent synthesis (and cf. Cunliffe 1991); Pryor 2003, 433–44, weakens his brilliant revisionist approach by taking too much of the source evidence on trust. The papers in Haselgrove and Moore 2007 offer the most authoritative synthesis of current thinking on late Iron Age society.

archipelago.[34] It is now widely recognized that, at the time of the Claudian invasion of AD 43, the southeastern region was dominated by two major kingdoms and that these had (or had previously had) some sort of formal client relationship with Rome (see fig. 3.2).[35] There is similarity here with the situation observed in other colonial contexts, wherein an expanding empire has a considerable impact on peripheral societies, leading to the emergence of higher forms of statehood.[36] The "eastern kingdom," with its main proto-urban centers (*oppida*) north of the Thames at Colchester (Camulodunon) and St. Albans (Verlamion), is often associated with the Trinovantes and Catuvellauni people, but is perhaps better conceived as the kingdom of the House of Cunobelin. The southern kingdom, with known centers at Silchester (Calleva) and Chichester, is generally associated with Atrebates, but again may more accurately be considered the House of Verica. These sophisticated states were built on the personal power of their ruling dynasties and the close ties the latter had with the Roman Empire.[37]

The ostensible reason for the Claudian invasion according to Cassius Dio was the flight across the Channel of Verica (or Berikos) as a result of an uprising in Britain;[38] he apparently persuaded Claudius to send an expedition. As noted already, Verica appears to have been king of a substantial territory south of the Thames around AD 10–42. There is an interesting symmetry with the account of Caligula's planned campaign of AD 40, when another refugee British prince was received by the emperor. Adminius was a prince of the ruling house of the eastern kingdom of Cunobelin to the north of the Thames.[39] The consensus view of these events has tended to be that the expansionism and profound anti-Roman tendencies of the eastern kingdom had got out of control, exacerbated by their annexation of neighboring territory (some commentators anachronistically and hyperbolically write of a growing "Catuvellaunian empire").[40] The flight of Verica and Adminius are seen as representing the expulsion of recognized Roman clients or of pro-Roman elements within the court of Cunobelin. Henig gives a particularly lopsided view of events, taking the Roman sources on trust and amplifying their innuendos:

When, at the end of Cunobelin's reign, his philo-Roman son Adminius, was driven out of Britain, to surrender himself to Gaius Caligula . . .

---

[34] Champion and Collis 1996; Gwilt and Haselgrove 1997; Haselgrove 1999, 130–33; 2004; Mattingly 2006c, 68–84.
[35] Creighton 2000 is the best account.
[36] Whitehead 1992.
[37] Creighton 2006, 19–31.
[38] Dio, *Roman History*, 60.19.1–2.
[39] Suetonius, *Caligula*, 44.2.
[40] Braund 1996, 101; Wacher 1998, 15.

it might appear that the situation was very different from that of 30 years before when Tincomarus was expelled from the southern kingdom. What had changed was that Cunobelin's other sons, Caratacus and Togodumnus, were bent on continuing an aggressive policy and building up a unified realm in the south-east.... Claudius could only nod thoughtfully, realising that the situation in Britain was a potential threat to the security of the neighbouring parts of Gaul.[41]

The same tendency to embellish the threadbare evidence is demonstrated also by John Wacher, who writes, "In [Cunobelin's] declining years ... power was increasingly transferred to his sons. One of these Adminius, held pro-Roman views ... two others ... Togodumnus and Caratacus revived the indifference towards Rome. By the time Gaius had succeeded Tiberius ... this pair had sufficient authority over their father to cause Adminius' expulsion."[42]

Although blamed by most modern commentators on the expansionism of the eastern kingdom, the flight of Verica to Rome in about AD 42 was actually attributed by Dio to "internal unrest" within his southern kingdom.[43] Modern textbooks generally present this as the final straw for Rome in its deteriorating relationship with a rogue state. This puts all the responsibility for the Roman invasion of Britain on the native princes, with Henig—among others—claiming that the restoration of the House of Verica in the southern kingdom was a prime objective of the invasion in AD 43. As we shall see, there is no doubting that the initial and prime target of the invasion was the annexation of the eastern kingdom. The fundamental assumption in most modern accounts concerns the presumed anti-Roman outlook of Cunobelin and his sons Caratacus and Togodumnus.[44] But how did the breakdown in relations come about, and was Rome blameless in this situation? What if the depiction of the House of Cunobelin as fundamentally and unwaveringly anti-Roman was a deliberate falsehood?

Despite the lack of more explicit testimony relating to the events of the late AD 30s and early 40s, I think some suggestions can be made for an alternative narrative to that most widely disseminated today. I suggest that the transformation from friendly king to "rogue state" was late, sudden, and precipitated by unilateral Roman actions.

---

[41] Henig 2002, 33–34.

[42] Wacher 1998, 15 (all highly speculative and accepting at face value the hints of motive/justification in Roman accounts of the invasion).

[43] Dio, *Roman History*, 60.19.1.

[44] The pair are described as "hot-headed" in Wacher 1998, 15, but on what grounds?

My understanding of the Roman conquest is built on a series of observations and suppositions that I shall acknowledge at the outset, though I think each can be justified:

1. The status of the eastern and southern kingdoms was as formal *client kingdoms* of Rome.
2. The increasing age of Cunobelin and Verica by the late AD 30s (both had been in power since about AD 10) was likely to have focused attention on the issue of political *succession* in both kingdoms.
3. The death of Tiberius in AD 37 marked an end of a nonexpansionist era in Roman foreign relations and put Roman *territorial annexation* on the agenda.
4. Roman *actions* provoked the crisis in relations; Gaius (Caligula) announced Rome's new intentions by assembling ships and troops for a British campaign at Boulogne, and building a lighthouse there.
5. Verica and Adminius may both have been pro-Roman voices in their respective kingdoms, but the fact that neither was restored as a client king postconquest suggests that they were useful *pretexts* rather than part of Rome's plans.

In the rest of this chapter I shall consider these key terms one by one.

CLIENT KINGDOMS

In the period between 30 BC and AD 43 a wide range of innovations appeared in the Iron Age coinage produced in southeastern Britain, heralding the emergence of two major kingdoms.[45] The use of Latin legends and the inclusion of imagery drawn from the visual language of imperial power are particularly interesting developments. We know that Caesar demanded hostages (*obsides*) and tribute payments from the British rulers as well as guarantees from them regarding their future conduct and acknowledgment of Rome's suzerainty.[46] It has sometimes been considered unlikely that such arrangements endured for long in the prolonged period of civil wars and internal strife that beset the Roman Empire.[47] The coinage evidence as interpreted by John Creighton suggests a different picture—that parts of Britain were effectively considered as integrated

[45] Here again Creighton 2000 is a fundamental study; see also Braund 1996, 76–90, for the historical background.

[46] Cicero, *Letters to Atticus*, 4.18.5; Strabo, *Geography*, 4.5.3. On the role of obsides in Roman "empire management," see Allen 2006.

[47] Frere 1974, 39–45, and Salway 1981, 48, for instance, suggest that there was some hiatus before Augustus renewed relations around 16 BC.

client states within the empire. Archaeological evidence is also starting to accumulate to suggest a much higher engagement with Roman material culture and continental innovations in social and religious behavior.[48]

The absence of these British *obsides* from their homelands could be prolonged. They established high level contacts in Roman society, they were very often given a period of service as officers in the Roman army, and they were firsthand witnesses of imperial politics at the center of power. The major innovators in the Iron Age coinages in Britain were thus most likely princes who had spent a period of time in Rome—or, at any rate, inside the empire. The seeming coincidence of approximate accession dates for both Cunobelin and Verica around AD 10 might hint at a late Augustan revisiting of the British situation and installation of two men with a particularly good exposure to and understanding of the new visual vocabulary of power at Rome.[49] However, one can also point to the earlier installation of Tincomarus and Tasciovanus around 30–25 BC as equally critical moments when new iconographic programs appeared in the British coinage, heralding the initiation of two long-lived reigns. The Roman sources highlight the importance of these relationships in the reign of Augustus.[50]

There is significant overlap between some of the imagery employed by British client rulers such as Tincomarus of the southern kingdom and that on the coins of Juba II and his son Ptolemy of Mauretania. The similarities among coinages of a number of Augustan clients are so close as to suggest at the very least a keen awareness of what other client rulers were doing.[51]

SUCCESSION

The dynamics of this contact situation were inherently unstable, as a political settlement based on individual power and agreements with Rome required renegotiation and renewal every time leadership changed, whether as a result of the incumbent's death or his overthrow. The transfer or prolongation of power in the next generation of a friendly kingdom could make headline news at Rome, especially if the emperor's preferred candidates were not immediately accepted—as may have happened in Britain around 27–26 BC.[52] Client kingship was something that had to be agreed by Rome, so anyone seeking to establish their own rule, no

---

[48] Creighton 2006, 35–45; Manley and Rudkin 2005.
[49] Creighton 2000, 95–125.
[50] Strabo, *Geography*, 4.5.3.
[51] Creighton 2000, 118–24.
[52] Dio, *Roman History*, 53.22, 53.25.

matter what their support in Britain, would have to seek recognition from Rome.[53] In succession matters, Rome may often have had a favored candidate, though it is clear that the diplomatic and military situation did not always resolve itself to Rome's liking, and we know of at least two British rulers who fled to Rome under Augustus in addition to those on the eve of the Claudian invasion.[54] The point is that such upheavals are most likely to have occurred at moments of succession to the two major client kingdoms that Rome recognized in Britain rather than being a continuous problem.

In a similar way, a famous series of inscriptions from the forum area at Volubilis in Mauretania refer to "altars of peace" being erected at colloquia between the Roman governor and the chiefs of one of the leading peoples of the Atlas Mountains, the Baquates.[55] Although at one time interpreted as evidence for recurrent warfare between Rome and hostile forces on its Moroccan frontier, more recent appraisals have tended to conclude that these represented periodic reaffirmations of a client relationship with successive chieftains.[56]

What was the relationship between the two British client kingdoms? Where is the evidence to suggest that one was attacking the other in the time leading up to the Claudian invasion? Overlapping with the latter stages of Verica's coinage is the series produced for another ruler called Epaticcus, centered on the northern part of Verica's zone of influence.[57] The iconography of the coins follows that of the eastern kingdom, though the denominations match the normal pattern of the southern kingdom, with gold and silver but no bronze issues. Epaticcus thus signaled a dynastic link to the ruling group of the eastern kingdom. This has often been presented as the prime evidence that the eastern kingdom was expanding in defiance of Roman wishes at the expense of its southern rival, provoking Verica's fall.[58] There are alternative scenarios to consider. If the eastern kingdom had indeed become predominant over the southern, there is a possibility that Rome had given explicit encouragement and support for this, perhaps favoring a situation where it dealt with a preeminent kingdom rather than maintain the potentially tricky balancing act of supporting two rival powers equally. It is also entirely feasible (and perhaps more likely in terms of Roman diplomatic management of its clients) that Epaticcus appeared as ruler at Calleva as a result of an

[53] Braund 1984, 24–27; 1996, 84–86.

[54] Augustus, *Res Gestae*, 6.32; Suetonius, *Caligula*, 44.2.

[55] *IAM* 2.348–350, 356–61, 384, 402.

[56] For the traditional interpretation, see Frezouls 1957 and 1980. Cf. Mattingly 1992; Shaw 1987.

[57] Creighton 2000, 104–5, 111–12.

[58] See, among others, Salway 1981, 70.

arranged dynastic marriage brokered by Rome; there are certainly many other examples of Rome arranging such matches between neighboring client states. It is surely significant that the few coin issues ascribed to Caratacus, who may have succeeded Epaticcus in this territory just ahead of the Roman invasion of AD 43, continued Roman-style themes, perhaps still in the hope that Rome would recognize his legitimacy as a client ruler.[59] It is thus by no means certain that the fall of the House of Verica was the equivalent of Saddam's invasion of Kuwait in provoking an imperial military response.[60]

The reign of Cunobelin marks the apogee of the late Iron Age kingdoms in Britain.[61] His coinage is estimated to have exceeded more than a million struck pieces, and dwarfs all the other pre-Roman kingdoms. He appears to have ruled over a wide region with Roman support and approbation. The Roman historian Suetonius described Cunobelin as *rex Britannorum* (king of the Britons), which implies that he ruled over a large group of British peoples with imperial blessing.[62] His client status is also indicated by the use of the *rex* legend on his coins.[63]

Cunobelin's coinage was the most classical of all the kingdoms. The proliferation and range of the imagery employed overall is astonishing. By identifying with the iconographic program of Augustus and the reinvention of Roman culture that took place in the Augustan age, the British dynasts both proclaimed their allegiance to Augustus and constructed their own identity as powerful rulers.[64] The coins reflect the close integration of these kingdoms within the Roman world; the complexity of the imagery would have made the message of the coins wholly accessible to a relatively small group in society or perhaps had been consciously designed with an external audience in mind. Indeed, some of the Cunobelin and Verica issues feature what are clearly imperial portraits of Augustus, Tiberius, or Gaius and the voluntary inclusion of such images must indicate an expression of allegiance.[65]

Succession issues are also indicated by the use of *F* or *FIL*, for *filii* ("son of"). These coins were a way of showing a sense of belonging to the Roman world and of seeking legitimation of power and authority by emulation of programmatic Roman imagery and wordplay. In presenting real or imagined dynastic links to other rulers, the kings reinforced their

---

[59] Creighton 2000, 219; 2006, 30.

[60] We might note, however, that Saddam mistakenly thought he had been given the nod by the U.S. ambassador ahead of sending in his troops.

[61] Cunliffe 1981, 37–39, 82–84; Creighton 2000, 109–11.

[62] Suetonius, *Caligula*, 44.2.

[63] This runs contra the views of Salway 1981, 56.

[64] Creighton 2000, esp. 80–125.

[65] Creighton 2000, 176–88.

own authority. It is conventional to take literally the family links implied by the coin legends, but while it is not implausible that Cunobelin, for instance, was the son of Tasciovanus, we should be cautious. After all, if the Roman Empire was their model, the relationship of Octavian to Caesar (or of a succession of presumptive heirs to Augustus) was that of adoptive son, not blood relation. Perhaps it is safer to assume that the claims of filiation on the coins were a legitimation device indicating "of the family of" or "descendant of," following good Roman precedents.[66] Given that Rome often wished to play kingmaker in succession issues, it was by no means certain that a client kingdom would have passed in a simple father-to-son pattern. The expression of such dynastic links may also have articulated the hope that the wishes of the present incumbent would be given due weight by Rome.

Client rulers were controlled and manipulated in a variety of ways, but interference in the succession process was probably the most significant and contentious area.[67] It was clearly in Rome's interests when a client king died to have him replaced by one of the educated hostages from the pool held at Rome. But hostages were sometimes at a disadvantage in terms of not always being on the spot when the ruler died, and were also potentially out of touch with the bulk of the people within the kingdom. To counterbalance these disadvantages, Rome made certain requirements of client rulers about their succession: that arrangements were openly discussed with Rome and the nominated successor approved by Rome, new client kings were expected to travel to Rome to be formally recognized, and so on. It was an exceptional case, as with Herod, for the emperor to grant a client king the privilege of appointing his own successor.[68]

The system did not always work smoothly, of course, and Rome could, if necessary, threaten annexation against client states keen to appoint a king other than a candidate endorsed by Rome. There might be a lengthy interregnum while the issue of succession was sorted out to the satisfaction of all.

ANNEXATION

The conquest of AD 43 saw the eradication of the eastern kingdom and the start of wider campaigning in Britain, coupled with the recognition of several new client kings. There was no return for Verica, the southern kingdom being handed over (though perhaps only after an interval of

---

[66] This has been argued already in Creighton 2000, 170–73.
[67] Braund 1984, 24–26.
[68] Josephus, *Jewish Antiquities*, 15.343, 16.92; Braund 1984, 26–27.

several years) to a certain Togidubnus, while new clients were recognized as rulers of the Iceni and Brigantes.

The identity of Togidubnus (or Cogidubnus, as some books still present him on the basis of the less likely version of his name in the classical sources) is a conundrum. It has generally been accepted that he was a British prince who happened to have a rather similar name to Togodumnus, the son of Cunobelin. The conventional view, on Dio's apparent testimony, is that Togodumnus was killed in battle early in the AD 43 campaign. However, as I have hinted at in *Imperial Possession*, Dio may have misinterpreted his source in reporting the death of Togodumnus, an idea now convincingly developed by John Hind to suggest that far from being killed in battle, Togodumnus was effectively "turned" by Rome and persuaded to collaborate.[69] This clears the way for correlating Togodumnus with Togidubnus, the client king postconquest. The possibility is very attractive, and is consistent with what we know of Roman use of clients elsewhere, while also highlighting the contrasting fates of the two premier princes/kings who led the opposition to the Roman invasion in AD 43. While Togodumnus was potentially persuaded to collaborate, his brother Caratacus fought on resolutely, eventually to be paraded at the triumph of Claudius in Rome.[70]

The kingdom assigned to Togodumnus/Togidubnus in the later AD 40s was eventually annexed peacefully (probably quite early in the reign of Vespasian), but some of the worst military problems in the first century AD attended the termination of other British client kingdoms, that of Prasutagus of the Iceni and Cartimandua of the Brigantes. The Boudican revolt erupted when the Romans overrode the wishes of the Iceni and annexed the territory of the client state after the death of king Prasutagas, ignoring his will that had attempted to leave only half his territory to Nero and the rest to his daughters.[71] The Brigantian problem is presented in the sources as the fall out from a sordid palace scandal, when Queen Cartimandua replaced her husband Venutius in her bed with his armor bearer, Vellocatus.[72] Venutius is sometimes presented as fundamentally anti-Roman, but he had in fact been described as the British leader after Caratacus who "excelled in military skill.... For a long time he was loyal and enjoyed the protection of Roman arms."[73] The marital discord seemingly opened up fault lines within Brigantian society, perhaps

---

[69] Dio, *Roman History*, 60.21.1; see Mattingly 2006c, 100, and Hind 2007, 96–100, for detailed discussion and proposed reappraisal of Dio's text and Togodumnus's presumed death.

[70] Hind 2007, 99–100.

[71] Hingley and Unwin 2005, 43–47; Mattingly 2006c, 106–8.

[72] Tacitus, *Histories*, 3.45.

[73] Tacitus, *Annals*, 12.40.

focusing on different readings of Rome's long-term intentions in northern Britain.[74]

So whose fault was the invasion of AD 43? Was it a catastrophic miscalculation by the ruling family of the eastern kingdom, or was it the result of political duplicity on the part of Rome, turning on a long-term ally? We shall never have the evidence to answer all our questions about the underlying story of Cunobelin's sons: Caratacus and Togodumnus who resisted the invasion (though with Togodumnus possibly being persuaded to switch allegiance at an early stage), Amminius (or Adminius) who was forced to flee to Gaius Caligula after a quarrel with his father, and unnamed other brothers captured by Ostorius Scapula in AD 52.[75] However, it is surely significant that following his final defeat and capture by Ostorius Scapula after almost ten years of warfare, Caratacus was spared from execution after being paraded in Claudius's triumph.[76] Tacitus implied it was the oratorical skills of Caratacus that gained his reprieve (and likely pensioned retirement within the empire), but if he had been a long-term friend of Rome prior to AD 43 there may have been an element of bad conscience behind Claudius's decision.

My reconstruction of events thus differs from the consensus view in putting greater responsibility on Roman imperial politics rather than on intransigence and unilateral action on the part of the House of Cunobelin. The territory under the influence of the eastern dynasty was exceptionally large—as already noted, Suetonius referred to Cunobelin as "king of the Britons,"[77] implying control of several distinct peoples in southern Britain. I have argued herein that there is actually no evidence to suggest that the expansion had been attained in defiance of Rome's wishes. Cunobelin had a long and prosperous reign as a friend of Rome. But he chose a bad moment to die and to create a succession issue, at a time when two new emperors came to the throne in Rome in rapid succession, each needing some quick military glory to establish their popular reputation. Client kingdoms, no matter whether loyal or not, were an attractive target in such circumstances, as if handled well, the glory and booty could be had fairly cheaply and quickly become victories, provided that some at least of the native elite order could be persuaded that their interests would be best served by compliance. Again, the decision to reward Togodumnus/Togidubnus with a new client kingdom south if the Thames, if the correlation of the names is correct, is much more plausible if Cunobelin and his sons were not directly responsible for provoking a crisis that necessitated Roman intervention.

---

[74] Creighton 2006, 33–34.
[75] Tacitus, *Annals*, 12.35–36.
[76] Ibid., 12.36–37.
[77] Suetonius, *Caligula*, 44.2.

It is thus an interesting paradox that annexation, when it came, should focus on the British client kingdoms that had been most closely aligned with Rome in the period between the campaigns of Caesar and Claudius. The accession of Caligula in AD 37 created the need for military glory to bolster his prestige. The first result of this political pragmatism was the execution of the king of Mauretania, Ptolemy. Mauretania erupted in revolt and Claudius was still mopping up the resistance in the early years of his reign.[78] Under the rule of the antiexpansionist Tiberius, the succession of Cunobelin's sons may well have been agreed in principle, but trouble and suspicion would have flared up quickly if, following the accession of Gaius, Roman missives suddenly become evasive on the issue of who was the approved heir. Cunobelin was evidently dead by the time Plautius landed with his invasion force in AD 43, with Caratacus and Togodumnus now cast in the role of rebels. Given Rome's invasion planning since at least AD 39, it is questionable whether Rome left them much of an alternative. Annexation here looks to have been a unilaterally "done deal."

ACTIONS

The evident deterioration in relations between the House of Cunobelin and Rome in the late AD 30s and early 40s was thus arguably a direct consequence of the realization in Britain that Rome intended to annex the kingdom on Cunobelin's death. Our sources imply that it was the British kings who became difficult and broke agreements, but it is at least as likely that it was the Romans who tangibly instituted a change in policy and whose actions preparing for the invasions sparked a crisis before Cunobelin was even dead. Although the detail of the abortive campaign under Gaius Caligula is fuzzy, there is little doubt that the construction of a lighthouse and improvements to the harbor at Boulogne, the assembly of an invasion fleet and the massing of troops on the Channel coast was an unambiguous threat that signaled a fundamental change in relations between the superpower and its British satellites.[79] The flight of another son of Cunobelin, Adminius, to Rome was perhaps a consequence of Roman attempts to convince some in the ruling elite to collaborate. It is likely that the same policy may have also affected the southern kingdom of Verica, or have had repercussions for him if he was perceived as accepting a Roman takeover as inevitable, since he was forcibly ousted just prior to the conquest of AD 43.

---

[78] Ibid., 46; Dio, *Roman History*, 59.25.
[79] Dio, *Roman History*, 59.25.1–3; Suetonius, *Caligula*, 44.2, 46.1; Todd 2004a, 44–46.

PRETEXTS

Adminius and Verica were used as pretexts for invasion in AD 40 and 43, respectively, but significantly neither appears to have been returned to power as a Roman client once the invasion was launched. Although in the event only the eastern kingdom was directly annexed in AD 43, with the southern kingdom being returned to the care of a new client ruler, one senses that realpolitik lay behind Rome's actions. Recent attempts to suggest that the Roman conquest was invited and encouraged by a large percentage of the Atrebates and other peoples threatened by the eastern kingdom's expansion seem to be far too accepting of a Roman perspective of these events.[80] If the new client king over the southern kingdom was in fact Togodumnus, son of Cunobelin and prince of the eastern kingdom, the events of the AD 40s appear in an altogether different light. Faced with a strong British force in the early stages of the invasion, the persuasion of one of the sons of Cunobelin to revert to a position of friendship to Rome—with the cynical promise one imagines of a client kingdom to follow—was a classic example of the pragmatic "divide and rule" mentality of imperial expansion.

The sequel to the invasion of AD 43 was far more than the annexation of a single client kingdom, in that a larger project for the conquest of the British archipelago was rapidly launched. The economic opportunities offered by newly annexed territories, in terms of control of natural resources and construction and supply contracts, can be readily paralleled in other imperial contexts. I remain dubious about the extent to which imperial grievances with the British client kings were anything more than a useful excuse for the habitual Roman pattern of exploitation and domination.

[80] Henig 2002.

CHAPTER FOUR

Power, Sex, and Empire

THE DYNAMICS OF POWER

This chapter concerns the workings of power on the body and the centrality of power as a sociological and historical theme. It explores the dynamics of power in imperial situations and assesses the value of comparative studies in colonial discourse by examining aspects of sex in the Roman world and more recent colonial societies. I owe much in this respect to my reading of Michel Foucault, but, as will become apparent, my argument diverges significantly from the line taken by his last works.[1]

The chapter is also written in reaction to much recent scholarship on the concept of power in the Roman world. While my specific subject is sexual power and its effect on shaping Roman sexual attitudes, the broader aim is to refocus interest on the distorting influence of power on social development and change in the Roman world. It has become common for discussions of cultural relations between Rome and its subject peoples to be put in terms suggestive of symmetry and equality. Although Rome was by no means as racist and exclusive as more recent colonial powers, the impact of Roman conquest on subject peoples cannot be assumed to have been negligible. Just as the presence of pollution, rubbish, and faecal material on Roman streets is enough to make us view Roman water and food sources as "presumptively contaminated,"[2] our starting point with Roman imperialism should be the presumption that it was based on significant power asymmetries, intrusion, exploitation, violence, and coercion. We can, of course, then consider the mitigating circumstances of the case and the degree to which Rome solicited

Earlier versions of this chapter have been presented at the Theoretical Roman Archaeology Conference in Sheffield, and in seminars at Leicester and Reading, England. The ideas have been substantially reworked and expanded for the Balmuth lecture. Special thanks go to Jane Webster for her comments on an early draft, and to Rob Young, who, knowing the track I was on, put vital reading matter in my path. Christine Kondoleon discussed some of the ideas with me in Boston and generously made available information on sexual imagery in the Roman collection of the Boston Museum of Fine Arts.

[1] At an early stage I was much influenced also by Gramsci (1971) and his reflections on power and hegemony.

[2] Scobie 1986, 407–9.

participation, accommodation, and negotiation. Older views of imperialism have tended to disempower the subject peoples from any active role in their destiny; what I also want to emphasize is that all acts of collaboration, selective participation, and resistance took place within a dynamic structure of power relations.

Postcolonial theory is increasingly recognizing the importance of the unprecedented "opportunities" presented to servants of empires to indulge in new and often extreme patterns of sexual behavior. Much attention in the past has focused on the misbehavior of emperors, salaciously presented to us by the ancient sources.[3] But these accounts have tended to *describe* more than to *analyze*, and also misdirect our gaze to the exceptional figures in society. The indulgences of individual emperors need to be understood in the broader context of changing sexualities in colonial societies. Mythic Roman orgies can thus be relocated in this discourse—Roman sources and the Latin sexual vocabulary reveal a pattern of domination and penetrative practices that cut across normative boundaries of morals, gender, class, and ethnicity.[4] Of course, not everyone in positions of power showed such lack of restraint. Indeed, striking parallels exist in Roman, U.S., and British imperialisms; for instance, for a polarization of attitudes about sex, with visibly increased sexual license in society being in part countered by purity or moral campaigns. Similar discourse could be constructed in relation to other areas of indulgence and consumption in Roman elite society that were fed by imperial opportunity.[5]

While the effect on subject peoples of degrading forms of sexual compliance could easily be overstated—especially in terms of the actual numbers directly affected—I believe that the psychological taint of sexual humiliation and degradation has been a powerful tool for sustaining social difference between rulers and ruled in many colonial societies. Such patterns of behavior in the sexual sphere may thus serve as a good index of the wider social impact of empires on their subject peoples. There are, of course, other issues involved in making a reading of the body in the Roman world,[6] but it is precisely because many recent studies have

---

[3] Blond 1994; Farrington 1994.

[4] The precise details of what societies consider normal in sexual behavior differ wildly, of course, but in focusing on transgressive sexuality I am emphasizing aspects that many communities find moral or legal difficulty with in relation to their core membership—such as rape and other forms of sexual coercion, sexual humiliation, and exploitation based on social power inequalities. Attitudes to the sexual exploitation of those seen as marginal or inferior to the core society are often a different matter.

[5] For instance, Dalby 2000, 10–13, highlights the fine distinction that might exist between the vices and the pleasures of empire and the social tensions that these created.

[6] Edwards 1993.

separated agency from structure that I have focused in this chapter on the links between power and the body. A secondary aim is to remind us of something lost sight of in a number of recent discussions of Roman imperialism: power and inequality lay at the heart of the discourse of the Roman Empire. Models that presuppose a "civilizing mission" or highlight unfettered native initiative rather miss the point. This chapter is thus a further contribution to continuing debate about postcolonial perspectives of Roman imperialism.[7] Whatever their structural and ideological differences, there are important points of comparison to be made between imperial systems ancient and modern concerning this question of the operation of power, both physical and psychological, in colonial societies.[8]

ROMAN PERMISSIVENESS

> From staid beginnings Roman sexual history moves towards a crescendo of eroticism such as the world has rarely seen.[9]

> The sexual temper of the age was randy and permissive and tolerant of fairly bad behaviour, but not vicious or orgiastic.[10]

The transformation of Roman society and its sexual attitudes from "staid beginnings" to a hotbed of licentiousness opens up a series of questions. When did this change occur and why? Was it something internal to Roman society, bound up in social structures at the center of the empire, or did it develop through colonial contact?[11] Our knowledge of Roman sexuality is not as detailed as we would wish, and primarily reflects the views and beliefs of the upper echelon of society.[12] It is clear that early Roman society put great store on respectability, with Roman chastity and virtue (based on that elusive ideal of heterosexual marital intercourse for procreative purposes) being contrasted with Greek and Etruscan wantonness and lust (see fig. 4.1a). It is also apparent, though, that from early times different standards of behavior were expected of men and women. Virginity, modesty, and sexual fidelity were the key characteristics demanded of a Roman aristocratic bride, while men clearly had greater license, both

---

[7] Webster and Cooper 1996; Mattingly 1997a.

[8] Cf. Webster 1996b.

[9] Benjamin and Masters 1966, 42.

[10] Blond 1994, 3

[11] Edwards 1993.

[12] Richlin 2006, is a wonderful attempt to construct a "Kinsey Report" of sorts on the Roman Empire, though it tends to be more descriptive of practices rather than analytical of why Roman sexuality evolved as it did.

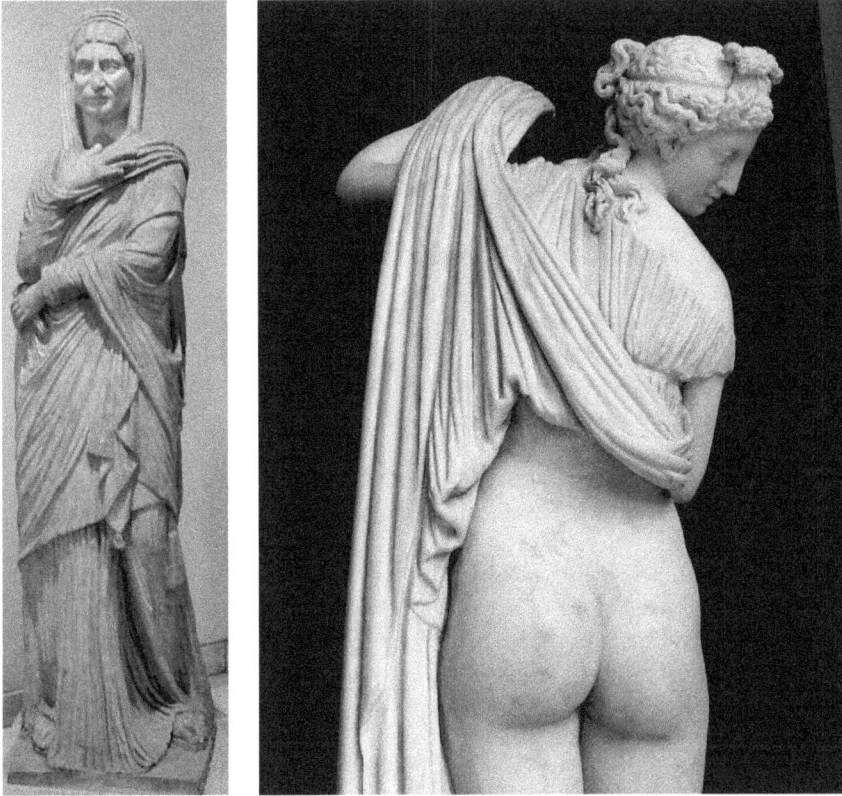

FIGURE 4.1 (a) The archetype of the Roman demure matron contrasts with (b) increasingly more explicit depictions of sexy Venus.

for prior sexual experience and external affairs after marriage. However, dramatic change seems to have occurred when Rome acquired its first imperial possessions outside Italy. Prior to the second century BC, Venus was a "sexless Italian spirit of well-tended herb gardens" until Rome's widening imperial horizons saw its being promoted as an equivalent to naked Aphrodite (see fig. 4.1b).[13] Several points follow. This was a time of new wealth, increased slave ownership, and greater Roman prestige and self-image. For the Romans active in and alongside the armies that were sent to Greece, Asia Minor, and Spain at this time, it was a period of unprecedented opportunity and experimentation.[14] Changes in sexual

[13] Hallett 1988, 1270; cf. Schultz 2006 and Staples 1998 on the role of women in Roman religion.

[14] For the evolution of Roman imperialism see, among others, Cornell 1995; Harris 1978, 1984; Lintott 1972; and chapter 1 of the present volume.

behavior were matched in the same period and for the same reasons by radical transformations in conspicuous consumption and experimentation with new forms of luxury—material, culinary, and artistic.[15]

Part of the problem in Roman society, but by no means unique to Rome, was that aristocratic marriages among the ruling senatorial and equestrian classes were generally political and economic arrangements between families rather than love matches. It was commonplace for men to marry much later than women and to take as wives young and sexually inexperienced girls.[16] The chief aim of these marriages was to produce heirs, not happiness, and while Roman matrons were expected to endure loveless marriages in perfect fidelity for the sake of the children, men had license to pursue pleasures outside.[17] The contrast between the normative Roman conditions for procreative marital sex and the range of sexual practices discussed below is striking: respectable couples were recommended to avoid lovemaking in daylight or in lit rooms, respectable women were not expected to remove all their undergarments in bed or to take a particularly active role. The contrast with what was demanded from prostitutes and slaves was marked (see fig. 4.2).[18] Contrary to the impression to be gained from watching the 2005 TV series *Rome*, Roman matrons were not nymphomaniacs (though our literary sources suggest there were a few scandalous exceptions). Indeed, there is evidence to suggest that aristocratic wives tried to reduce sexual contact with their spouses to a minimum and to avoid numerous pregnancies.[19] Many members of the ruling class might be away from Rome for long periods of time, serving in administrative roles in the provinces, and this could further weaken the bonds between man and wife, especially if the wife chose to (or was instructed to) remain at home.

In these circumstances, Roman permissiveness in a colonial situation was exacerbated by the sexual limitations of the social strategies aimed at protecting the reputation of aristocratic marriages and by implication the legitimacy of the children that resulted from such unions. Much analysis of Roman sexuality had followed the sort of line expressed by Anthony Blond in the quotation that opens this section—specifically that, though different from today's mores, it was permissive rather than violent. I believe, however, that we can locate the phenomenon of Roman permissiveness in a specific discourse of colonial sexuality and that this casts a new light on the violent and exploitative nature of some practices.

[15] See Dalby 2000 for a thorough overview of the "empire of pleasures."

[16] See Veyne 1987, 34–35, on the difficulties of Roman wedding nights.

[17] On Roman marriage in general, see Dixon 1992, 61–97; Rawson 1986, 1–57; Treggiari 1988.

[18] Veyne 1987, 203.

[19] Hallett 1988, 1276–77.

FIGURE 4.2 The objectification of female sexuality; brothel picture from Pompeii.

THE COLONIAL DISCOURSE OF SEXUALITY

Colonialism was a machine: a machine of war, of bureaucracy and administration, and above all, of power . . . enormous power put forth and resistance overcome . . . it was also a machine of fantasy and desire.[20]

Sex and desire in the ancient world have been studied from many angles, literary and artistic,[21] but—notably—the terms *colonialism* and *imperialism* do not feature in the indexes of these works. However, that there have been colonial discourses of sexuality is made clear from work on modern empires.[22] In modern colonialism, of course, the issue is intertwined with another larger and nastier one—that of race.[23]

[20] Young 1995, 98.
[21] Clarke 1998, 2003b; Edwards 1993; Hallett and Skinner 1997; Kampen 1996; Kiefer 1932; Richlin 1983, 2006; Rousselle 1988; Skinner 2005; Taylor 1953; Veyne 1988; Vout 2007; Winkler 1990.
[22] Gill 1995; Hyam 1990; Trexler 1995; Young 1995.
[23] Fanon 1986; Young 1995.

FIGURE 4.3 "America" surprised in her hammock by Amerigo Vespucci, by Jan van der Straet (Giovanni Stradano). (Bridgeman-Giraudon / Art Resource, NY.)

The language and iconography of empire is full of sexual imagery and innuendo. Jan van der Straet's famous image of a naked female "America" surprised in her hammock by Amerigo Vespucci is a classic example of the representation of the colonizer as armed male and the colonial territory as a vulnerable (and endangered) woman (see fig. 4.3).[24] The scenes of Claudius with female personifications of Britannia and Armenia from the Sebasteion at Aphrodisias are likewise graphic depictions of violent conquest of female provinces by the armed emperor.[25] Rape is implicit in all these scenes, as it is in numerous other scenes of Roman martial art, where (often bare-breasted) women captives are seized by the hair.[26] As both Roy Porter and Dick Whittaker have argued, the Roman Empire generated a large volume of "phallic aggression" in its frontier regions.[27]

[24] See Whittaker 2004b, 115–16 for the image and discussion.

[25] Ibid., 117–18.

[26] Cf. Smith 1987, 116–17, which interprets Claudius as (merely) slaying Britannia and Armenia in the Aphrodisias reliefs.

[27] Porter 1986, 232; Whittaker 2004b, 120, 128–29.

The discourse of sexuality is multidirectional and operates at different levels within society. As Robert Young notes, the desire for territory and dominance in the political field entrained another set of colonial desires: "In that sense, it was itself the instrument that produced its own darkest fantasy—the unlimited and ungovernable fertility of 'unnatural' unions."[28] The role of the state is thus an ambiguous one; its power and rapacity can encourage or enable individual colonial servants to behave in ways that threaten the very stability of the empire. So the colonial state is often found to be using its power to curb or discourage certain types of sexual activity that are made possible by the empire's existence. Sexual discourse thus commonly involves imperial powers in mitigation strategies. Changing attitudes to sex, power, and the body in colonial situations are thus both a *function* and a *consequence* of empire. The work of Michel Foucault suggests some ways of addressing this discourse.

FOUCAULT ON SEX, POWER, AND THE BODY

> It seems to me that power is always there, that one is never 'outside' it, that there are no 'margins' for those who break with the system to gambol in.[29]

> Power is not simply what the dominant class have and the oppressed class lack. Power, Foucault prefers to say, is a strategy and the oppressed are as much a part of the network of power relations and the particular social matrix as the dominating.[30]

Much of Michel Foucault's oeuvre—indeed, by far his most significant works (and his enduring reputation)—concern the philosophy of knowledge and power.[31] Although in his formative works the word *power* was rarely used, Foucault could claim later that it was nonetheless the key and underlying theme all along.[32]

Several key points emerge. First, he suggested that power is not simply a negative force (power that "says no"): the "relations [of power] don't take the sole form of prohibition and punishment, but are of multiple

---

[28] Young 1995, 98.

[29] Foucault 1980, 141.

[30] Hoy 1986b, 134.

[31] Foucault 1975, 1979, 1980, 1981; see also Hoy 1986a; Giddens 1995, 199–215, 263–68; Goldstein 1994; Lemert and Gillan 1982, 32–91, 110–24; McNay 1994, 95–100.

[32] Lemert and Gillan 1982, 58–59; Rabinow 1984 provides some good insights into the crystallization of Foucault's writing on power.

form."[33] Actually, he had modified his position on this issue, in his mature works stressing the empowering aspects of repressive power.[34] There he envisaged power as a strategy, a network of relations that not only constrain but enable.[35] Moreover, Foucault argued strongly that "all knowledge is embedded in power relations."[36] He also warned against the use of simplistic oppositions: dominators/dominated—the power web is to be seen as more complex than that.[37] Some of his finest work concerned the minute analysis of the societal changes that brought about new structures of discipline and control, the asylum and the prison (although he eschewed historical specificity at one level, many of his works focused on the peculiar conditions of the eighteenth century).[38] Here power was represented as power over others, the power of surveillance and discipline, but it was still not a wholly repressive force. Rather, it created new conditions and relations.

What are the weaknesses of Foucault's approach to the "microphysics of power"? Several critics have found that while identifying the significance of power networks, Foucault had scrupulously avoided analyzing in detail the historical contingency of the structures he identified.[39] Others have seen his vision of the nature of power as too fatalistic and negative.[40] In a particularly interesting critique, Edward Said has suggested that Foucault was far more concerned with power than with factors opposing it. Power presupposes resistance, and Said rightly questioned Foucault's commitment to the study of this aspect.[41] Said suggests that there are four ways of thinking about power:

1. imagine how you as an individual would use it if you had it;
2. imagine what you would imagine if you had it;
3. assess the power needed to vanquish present power;
4. imagine things that cannot be commanded by the present extent of power.[42]

According to Said's analysis, Foucault had largely written on aspects 1 and 2, ignoring 4 (the utopian vision) altogether and neglecting 3. To

---

[33] Foucault 1980, 139, 142.

[34] McNay 1994, 3.

[35] Lemert and Gillan 1982, 77–78.

[36] McNay 1994, 2; Sarup 1993, 73–75.

[37] Foucault 1980, 142.

[38] Foucault 1963, 1975.

[39] Giddens 1995, 265; Hoy 1986b.

[40] This tendency may, however, represent a misreading of his theoretical position; see Hoy 1986b, 144.

[41] Conversely, however, Foucault did not investigate the nonjudicial forms of coercive power available to states either; see Sarup 1993, 83.

[42] Said 1986, 151; cf. Sarup 1993, 81–82.

these criticisms, Madan Sarup adds the failure of Foucault to develop a more specific analysis of the broad concept of power or of the state and its infrastructure.[43]

When we turn to Foucault's writings on sex and sexuality, power is once again a dominant theme. Although the relationship between power and sex is characterized by repression and prohibition, he is also adamant that sexuality is not a natural condition but the product of power (more so than sexuality is repressed by power): "sexuality is not an animate or natural quality of the body but is, in fact, an historically specific effect of the operations of different regimes of power on that body."[44] In other words, sexual mores and practices are not unvaried through human history, but are contingent on specific historical and social conditions. Thus, sexuality in any era will be a product of the "system of discourse."[45] As such, "sexuality becomes a dense transfer point for relations in power."[46]

The manifesto of volume 1 of Foucault's *History of Sexuality* promised much: he attacked the repressive hypothesis that saw the creation of sexuality as the product of nineteenth-century capitalism and made strong links between power and the body in the definition of sexuality.[47] However, the second and third volumes are a disappointment, all the more so as they are devoted to ancient Greece and Rome—though Foucault acknowledges his lack of prior training and research in this area.[48] In contrast to the prolegomena of volume 1, with its emphasis on the centrality of power, these later works reflect Foucault's changing perspectives about sexuality and the body. Now Foucault asserted the importance of the self-fashioning body and the inner constitution of the individual and his pleasures (for it is mainly of "he" that Foucault wrote). This seems to have more to do with the author's sudden awareness of his own fragile mortality than with the philosophical positions he had earlier created so brilliantly, and these volumes have been criticized as a simplistic misrepresentation of the realities of the Greco-Roman world, based on highly selective use of sources.[49]

The body, whether written upon by experience or self-fashioning, takes center stage in these later works. But several commentators have noted that this strategy isolates the body from the "affective mechanisms of

[43] Sarup 1993, 84; see also Giddens 1995, 265–67.
[44] McNay 1994, 9.
[45] Sarup 1993, 70–72.
[46] McNay 1994, 98; cf. Foucault 1981, 103.
[47] Foucault 1981; cf. Lemert and Gillan 1982, 69–82; cf. Parker et al. 1992 for some exploration of the links between nationalism and sexuality.
[48] Foucault 1985, 1988.
[49] See Cohen and Saller 1994; Foxhall 1994; Halperin 1994; Poster 1986.

power" at work on it, which Foucault had earlier promised to study.[50] If we are to make best use of Foucault's frame of analysis, therefore, it is vital that the body is not separated from the power network within which it is situated. In what follows I shall try to demonstrate the importance of the colonial discourse in shaping sexuality and societal power.

THE OPPORTUNITIES OF EMPIRES

Ronald Hyam has offered a brilliant analysis of the corrupting force of the opportunity of empire, focusing on the modern British experience.[51] The colonial agent (predominantly male) had social, administrative, economic and, often, legal influence over subject men and women who came in contact with him.[52] This power was easily translated into sexual opportunity—and not just by the unscrupulous. The opportunity was reinforced by strong desires, the product of (spatial, social, and moral) distance from home and by the hardships and inconveniences of life in remote territories.[53] Colonial mythology created its own order of sexual delights, and the freedom from traditional restraints is a notable feature of the patterns of sexual behavior that resulted.[54] Some modern colonial servants drew direct inspiration from imperial Rome in living out their fantasies. After his retirement from colonial service in the eighteenth century, General James Dormer had his house and garden at Rousham, Oxfordshire, embellished to reflect his lusty appreciation of Roman eroticism and the "confident bisexuality" of that age.[55]

Female prostitution and concubinage were routine devices for servicing desire without responsibility. The well-being and rights of these women and any offspring were highly insecure even when they were treated with some degree of gentleness. Pederasty is commonly attested, with some individuals seeking out young boys in a particularly predatory and promiscuous manner.[56] Servants and slaves were routinely abused by masters as a right. There was much interest in experimentation and sexual license— take the lonely British official in India who, as opportunity presented

[50] Foucault, in Lemert and Gillan 1982, 81.

[51] Hyam 1990, 88–110.

[52] MacMullen 1990, 190–97, offers some pertinent reflections on the limits of personal power in the Roman Empire.

[53] Gill 1995, 57–87; Hyam 1990, 88–90.

[54] The sexual connotations of orientalism are well known; see Said 1978, 179–97.

[55] Mowl 2007, 68–76 (Tiberius would have approved).

[56] One such was Kenneth Searight, who left a detailed account of his encounters with 129 boys during nine years' army service in India; see Hyam 1990, 128–31.

itself, satisfied his urges with masturbation, boys, men, married women, servants, prostitutes, animals, and melons![57]

Sodomy of men and women is a notable and repeated feature of the colonial sex life, and much of the former appears to have been opportunistic bisexuality rather than homosexuality.[58] There is a long, cross-cultural history of sexual violence toward defeated enemies on the battlefield,[59] but colonialism presented a more persistent threat of sexual humiliation of subject men and women. In a nasty racist pamphlet of the mid-nineteenth century titled *Inequality of Races*, Count Gobineau revealed the potential sadistic violence of colonial desire and the linkages among sexuality, mastery, and domination.[60] Gobineau assigned gender characteristics to racial difference, writing of the "male" Aryan race in contact with the "female" black and yellow races. By subsuming both male and female native identities in a female (that is, passive) group, he emphasized the likelihood of white males being attracted to both. Colonial desire is thus exposed as a conduit for sexual license in situations where traditional constraints on sexual conduct fail and are replaced by new normative patterns of dominating behavior. In place of the safety and responsibility of marriage, sexual relationships in the colonial world are often characterized by "careless sensuality . . . frivolous, adolescent, reckless" behavior.[61] Furthermore, the eroticism of empire entails a broader impact in society at large, also affecting sexual habits and outlook in the metropolitan country at the heart of the empire.[62] As we shall see, in such cases colonial desire leads not only to licentiousness, but also to increased calls for morality to combat the perceived decline in personal standards.

LATIN SEXUAL VOCABULARY AND ROMAN SEXUAL PRACTICES

How does the Roman world fit in with such a model of colonial sexual discourse? Roman views on the body and its social and sexual functioning evolved over time, becoming increasingly male-oriented.[63] The Latin

[57] Hyam 1990, 132–33.

[58] Hyam 1990, 91–92, 212.

[59] Trexler 1995.

[60] Young 1995, 99–117, esp. 108.

[61] Hyam 1990, 210. Paradoxically, the importation of British women into India, aimed at redressing the reliance on native prostitutes and concubines for satisfying the sexual needs of the British army and administration, had the unexpected effect of discouraging engagement with Indian languages and culture and resulted in an increasing distance between British officers and native sepoys, James 1997, 206–30.

[62] Hyam 1990, 56–79.

[63] Brown 1990, 1–25.

sexual vocabulary was extensive and its content is highly instructive about the social context in which it was deployed.[64] Despite the obvious anatomical similarities, it is soon apparent that this was a different world to our own.[65] However, it is possible to perceive development and change in sexual attitudes. For example, the basic terms for the sexual organs and a number of the most common acts were of Latin origin, whereas the vocabulary for male same-sex relations was primarily derived from Greek terms, suggesting that the widespread experimentation with the latter was a secondary development in Roman sexuality following increased contact with the Greek world from the late third century BC. Learned in the East in a time of imperial conquest, "Greek love" took on a very different social meaning in Roman society to its traditional role in Greek societies.[66]

The penis (*mentula*) dominates the Latin sexual scene; indeed, the phallocentric nature of Roman society is emphasized by the fact that there were 120 separate terms for the penis, far more than for the female genitalia.[67] Phallic imagery included many religious uses (herms and other boundary markers, as a symbol against the evil eye, and as representations of the god Priapus (see fig. 4.4).[68] In Latin literature it "is not treated as exciting disgust, so much as fear, admiration and pride. It was a symbol of power which might present a threat to an enemy."[69] Of the metaphorical synonyms of the penis, the largest grouping was that of weapons, whose sexual symbolism was instantly recognizable in an imperial world.[70] By the same token, the metaphors for sexual intercourse are predominantly ones of striking, cutting, wounding, penetrating, digging, triumphing, dominating—typical soldier's work.[71]

The vagina (*cunnus*) has a range of metaphorical synonyms, mainly connected with animals, fields, caves, ditches, and household objects,[72] perhaps merely intended as descriptive or coincidentally also representing things the Roman man liked to have control over (land, animals, the household). Many of the descriptions of the female genitalia are unflattering, and some plain abusive, reflecting a strongly misogynist streak in

[64] Adams 1982, lists eight hundred terms in his classic study; see also Richlin 1983, esp. 1–31.

[65] Clarke 2003b, 11–15; Wiseman 1985, 1–14.

[66] MacMullen 1990, 177–89, on Roman attitudes to Greek love.

[67] Adams 1982, 9–79, esp. 77; cf. Johns 1982, 62–75, for a similar bias in iconographic representation.

[68] See Parker 1988 for the *Priapeia*—poems celebrating the ithyphallic god.

[69] Adams 1982, 77; cf. Parker 1988, 89, 105 for poems making explicit threats of sexual outrage against thieves from the orchard guarded by Priapus.

[70] Adams 1982, 19–22.

[71] Ibid., 145–49.

[72] Ibid., 80–109.

FIGURE 4.4 Phallic imagery was very much "in-your-face" in ancient Roman society; here a street marker from Lepcis Magna, protecting townsfolk from the evil eye, not pointing the way to the nearest brothel.

the male writers. The rectum (*culus*) has a very similar range of metaphors to the vagina; indeed, many of the terms for *cunnus* were interchangeable with those for *culus*, suggestive of a certain sexual ambiguity between the two sites.[73]

This impression is reinforced when terminology for the three principal forms of sexual congress is considered. These were vaginal intercourse (*fututio*), anal intercourse (*pedicatio*) and oral intercourse (*irrumatio*), normally used in the active sense, but occasionally in their passive forms to describe (with derogatory undertones) the experience of the penetrated party. It is interesting to note that, once again, there are instances of *fututio* being used as a synonym for *pedicatio* of a male.[74] There was also an active term for the act of performing oral sex on a man (*fello*), and this raises an important distinction not easily understood in the modern term *fellatio*. A *fellator* (m) or *fellatrix* (f) was someone of low social status who could provide the specific service of oral sex, but such an active response from the penetrated person was not always required or expected. The point is that oral penetration was not necessarily a consensual act; indeed, it was considered shameful and humiliating to have to submit to it. Oral intercourse was in many instances nothing less than oral rape.

[73] Ibid., 96, 112–15.
[74] Ibid., 118–30.

The *Priapea* poems clearly demonstrate by reference to the threats of Priapus against would-be-thieves from his orchard that oral rape was seen as much more shameful to the recipient than anal penetration.[75] Performance of this act was as much about the humiliation of the passive partner at it was about the gratification of the active male.

A final point about vocabulary: Much humor and invective in Roman writing about sex depends on a perception of the genitals as unclean or foul. In particular, oral-genital contact was seen as a filthy act, leaving a bad-smelling mouth to mark out perpetrators.[76] Cunnilingus was considered an even more shameful act for a free man to undertake than fellatio, echoing a strong sense of repugnance in descriptions of female genitalia in general.[77] As Amy Richlin observes, the universally bad press accorded the vagina by male Latin authors is part fear of the unknown, part denial of value in a male-dominated society.[78] In the same way, we may note that the surviving literature places value entirely on acts of male sexual gratification while placing opprobrium on acts designed to give pleasure to others. That is not to say that Romans did not ever value their women or that women were passive victims in Roman society.[79] Lin Foxhall has suggested for the Greek world ways in which women could develop a very different construction of sexuality to that of their menfolk.[80] I am sure that it also existed in the Roman world, but the essential point I wish to make here is that the dominant male view of sexuality was profoundly affected by the experience of imperial success. As we shall see in the next section, the massive increase in the availability of slaves to serve elite Roman households was a further factor in changing sexual behaviors.

The Importance of Social Status

A point that emerges time and again in looking at the Latin literature on sex is that it was not what one did that defined whether it was decent; rather, it was a question of whom one did it with and what role was played. Artemidorus, in his second century AD book *The Interpretation of Dreams*, presented a view of sexuality that was clearly not simply limited to the elite in society. Although discussing the portent of sexual dreams, many of the value judgments made by him about different sexual

---

[75] Parker 1988, 50, and poems 28 and 35.
[76] Edwards 1993, 71; Richlin 1983, 26–27.
[77] Kay 1985, 126–27.
[78] Richlin 1983, 68–69.
[79] Hemelrijk 1987.
[80] Foxhall 1994.

acts reflect this importance of social rank. As elsewhere in Roman literature, the sexual exploitation of slaves by the master of a household is
taken for granted.[81] In his helpful analysis of this account Foucault observed, "The sex of the partner makes little difference . . . what matters is
that one is dealing with a slave."[82] On the other hand, there were property
laws that prohibited messing around with someone else's slave, though
the well-known erotic escapade of Lucius and Photis in *The Golden Ass*
suggests that ownership might not always have been respected.[83] Men
were commonly expected to pursue liaisons outside the home, with prostitutes and mistresses, though they were required to observe the laws of
adultery protecting married women.[84] In relations with men and boys,
the Roman freeborn citizen could escape censure by taking the active role
(see below) and by respecting certain social rules about such encounters.[85]

Looked at from another perspective, the judgment of an individual's
sexual behavior was often dependent on social status rather than specific
knowledge. Thus, slaves and freedmen were generally presumed to have
the stain of sexual submission and degradation about them, whether or
not there was evidence to support this. Seneca summed up the distinctions neatly: "Unchastity is grounds for accusation in a freeborn man, a
necessity for a slave, a duty [*officium*] for a freedman."[86] Note here that
the continued sexual domination of freed slaves by their ex-owners was
a recognized occurrence, whether as female concubine or passive male
partner.

Another interesting sidelight on the sexual exploitation of slaves is provided by a recently published writing tablet from London that details
the purchase of a slave girl called Fortunata ("or whatever name she is
known by") by a man called Vegetus.[87] Vegetus was himself the slave of
an imperial slave called Montanus, so the tablet in effect details three
tiers of slaves owning others—in the case of both Vegetus and Montanus,
as a result of their ability to accumulate a substantial savings account
(*peculium*) from their lucrative work in imperial administration.

---

[81] Rousselle 1988, 82; cf. Hopkins 1979, 99–132, on the growth and practice of slavery.

[82] Foucault 1988, 19.

[83] Apuleius, *The Golden Ass*, 2.7–10, 16–18. As one of my anonymous reviewers has
suggested, it is equally possible that Lucius was quite literally making an ass of himself in
his behavior.

[84] Rousselle 1988, 78–92.

[85] Kay 1985, 118–20, 126–7, 163, 197; Richlin 1983, 34–44, 220–226; cf. Clarke 2003a,
163, for a more restrictive view suggesting that freeborn individuals were generally off-
limits.

[86] Seneca, *Controversiae*, 4.10.

[87] Tomlin 2003.

Active and Passive Roles and the Concept of Sexual Shame

> The material . . . gives ample testimony that normal male sexuality was aggressive and active, also that it was directed at both male and female objects.[88]

The most vital aspect of sexual relations for a Roman man concerned his position and role in the act.[89] As we have seen, the terminology prioritizes acts of penile penetration; indeed, it loads those acts with connotations of violent conquest and dominance. Women in ancient Rome were devalued in this formulation of sexual interaction, relegated to a passive, indeed submissive role. Roman matrons, no matter that they commanded respect in society, were not immune from the more extreme sexual demands of men. Martial's famous epigram concerning a man trying to persuade his unenthusiastic wife to follow the lead of a clutch of wives of famous Romans in allowing him anal intercourse with her is one of the most striking pieces of evidence of the domestic impact of the sexual liberalization of Rome.[90] The wife's passivity, her prudery and lack of adventure are contrasted unfavorably with the man's liking for drink, naked flesh under bright lights, and "abnormal" couplings. Perhaps unsurprisingly, by far the majority of Latin erotic literature deals with promiscuous sexual relations outside marriage.

On the other hand, a man taking on the passive role in sex adopted the woman's part (*muliebria parti*) and submitted to another man's power. While the Romans found nothing disgraceful in playing the active role in male-on-male pedicatio and irrumatio, submission to either form of penetration was a source of shame (*stuprum*) and degradation for a Roman citizen to have to undergo (see fig. 4.5). This shame might be slightly lessened if the active partner was someone of greater wealth or higher status, but if a person of equal or lower status it was far more damaging to reputation. To be sodomized or orally penetrated by another man was to be demeaned, while the act showed the superiority of the penetrator. Most discussions of the shaming nature of such relations have focused on the loss of reputation for upper-class Roman citizens who submitted to such acts. The Warren Cup, with its paired scenes of a man sodomizing a youth (see fig. 4.5) and two adult males of apparently similar status hard at it, hints that "Greek love" regularly extended beyond the pursuit of slave boys.[91] What has been missed, I think, is the implication

---

[88] Richlin 1983, 58.
[89] Wiseman 1985, 10–14; Veyne 1987, 204–5.
[90] Martial, *Epigrams*, 11.104; Kay 1985, 276–82; Richlin 1983, 159–60.
[91] Clarke 2003a, 77–93.

FIGURE 4.5 Male youth being sodomized by an older man; relief decoration on the Warren Cup. (© The Trustees of The British Museum / Art Resource, NY.)

that such demeaning acts were frequently enforced by Roman citizens on subject males in the provinces (see fig. 4.6). Bisexual relations were very prevalent in Roman society and clearly played an important part in social power games as a consequence.[92] The story reported by Tacitus of a Roman military commander in the Rhineland demanding from the local community a supply of young boys for his pleasure cannot have been an

[92] Richlin 1983, 220–26; this is contra the views of Matthews 1995, which tends to view all male-male sex as evidence for homosexuality.

isolated case.[93] It is an excellent example of the systemic side-effects of imperial power in operation.

The law allowed wronged husbands a lot of leeway in dealing with adulterers caught in the act with their wives. Anal rape of the adulterer was seen as a fitting punishment, following the imagined retribution of Priapus.[94] If the wronged man's slaves also participated in the gang rape of the male transgressor the humiliation was made even worse and the revenge more complete.[95] Not all Romans, of course, could go around physically dominating their enemies and acquaintances with acts of sexual violence, but it is notable that much of the extant Roman sexual graffiti and other obscene threats aimed at men contain orifice-specific promises to "fuck you."[96] Sexual violence was no doubt often latent rather than actual, but the close linkage between sexual power and sociopolitical power is clear from numerous examples in elite society of verbal attacks of a sexual nature on prominent people. Cicero subtly made a link between Clodius's deviant sexual behavior and his poor reception in the theater.[97] Much slander consisted of rumors that well-known Romans, even emperors, had played the passive role in male-male sex.[98] Similar attitudes operated down the social scale.[99]

The Moral Backlash and Purity Campaigns

Not everyone misbehaves sexually in colonial society, though the scandals surrounding the worst miscreants have a long life.[100] Indeed, many individuals may choose to register their protest against the decline in moral standards; in ancient Greece and Rome it was typically intellectuals and philosophers. Moreover, the state itself may take action to curb the worst excesses of individual licentiousness. In Augustan Rome, a wave of imperial edicts addressed moral standards and sexual misbehavior. While this might in part be seen as a recognition of the danger to colonial rule of sexual outrages (the rape of the daughters of Boudica in Britain was, after all, to be a contributing factor in the revolt of AD 60),

---

[93] Tacitus, *Histories*, 4.14.

[94] Parker 1988, poem 25.

[95] Richlin 1983, 215.

[96] Catullus, *Poems*, 10.

[97] Cicero, *Pro Sestio*, 108–18; see also Parker 1999, 175–76.

[98] Cicero, *Philippics*, 2.44–47, on Mark Antony; Suetonius, *Caesar*, 49–52, on Julius Caesar.

[99] Edwards 1993.

[100] Hyam 1990, 214–15.

the more immediate cause of this legislation would appear to be concern for the sanctity of aristocratic marriages. Female adultery in high society was to be harshly punished, male transgression similarly so when a married woman was involved and in general after the Augustan era male extramarital activity was more closely circumscribed. The effectiveness of these measures has been questioned,[101] but Augustus was not afraid to take action and to set an example, even when it was his own daughter Julia at the center of scandal.

In the provinces, the conduct of governors and high officers of state was constrained by legislation prohibiting them from contracting marriages with provincial women while holding office. This measure was primarily designed to prevent governors using their power to coerce local heiresses into wedlock. It was also an extension of the protection of elite marriages, which were seen as crucial for the stability of society. Just how disruptive to provincial societies was the prospect of wealthy women being married off to outsiders is revealed in the famous trial of Apuleius at Sabratha in AD 158. Perhaps understandably in an age when love was not expected to feature in elite marriages, he was accused of witchcraft by the local aristocracy because he had successfully courted a local millionairess without being either particularly rich or powerful.[102]

The key concern of this sort of legislation was not to protect imperial subjects at large as much as it was to protect the status of aristocratic marriage. Similar moves in the British Empire went further, partly because of the issue of race. The purity case was forcefully put in the *Pall Mall Gazette* in 1887, where approximately 500,000 British people associated with or serving the empire overseas were castigated as almost entirely corrupted by sexual vice as a result of "immoral relations with the heathen."[103] Such views led to policies variously promoting earlier marriage of men to British women in the colonies, advocating chastity in cases where this was not possible, and in any event trying to discourage concubinage and interracial marriages.[104] However, in neither the Roman nor the modern case could such reactions of the state entirely reign in the sexual forces unleashed by the colonial situation. Literature in the modern English imperial age often presents the "stubbornly nonsexual English gentlewomen" as the "antithesis of the teeming sexuality of

---

[101] Richlin 1983, 215–19.

[102] See Mattingly 1995, 53, 123, for the circumstances. The real issue at stake was no doubt the fear of the nonlocal person making off with a fortune that the family had hoped to keep within its extended local group.

[103] Hyam 1990, 91; cf. Gill 1995; Mason 1994.

[104] Hyam 1990, 137–81.

FIGURE 4.6 Still photograph from the original production of Howard Brenton's play *The Romans in Britain*. The young Britons have just emerged from a swim and are about to encounter Roman sex and violence up close and personal. (Photograph by Alastair Muir; used with permission.)

empire and its torrid zones."[105] Here we may reflect on Foucault's diagnoses that sexuality was not a natural condition, and that it was a product of power to a greater extent than it was repressed by power.[106] The key point is that sexual exploitation of the colonial subject is not just about lust and desire, it is also about power and domination.

PROSTITUTION, CONCUBINAGE, AND THE ARMY

The sexual behavior (and misbehavior) of individual Romans in the provinces represents only one strand of the colonial discourse of sexuality. Even greater importance may have attached to the sexual servicing of the Roman army, a matter in which the state could hardly be indifferent.[107] Here we need to consider the harsh realities of ancient prostitution—much more sordid than the idealized couplings amid plush furnishings in the Pompeian paintings (see fig. 4.2)[108]—and commonly involving enslaved women.

[105] Nussbaum 1995, 150–51.
[106] Sarup 1993, 70–72.
[107] Yet this has attracted surprisingly little scholarly attention; see Whittaker 2004b, 132–38.
[108] Clark 2003b, 60–75, 121–31.

From the reign of Augustus, service conditions for soldiers were standardized on extremely long terms (the age of enlistment was about eighteen, and soldiers normally served for twenty-five or twenty-six years). In the first centuries AD soldiers were not allowed to marry while in service, and though many might take concubines, children were not recognized by the state.[109] Inscriptions make it clear that soldiers did often take unofficial wives and families, though typically these are recorded in the later stages of their service terms and not in the early years. Such partners were typically ten to twenty years younger then the soldiers who "married" them. In the earlier stages of their careers, soldiers seem to have demonstrated a greater degree of commitment phobia.

Clearly, the half million men under arms were hardly to be expected to live out their young lives in chaste sublimation of desire. The alternatives were all potentially threatening for morale and discipline: the use of prostitutes or slaves, unofficial marriages, and the rape of civilians, not to mention buggery in the barracks or masturbation in the milecastles. Centurions and higher-ranking troops might have been able to buy a slave girl—as was perhaps the case with the aptly named M. Cocceius Firmus, centurion at Auchendavy on the Antonine Wall.[110] His was a complicated case, as he had inadvertently bought from foreign traders a (British?) girl who had earlier been condemned to hard labor in the saltworks prior to being carried off by brigands.[111] However, buying a slave girl outright might cost the equivalent of a lower rank soldier's annual salary, while buying a small amount of a sex slave's time was more suited to the ordinary soldiery. It is likely that many prostitutes servicing the army were slaves, bought and controlled by individual entrepreneurs.

In the conquest phase, armies were allowed a fair amount of license to plunder and humiliate civilians. The testimony of the columns of Trajan and Marcus Aurelius is clear on this and, as noted already, imagery of rape is even utilized by the state in celebrating its own conquests, as in the famous Aphrodisias relief of Claudius "subduing" Britannia.[112] The accusations against British and American service personnel in Iraq are therefore nothing new and would be less shocking to us if we acknowledged more openly the past history of the violent use of sex in imperial domination. On the contary, though, British public opinion has not always taken kindly to postcolonial criticism of imperialism. In 1980 the first performances of Howard Brenton's play *The Romans in Britain* caused a sensation because of the staged rape of a male Briton by a group of

[109] Dixon 1992, 92.
[110] Birley 1979, 146.
[111] *Digest*, 49.15.6.
[112] See Ferris 1995.

Roman soldiers (see fig. 4.6).[113] In part the outcry was provoked by this being a graphic and shocking piece of theatrical sex and violence, but for some this was compounded by the fact that parallels were being drawn between Roman imperialism and the modern experience of Northern Ireland being patrolled by British troops. The violence is the sort of plausible outrage that imperialism begets (and that we would prefer not to be reminded of). The revival of the play in February 2006 in Sheffield was timely, precisely because of current events in Iraq; indeed, the play's run coincided with renewed allegations in the media about sexual abuse of civilians at the Abu Ghraib prison.[114]

Clearly, in the longer-term administration of a region, the power of the state needed to be used to channel and control such behavior without ever neutralizing its latent threat to the subject peoples. Given these conditions it is implausible that the Roman state did not seek to regulate to some extent the provision of sexual services for the army. At the very least, prostitutes would have been registered with the military authorities.[115] But the interests of the state may have extended to proactive control of their numbers and availability,[116] as the British army did in India (with seventy-five regimental brothels being set up in the mid-nineteenth century) and the Japanese in their Pacific empire—where a ratio of about one prostitute per forty men seems to have operated.[117] If this ratio is applied to the Roman case study as an order of magnitude figure, the 500,000 troops of the second century AD would have required the services of 12,500 women; Britain, with a garrison of approximately 50,000, would have needed 1,250 women in close proximity to the garrison posts. Rather than "regimental brothels," for which there is no evidence, we might envisage the issuing of contracts to individual entrepreneurs to lay on an appropriate numbers of girls at specified garrison posts. If we assume an average ten-year "career" for these women, this would suggest a total recruitment of 12,500 prostitutes in the course of a century in Britain alone (or 25,000 if the average working life was only five years). Perhaps as many women again would have been enslaved or pressed into prostitution in the towns of the province.[118] In addition,

[113] Brenton 1989; Lawson 2005.

[114] The story of how the transgressive abuses of power at Abu Ghraib occurred, with complicit negligence on the part of the U.S. command is told in Gourevitch and Morris 2008.

[115] Prostitutes were registered in towns, where their activities were taxed; see Krenkel 1988, 1294.

[116] Gill 1995, 121–41.

[117] Hyam 1990, 121–29, 137–53.

[118] On urban prostitution, see Krenkel 1988; Laurence 1994, 70–87; McGinn 2002; Vanoyeke 1990; and Wallace-Hadrill 1994, 43–55.

longer-lasting relationships would have been formed by many soldiers with native women of free birth. Given the prevailing sexual ethos of Roman society, such concubinage may well have been exploitative and unstable (*unofficial marriages* may be an overoptimistic term). Native women in the frontier zone would also have been targets of amorous desire, harassment, and rape. Soldiers were seen as a real danger to women in some provinces—rabbinical texts, for instance, reveal that women captured by soldiers were assumed likely to have been raped, whereas with women taken hostage by brigands this was not necessarily the case.[119] The rape by soldiers of the royal daughters of Boudica may have been a licensed and calculated act of humiliation, but it extended to a hitherto favored elite behavior that was no doubt commonplace at lower levels of society. The impact of Roman army morals and military occupation on women in a province like Britain would thus have been on a significant scale. How this affected the relationships between native British men and women is another issue again.

One of the most disturbing scenes on Trajan's Column concerns the apparent torture of a group of naked Roman soldiers by Dacian women.[120] R. R. R.Smith has argued to the contrary that the men were in fact Dacians being tortured by provincial women who had suffered during Dacian attacks.[121] The scene is unexplained in extant literary sources, but either explanation raises the specter of sex, power, and violence, though with altogether different implications depending on the identity of the women. The sequel to the scene is to be found in the remorseless subjugation of the Dacians, the burning of villages, the slaughter of livestock, the execution of male Dacian prisoners, the seizure of Dacian women, and the dispatch of the sorry survivors into exile (see fig. 4.7).[122] There are equally explicit scenes on the Aurelian Column, especially of German villages burned, civilians massacred, and bare-breasted women being grabbed by the hair in preparation for rape (see fig. 4.8).[123] The true story of the "torturing Dacian Harpies/Roman women exacting just revenge" must have been tabloid news in Rome and among the troops at the time of the Dacian Wars. No doubt it was used in either case to justify the

---

[119] Potter 1999, 13; Isaac 1990, 85–86 (with references to the rabbinical texts).

[120] Trajan's Column scene XLV, 117 (Chichorius numbering); Ferris 2000.

[121] Smith 2002, 79–81.

[122] Burning of villages: Trajan's Column scene XXV, 64; LVII, 141; LIX, 144; CLIII, 405). Slaughter of livestock: XXIX, 72. Execution of male Dacians: LVI, 140; LXXII, 183. Seizure of Dacian women: XXIX, 72. Refugees: LXXVI, 200–201, CLIV, 409–10.

[123] Aurelian Column, scenes XCVII and XX. See Smith 2002, 78–83, for an extended discussion on the interpretation of scenes that to us appear to represent the horrors of war, but that in Roman eyes may have been intended simply to celebrate Roman justice being meted out on oath-breaking barbarians.

FIGURE 4.7 The frieze on Trajan's Column: Roman soldiers burning a Dacian village, framed by Dacian casualties and fugitives of war and overlooked by a Roman camp (with totemic heads) and the emperor Trajan. (Photograph by Mary Harrsch; used with permission.)

extreme violence meted out to their communities by the Roman army as the advantage was pressed home. But we should not ignore the possibility that these women, if they were Dacian, had been moved to their act of inhumanity by the enormity of violent acts already enacted by Roman soldiers on them and their families at earlier stages in the campaigns.

SEX AND VIOLENCE: THE OPERATION OF POWER

Enslavement and sexual domination or humiliation were effective tools in undermining old power relations and in creating a new social hierarchy. At its most extreme, Roman sexuality was nasty, pornographic, misogynist, violent, dominating, and humiliating.[124] Sexual humor in Roman society—typified by paintings from Pompeian bars and baths—was laced with allusions to power and humiliation.[125] The same

[124] Richlin 1983, 77–80.
[125] Clarke 2003a, 134–36, 160–70; 2003b, 116–33.

FIGURE 4.8 The frieze on the Aurelian Column: violence against civilians; an old man pleads with Roman soldiers ransacking a German village.

dubious qualities underlined much other entertainment in the Roman world. Public executions were played out as theater in the arena, and there was a vast array of violent or dangerous entertainment from boxing to gladiatorial combat, from animal baiting and hunting displays to circus races with spectacular crashes.[126] As with sexual relations, the discourse of violence had a purpose—sustaining the social and political order through its exemplary use of force. Similar excess was demonstrated by increasing judicial savagery during the principate.[127] Power in Roman society was indeed written on the body of its subject peoples, but in a selective and controlled manner.

Although sexual domination might seem to exclude and subjugate the individual, in reality the door was open for many provincials to pass through to the other side. Even the stigma of sexual shame had a limit on it. Slaves, freedmen, and freedwomen were condemned for their life to a lower social status because of their assumed uncleanliness as a result of having been the passive sexual partners of those of higher status (the argument of presumptive contamination again). Yet the character stain was

[126] Hopkins 1982, 1–30; Kiefer 1932, 64–106.
[127] Garnsey 1968; MacMullen 1990, 205–17.

not inherited in perpetuity and a son of a freedman could aspire—providing he had the financial means—to become part of local high society, to a place on the local town council, to a career in imperial service. Similarly, subject peoples, some of who may have endured sexual outrages in the conquest phase, could also choose to participate in the government and society of the empire.

However, these were not necessarily the choices of free agents, as imperial subjects were never outside the constraints of power. To take one's place in Roman society involved a process of negotiation with the imperial authority (or with an individual representative of it). That negotiation and the choices taken by subject peoples (collectively or as individual bodies) were thus not made in a power vacuum. On the contrary, the power asymmetries in these colonial discourses influenced the behavior of both rulers and ruled. Many may have chosen ostensibly unsatisfactory courses of action because the alternatives were worse. For example, one might chose to be a soldier's concubine not because one thought the army a terrific organization or because one liked the fancy uniforms or the individual man but because this was a way out of prostitution, or a potential meal ticket in an impoverished frontier region, or an acknowledgment of the latent power of the other party should he be rejected. Participation in the Roman Empire cannot then be read simply as compliance and approval. From this analysis, the historical contingency of Roman sexual relations is self-evident: the body (agency) cannot be divorced from the power networks of the society. Yet a purely structuralist approach is no more able to elucidate the critical issue of the negotiation of power; what is required is a more explicit body of theory on the nature and workings of power.

CONCLUSION

Roman sexual humor is often disturbing for the images it throws up, and Richlin's analysis suggests that these may be indicative of a normalizing of extreme behavior—there are obvious similarities with modern-day pornography and violent male fantasy.[128] In response to her statement that "it is impossible to ask the question 'What end does this humour serve?' without wonder and unease,"[129] my conclusion is that it served a very specific function of power in the ancient world.

Changes in sexual practices in the Roman world, intensifying from the second century BC, and the development of an underlying ideology

---

[128] Richlin 1983, 77–80.
[129] Ibid., 80.

of active domination and passive submission, correlate chronologically with the rise of the overseas empire. The historical contingency of these practices identifies them as a specific discourse of Roman colonialism. Indeed, the similarity with the modern British case study is also striking and suggests that the power dynamics in these cases were similar, whatever the overt social, economic and political differences between ancient and modern imperialism. The inequality of status of the participants, the use of violent, degrading, and humiliating forms of sexual dominance on passive partners of both sexes; all this confirms that colonial desires can give rise to nonconsensual and asymmetrical sexual relations.

The experience of sex and power in the Roman world was widely discrepant along gender and social lines (that is, among man, woman, slave, freedperson, freeborn, citizen, noncitizen, soldier, civilian, rich, poor, etc. But those perspectives were all to some extent conditional on the power structure and the individual's place within it. To accept that is to recognize that Foucault's idea of the self-fashioning body is out of line with his own diagnosis of the contingency of power.

PART THREE

Resources

CHAPTER FIVE

Ruling Regions, Exploiting Resources

INTRODUCTION

Since Moses Finley shredded the modernist views of Michael Rostovtzeff, the consensus model of the Roman economy has tended to emphasize its primitiveness and underdevelopment, its subsistence base, and its relative lack of growth.[1] Finley was strongly influenced, of course, by Karl Polanyi's theoretical work on the embedded nature of ancient economies.[2] Polanyi is also to be credited for introducing to the debate on the ancient economy the social structures of redistribution and reciprocity, and these have become important concepts alongside market exchange in our exploration of the Roman world.[3] The formalist/substantivist debate that Polanyi's work sparked has reverberated far longer in ancient history than it has in the social sciences and I have no wish to add to it. However, it is worth stating that it is possible to challenge Finley's minimalism while at the same time endorsing parts of the substantivist view.[4] Indeed, since Keith Hopkins made his first revisions to the minimalist model in 1980, the pendulum has started to swing back toward a more positive appraisal of the scale of activity and the possibilities of growth in the Roman economy.[5] A compromise position is to recognize that the Roman economy possessed both primitive and progressive characteristics.[6] As Henk Pleket has written, "primitive pre-capitalistic features were typical

Early versions of this chapter were presented at the Theoretical Roman Archaeology Conference in Cambridge in March 2006 and for the Miriam S. Balmuth Lectures in Ancient History and Archaeology series at Tufts Universty. I am grateful to several members of both audiences for constructive comments.

[1] See, for example, Finley 1985, 33–34, 58–59, 78; Rostovtzeff 1957. For more recent debate on the primitivist/modernist divide, see, among others, Andreau 2002; Bang 1997; Drinkwater 2001; Garnsey and Whittaker 1998; Jongman 2002; Meikle 2002; and Saller 2002.

[2] Polanyi, Arensberg, and Pearson 1957.

[3] See, for example, Peacock and Williams 1986, 55–63.

[4] Such challenges come in Horden and Purcell, 2000, 146–47, 150–51, 606. See also various papers in Harris 2005.

[5] Harris 1993b, 2000; Hitchner 1993, 2005; Hopkins 1980, 1996; Horden and Purcell 2000, esp. 143–52, 342–77; Mattingly 1996a, 2006b; Temin 2001; Wilson 2002, 2006.

[6] Mattingly and Salmon 2001b, 8–11.

of large sectors of the economy ... but at the same time ... there were 'niches' of a more capitalistic economy, characterized by structural long-distance trade in staples (wine, oil, grain) and luxuries (textiles, spices, marble) and by production of those goods for the market."[7]

Markets, both physical and conceptual, are increasingly recognized to have been of sophisticated type—at least at certain times and places.[8] It is perhaps time that debate on the Roman economy moved on to discuss other issues, such as how this hybrid economy came into being and how it functioned.

Another important question concerns the nature of intervention by the Roman state in the economic sphere. Modernists have tended to extol the economic benefits of empire—though this view is also symptomatic of the modern colonial discourse. As Jules Toutain expressed it, "Economic life, within the actual bounds of the empire was at once national and international. ... This very important evolution was favoured ... by the fact of the empire itself and by the benefits which it shed for at least two centuries on all countries subject to Roman rule."[9]

Primitivists have also let the empire off lightly by insisting on the limited impact of Rome on peasant subsistence economies.[10] A key conclusion of this chapter, as we shall see, is that state intervention was in fact significant both in terms of scale and impact.

The work of Hopkins is of particular importance for my theme in that he attempted to establish a series of propositions about the Roman economy that focused on the impact of taxation on the development of trade.[11] Specifically, Hopkins argued that frontier provinces were often net recipients of taxes raised elsewhere in the empire and that core Mediterranean provinces were net exporters of tax. In order to furnish the demands for specie, the tax exporting provinces were obliged to expand their involvement in interregional trade, with significant consequences for the Roman economy overall. In reaction to some critical responses,[12] he returned to the theme in a 1996 article, defending his position and en-

---

[7] Pleket 1993a, 317. Cf. the conclusion of Rathbone 2003b, 227: "Financing of marine commerce in the Roman world in the first two centuries AD cannot easily be constrained within the primitivist model of the ancient economy."

[8] Bang 2006; De Ligt 1993; Giardina 1986; Temin 2001.

[9] Toutain 1930, 253.

[10] See Garnsey and Saller 1987, 43: "The Roman economy was underdeveloped. This means essentially that the mass of the population lived at or near subsistence level. In a typical underdeveloped, pre-industrial economy, a large proportion of the labour force is employed in agriculture. ... The level of investment in manufacturing industries is low. ... Backward technology is a further barier to increased productivity."

[11] Hopkins 1980.

[12] See Duncan-Jones 1992, 1994.

larging his view.[13] Both articles are excellent examples of how theoretical studies can be presented in clear models, backed up by imaginative use of order-of-magnitude estimates and comparative approaches. Although my overall conclusions here will place a different emphasis, I endorse Hopkins's general point that there was a potentially significant relationship between the economic exactions of the state and the overall relative patterns of economic growth and stagnation.

In recent years, debate has started to explore the tensions between global and local aspects of the Roman economic world.[14] Peter Temin has stated, "Finley was wrong; ancient Rome had an economic system that was an enormous conglomeration of interdependent markets,"[15] a point supported by Greg Woolf, who has made a strong case for identifying significant regional economic foci.[16] There has been some fertile engagement with "new institutional economics" in recent discussion about the role of the state in the imperial economy.[17] However, there is still a tendency for commentators to write about the Roman economy in the singular. I shall argue in this chapter that the economy is not only best understood as an agglomeration of globalized regional economies but that we can also define a series of major mechanisms at work that governed discrete areas of economic activity. In particular I shall focus on the role of the state as a motor of economic activity through its status as an imperial power. I am going to construct some simple models of my own, built around colonial discourse analysis, rather than complex economic theory. It needs to be stated at the outset that I am aware of the dangers of oversimplification inherent in such an exercise. Detailed consideration of individual economic instruments, such as the imperial *fiscus* or the taxation system, will no doubt reveal greater complexity due to regional specificities or evolution over time.[18] The main purpose of this chapter, however, is not to outline a new general model for the Roman economy but to reignite debate about the economic face of Roman imperialism.

I want to start by contrasting two views on the economic face of colonialism:

Britain . . . had no reputation as a source of wealth. It is very doubtful that wealth was expected to accrue from its conquest, at least after the initial spoils of war had been claimed by the invading army. The

[13] Hopkins 1996 essentially updates and supplements the 1980 article and attempts to answer the critics.

[14] See Geraghty 2007 on globalization and the Roman economy.

[15] Temin 2001, 181.

[16] Woolf 1992a.

[17] See, for example, Lo Cascio 2006, 2007; Kehoe 2007.

[18] See for example, Alpers 1995, on the *fiscus*; and Cottier et al. 2009 on tax law in Asia Minor.

empire's provinces were an accidental by-product of politically motivated conquest and were rarely viewed as an economic resource to be exploited systematically.[19]

An imperial power which has just acquired a new province faces the huge task of organizing the territory and implementing its power. . . . Once the new imperial power has quelled any substantial military resistance, it needs to carry out some sort of census or survey to evaluate what it has acquired, make sure that the necessary communications systems are in place, and above all set up a system for the extraction of surplus by means of taxation. This "settlement" is the material face of the colonial project as a whole: the creation of order, government and infrastructure, often with ideological trappings of paternalism and altruism.[20]

Empires exploit territory and people, and there tend to be common patterns in the sequence of events that follow armed conquest of a region.[21] When the French general Thomas-Robert Bugeaud set out to crush resistance in Algeria led by Abd el-Kader, his treatment of defeated tribes included a variety of measures—burning of settlements and crops, forced military recruitment, taking of hostages and female prisoners, exaction of tribute, forced resettlement and reallocation of lands, disarmament, placing of garrisons and imposition of military road networks, requisition of transport animals, and demands for labor corvées.[22] This account of the multiplex exploitation of people and resources could equally be applied to the Roman Empire. The Roman sources, and the (rare) testimony of subject peoples such as the Jews, certainly suggest that the Roman state had an extraordinary capacity for swallowing up the wealth of the world.[23] Yet many modern scholars have chosen to downplay the economic underpinnings of Roman imperialism.[24]

While I would agree that the motivations behind further conquests in the Roman Principate were often highly political, the emperors sought not only military glory but also to fulfill their responsibilities to keep an expensive show on the road.[25] "Good emperors" were expected to bal-

---

[19] Millett 1995a, 12.

[20] Given 2004, 49–50.

[21] Barrett 1989; See Bang 2002, 2006 for reflections on the nature of the economic structures of tributary empires, comparing Rome and the Mughal Empire.

[22] Germain 1955, 19–29.

[23] *Sibylline Oracles*, 3.179, 3.189; cf. *Ecclesiastes Rabbah*, 1.7.

[24] See chapter 1 of the present volume.

[25] This is contra Love 1991, 272–74, which seems to argue that economic competition between the princeps and the patrician elite was a main driver behind the creation of the economic systems of the principate.

FIGURE 5.1 The spoils of victory (short-term): the temple treasure from Jerusalem paraded through the streets of Rome as part of the triumph of Titus.

ance the budget—that is, to ensure that revenues met or exceeded core expenditure—and to have control of financial records.[26] Moreover, the annals of Roman history were full of details of the spectacular spoils of expansionism: Carthage's indemnity after the Second Punic War was the equivalent of 100 million sesterces; in the second century BC Antiochus paid over 340 million sesterces; Pompey the great claimed to have raised provincial tax revenue by 140 million sesterces as a result of his Eastern triumph.[27] As we shall see these were very substantial sums when set in the context of the overall imperial budget. Those at the center could not afford to ignore the potential importance of conquest for the imperial coffers (see fig. 5.1).[28] The creation and maintenance of empire has ultimately to be linked to the exploitation of resources.[29]

Comparative studies suggest that the economic encounter of colonizer and colonized is a defining aspect of most imperial systems. Michael Given's perceptive book *The Archaeology of the Colonized* could equally be subtitled "the archaeology of taxation and tax evasion," as it deals with the competing economic forces of imperial exaction and individual strate-

---

[26] Following the model set by Augustus, see Suetonius, *Augustus*, 101.4; Tacitus, *Annals*, 1.11.

[27] Polybius, *Histories*, 3.27; 21.43.19; Plutarch, *Pompey*, 45.3.

[28] For other ancient evidence, see Frank 1933, 1:127–38.

[29] Fulford 1992.

gies of fiscal subterfuge.[30] The difficulty for archaeologists is to demonstrate conclusively the traces of this recurrent battle, when so little of the written documentation of the census and taxation systems survives. Yet to ignore the impact of the encounters between subjects and the tax man is to turn our backs on what must have been key experiences of empire. In the Roman world, paying taxes was not a neat payroll deduction but an act of "public dispossession" on the part of an imperial agent. As Given writes, "Through the physical actions of paying taxes and working in labour gangs, people experience imperial rule in their bodies."[31] Taxation and other exactions thus represent the quiet violence of empires. In the Roman Empire, exploiting resources covered a wide range of activities in addition to taxation, including measures to exploit land, natural resources, and, above all, the labor of subject peoples. A recurrent problem for empires concerns how to promulgate and enforce rule-based order. Opposition to imperial systems is often rooted in economic and power inequalities, and while these inequalities are integral to the efficient functioning and maintenance of the empire, they are also a constant danger to its existence.[32]

The Roman Empire is sometimes presented as inefficient and disorganized in its attempts to collect taxes—witness the fact that practice varied hugely from province to province and that periodically there were general write-offs of arrears—with Hadrian seemingly absurdly generous in this respect in canceling 900 million sesterces of arrears.[33] Yet this apparent failure could be taken another way—the Roman Empire was able to remit taxes periodically precisely because of its overall *success* in assessing tax liability across all provinces and a wide range of activities. Raising taxation from large and diverse territories is never easy—as the British Empire found to its cost in Boston—and by the standards of the ancient world, Rome was pretty good at it.[34]

Monetization and the rate of circulation of coinage are clearly important issues of debate, not least because of the extent to which the Roman Empire collected tax and rent in coin (see fig. 5.2).[35] But it is clear that

[30] Given 2004.

[31] Ibid., 93. There are echoes here of the views expressed by Barrett 1997. It is true, of course, that nonimperial regimes also exact taxation and labour, but the "paper trail" efficiency and the sometimes long-range nature of imperial impositions/exactions often give them a special character.

[32] This theme is developed in Jones 2006 as a "Roman predicament facing the United States today."

[33] See Johnson 2006 for the "lax tax" view; on Hadrian's generosity with tax arrears, see Duncan-Jones 1994, 59–63; *Inscriptiones Latinae Selectae*, 309; Dio, *Roman History*, 69.8.1.

[34] Goldsmith 1987, 34–59, provides an overview of the Roman financial system, but the value of the book lies in its comparative framework of a number of preindustrial economies.

[35] Aarts 2005; Duncan-Jones 1994, 95–247; Howgego 1992, 1994.

FIGURE 5.2 The spoils of victory (long-term): rents being collected in coin and recorded by scribes in a funerary relief from the Moselle region.

the state also extracted resources in other ways, too: in kind, through monopolies of key natural resources and in terms of labor, transport, and liturgical commitments.[36] Thus, if I seem to give less attention here to coinage that you might expect, this is not for lack of interest or relevance but more so that I can open debate on a wider array of ways in which the empire was exploited economically.

In this chapter, then, I want to turn away from individual economic agents and focus on the state and its economic needs and systems. Just as the globalizing reach of Rome had an important role in the emergence of discrepant social identities, it also spawned discrete economic "identities." A recent paper by Lisa Fentress has tried to refocus the debate about the Romanization of Africa around a fuller appreciation of the economic effects of empire and the process of disembedding that followed Rome's attempts to mobilize the economic potential of its territories.[37] While I reject her use of the word Romanization to describe this process, I think that Fentress and I are both broadly concerned with the same phenomenon—the behavioral consequences (intended or otherwise) of an empire's efforts to exploit its subjects economically.

[36] Adams 2001, 2007; Carreras Montfort 2002; Kolb 2002.
[37] Fentress 2006.

TABLE 5.1

Estimates of imperial annual budget in millions of sesterces

	AD 150		AD 215	
	Low figure	*High figure*	*Low figure*	*High figure*
ARMY	643	704	1,127	1,188
OTHER IMPERIAL SERVANTS	75	75	75	75
CONGIARIA	44	44	140	140
BUILDING PROJECTS	20	60	20	60
OTHER	50	100	100	150
TOTAL	832	983	1,462	1,613

Source: Duncan-Jones 1994, 45.

Note: To put this annual budget of around HS1,000,000,000 in perspective, we should first note the minimum census qualification for a senator of HS1,000,000.

THE IMPERIAL BUDGET

The cost of running the Roman Empire must have been a major preoccupation of those at the center of power. One of the paradoxes of the Roman Empire is that the costs of its conquest were drastically lower than the recurrent expense of its defense thereafter. The progression from an annually levied army of generally less than ten legions strong to a permanently maintained force of twenty-five to thirty legions, plus equivalent numbers of auxiliaries (for a total force of between 300,000 and 500,000 men), was a singularly important economic shift. Modern European states did not acquire similar standing armies until eighteenth-century France or nineteenth-century Britain—in the medieval era, the resourcing of periodic levies of tens of thousands of troops for war was a major challenge to European states.[38] In this light, the Roman state's economic achievement is striking.

There have been few attempts to calculate the likely revenues and expenses of the Roman Empire at the height of the Principate.[39] Table 5.1 suggests that a round figure of about 1 billion sesterces may have been required by the mid-second century AD. Although there are large lacunae in

[38] Tilly 1990, 79.

[39] See for instance, Duncan-Jones 1994, 33–46 (on which table 5.1 is largely based); see also the important discussion in Mattern 1999, 123–61, and the more speculative figures in Goldsmith 1987, 34–59.

our knowledge, military expenditure was evidently a huge and recurrent element of the total. Richard Duncan-Jones's figures are slightly higher than some previous estimates; these vary from as low as 300 million sesterces under Augustus to around 900 million in the Severan period.[40] Taken together, the cost of the army and of salaries for officials involved in provincial or central government functions made up over 85 percent of the estimated total budget. States have a number of options over how to fund warfare and organize supplies for armies: seizing, making, buying, coercing, or taxing.[41] For the Roman state, with its habitual approach to war in the Republic and its large standing armies in the Principate, ad hoc measures had to cede increasingly to systematic levying of tribute. This was the bottom line of running the empire—taxation simply had to deliver at least these levels of resources. The comments attributed to Cerialis by Tacitus convey the message clearly: "[N]o peace ... without arms, no arms without pay, no pay without tribute."[42] Despite the many uncertainties in our knowledge of the imperial budgets and of revenues, it is clear that emperors were in a better position to understand their financial position because of detailed record keeping and a growing bureaucracy under control of financial specialists, the secretaries *a rationibus*. "Bad emperors" could impact negatively on their secretariat's best efforts by emptying the coffers and cause headaches for those who followed after (succession was always an expensive moment for any *princeps*). Pertinax found only 1 million sesterces in the treasury on his accession, a fact that contributed significantly to his rapid fall from grace with the praetorian guard.[43] The emperors Nerva, Marcus Aurelius, and Pertinax were obliged to auction off artworks and furniture to raise emergency funds.[44] But by and large the system worked tolerably well in the first two centuries AD.

It is clear that there were major differences between the Late Republican tributary systems and the more regularized direct rule and taxation of the Principate; further changes occurred in late Roman times.[45] But "bean counters" were common to all phases of Roman imperialism, as were fraud, bribery, malpractice, unjust impositions, and tax evasion. Many one-off taxes—such as those on trade goods at borders, on slave purchases, and on inheritance were around 5 percent of the value of the

---

[40] See Duncan-Jones 1994, 33–37, for the detailed arguments. See also Mattern 1999, 130, n. 27.

[41] Tilly 1990, 84–91.

[42] Tacitus, *Histories*, 4.74.

[43] Dio, *Roman History*, 73[74].5.4.

[44] Mattern 1999, 136.

[45] Duncan-Jones 1992, 187–210; 1994, 47–63; Lintott 1993, 70–96; Nicolet 1976, 1988, 2000.

goods. These base levels of taxation may seem relatively low, but recurrent tribute on land was much more varied and could be as high as 25 percent, and "rents" on imperial estates in Africa, for instance, were levied at 33 percent of the main crops produced. In Egypt it is clear that there was a multiplicity of different taxes and that arrangements varied wildly within the province and across social groupings.[46] In Judaea there are also hints in the Talmud and other ancient sources of heavy taxes being endured.[47] The varied nature of provincial arrangements, often building on preexisting structures, and the accretion of additional exactions over time cumulatively represented a burden for many communities—made worse by the fact that some groups and communities were much more favorably treated. In the face of provincial disquiet at the impositions, Roman writers were conscious of the need to stress the necessary link between taxation and security: "And since it is quite impossible to maintain the empire without taxation, let Asia not begrudge its part of the revenues in return for permanent peace and tranquility."[48]

For much of the Republican imperial age, the state took a somewhat backseat approach to taxation, appointing tax farmers (*publicani*) or enlisting local authorities to act on Rome's behalf. In the Principate, the *publicani* were replaced by a combination of imperial financial officials and local agencies (urban magistrates or councils who oversaw collection). The conventional view is that the Roman officials simply dictated the sums required from a particular city or region and left to "local responsibles" the more complicated decisions about how that liability was to be apportioned to individuals.[49]

The Achaean town of Messene in the first century AD appears to have had an overall demand equivalent to 400,000 sesterces.[50] The inscription that records the arrangements for dividing this large demand among the constituent groups in the town's population reveals that the tax represented about 2 percent of the capital value of land. Evidently detailed census records underlay both the state's appraisal of regional tax capacity and the calculations of local officials in apportioning shares of this across the community. Knowledge was thus crucial to power.[51] The Messene inscription records how, under the watchful but approving gaze of the Roman praetorian legate, the council secretary Aristocles reported to the assembled townsfolk his success in collecting in 83.5 percent of the required total. Some of the local inhabitants appear to have been more

---

[46] See Capponi 2005, 123–55, for an up-to-date summary.
[47] This is summarized in Roth 2002, 382.
[48] Cicero, *Letters to His Brother Quintus*, 1.1.34.
[49] Galsterer 2000, 353.
[50] *Inscriptiones Graecae* 5.1.1432f; translation in Levick 1985, 75–85, no. 70.
[51] Nicolet 1991.

successful than others in evading their obligations. For instance, Roman citizens and aliens living at Messene were responsible for 10 percent of the tax liability, but 33 percent of the net arrears. It is not improbable that the tax system was operated with built-in assumptions about acceptable levels of arrears and that provincial officials were perhaps only required to take action if revenue fell far short of the notional target or their overall provincial target was not reached. Aristocles seems to have been congratulated for his nearly 84 percent return by the provincial governor and his legate and by his fellow townsfolk.

The total *tributum* yielded by individual provinces no doubt varied greatly, but we should envisage that the expected returns were probably firmer target figures, as ultimately the imperial budget depended on these sums. Rogue emperors could blow holes in their own budgets through extravagance—at least this was part of the standard diagnosis of the "bad emperor." So Caligula, we are told, spent 10 million sesterces, "the tribute of three provinces," on a single banquet.[52] These must have been small provinces as the average sum required of provinces in the mid-first century ought to have been closer to 20 million sesterces. Although the Hopkins model envisages net flow of tax income from the core Mediterranean provinces to those with large military garrisons (and thus high costs), it is also entirely plausible that frontier provinces were squeezed harder to meet financial targets. If so, that has major implications for the observed pattern of economic development in provinces such as Britain.[53] Conversely more easily achievable targets in core provinces could have allowed officials on the spot considerable discretion on what sort of arrears were acceptable from different communities under their purview—providing ample scope for corruption one suspects.

The ability of some emperors exceptionally to write off arrears (and have the records of those tax debts publicly burned to reassure provincials) is testimony to the fact that for long periods, notwithstanding a shortfall on individual assessments, the empire raised more than the minimum sums required to meet its core costs. It is arguable, however, that the large army pay rises initiated by Septimius Severus and Caracalla in relatively quick succession did mark a turning point of sorts—in Duncan-Jones's figures this represents a near doubling of the military budget in the space of a decade.[54]

While today we tend to discriminate between direct and indirect taxes, in Roman times the main difference was in terms of regularly levied taxes such as the poll tax (*tributum capitis*) or the land tax (*tributum soli*) and

[52] Statius, *Silvae*, 10.4.
[53] On the economy of Britain, see Fulford 2004; and Mattingly 2006c, 491–520.
[54] Cf. Duncan-Jones 1994, 33–35.

irregular liability for tax on sales or manumission of slaves, on inheritance, and so on.[55] The 5 percent inheritance tax came to be of particular importance as it underwrote the retirement fund for the army. It was levied only on Roman citizens, whose numbers grew steadily in the provinces in the first two centuries AD and then exponentially so with the massive extension of citizenship by Caracalla in 212. As in many other areas of bureaucracy there is evidence of an increase in direct supervision of various taxes over time—accounting in part, at least, for the huge growth in the procuratorial service from 23 people under Augustus to 182 posts by the mid-third century.[56] It is plausible that imperial officials with financial responsibilities had performance targets to meet and when a shortfall occurred might even have had discretion to make an additional tax levy, as the praetorian prefect Florentinus evidently proposed for Gaul in AD 357.[57]

Taxation and other revenue raising by the state was (unsurprisingly) unpopular and complaints about it were common. However, there is a general assumption in many books that the rates of taxation were low in comparison to modern times.[58] There are several reasons to believe this may not be entirely accurate. Recurrent taxation, such as the land tax, may have been 25 percent of grain production in Egypt (and there was a plethora of additional taxes in Egypt).[59] Although views vary on the extent of change to preexisting Ptolemaic landholding and tax systems under Rome, it is generally agreed that Egypt was effectively exploited for the benefit of both the Roman state and the uppermost tier of local landholders.[60]

The highest tribute rates may have applied to peoples that Rome wanted to make an example of or whose lands happened to be occupied by large garrisons. The taxes we generally hear about in the sources were those that were most resented by the Roman elite, close to the center of power. The 5 percent inheritance tax on Roman citizens—introduced by Augustus specifically to fund the discharge bonuses of the army—had a particularly large impact on the wealth in land and capital of the Italian elite and was a crucial exception to the general avoidance of putting a financial burden on the imperial elite.[61] At the very least, this might suggest that the fiscal burdens imposed on subjects were heavier than is sometimes assumed, though the mixture of regular and irregular deductions must have

---

[55] Eck 2000b, 282.
[56] Eck 2000a; 2000b, 284–87; cf. Shipley et al. 2006, s.v. "equestrians."
[57] Ammianus Marcellinus, *Histories*, 18.3.
[58] Mattern 1999, 132, n 35.
[59] Duncan-Jones 1994, 54–55.
[60] Bagnall 2005; Rathbone 2002.
[61] Mattern 1999, 126, 132–33.

made it hard for people to work out their overall burden. The expressive list of epithets for tax men contained in a second-century AD source gives a good flavor of public opinion about their work: "Should you wish to abuse a tax farmer, you might try saying: burden, pack-animal, garotter, sneak-thief, shark, hurricane, oppressor of the down-trodden, inhuman, nail in my coffin, insatiable, immoderate, Shylock, violator, strangler, crusher, highwayman, strip-jack-naked, snatcher, thief, overcharger, reckless, shameless, unblushing, pain in the neck, savage, wild, inhospitable, brute, dead weight, obstacle, heart of stone, flotsam, pariah, and all other vile terms you can find to apply to someone's character."[62] We might also note the observation in Cassiodorus that sailors feared customs officials more than storms.[63]

As noted already, the actual rates of *tributum* imposed on provincial peoples reflected a settlement between them and the state based on their perceived merits. Siculus Flaccus summed up the situation well: "Certain peoples, with pertinacity, have waged war against the Romans, others having once experienced Roman military valour, have kept the peace, others who had encountered Rome's good faith and justice, declared their submission to the Romans and frequently took up arms against their enemies. This is why each people has received a legal settlement according to merit: it would not have been just if those who had so frequently broken the peace and had committed perjury and taken the initiative in making war, were seen to be offered the guarantees as loyal peoples."[64]

It is certainly plausible that these impositions could have been quite punitive on occasion. The ancient sources contain several explicit references to revolts being sparked by the nature of tribute exactions. For example, Dio on the Pannonian revolt in AD 6 noted the Illyrian view that it was Rome that was responsible, "for you send as guardians of your flocks not dogs or shepherds, but wolves."[65] A major grievance underlying the widespread uptake of the Boudican revolt in AD 60–61 evidently concerned taxation.[66] In the reign of Domitian, the Nasamones of Syrtica revolted against the imposition of tribute, "exacted from them by force."[67] Similarly, in the reign of Tiberius a reinterpretation of the tribute levied in ox hides on the Frisians lying to the north of the Rhine River's mouth by the centurion in charge of this region led to severe hardship followed by revolt.[68] There was a careful balance to be struck between

---

[62] Pollux, *Onomasticon*, 9.30–31.
[63] Cassiodorus, *Variae*, 4.19.
[64] Siculus Flaccus, *De condicionibus agrorum*, 7–8.
[65] Dio, *Roman History*, 56.16.3.
[66] Ibid., 62.3.3.
[67] Ibid., 67.4.6.
[68] Tacitus, *Annals*, 4.72.

the precise level of tribute exacted and the ability of local communities to pay. Punitive levels of tribute imposed by Rome carried the risk of armed resistance. The examples cited above are a selection from a number of cases where things went wrong. Perhaps more surprising is how often the Romans managed to get the balance right.

The exact detail of Roman censuses, taxation, and tribute exactions will always be elusive because of the nonstandardization of Roman practices across the empire. It is simply not possible to model the picture in Britain in comparison with what we see in Egypt. However, the snippets of extant primary documentation relating to landholding, land management, census activity, and tax collection should encourage us to envisage a series of provincial systems that were based on systematic data gathering and rational accounting principles.[69] The bottom line was the bottom line. Through a variety of methods it appears that the Principate was able to meet its budgetary needs most of the time. If we take 800 million sesterces as the average annual income figure for the first two centuries AD, that represents an aggregate tax take of 160 billion sesterces.

ROMAN ECONOMIES

In this section I shall argue for the existence of three distinct economic entities in the Roman world: an imperial economy, an interconnecting series of extraprovincial economies, and a series of regionally centered provincial economies (see table 5.2). I shall explain each of these in turn in simple terms and then consider how they may have operated in harness with each other.

The raising of the revenues needed to pay for the costs of running the empire were one part of what we might define as the *imperial economy*.[70] The other element of this concerned the economic structures set in place over time to transport and deliver needed resources to Rome and to the key functionaries of imperial rule—the armies and administrators in the provinces.[71] The imperial economy thus concerned the revenues and disbursements of the state, incorporating the army and infrastructures of governance, the taxation system, the exploitation of resources and the supply issues relating to the needs of the state. A huge amount of economic activity is covered under this heading, though only

[69] Ørsted 1985; Peña 1998; Rathbone 1991.

[70] See also Harris 2007 and Lo Cascio 2007 for the evolution from Late Republic to Early Principate.

[71] For the supply of Rome, see Aldrete and Mattingly 1999; Garnsey 1988; Morley 1996; Pleket 1993b; and Sirks 1991, 2007. For the armies, see Erdkamp 2002; and Papi 2007.

TABLE 5.2
Different Roman economies?

Economic structure	Location	Economic mechanism	Archaeological correlates
IMPERIAL ECONOMY	Empirewide and beyond frontiers	Taxation, imperial exploitation of land, labor, resources, redistribution, largesse, and salary commitments	Monetization focused on military needs, tax gathering (Egyptian tax grain arrangements, etc.); long-range movement of many commodities to frontier provinces or Rome, military bias in distribution patterns
EXTRAPROVINCIAL ECONOMIES	Empirewide and beyond frontiers	Free-market economy, response to opportunities of imperial supply, gift exchange	Interprovincial movement of goods to local markets, consumption of imported goods on civilian sites
PROVINCIAL ECONOMIES	Within provincial borders, often localized around major towns	Free-market economy, response to taxation, monetization	Local market distributions of locally produced goods, spread of monetization to smaller market centers, etc.

occasionally can it be unambiguously identified from the archaeological evidence.

The imperial economy intersected with *extraprovincial economies*, whereby interregional movement of goods took place across customs zones at provincial boundaries. Archaeological evidence is now clear-cut on this point: there was a huge expansion in the scale and nature of interregional movement of goods (including agricultural staples), only part of which can be attributed to the imperial economy.[72] It can be difficult to differentiate between the mechanisms from the archaeological assemblages alone, but in Roman times the extraprovincial commercial trade should have been easily distinguishable from the imperial economy. The fact that there were specific exemptions from the customs dues (*portoria*) for goods carried under state contracts—for instance, for military supply—demonstrates that officials on the ground could in principle differentiate between the operation of imperial and extraprovincial economies. The former area was governed by paperwork—contracts, orders, and so on—as is clear from a number of detailed customs tariffs for example.[73]

---

[72] Bonifay 2004; Greene 1986; Mattingly 1988a, 1996a; Panella and Tchernia 2002; Parker 1992.

[73] Horden and Purcell 2000, 354–56.

Of course, there was considerable scope for fraud and tax evasion in the movement of goods and the blurring of the distinctions between different categories of cargo would have been to the advantage of the merchants and shippers involved.[74]

I suggest that *provincial economies* relate to the emergence or further evolution of local market systems and networks, increased rural productivity, and manufacturing activity—even where these were in part at least a response to the pressures/demands of the imperial economy. The provincial economy also integrated aspects of pre-Roman economic structures, in northern Europe often involving practices embedded in social customs.

To conceptualize the Roman economy in this way is, of course, to disaggregate elements that were not always clearly divisible in practice and which were in many respects interdependent. Like a complex financial spreadsheet, changes to one of these economic areas would have generated automatic adjustments in other areas as well.

What I think my model achieves is a clearer appreciation of how it was that the Roman economy could appear both so modern and so primitive at the same time, why scholars can recognize both formalist and substantivist elements, and how it was capable of generating both globalized and highly localized distributions of material culture. Above all, it focuses attention on the extent to which Rome's financial needs acted as a driver of economic development and monetization in the provinces. A corollary of ruling regions was that the Roman state needed to capitalize on the possibilities for the exploitation of resources (natural, human, and in terms of farmed and manufactured products). The operation of the imperial economy might have had particularly large effects at certain times and places.

There were five key drivers in the imperial economy: the census, land, tax/tribute, resources, and supply systems. Each of these had large effects on the evolution of provincial and extraprovincial economies (summarized in Table 5.3). We can visualize these as links in a chain: knowledge–resource allocation–resource collection–resource exploitation–resource distribution. The overall aims were to assess and mobilize the economic potential of the empire and to collect and deliver the resources needed for the maintenance of the empire and the well-being of its key constituents. The imperial economy evolved and changed markedly over time, but the key proposition here is that at its peak it operated on a scale and at a level of sophistication that differentiates it from the vast majority of other ancient states.

---

[74] Whittaker 1994, 110–13.

The Census

The "road map" for the imperial economy was the census, working on the principle that knowledge equals power. As a vital fact-finding procedure that was coordinated by financial officials (and the army in frontier areas) the census underlay the exploitation of every province.[75] It established the extent and value of provincial lands and the size of regional populations. These data enabled the state to set down figures for tax/tribute assessment, compulsory army recruitment, labor and other services (corvées, liturgies) to be rendered. Records were held centrally within provinces (and arguably in summary form, at least, at Rome; there were periodic revisions and adjustments to population figures, information on land productivity, and so on. There is no doubt that the census was far from perfect or infallible in representing the regional resources of the empire, but by premodern standards it must have been an extraordinarily useful instrument of imperial government, providing an empirewide basis for the effective exploitation of land, resources and people

Land

Land was routinely "confiscated" from defeated enemies and accrued to the territory of Rome. Rome is often praised for the extent to which it subsequently returned control/ownership of such land to its previous owners, but it is clear that this was very often conditional on the terms of their surrender and their continuing good behavior. Put bluntly, loyal subjects were rewarded with generous land settlements, while those who resisted more fiercely or broke treaties were liable to be subjected to far less favorable settlements. Some of the land that was seized from defeated enemies was reallocated to colonists—often army veterans; some land was sold, some land became state land (*ager publicus*) or imperial estates for rental (a portfolio that grew over time). The nature and sophistication of Rome's arrangements relating to conquered land changed significantly in the last centuries BC, developing from a complex series of ad hoc measures in the early stages of Roman expansionism into a fully imperial system of exploitation at a comparatively late date.[76] Land was thus a significant lever to encourage the compliance of subject peoples and

---

[75] Nicolet 1988, 2000; cf. Capponi 2005, 83–96 (on Egypt). For the significance (and sophistication) of census records in the administration of the Ottoman Empire, see Given 2004; and Zarinebaf et al. 2005.

[76] Rathbone 2003a.

TABLE 5.3

Mechanisms of the imperial economy

CENSUS (KNOWLEDGE)	•The census was a vital fact-finding procedure that underlay the exploitation of the provinces. Coordinated by financial officials (and the army in frontier areas), it established the extent and value of provincial lands, size of population, etc., and set down markers for tax/tribute assessment, compulsory army recruitment, labor, and other services (corvees, liturgies) to be rendered, etc. •Periodically revised and records held centrally. •Census is crucial in providing solid basis for exploitation of land, resources, and people. •Knowledge = power.
LAND (RESOURCE ALLOCATION)	•Land was routinely confiscated from defeated enemies—the extent to which it was returned to previous owners very often conditional on terms of surrender and subsequent good behavior. •Loyal subjects rewarded with control of land. •Some land reallocated to colonists—often army veterans, some land sold, some land became state land (ager publicus) or imperial estates (growing over time). •Land was thus a significant lever to encourage compliance. •Land sometimes surveyed, divided, and reallocated (centuriation). •Land was also subject to rules (especially imperial estates).
TAX/TRIBUTE (RESOURCE COLLECTION)	•Taxation/tribute levied from neighbors and conquered peoples. No standard package, varied from case to case and many exemptions and special dispensations for communities seen as deserving. •Taxation could be based on land or on capitation. Customs dues and market taxes on movement/sale of goods, inheritance tax on wealth. •Taxes collected by: tax farmers (*publicani*), local civic authorities, imperial officials—variable practice. •Tax collection not always efficient—periodic remissions of tax arrears (HS900 million under Hadrian), but note that the rich were more successful in deferring tax payments and benefiting from remissions. •In general, tax probably quite burdensome for poor, and some provinces and regions harder hit than others—explains some of visible differences in wealth accretion.
NATURAL RESOURCES (RESOURCE EXPLOITATION)	•Natural resources were often exploited by Rome—gold, silver, copper, even iron mines; marbles and other decorative stones; salt; cedars of Lebanon; etc. •Rise in scale of mining activity in first and secong centuries AD—especially for production of gold and silver coinage. •Much in imperial or state ownership, though some subcontracted.
SUPPLY (RESOURCE DISTRIBUTION)	•Supplying the system involved Rome and the armies. •Economic impact of the empire went beyond moving specie to pay troops—major infrastructure for supplying food and other necessities to city of Rome and the frontier armies. •Population of city of Rome: c. 1 million. •Total size of army: c. 0.5 million. •Huge undertaking—fulfilled mostly by private shippers and traders working with state supply contracts. •Bureaucracy evolved over time, especially from time of Augustus onward. *Praefectus annona* in overall charge of supply system. •Imposes measure of price control and price fixing.

communities. Conventional studies of the Roman countryside emphasize the supposedly ubiquitous and irresistible rise of the villa estate in place of indigenous homesteads and farms,[77] but the reality appears a good deal more complex, with some regions undergoing significant change and economic growth and others entering prolonged periods of material and social stasis.

Certain land was surveyed, divided, and reallocated in the process we know as *centuriation*.[78] This was often linked to the census process as a means of evaluating a region's worth and productive capacity. Land was also often subject to complex legal rules (especially imperial estates).[79]

TAX

As has already been described, taxation/tribute was levied from neighbors and conquered peoples alike. There was no standard package to be applied across the empire; the tax settlement varied from case to case and there were many exemptions and special dispensations for communities seen as deserving. Taxation was fundamentally based on land or on capitation, but there were many additional taxes that we should take account of. Customs dues and market taxes related to the movement/sale of goods, while inheritance tax was imposed on the property of Roman citizens.[80] Taxes were collected by diverse means, often building on earlier local practices. In the Late Republic greater use was made of tax farmers (*publicani*), but under the principate the task was increasingly taken up by local civic authorities supported and cajoled by dedicated imperial financial officials.

Tax collection was certainly not always efficient, and it has often been noted that tax arrears built up recurrently in many provinces. The periodic remissions of these tax arrears (900 million sesterces under Hadrian), were more likely to benefit the rich who were probably more successful in deferring tax payments. In general, taxes were probably quite burdensome on the poor and some provinces and regions were harder hit than others. This may explain some of the visible differences in wealth accretion across the empire.

---

[77] Dark and Dark 1997; cf. Bayard and Collart 1996.

[78] Campbell 2000; Dilke 1971.

[79] Kehoe 1988, 2007.

[80] Inheritance tax was closely linked to the military budget, being set up under Augustus to fund the discharge packages for time-expired soldiers. The extension of citizenship by Caracalla increased those liable to inheritance tax by many millions, at a time when army pay had increased dramatically.

RESOURCES

Natural resources were often exploited by Rome; there were imperial gold, silver/lead, copper, and even iron mines; quarries for marbles and other decorative stones: saltworks and brine springs; and even the cedars of Lebanon were decreed an imperial resource.[81] The archaeological evidence suggests a substantial increase in the scale of mining activity in the first and second centuries AD, especially linked to the production of gold and silver coinage. Certain resources were placed under direct imperial control, while others were exploited by means of subcontracts with individuals or companies (socii) who shared the capital expense and risk. The overriding requirements of the state to exploit some key regional resources had a major impact on the socioeconomic evolution of communities living close to the resources. In northwest Spain, for instance, it is clear that the hundreds of Roman gold mines now known could not have been worked without significant labor inputs from the local people. In other words, Rome often mobilized the human resources of regions rich in natural resources to facilitate and bring down the direct cost of the exploitation of those resources.[82]

SUPPLY SYSTEMS

The Roman Empire was an unusually well-connected world by the standards of preindustrial ages.[83] The economic impact of the empire went far beyond moving specie to pay troops. The Roman state moved raw material, agricultural staples, and manufactured goods on an unprecedented scale across large distances.[84] "Supplying the system" involved mechanisms for the provisioning of the city of Rome and the armies.[85] Over time a major infrastructure was created for satisfying the vast consumption needs of Rome (with a population of about one million) and the frontier armies (about half a million men). This was a huge undertaking for a preindustrial state—another area where we find the best comparisons among other imperial powers rather than the normative preindustrial states. This was fulfilled to a large extent by private shippers and trad-

---

[81] Wilson 2007.

[82] See chapter 7 below.

[83] Adams 2007; Adams and Laurence 2001; Horden and Purcell 2000; Morley 2007; Purcell 2005a; Purcell and Horden 2005.

[84] This is perfectly exemplified by the physical structures of the port of Rome; see Keay et al. 2005.

[85] Aldrete and Mattingly 1999; Funari 2002; Papi 2007; Stallibrass and Thomas 2008; Whittaker 2002.

ers working with state supply contracts.[86] The bureaucracy evolved over time, especially from Augustus onward, and a high equestrian post—the *praefectus annona*—was created. The existence of the *annona* and the supply mechanisms that went with it created conditions in which by accident or design there was a measure of price control and price fixing.

DISCREPANT ECONOMIES

The broad spectrum of socioeconomic structures and practices that made up what we term the Roman economy ensured that individual experience of it was extremely varied. As a Talmudic source has put it, "The [Roman] government gives abundantly, and takes away abundantly."[87]

This variation was conditioned partly by social factors (as noted already, wealthy people were often better at evading full payment of their liabilities), partly by geographical differences, and partly by historical and institutional differences. Where suitable structures of taxation already existed in pre-Roman societies, these were often adopted as a basic starting point for Roman exactions. It was comparatively rare for Rome to introduce universal measures of taxation and the patterns in most provinces reflected the gradual accretion of regionally focused impositions. Individuals and communities faced both opportunities and challenges from Rome's exploitation of empire with varying levels of financial success. An economic theme I have been attempting to understand for a number of years concerns the extent to which Roman provinces appear to have been landscapes of opportunity or resistance.[88] I hope to have shown how the unequal impact of the imperial economy provided new and unheralded scope for wealth creation in some areas, while at the same time denying opportunity in others because of the relative scale of exactions of regional surpluses. The diverse patterns of economic behavior that we can recognize in the archaeological record represent in part at least the emergence of distinctive economic identities. As with social identities, our understanding of the individual choices that contributed to the formation of different economic identities needs to recognize that these were often responding to a fundamental colonial discourse.

---

[86] Sirks 1991, 2007.
[87] *Midrash Sifre de Bei Rab* (*Deuteronomy*) 354.
[88] Mattingly 1997c, reprinted in the present volume as chapter 6.

CHAPTER SIX

Landscapes of Imperialism

AFRICA: A LANDSCAPE OF OPPORTUNITY?

ECONOMIC GROWTH IN ROMAN AFRICA

In recent years a strong case has been made for identifying intensive economic growth in the provinces of Africa Proconsularis and Numidia—notably, between the second and fourth centuries AD.[1] This thesis is supported by comparative studies of other preindustrial societies,[2] since Roman Africa reveals virtually all the classic elements associated with this phenomenon. These include growth in agricultural production and rural population, an increase in exports of primary products, raised levels of import substitution, larger-scale units of production (farms to oileries, workshop to manufactory pottery production), the emergence of a society that was patently involved in risk taking, economic calculation, technological innovation, and other "rational" economic behavior.[3] In this respect, Africa stands out from many other provinces of the Roman Empire, where growth of this sort did not occur. By way of comparison, Achaia (Greece) may have been a province that contracted economically and demographically in the early Roman period.[4] What accounts for this

This chapter retains its essential character from its original publication (Mattingly 1997c), where it formed one half of a paired discussion with Susan Alcock. It can survive separation from its Siamese twin in the context of the present collection of essays, and I have made a small number of editorial emendations to reflect this, as well as adding a couple of extra figures. Interested readers may also wish to note that I have explored the theme of discrepant landscapes somewhat further in subsequent publications—notably, Mattingly 1998; 2006a, 379–452; 2007b; and Leone and Mattingly 2004. Note also the work on this theme of my PhD student (Fincham 2000, 2002). Recent publications on African landscapes add interesting details (De Vos 2000, 2007; Fentress 2000; Ørsted et al. 2000; Stone 2004; Stone, Stirling, and Ben Lazreg 1998) and work on colonial landscapes of other periods suggest that there is further potential in comparative approaches (Hauser and Hicks 2007). However, they do not substantially contradict the picture offered here.

[1] Hitchner 1993; Mattingly 1988a, 1988b, 1994b; Mattingly and Hitchner 1995, 198–204.

[2] Jones 1988; Reynolds 1985.

[3] Mattingly and Hitchner 1993.

[4] Alcock 1997; cf. Alcock 1993 and Mattingly 1994a.

difference? This chapter does not have answers, but hopefully will suggest a few pointers for further work in this developing field of research.

First, however, a word of caution: Is it right to even talk of landscapes of opportunity and resistance? One of the dangers of generalizing about provincial landscapes is that we may obscure the "discrepant experiences" and changing perspectives of Roman imperialism that they also encapsulate.[5] Moreover, the modern vision of Roman Africa is heavily influenced by the events of more recent colonial rule there, with potentially distorting effect.[6] Africa should not necessarily be accepted as a landscape of opportunity, without close consideration of spatial, social, and chronological exceptions to this supposed rule. In my view, provincial landscapes were the product of complex processes of coercion, negotiation, accommodation, and resistance—exploitative of, but also exploited by, some of the local population.[7] Just as important, perhaps, is the fact that they were not static entities, but continually evolving and/or devolving.

LANDSCAPES OF IMPERIALISM

The conquest of Africa Vetus (following the destruction of Carthage in 146 BC) and of Africa Nova (with the defeat of Juba I and the Pompeian forces by Caesar in 46 BC) put huge amounts of land at the disposal of Rome (see fig. 6.1). The consequences of this can be read in the archaeological record of centuriated landscapes and the epigraphic evidence of lands assigned to towns, tribes, emperors, senators, other wealthy individuals, or people of lesser means. The landscapes of Roman Africa vary greatly from region to region, yet most are classifiable as artifacts of imperialism on account of the evidence of profound changes detectable within them. In view of the later wealth and growth of the countryside, it would be easy to underestimate the potentially negative impact of Roman conquest on traditional structures and population. Yet the archaeological and epigraphic data are clear-cut as regards the initially dramatic effects of Roman conquest. This should not surprise us—the interests of the state plainly lay in the measurement, assignment, assessment, and taxation of land.[8]

The clearest evidence comes from the extensive areas of centuriation, especially in the original province of Africa Vetus, where over 15,000

---

[5] Cf. Said 1993, 35–50; and Webster 1996b, on postcolonial theory in general.

[6] Mattingly 1996a; Mattingly and Hitchner 1995, 169–74. See also chapter 2 of the present volume.

[7] Whittaker 1995 provides an important complementary analysis of cultural impacts of Rome on Africa, though with different emphases to my own.

[8] Mattingly 1992.

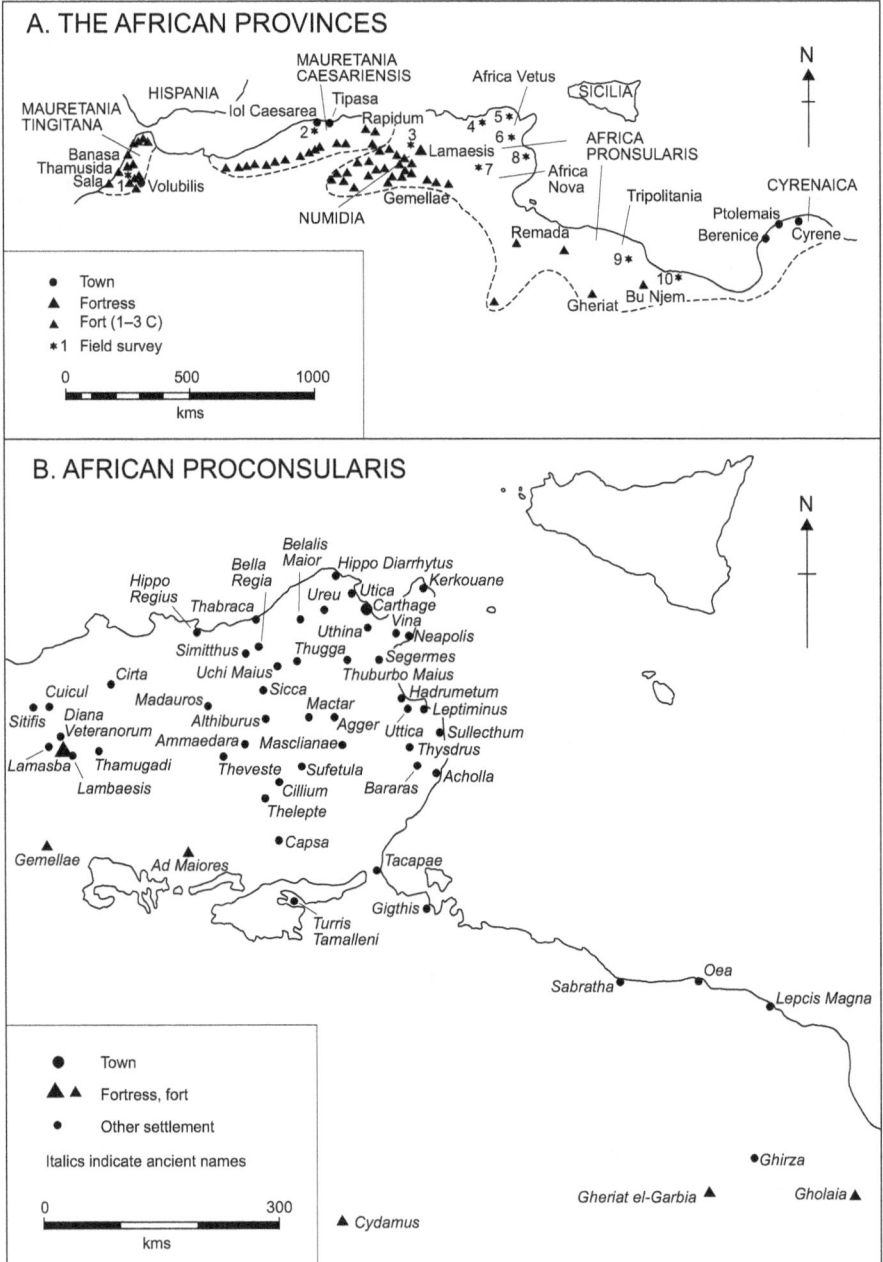

FIGURE 6.1 General maps of Roman Africa. Numbers indicate the location of the main rural surveys: 1 = Sebou area; 2 = Caesarea; 3 = Diana Veteranorum; 4 = Tunisian Tell; 5 = Carthage; 6 = Segermes; 7 = Kasserine; 8= Leptiminus; 9 and 10 = Libyan Valleys.

square kilometers were surveyed in the second and first centuries BC.[9] The physical manifestations of these systems have been mapped in detail and several distinct alignments have been discerned: a major program covering most of Africa Vetus, with smaller-scale additions in the region of Hadrumetum and Acholla. Some areas show evidence for several successive phases of survey. Other examples of centuriation are known or suspected from inland Numidia and probably date from the first and second centuries AD.[10] A number of studies have shown that the cardinal measurements of the land allotments relate to Roman metrology. For instance, in the area to the east of El Jem, François Favory has demonstrated that many of the subdivisions within the *centuriae* are based on multiples of 1 or 2 *iugera* (0.65–1.3 acres, or 0.25–0.5 hectares).[11] Sadly, we still lack detailed studies of the surface archaeology in these centuriated regions.[12]

Centuriation schemes were, of course, primarily utilized for land seized by conquest and/or for the lands intended for distribution to Roman colonists. But it is also clear that, as the African cities which had initally been independent allies of Rome were absorbed into the territorial empire, their lands were at the very least subject to review by Roman surveyors. The point is well illustrated by the example of Lepcis Magna, where a milestone of Tiberius referring to a road leading into the hinterland for 44 Roman miles can now be understood as a disguised reference to the southwestern territorial limits of the town. After a dispute over its mutual border with Oea led to open war between the two towns in AD 69, the *territorium* of Lepcis Magna was resurveyed (though not centuriated) and boundary stones erected along the disputed sector.[13] Lepcis Magna was one of the most independent African towns in the early empire, with an exceptionally strong and wealthy local elite and little evidence for immigrant families, however, this evidence suggests that Rome took a deep interest in the territories of all its subject towns.

Many noncenturiated areas of the Maghreb were nonetheless divided up by highly visible markers (walls, irrigation canals, field systems). The process had pre-Roman origins and was the work predominantly of native Africans, but the increased scale and extent of such constructed landscapes is a key characteristic of the Roman period.[14] John Barrett contends that the Roman Empire was something experienced by individuals

[9] Dilke 1971, 155; Peyras 1986.

[10] Soyer 1973; 1976; 1983, 336–39.

[11] Favory 1983, 131–35; cf. Trousset 1977, 1997.

[12] Although, cf. Maurin and Peyras 1991; Peyras 1975, 1983, and 1991 for some extensive reconnaissance in centuriated areas.

[13] Di Vita-Evrard 1979; Mattingly 1995.

[14] Baradez 1949; see also Birebent 1962 for the data, but a colonialist interpretation.

("written on the body"); but this evidence (and much like it elsewhere) suggests that imperialism was imprinted as indelibly on the landscape.[15] My strong suspicion is that different landscapes of Roman date reflect divergent experiences of Roman imperialism. The extent of Roman period land delimitation and demarcation in Africa suggests massive intervention in preexisting landholding patterns. Roman landscape change in Greece was different. There, confiscation and reallocation/confirmation of lands led to a thinning of settlement and markers; in Africa the reverse applied.

In addition to the formal centuriation schemes and delimitation of urban lands, the state carried out other surveys of conquered land. The most famous instance is the *delimitatio* of the lands of the Nybgenii people of southern Tunisia, first achieved in AD 29–30, when a baseline over 200 kilometers long was laid out, extending from the legionary fortress at Ammaedara to the area of the Chott Djerid/Fedjedj.[16] The few extant boundary stones from this survey suggest that although it was no doubt recorded in the primary archive copy as a centuriated grid, only a few cardinal points were ever in fact marked on the ground. The purpose would seem to have been to survey the extent (and potential value) of the lands of the Nybgenii and to delimit them with boundary markers from those of the neighboring civic communities, notably Tacapae (modern Gabes) on the coast.

Many other tribes had their lands surveyed and demarcated by boundary stones, an action sometimes wrongly interpreted as the penning up native peoples in "reservations."[17] In fact, the dates of the main phases of these surveys (AD 70s, 100–110) correspond with periods of major advance of the African frontier, creating the conditions for releasing large amounts of territory variously to Roman colonies, self-governing local communities, imperial estates, and individuals. These lands would have been held by the state during the phase of direct military occupation. The forward movement of the army allowed the reallocation of these lands in various forms. Some of the land was centuriated, some surveyed in lesser detail. In the well-known case of the Musulamii of central Tunisia and eastern Algeria, boundary markers indicate the separation of the Musulamian lands from city lands (including two Roman colonies) and imperial and private estates. Many similar examples can be produced from the rich epigraphic records of Roman Africa, but the surviving evidence must represent only a tiny proportion of the actual activity of this sort.[18]

---

[15] Barrett 1997; cf. Shaw 1984, 1991; and Trousset 1987.
[16] Trousset 1978.
[17] This is discussed in Février 1990, 127.
[18] Février 1990, 80–81, 125–30 (see 125–27 for the Musulamii).

Land survey of different kinds and the maintenance of current records would have been long-term preoccupations of both provincial and local bureaucracies. Knowledge of the extent and quality of land was the basis for tax assessment and thereby a vital component in the exploitation of subject peoples.

The power asymmetries that underlay the mechanics of imperial land surveys should alert us to the probability that such large-scale operations, often carried out by military personnel, would almost invariably have gone beyond providing a simple record of existing arrangements. Land (and especially its distribution and redistribution) was one of the most effective tools of Roman imperialism and its potential as a coercive mechanism or as a reward for appropriate behavior must have been clearly perceived by both conqueror and conquered in their unequal negotiations. It is worth noting that most of the attested surveys of native lands occurred a generation or more after the submission or subjugation of the indigenous group. The formal return and recognition of territory was not the first conciliatory act by Rome after a conquest, but in many cases came at the conclusion of a longish period of direct military occupation or supervision of an area. A satisfactory solution for a native people had to be earned; in the interim any arrangements made were purely temporary and might be deliberately punitive. When revolts occurred under Augustus and Tiberius, a prime cause appears to have been Rome's interference in traditional landholding arrangements. Furthermore, Roman interference was not limited to landholding arrangements and it had means of persuasion beyond force and threat: army recruitment, supervision of native peoples by Roman prefects, and the recognition of specified settlements as administrative centers could all be used to undermine traditional power structures within a community.[19]

Of the land conquered or surrendered to Rome in Africa, some remained *ager publicus*, while a large amount was returned to native communities or passed into private ownership.[20] The principal individual beneficiary of land redistribution in Africa was the emperor, whose estates were both numerous and large.[21] This was a cumulative process, of course. In some regions, such as the northern Bagradas Valley, imperial holdings were particularly extensive, and after Nero's confiscations of the estates of six prominent senators it was said that the emperor controlled half of the lands of Africa.[22] Although that figure is clearly exaggerated, by the early fifth century imperial lands allegedly comprised over 15,000

[19] Mattingly 1992, 1995.
[20] See Duncan-Jones 1990, 121–42, for the different categories of land.
[21] Crawford 1976.
[22] Pliny, *Natural History*, 18.35; analysis in Kehoe 1984; 1988, 11, 49. See also Kehoe 2007 for a refined analysis.

square kilometers in Proconsularis and Byzacena alone (about one-sixth of the total land area).[23] Two reasons can be advanced for why these estates were of great significance in the pattern of rural development. First, the emperors clearly viewed Africa as a vital source of food for Rome; they established a close link between rural production and the food supply mechanism (the annona). Second, they made changes to the organization of these estates as a means of increasing productivity. Such institutions also had an impact on private estates.

From an early date in the life of the province, senatorial families at Rome owned estates in Africa. These property portfolios were often consolidated during periods of office holding in Africa; at least this is clear in the best known cases (for example, Galba or Gordian I). It is likely that the management of these estates on behalf of their absentee landlords was closely similar to, if not modeled on, that of imperial estates. In theory, these estates involved outside investment in African production, though the effects of this could easily be exaggerated, since the greater responsibilities for investment and risk seem to have been placed on managers or chief tenants (*conductores*) and share-cropping tenants (*coloni*). On the other hand, like the imperial properties, senatorial estates may have produced surpluses for export (whether for sale overseas or for the private consumption of the large *familiae* of Roman aristocrats).[24] This is important because it offers a clue as to how traffic may have built up on shipping routes to and from Africa.

By the second century AD, of course, there was a significant group of African-born senators, representatives of a larger body of private estate holders. These people were active in the development of rural infrastructures (estates, villas, villages, oileries, minor roads, irrigation schemes, etc.), but always within a political framework that depended on the state. Of critical importance is the observation that the growth of private landholding in some areas may have been achieved at the expense of previous communal patterns of land use. Tribal ownership or control of lands may increasingly have given way to estates owned by an elite or favored group within the community.

However, large estates do not appear to have been ubiquitous. The Lamasba inscription, detailing arrangements for the distribution of water for irrigation to a group of over eighty named farmers, suggests that a substantial body of smallholders lived there.[25] On the other hand, this text is from a town and presumably related to olive groves in very close

---

[23] Lepelley 1967.
[24] Whittaker 1985.
[25] Février 1990, 88–89; Duncan-Jones 1990, 135–36.

proximity, and in an area where one might expect to find parcels leased from the municipality.[26] For this reason, I suspect that the Lamasba data cannot be regarded as typical of the general pattern of rural settlement. Nevertheless, there must have been vast numbers of small-scale holdings dotted across the landscape, some assigned to or bought by retiring army veterans (and from the second century AD onward, these were predominantly men of African birth).

There were thus several factors and groups of individuals contributing to the pattern of rural settlement in Africa. In all regions, control of water resources was of prime importance, with hydraulic technology varying according to local topography, hydrology, and tradition.[27] Indigenous labor and know-how seem to have predominated over immigrant colonists and imported technology. The resultant landscapes are notable in several ways. As we shall see, field survey demonstrates a significant rise in sedentary agriculture and in agricultural productivity in many regions—especially those that had hitherto been comparatively underdeveloped. This is matched by a dramatic increase in the numbers of towns, both in regions already somewhat urbanized (the coastal Libyphoenician centers and the Numidian kingdom) and in some sectors where they were previously unknown.

The Organization of Labor

The available evidence suggests strongly that tenancy was by far the commonest form of labor organization on imperial and private estates in Africa. Slave labor does not seem to have been significant in the countryside, though its importance may have varied regionally.[28] Our most detailed information on tenancy comes from a well-known series of inscriptions from imperial estates in northern Tunisia that detail terms and conditions laid down by law (the *lex Manciana* and *lex Hadriana*). Kehoe has argued that the Mancian tenure applied to all lands of these estates and set fixed shares of each type of crop (normally one-third) that tenants were to hand over to the *conductores* of the estates. In return, the tenants (*coloni*) and their heirs obtained rights to cultivate the land they leased in perpetuity, providing the land was not left unproductive for two consecutive years. Incentives were offered to encourage tenants to bring uncultivated areas of the estate into production.[29]

---

[26] Cf. Shaw 1982a.
[27] Euzennat 1992; Shaw 1984; Slim 1992; Trousset 1986, 1987.
[28] Carlsen 1991; Mattingly 1987b; Whittaker 1978a, 1980.
[29] Kehoe 1984, 1988, 2007; Kolendo 1992; Vera 1987, 1988; Whittaker 1978a, 1995.

The appearance of Mancian cultivators outside imperial estates indicates that, whether or not the terms of the surviving laws were limited to imperial estates, the type of tenancy arrangement embodied therein was imitated in private leases also. The clearest evidence of this is provided by the late-fifth-century Albertini Tablets, where Mancian sharecropping plots were ostensibly sold without reference to the absentee landowner. The answer to this apparent contradiction sheds further light on the incentives that Mancian sharecropping tenancy arrangements offered to the *coloni*. Close examination of the transactions reveals that what was sold was not in fact an exact area of ground but instead the use of a defined area and ownership of things that had been placed on that patch of earth. Thus many of the documents concern the sale of olive trees and the leasing of cultivation rights (under normal sharecropping terms) of individual fields on the estate.[30] This separation between ownership of the land and ownership and use of what was placed on the land (olive trees, hydraulic systems, farm buildings) is a distinctive feature of North African tenurial systems and may be suspected to be in origin a pre-Roman tradition. The development of rural estates, both imperial and private, may have exploited the resources and aspirations of tenant farmers. Thus, the expansion of sedentary agriculture into more marginal districts may to some extent have relied on what were in effect partnerships between landowner and tenant. The full significance of this peculiarity of African tenancy in promoting growth and opportunity in the regional economy cannot be known, but it offers a clue as to how the "discrepant experience" of a peasant farmer might at a certain point overlap with that of a richer landowner or chief tenant.

Interesting comparisons exist in the modern colonial period, where a somewhat similar system of investment was used to create the massive olive orchards of the Sfax area in Tunisia. Foreign capital bought the land, but native tenants were encouraged with loans to participate in the planting of olive orchards (where they provided the labor, of course) and to which they would in time have a share of property rights. Perhaps equally significant is the fact that these modern Tunisian sharecroppers were frequently obliged to hand over to their absentee landlords a larger part of the fully productive orchards than they were contracted to, in order to settle debts they had run up during the years of development.[31] It is possible that Roman-period expansion may also have been cruelly exploitative of the aspirations of peasant farmers. Such people were notoriously conservative and averse to risk-taking, yet in this situation they appear to have gambled with their livelihoods on a significant scale.

[30] Mattingly 1989a; Hitchner 1995.
[31] Poncet 1963, 396; Mattingly 1994b, 97–103.

However, the important point to note is that, although the sharecroppers were not coerced to participate, they made their choice on the basis of their reading of the imperial situation. Whether their actual experience proved them right (and common sense would suggest that there were winners and losers in this type of speculative agriculture), it seems a fair interpretation that they perceived a landscape of opportunity.

The Evidence of Field Surveys

The archaeology of rural sites and landscapes in Africa, despite early achievements by the colonial mapmakers,[32] is still an underdeveloped area of research.[33] There are hardly any published excavations of rural sites to a modern standard.[34] Field survey evidence has increased greatly in recent years, though coverage is still very patchy, and interpretation and analyses are still evolving.[35] Yet because of the level of site preservation, the quality of survey data is extraordinarily high in comparison with many other Mediterranean regions. A few brief examples must suffice (see fig. 6.1).[36]

Philippe Leveau's groundbreaking study in Mauretania Caesariensis of the city of Caesarea and its territory recorded 241 sites in a semicircular zone of about 500 square kilometers, with the rural settlement hierarchy dominated by around 60–70 villas. Of 36 villas investigated in detail, eight sites had an area of more than 2,400 square meters; the rest had areas between 600 and 2,400 square meters. Leveau suggested that five of the 36 villas were major estate centers, 17 were important villas, and 14 were more moderate establishments. However, these villas were essentially functional structures, not luxurious dwellings. This is supported by the important evidence for olive presses (about 100 were recorded), which in at least four cases occurred in multiple units and in specialist buildings (oileries).[37]

Apart from the villas, Leveau found evidence for smaller rural sites built of less durable materials (representing tenant farms and/or farmsteads of independent smallholders?), along with an important number of

---

[32] See, for example, Gsell 1911.

[33] See Stone 2004.

[34] Barker and Jones 1984 (el-Amud, Libya); Brogan and Smith 1984 (Ghirza, Libya); Anselmino et al. 1989 (Nador, Algeria).

[35] Cf. Lassère 1977, 295–363; Leveau, Sillières, and Vallat 1993, 154–200.

[36] Note in addition the important extensive survey work of Ben Baaziz 1985, 1988, 1991b, 1993a, 1993b; Morizot 1991, 1993; Peyras 1991; and Rebuffat, Lenoir, and Akerraz 1986. This section is based on the summary in Mattingly and Hitchner 1995, 189–96.

[37] Leveau 1984.

"agglomerations" (villages?), the latter occurring sometimes in association with villas, sometimes in isolation, and in one case covering about 10 hectares, though more normally 2–3 hectares. At the fringes of the economic territory of the city (as defined by the distribution of villas), such agglomerations appear to represent the top of the settlement hierarchy. Dating evidence, based on collections of fineware diagnostics at a sample of sites only (1,063 shards from 34 sites), allows little conclusive to be said about pre-Roman settlement, or indeed about villa development before the late first century AD, though the heyday of the villa economy (judged purely on ceramic evidence) lay in the second to fourth centuries. The paucity of later fineware from the survey suggests a significant decline of settlement.[38] Comparison with the region around Volubilis in Mauretania Tingitana, where pre- and post-Roman pottery has been recognized, also indicates that the Roman period saw peak levels of dispersed rural settlement.[39]

The Tuniso-Danish Africa Proconsularis project (1987–89) involved both survey and excavation at the Roman town of Segermes and in its territory. Within a zone of 600 square kilometers, intensive field walking was carried out over a total of 26 square kilometers split among eleven sample sectors. All pottery observed by the field teams was counted (114,000 shards) and its density across the landscape mapped, though only diagnostics were collected (about 10,000 shards). In an area with 74 previously known sites, a total of 193 is now reported.[40] This dramatic rise in the number of sites over those mapped on the *Atlas archéologique de la Tunisie* is a salutary lesson about the comprehensiveness of the French colonial mappers and the value of intensive methods. As regards site morphology, Peter Ørsted differentiates between villas (sites of large size, with evidence of baths) and olive farms, though most of the latter would count among the villas of Leveau's work.[41] Many of the farms/villas comprise three ranges in a distinctive U-shaped layout around a court; olive presses are also common, though never more than two have been found at a site, suggesting a lesser degree of olive specialization here than in some other areas.

The phasing of settlement is significant because of the comparatively large sample of pottery processed. Punico-Libyan settlement was certainly present, though possibly sparse, in the region, with a major intensification of sites and land use in the first and second centuries AD.

---

[38] Subsequent excavation at one site has revealed a very active late antique phase; see Anselmino et al. 1989.

[39] Akerraz and Lenoir 1990; Rebuffat 1986; Rebuffat et al. 1986.

[40] Carlsen and Tvarnø 1990; Dietz, Ladjimi Sebaï, and Ben Hassan 1996; Gerner Hansen et al. 1993; Ørsted et al. 1992; Ørsted et al. 2000.

[41] Ørsted et al. 1992.

The bulk of the ceramics suggest that settlement peaked in the third and fourth centuries, with some decline in site numbers in the fifth and sixth centuries.

The Kasserine survey (1982–89), directed by Bruce Hitchner, has investigated rural settlements around ancient Cillium (Kasserine) and Thelepte.[42] Over 200 sites were recorded within a series of sectors covering 75 square kilometers, though in the most intensively surveyed area, there was a total of about 20 settlement sites in an area of only about 3.5 square kilometers. The morphology of settlement comprizes a full hierarchy of farming sites from large villas and purpose-built oileries, through smaller villas and farms in *opus africanum* masonry, to minor farmsteads and isolated buildings built in rough, drystone techniques. There is also a hierarchy of nucleated sites with the three largest being described provisionally as "agrovilles," since they possess some of the characteristics of urban centers, but reveal a profoundly rural function—that at Ksar el-Guellal covering 53 hectares and containing over twenty olive presses.[43] The chronology of Roman settlement in the Kasserine region ranged from the first century AD, when large-scale sedentarization appears to have begun, to the sixth and seventh centuries AD, with the peak period, based on pottery supply, being the third to fifth centuries AD.

The total survey of a 3.5 square kilometer area of Sector 1 provides a dramatic picture of the spatial dynamics of settlement.[44] Within this small area, there are two major oileries, each with a bank of four presses, five other substantial farms, seven or eight minor farmsteads or isolated structures, and thirty-four tombs and cemeteries. Stock enclosures are a feature of all types of settlement.[45] Given the scale of olive oil production and pastoral activity attested to by the major sites, it seems appropriate to interpret many of the minor sites as tenant or dependent farms within one or more large estates. Study of the archives of the French "brigades topographiques" suggests that this picture may be fairly typical of settlement on the high steppe zone.[46] There are quite a number of major mausolea alongside villa estates, some relating to families attested in the municipal aristocracies. The role of oleoculture in this marginal zone of about 1000 square kilometers in extent was clearly very significant, with over 300 presses recorded, including a notable density of major oileries with four or more presses. This would appear to be a highly specialized, capital intensive, and estate orientated landscape.

[42] Hitchner 1988, 1989, 1990.

[43] Hitchner and Mattingly 1991.

[44] Hitchner 1990, 258–59. The map is also reproduced in Mattingly and Hitchner 1995, 193.

[45] Hitchner 1994; Leveau 1988.

[46] Mattingly 1988b; Hitchner 1989.

The UNESCO Libyan Valleys Survey in northwestern Libya was launched at the behest of Libyan leader Muammar al-Ghaddafi to investigate the abundant traces of Roman period farming in the Libyan pre-desert. An Anglo-Libyan team led by Graeme Barker and Barri Jones investigated the wadi systems of the Sofeggin and Zem-Zem basins about 100 kilometers south of Tripoli. This region (around 50,000 square kilometers in extent) was studied across five seasons (1979, 1980, 1981, 1984, 1989), with more than 2,500 sites recorded, over 55,000 shards of pottery collected and processed, and over thirty preliminary publications and a two-volume final report resulting.[47]

The settlement distribution here was related to the exploitation of the soils of the dry river beds, or wadis, that bisect the pre-desert plateau. Surveys of walls and hydraulic features on the wadi floor have elucidated the technology of wadi agriculture.[48] The site hierarchy was dominated by elite farms, initially undefended and later often fortified. There were also large numbers of less substantial farms and farmsteads, small settlements, huts, and tent bases (occurring singly and in groups).

From studies of inscriptions on mausolea, it is now clear that the wadi farmers were indigenous Libyans, engaging to varying degrees with Roman or Punic culture, and not settlers from outside the region (let alone from overseas), as was once posited.[49] The economic success of a sizable elite group among them, despite the harshness of the pre-desert climate, is indicated by the more than 70 mausolea and by the architectural pretension of the major sites. It is therefore presumed that many of the minor structures were held in some sort of dependency relationship by the upper echelon settlements, and an estate system may again be indicated. This conclusion has received support from a geographic information system analysis of the spatial patterning of early settlement (see fig. 6.4).[50]

The earliest settlement in the pre-desert is hard to date, since no pre-first century AD fineware has been identified.[51] However, it is clear from the study of both fine and coarse pottery that there was a dramatic and sustained development of undefended farms from the third quarter of the first century and into the second century AD. In the third century, there was some slight relocation of settlement, partly a result of the growing preference for fortified farms.

[47] See, among others, Barker and Jones 1981, 1982, 1984, 1985; Barker et al. 1996a; 1996b; Jones and Barker 1980, 1983; and Mattingly 1989b. For complementary French work in Syrtica to the southeast, see Rebuffat 1988; and Reddé 1988.
[48] Barker 1985; Barker et al. 1996a, 191–225, 265–90; Gilbertson et al. 1984; Hunt et al. 1986.
[49] Mattingly 1995.
[50] Flower and Mattingly 1995.
[51] Dore 1985, 1996.

What links all these different landscapes—from a Mediterranen coastal zone to the Saharan pre-desert—is that their archaeology demonstrates settlement expansion and economic change (in favor of more specialized and cash-crop-orientated production). The wealth generated by this rural revolution is manifest not only in the capital reinvested in prestige forms of rural construction and in large-scale estate buildings but to an even greater extent in the fabric of the hundreds of towns that Roman Africa sustained. Exploitative and unpromising as imperial rule may have at first appeared, Africans (or some, at least) turned opportunity to advantage.

IMPERIAL POLICY AND AFRICA: THE *ANNONA*

The large-scale export of foodstuffs from Africa to Rome was a significant factor behind agrarian and trade development. The concerns of the *fiscus* with the imperial estates and with the evolving structures of the *annona* organization are clear in principle, if occasionally hazy in detail.[52] The emperors had the need and the resources to encourage rural growth and investment, just as they provided incentives to the shippers responsible for carrying *annona* cargoes to Rome. Although olive oil was not regularly included in the monthly handouts of foodstuffs in Rome until the third century AD, it seems clear that the actual scope of the activities of the *annona* officials was a good deal broader than simply arranging the import of grain for the dole.[53] Spanish and African olive oil imports were evidently partly regulated by then in the second century AD (if not earlier) and the influence of this state-directed trade on the subsequent boom in African olive oil production should not be overlooked. Here perhaps is a crucial distinction between Africa and Achaia. The existence of a substantial level of tied or subsidized traffic between Africa and Rome created different opportunities for agricultural growth.

AFRICA AS A LANDSCAPE OF RESISTANCE?

How can we identify landscapes of resistance in Africa? Several examples can be suggested from the field survey data. The limit of villa estates in the hinterland of Caesarea seems to define an economic territory, beyond which other settlement types—especially nucleated villages—dominated, perhaps indicative of a different system of rural exploitation or of eco-

---

[52] Sirks 1991.
[53] Mattingly 1988a, 1996a.

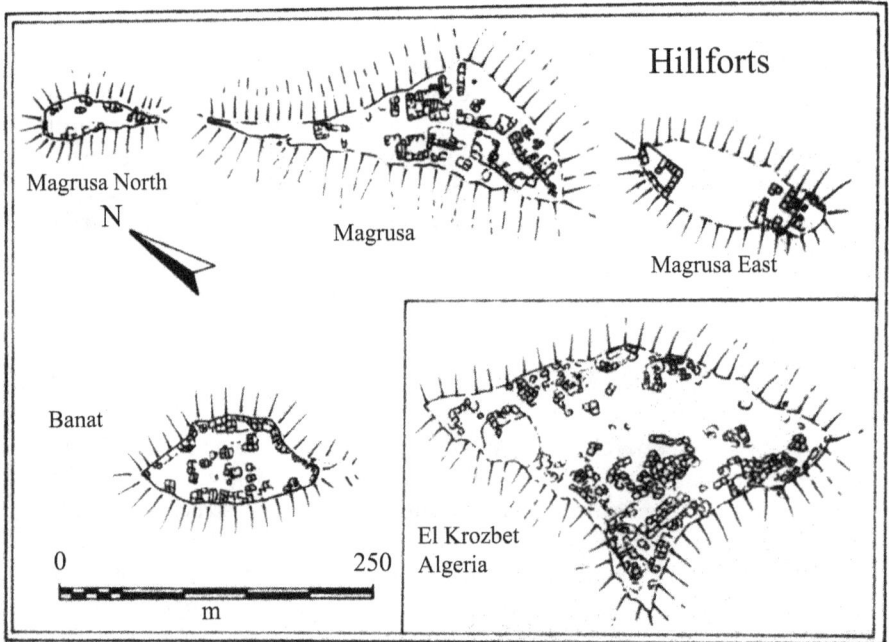

FIGURE 6.2 Hill villages (hillforts) from the pre-desert zone of Tripolitania, with an Algerian example for comparison.

nomic organization.[54] Comparable differences have been noted in the morphology of settlement in mountainous areas bordering plains that were evidently exploited by large villas and Roman-style farms. Near Diana Veteranorum, Lisa Fentress has recorded a radically different form of settlement pattern in the mountainous margins of the territory.[55] Similarly, the Kasserine survey has also recorded mountain communities living in small irregular farmsteads or hamlets comprising several of these family units, the form of which is entirely different from the farms of the plains below.[56] In the Libyan Valleys Survey, a number of hillforts were discovered showing evidence of occupation from the first century AD to at least the third or fourth centuries. These are generally away from the main areas of wadi agriculture and the morphology of the buildings within them differs from that of the wadi agriculturalists (see figs 6.2–6.3). It is hard to avoid the conclusion that these sites represent a different set of values and realities to those already discussed.[57]

[54] Leveau 1984.
[55] Fentress, Aït Kaci, and Bounssair 1993.
[56] Hitchner 1988.
[57] Barker et al. 1996a, 116–18, 147–50; Mattingly 1995, 41–49.

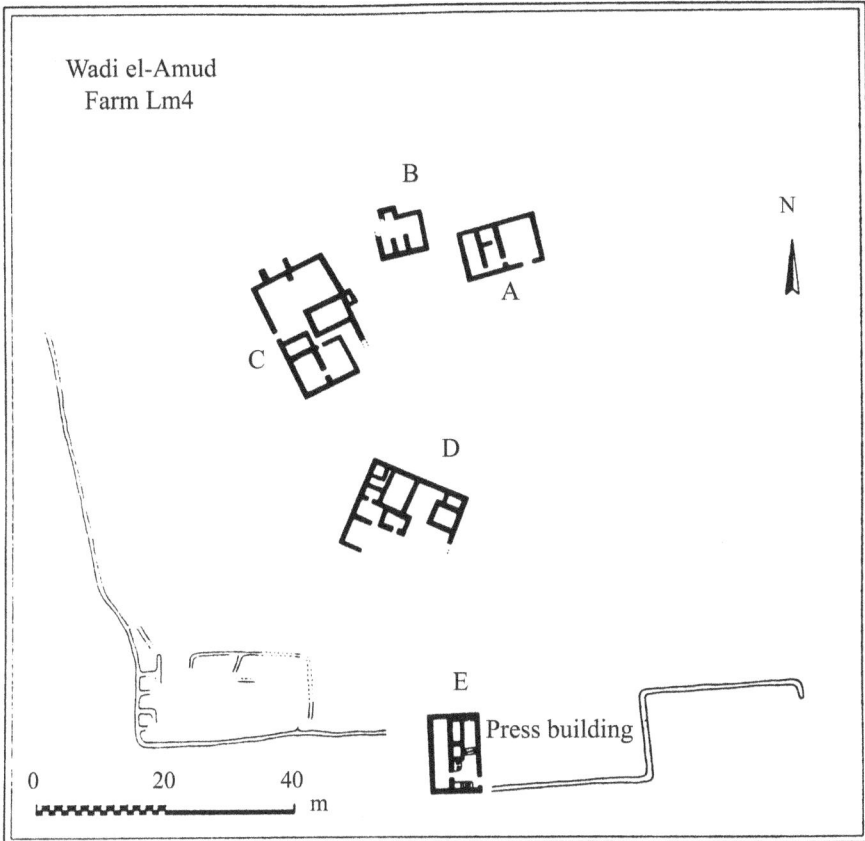

FIGURE 6.3 The Roman period open farm Lm4 (Wadi el-Amud) in the Tripolitanian pre-desert.

The late Roman trend toward defended dwellings and fortified farms, particularly evident in the frontier zones, is another tendency that may reflect changes in perceptions of Roman imperialism and not simply increasing insecurity or a new fashion among the rural elite. We are dealing with new power relationships, with the state obliged to tolerate many forms of private fortification that would not have been acceptable in the immediate postconquest phase. If at first intended more to perpetuate the power and wealth of the elite, some fortified farms undoubtedly had become regional power bases by late antiquity.[58]

Another landscape of resistance may be traced through the study of linear barriers (*clausurae*) that were part of the Roman frontier works.

[58] Barker et al. 1996a, 319–42; Mattingly 1995, 194–201.

The consensus view is that these walls and earthworks were not defensive barriers but filtering mechanisms and control points for the passage across the frontier of transhumant peoples, whether with their flocks or with letters of passage going in search of employment within the province.[59] The Roman perspective of mobile populations was cautious but pragmatic: exclusion was impractical and the controlled crossings offered opportunities for the levying of tax, tribute, and customs dues on people who might otherwise have been hard to bring to account. But in desiring to limit and control access to pasture, wells, markets, and work inside the frontier, the state was obliged to police the frontier zone and periodically to enforce its will. Regardless of whether the transhumant peoples desired to participate in the economic structures of the sedentary farming zone (as harvesters, shepherds, crop watchers, etc.), the unilateral rules of the cross-border relationship were hardly consensual. Although the *clausurae* were, in effect, part of a landscape of imperial control, their location is a useful diagnostic for identifying points of contact between areas of sedentary farming and traditional pastoralists, whose lifestyle can at a certain level be read as one of latent resistance to the state.

The vertical divisions of rural society could also foster highly differentiated perspectives on events. The specialized harvesting of cereals and olives was accomplished by the annual formation of large harvest gangs. From time to time these labor pools provided a focus for civil violence or rebellion (as seems to have happened in the revolt of the Gordians in AD 238 or the Donatist schism). Resistance in this case, as in most of the others referred to herein, was latent even at the height of the region's prosperity.

Conclusion: A Contrast with the Landscapes of Roman Achaia

The background conditions of the incorporation of Africa and Achaia in the Roman Empire were sufficiently similar for their subsequent divergence in economic and demographic profiles to be of considerable interest. Both experienced the violent passage of the armies of Rome and its enemies (Carthage, and the Macedonian and Seleucid kingdoms) and both regions were involved more culpably in acts of resistance against Rome (the Achaian revolt and sack of Corinth, and the destruction of Carthage, the Jugurthan War, the civil war of 46 BC, the Tacfarinan war, etc.). In each province much land was confiscated for a time and held in the gift of the state. There is evidence for the imposition of new

---

[59] Mattingly 1995, 106–15; Trousset 1987.

MODEL A

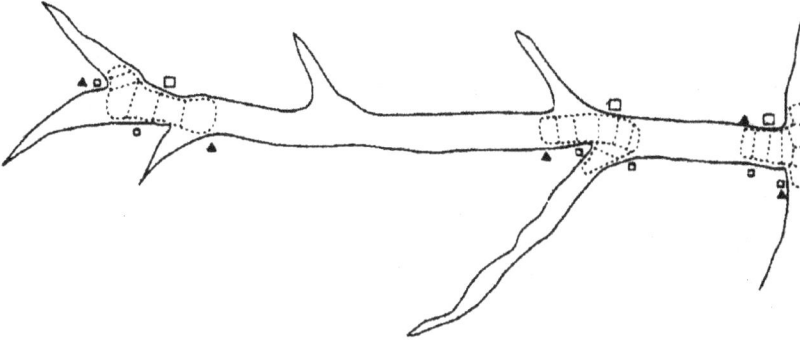

MODEL B

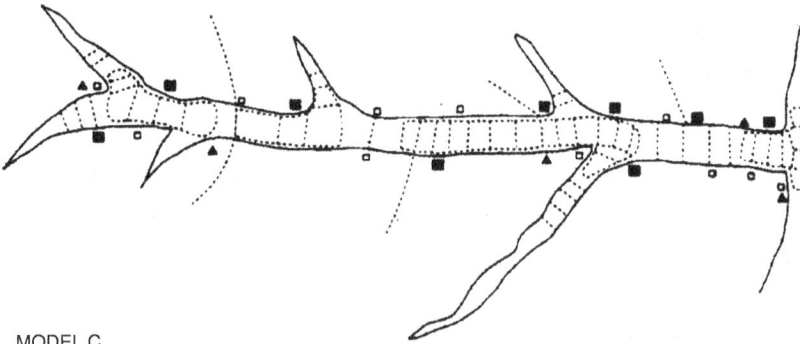

MODEL C

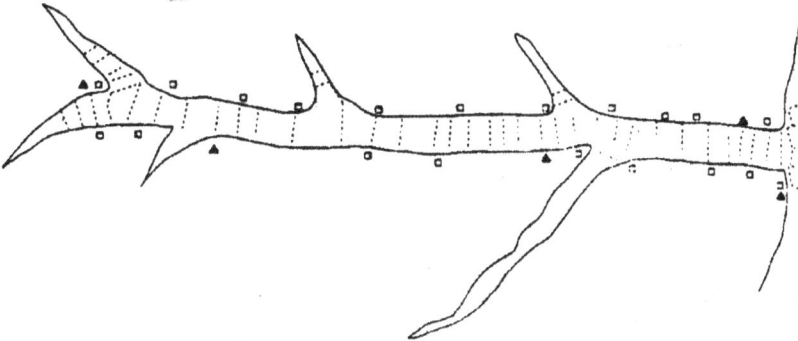

FIGURE 6.4 Models of rural development in the main zone of wadi farming: (a) initial stage (first–second centuries AD) based on estates at favored locations only; b) evolved system (third–early fourth centuries AD), with eventual infilling between initial estates and replacement of some open farms with fortified farms; (c) less likely alternative initial model envisaging equal partition of landscape and relative equality of status of all wadi farmers.

colonies of Roman veterans on some of this confiscated and centuriated land (Corinth, Pattras, Carthage, etc.

The short-term effects of Roman conquest and assimilation into the provincial structures were undeniably traumatic in both Africa and Achaia. Yet Susan Alcock's evidence suggests that the longer-term manifestation of Roman government in Achaia does not reveal a significant recovery of population or economy until the late Roman period. In Africa, there are signs of significant growth in urban and rural settlement from the first century AD, perhaps reaching peak levels in the second to fourth centuries.

The Roman Empire was not run on altruistic lines; it developed mechanisms for the exploitation of land and people. It would be implausible, therefore, to suggest that there was a master plan for the creation of landscapes of opportunity. However, the combination of several factors may have been particularly important in shaping the outcome in Roman Africa. First, the extraction of agricultural surpluses for the *annona*, which though undoubtedly exploitative of the province, may over time have offered greater possibilities for local profit-taking and for capital investment in agricultural expansion. I suggest that trade from Africa was initially substantially based on carriage of *annona* cargoes, but later expanded well beyond it. We may note, in passing, the coincidental timing of the resurgence of Greek rural settlement following the creation of an *annona* system to feed Constantinople and the consequent relocation of trade routes. Second, the presence of a military garrison in Africa may have helped to stimulate production in the interior of Numidia and the Regio Tripolitana.[60] A third factor is the partnerships that were possible between landowner and sharecropper under the Mancian or similar sharecropping tenancies, linking elite capital investment in processing facilities on their estates (for example, oileries) with investment by the tenant in land clearance, trees, irrigation walls, and the like. Fourth, one might consider the social novelty of the situations created by imperialism in parts of Africa. Peoples that had been only partly sedentarized hitherto came to accept significant changes in their lifestyle, with their traditional leaders commonly emerging as major landowners. I would suggest that many Africans, and not just those at the highest elite level, perceived opportunity. Whether all of them were correct in their estimation of the situation is irrelevant. The degree of indigenous participation in creating new landscapes may reflect a different type of negotiation and a broader level of accommodation between Rome and its subjects in Africa than was the case in Greece. What is clear from both the Libyan Valleys Survey and from the evidence of the Albertini Tablets, for instance, is that new

[60] Fentress 1979, 176–87; Mattingly 1995, 152–53.

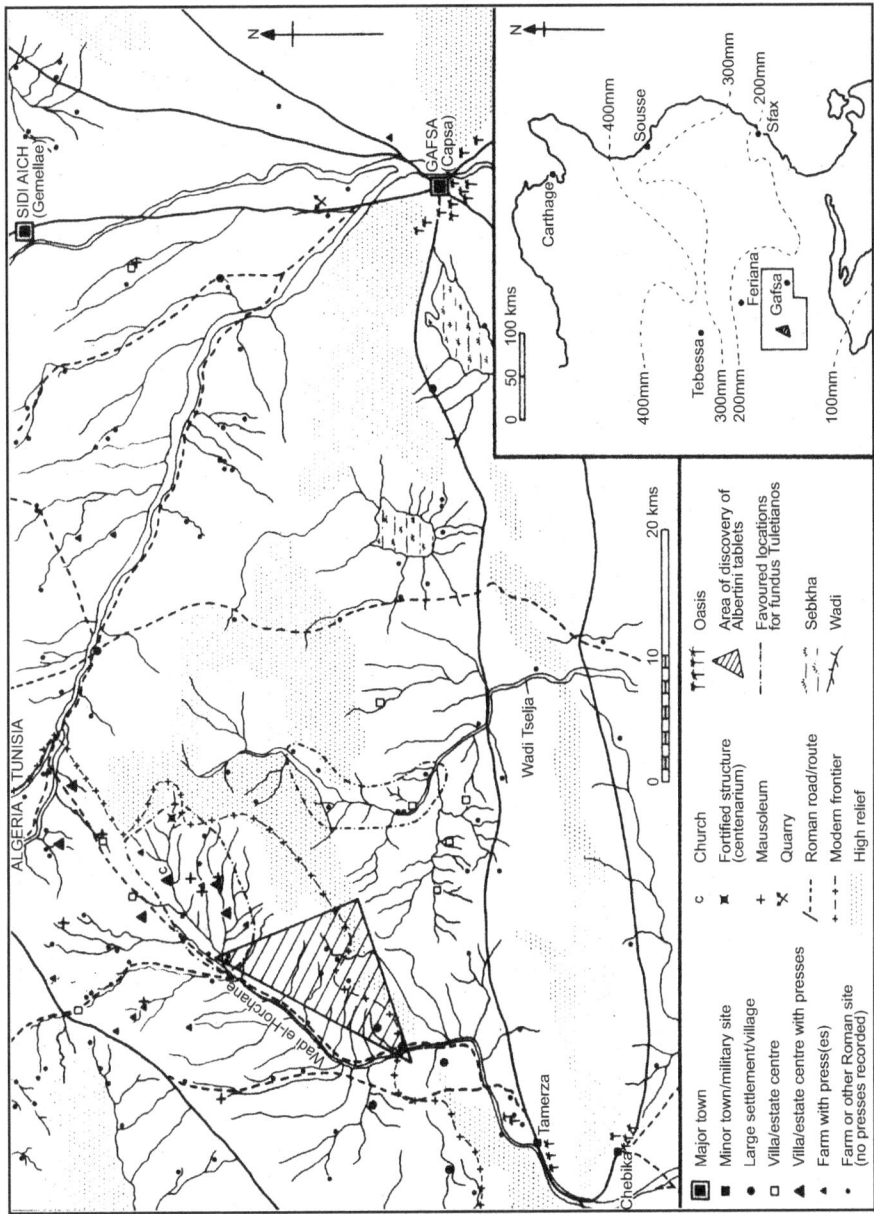

FIGURE 6.5 The approximate findspot of the Albertini Tablets in relation to archaeological knowledge of agricultural estates. These wadi farms are reminiscent of those in the Libyan pre-desert.

structures of landholding based on estates were a crucial element of the imperial landscapes that emerged in many areas of the province. In the Tripolitanian pre-desert, the evidence favors the view that the evolution of the floodwater farms was achieved through Roman authority over the region, creating the conditions for a drastically unequal division of land within existing Libyan communities and leading to the formation of elite-run estates (see fig. 6.4).[61] Similar archaeological traces exist in the pre-desert landscape from which the Albertini Tablets originated, close to the Tunisian/Algerian border, reinforcing the links between text and archaeology (see fig. 6.5).[62]

My conclusion would be that no one factor can be pin-pointed as critical. Imperial discourse involved a complex interplay between the different aims and aspirations of the principal actors against a background of drastically unequal power relations. The choice of Africans to moderate a tendency for resistance in favor of increased participation was a dynamic outcome. But this was not a simple opposition between accommodation and resistance. Postcolonial studies would do well to explore the interplay of resistance and accommodation, and the gradations of behavior in between, rather than simply to promote the significance of evidence for the former. That is what I would characterize as the discrepant experience of empire.

[61] Mattingly 1997c, 168–73.

[62] Cf. Mattingly 1989a (from which the map included in the present volume as fig. 6.5 was originally omitted through the error of the publisher).

CHAPTER SEVEN

Metals and *Metalla*

ROMAN COPPER-MINING LANDSCAPE IN THE
WADI FAYNAN, JORDAN

MINING AND METAL PRODUCTION IN THE ROMAN EMPIRE

The prospect of increasing state revenues may not have been the prime motor of imperial expansion, but the Roman state and its ruling order became adept at exploiting the opportunities that conquest and domination afforded them. Indeed, this was a necessity for the maintenance and prolongation of the empire. Just sustaining an army of 500,000 men should have been challenge enough; but the Roman Empire was extraordinarily profligate in other ways.[1] Conspicuous consumption at the center ran at a terrifying level (whether on the imperial court, on the building schemes of emperors, or on luxuries and status symbols in elite society). This was an empire whose elite class allegedly spent up to 100 million sesterces on the annual trade for eastern exotics.[2] It is no wonder that Rome was known as Daqin in fourth-century China—literally, "treasure country."[3] A particular problem with this sector of the extraprovincial economy was that it was extra-empire, too, and took wealth beyond the range of state taxation. How did the Roman Empire make good the loss of specie beyond its borders? One measure, of course, was to tax the Eastern import trade more highly than other interregional trade (25 percent instead of 5 percent). However, that still left a substantial potential trade gap, represented by a large net outflow of gold and silver coinage.

Mining and metallurgy were key operations used by Rome to plug this gap. The scale of Roman mining activity is demonstrated by the emerging picture of global pollution registered in the Greenland ice cores (see

Versions of this chapter have been delivered as lectures or at various conferences in Oxford, Leicester, St. Andrews, and London, England and Aberystwyth, Wales.

[1] Comparison with the Chinese empire may be instructive to set this profligacy in perspective; see Portal 2007. At the very least, the Roman emperors' behavior does not seem to have been particularly unusual.

[2] Pliny, *Natural History*, 6.101, 12.84; De Romanis and Tchernia 1997; Tomber 2008.

[3] Ying 2004.

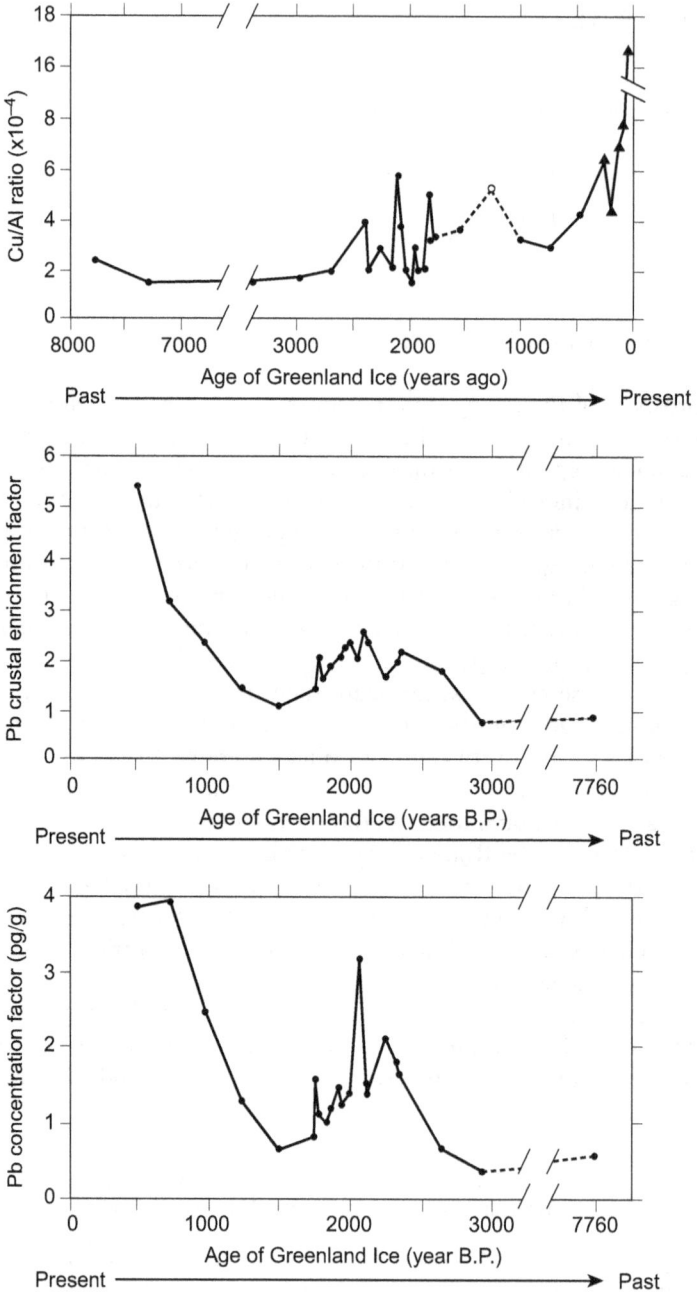

FIGURE 7.1 Summary charts of the Greenland ice-core data on hemispheric copper and lead pollution levels, showing significant peaks in the Roman era. (Redrawn from Hong et al. 1994.)

FIGURE 7.2 The largest of several hundred known Spanish gold mines; the main opencast mine at Las Medulas is 2–2.5 kilometers across.

fig. 7.1).[4] Analysis of the ice cores has revealed that fresh layers of ice are formed each year and that by counting back, the ice can be accurately dated, much as tree rings. The chemical analysis of ice across time has now shown that the major pre–Industrial Revolution peak in hemispheric pollution occurred in the Roman period, with notable peaks in both copper and lead.[5]

The evidence of mining and quarrying in the Roman world is cumulatively impressive, but difficult to evaluate in quantifiable ways.[6] It is clear from analysis of literary and epigraphic data that Rome did not have a single centralized bureau for the management of mines and quarries but a range of provincial posts was created over time to deal with particular local circumstances. There were inevitably some strong similarities in regional practice, but no overall blueprint.[7]

Literary and archaeological evidence for the scale of mining fills out the picture. We are told that the mines in Spain yielded 36 million sesterces annually in the second century BC.[8] By the first century AD, the

[4] While the hemispheric pollution represented on Greenland could have implicated China, India and Parthia/Persia also, there is general agreement that the Roman contribution to this pollution picture was likely to have been large.

[5] Hong et al. 1994, 1996. See Wilson 2007 for reflections on the implications of this for Roman metallurgical production.

[6] Mines: Davies 1935; Domergue 1990, 2008; Orejas 2001, 2003. Quarries: Maxfield 2001; Maxfield and Peacock 2001a, 2001b; Peacock and Maxfield 1997, 2007.

[7] Hirt 2004; Granino Cecerere and Morizio 2007.

[8] Polybius, *Histories*, 34.9.9; Strabo, *Geography*, 3.2.10.

substantial gold fields of northwest Spain were contributing 20,000 pounds (over 6 metric tons) of gold a year, the equivalent of about 85 million sesterces.[9] The Las Medulas mining complex was the largest of more than 230 gold mining sites in northwestern Spain, and its scale illustrates the human dimension of this activity (see fig. 7.2).[10] The main opencast mine here was about 2–2.5 kilometers across and more than 100 meters deep—almost certainly the largest preindustrial, constructed hole on the planet. The deposits of gangue and other mine waste were spread across 5.7 square kilometers around the 5.39 square kilometers of opencast mines. The extraction of over 93.5 million cubic meters of the landscape here was assisted by impressive hydraulic technology, with mountain-ridge aqueducts traversing over 100 kilometers of incredibly difficult terrain to reach the vast header tanks at the top of the Las Medulas mine.[11]

However, the large scale and sophisticated technologies of early imperial mining operations masks a paradox. One of the great anomalies of the Roman economy is the fact that many of the Spanish mines went out of production or declined markedly in scale by the later second century AD.[12] The same is also true of mining activity in many other provinces—initial large activity that was not sustained on the same scale into later antiquity.

Table 7.1 illustrates some of the potential changes in the fiscal policies of the empire from the Late Republican era until the late fifth century AD. A key question that arises here concerns why an imperial power would tolerate a massive reduction over time in its capacity to make good through mining a recurrent shortfall in the availability of metal for coinage. Yet that is what seems to have occurred in the Roman Empire. From a peak in the first and second centuries AD, Roman mining productivity appears to have declined significantly thereafter, a position exacerbated by the loss of the Dacian gold mines in the late third century.[13] This does not mean that the empire no longer had need for generating reserves of precious metals, and mining certainly continued at a large scale in some regions (as the Faynan case study below illustrates). However, it seems clear on current evidence that the mining output of the late Roman Empire was considerably less than that of the High Empire. The idea that the most abundant and accessible deposits were becoming worked out can only be partly true—the medieval and early modern miners in Europe, for instance, successfully revisited many of the same deposits with essentially

---

[9] Pliny, *Natural History*, 33.4.78.

[10] Sánchez-Palencia. 2000, esp. 156–57.

[11] Sanchez Palencia 2000, 189–207; cf. also, Sanchez Palencia et al. 1996.

[12] See Wilson 2007 for a good discussion of the archaeological, epigraphic, numismatic, and environmental data.

[13] Hanson and Haynes 2004; Oltean 2007.

TABLE 7.1
Revenue streams, availability of metals and coinage

Phase	Sources of revenue	Sources of metals for coinage	Problems affecting coinage supply
LATE REPUBLIC	Ad hoc taxation, conquests yield lands and booty	Some mining, treasure from conquests, tax coin, payments for contracts	Limits on state control of mines, mint infrastructure
EARLY PRINCIPATE	More regularized taxation, rents and dues, diminished wars/conquests, state exploitation of natural resources, land sales	Huge mining investment, payments of tax, dues and other contracts, diminished chances of booty, progressive reductions in purity of coinage	Higher costs of military, luxury trade with east, slow-up of wars of conquest
THIRD CENTURY	Taxation, rents and dues, diminished exploitation of natural resources	Few mines, higher emphasis on recycling tax coinage, massive debasement of coin purity	Revenue losses due to civil wars and "barbarian" invasions, higher cost of army, loss of mining capacity and noninvestment in replacement, payment of subsidies to barbarian peoples, loss of coinage from circulation in emergency hoards
CONSTANTINE	Taxation, rents and dues, confiscations from estates of enemies and of pagan temple treasures, booty from civil wars	Fiscal reforms and influx of treasure allowed new standard for coinage. Higher taxes, few active mines	Continued loss of mining capacity, loss of coin into nonrecovered hoards during civil wars, subsidies and extraempire trade continue
FOURTH CENTURY AND LATER	Taxation, rents and dues	Higher taxes, few active mines	Continued loss of mining capacity, subsidies and extraempire trade continue, periodic debasements to coinage

similar technology.[14] What this suggests is that the later Roman Empire put greater emphasis on other methods of securing the supply of coinage needed for the imperial budget.

We need to distinguish here between apparent cycles of economic decline and the application of different strategies to the problem of producing/raising specie. In the Early Principate the solution was to embark on remarkable, but costly, mining operations; in later Roman times the emphasis had shifted somewhat to the alternatives of exacting higher levels of tax, debasing the purity of the coinage and translating part of the cost of the army into payments in kind. Taxation in kind also became more

[14] Bartels et al. 2008, 113–96.

significant in some regions. Prospecting and developing mineral resources was expensive and not necessarily productive in full proportion to the effort expended. Costs tended to rise over time because mining worked out the most accessible deposits, necessitating deeper and more dangerous galleries. Fundamentally, then, the scaling down of mining activity does not indicate a collapse of Rome's attempts to exploit resources; rather, this represents a refocusing of attention onto other forms of exploitation and other resources. This is surely reflected more generally by the increased evidence for state intervention in economic activity from the time of Diocletian onward, as indicated by maximum price edicts, state-run workshops for army supply, enforcing hereditary occupations, and so on.[15] The empire may also have attempted to make up some of the shortfall in precious metals by importing gold from West Africa via the Saharan trade routes.[16]

MINING AND THE COLONIAL BODY

Study of the mining regions also illuminates the human dimension of the Roman Empire's exploitation of resources. Even with water to assist with the moving and washing of ore-bearing deposits at Las Medulas, that mine must have involved the labor of a huge number of people in scenes that can best be imagined from the photographs by Sebastião Salgado of the Brazilian gold mine of the Serra Palada—a modern relic of preindustrial labor conditions (see fig. 7.3).[17] How was this labor mobilized and paid for? The common assumption is that such mines involved a combination of salaried free labor and forced labor, particularly in the form of criminals condemned to the *metalla* for serious offenses. However, other forms of labor exploitation are also to be expected in Roman mining districts. Some degree of forced labor may have been more generally imposed as *munera* (required duties) on whole communities. In some of the main mining areas of the empire it is likely that the provision of labor was an obligation imposed by Roman peace settlements with local peoples—especially as in northwestern Iberia where armed resistance had been protracted. Studies of the settlement pattern around the northern Spanish mines suggest a significant level of reorganization of local communities to support the mining activity—a point now backed up by the discovery of an edict of Augustus from El Bierzo.[18] This document details

---

[15] Garnsey and Whittaker 1998.

[16] Garrard 1982; cf. Wilson 2007, 122–23, for an up-to-date review of the evidence.

[17] Salgado 1993.

[18] Sanchez-Palencia 2000, 252–306. For the edict, see Sanchez-Palencia and Mangas 2000.

FIGURE 7.3 A glimpse of preindustrial labor conditions? Brazilian gold mine at Serra Palada. (Photograph © Sebastião Salgado / Amazonas Images).

the favorable treatment of one small community (the Castellani Paemeio-brigenses of the Susari) who had not joined a rebellion against Rome. The clear implication is that other communities were harshly penalized and that Rome's exploitation of this region involved not only natural resources but human labor as well.[19]

Roman mines and quarries provide evidence of other forms of violence to the body. The *metalla* attained the direst repute through the writings of Christian accounts of martyrdoms, but they operated across longer time frames and against a broader range of people deemed socially unfit. The committal of people for extreme punishment was clearly designed to be exemplary and in addition to the customary floggings inflicted on people before they were even sent to the *metalla*, there were additional indignities such as being shackled, having marks tattooed or branded on the forehead, the head being half-shaved. In extreme cases people were emasculated, blinded in one eye, or maimed in one leg.[20]

However, the ugliness of imperial exploitation of people in such places went beyond visible marks on the bodies of slave workers or the mass imposition of some degree of forced labor on communities. The hundreds of imperial mines in Spain and elsewhere must also have relied heavily on free labor, in much the same way that gold and diamond mines in southern Africa lure workers with promises of higher than average wages, but at the cost of drastically shortened life-expectancy. The deliberate, accidental, and incidental side effects of Rome's exploitation of resources all had a sociopolitical as well as an economic dimension. They serve to illustrate the way in which subject people experienced the imperial economy in a physical way.

Introduction to the Wadi Faynan

The rest of this chapter will present a single case study of a Roman imperial mining operation (*metalla*) as an example of the potential environmental and human consequences of large-scale Roman metal production. As such, it stands for many instances of Rome's exploitation of the key natural resources of provincial territories. Tacitus, for instance, was explicit in describing the mineral resources of Britain as the "spoils of victory."[21] However, as we shall see, the consequences of Rome's pursuit of economic gain carried a high human and environmental cost. Here I

---

[19] Hingley 2005, 102–5.
[20] See Millar 1984 for an excellent overall review.
[21] Tacitus, *Agricola*, 12.6: *Fert Britannia aurum et argentum et alia metalla, pretium victoriae.*

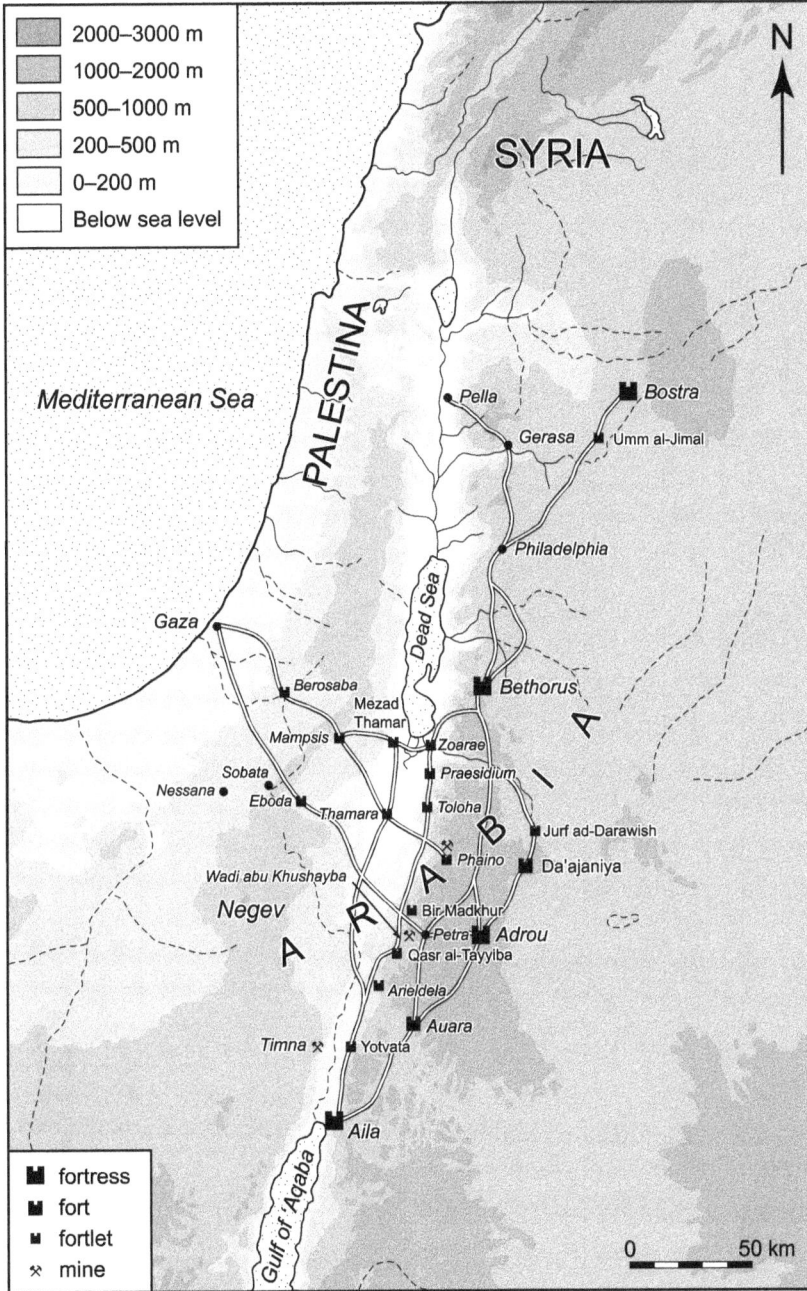

FIGURE 7.4 Map of Jordan showing mineral resources and location of Wadi Faynan, ancient Phaino. (From Barker, Gilbertson, and Mattingly 2007.)

FIGURE 7.5 Overall plan of Khirbat Faynan, ancient Phaino, showing main structures and slag heaps. (From Barker, Gilbertson, and Mattingly 2007.)

draw on the results of the Wadi Faynan landscape survey (1996–2000). Directed by Graeme Barker, David Gilbertson, and myself, this project was an interdisciplinary and diachronic investigation of evidence of environmental and climatic change, settlement pattern, and human activity.[22]

The sedimentary copper ores of southern Jordan represent one of the rare abundant copper sources in the Levant and have through many phases of prehistory and history been a key resource at the regional scale (see fig. 7.4). Copper mining on both sides of the rift valley south of the Dead Sea has a long history, with Beno Rothenberg's studies at Timna on the west side being particularly well known. But as recent work of the Deutches Bergbau-Museum has shown, the evidence from the eastern side of the Wadi Araba is, if anything, even more impressive.[23] Copper sources there have been exploited since the seventh millennium BC, with early peaks of activity in the Early Bronze Age and Iron Age. It is also clear that the Roman phase of exploitation was on a very significant scale. In the Roman phase, large tap furnaces were the norm, with separation of slag and metal within the furnace and the tapping process producing large plates of distinctive vitreous slags.

The total volume of slag at sites in the Wadi Faynan region far exceeds the quantities reported by Rothenberg for Timna or recorded at the lesser Jordanian sites in Wadi Abu Kusheiba.[24] Andreas Hauptman and his collabrators have estimated that the slag heaps at the four largest Iron Age production sites contain a total of over 100,000 metric tons of slag, representing perhaps 6,500–13,000 metric tons of copper. Although there appears to have been a decline in production in the late Iron Age and early Nabataean period, there is some evidence to suggest continuing or reviving mining activity under the Nabataean kingdom.[25] Roman interest in annexing the Nabataean kingdom under Trajan may have been influenced by knowledge of the copper resources. In the Roman period, the smelting of copper is thought to have been particularly concentrated at the site of Khirbat Faynan (ancient Phaino), where Hauptman estimates that about 40,000–70,000 metric tons of slag and 2,500–7,000 metric tons of Roman copper were produced (see fig. 7.5).[26] It appears that ore was brought into the smelters at Khirbat Faynan from quite a

[22] See Barker, Gilbertson, and Mattingly 2007 for the published final report; see also Barker 2000, 2002; Barker and Mattingly 2007; and Barker, Gilbertson, and Mattingly 1997, 1998, 1999, 2000 for interim statements and other relevant publications.

[23] On the impressive work of the Deutches Bergbau-Museum see, among others, Hauptmann 2000, 2007; on Timna, see Rothenberg 1999a, 1999b.

[24] Hauptmann 2007, 94–109; Hauptman et al. 1992, 3, 21.

[25] Barker, Gilbertson, and Mattingly 2007, 291–303.

[26] Hauptmann 2000, 97; 2007, 52–53, 147.

Legend:

- Major site (■)
- Other site (●)
- Tower (+)
- Mine (✕)
- Modern settlement (○)
- Main route (——)

Elevation:
- >1000 m
- 500–1000 m
- 400–500 m
- 300–400 m
- 200–300 m
- 100–200 m
- 0–100 m
- –100–0 m
- Below –100 m

Map labels: N, Gaza, Wadi 'Arabah, Wadi Fidan, Wadi-Fidan 50, Jabal Hamrat Fidan, QUARAYQIRA, Wadi Faynan, WF1415, Wadi al-Abyad, Qalb Ratiye, WF1, WF2, WF3, WF4, WF11, Khirbat Faynan, Wadi Shayqar, Wadi Ghuwayr, DANA, Wadi Dana, Mountains of Edom, 'Aqaba, Umm al-Amad, 0 — 4 km

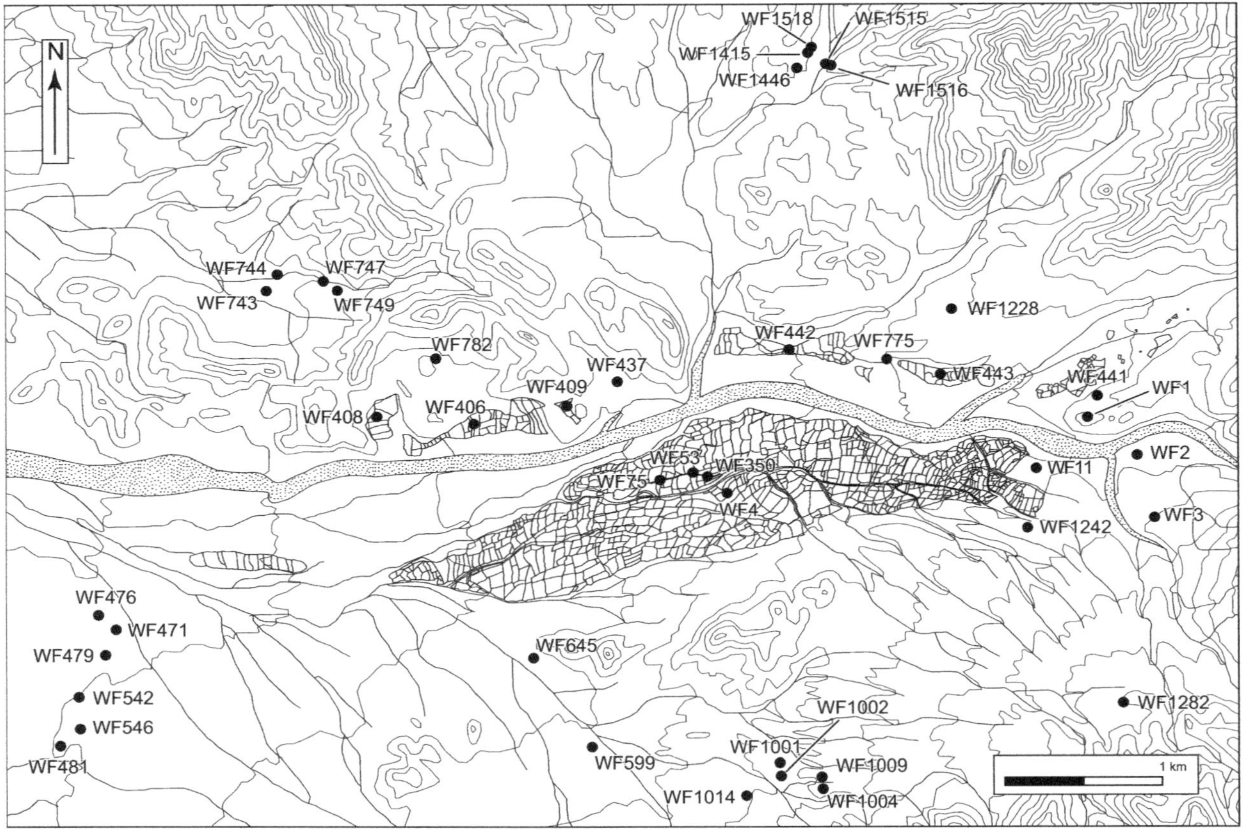

FIGURE 7.6 (a) and (b) The Wadi Faynan in Roman and Byzantine times, showing the location of the mines, the mining control site (Khirbat Ratiye WF1415), the smelting and administrative center (Khirbat Faynan WF1) and the field system (WF4). (From Barker, Gilbertson, and Mattingly 2007).

large region and not simply from the nearest cluster of mines, located a few kilometers to the north.

Phaino was set back from the main Roman road up the Wadi Araba, linking the Red Sea port of Aqaba (Ailat) and the Dead Sea (see fig. 7.4). It was the terminus of an eastward spur of the route that ran across the Negev connecting the Mediterranean port of Giza with the Wadi Araba road. The mining center sat just at the mountain front, where tracks ascend to the Jordanian plateau, on top of which ran the major eastern frontier roads and the routes connecting Petra with the trans-Jordanian cities.[27] The site was thus both isolated, but tied into Roman communications networks. As this region comprised a pre-desert environment in Roman times (as today), the location presented considerable challenges for maintaining and supplying a substantial mining and smelting workforce.

The Archaeology of the Mining Landscape

The Wadi Faynan survey concentrated on an area of just over 30 square kilometers of landscape, with some reconnaissance beyond—notably to locate the more remote mining sites.[28] Over 1,500 archaeological structures have been recorded in this small zone, allowing our team to construct a multiperiod analysis of settlement, mineral exploitation, land use, and environmental change.[29] The mines themselves are focused in several groups, with the main cluster just to the north and northeast of the main Roman smelting sites (see fig. 7.6). Detailed survey and classification of the workings, which comprise extensive shafts, adits, and galleries has been carried out by the Bochum mining museum, but the results are still only partially published.[30]

The mining works are far harder to date than production sites, and many of the more obvious adits and shafts may well have been exploited in more than one phase of extraction. Some of the most impressive evidence is found in the Wadi Khalid and the Qalb Ratiye about 1–3 kilometers north of the Wadi Faynan. The main Roman mines appear to have targeted low-grade massive brown sandstone (MBS) ores in the

[27] Freeman 2001, 433–44; Talbert 2000, maps 70–71; Tsafrir, Di Segni, and Green 1994.

[28] See Barker, Gilbertson, and Mattingly 2007, 3–57, for the topography of Faynan and the background to the survey.

[29] See Barker, Gilbertson, and Mattingly 2007, 98–140, for an overview of site typology, and 305–48 for a summary of the Roman and Byzantine evidence.

[30] Weisgerber 1989, 1996, 2003; a general listing of the Bochum Bergbau Museum's surveys of mining and smelting sites is provided in Hauptmann 2000, 62–100, and 2007, 85–156. Cf. Willies 1991 for a detailed survey of a Roman mine close to Timna.

FIGURE 7.7 The Umm al-Amad mine gallery.

Qalb Ratiye, 2 kilometers north of Khirbat Faynan and at Umm al-Amad in the mountains to the south of the Faynan. The higher-grade dolomite-limestone-shale (DLS) ores previously exploited in the Bronze Age and Iron Age mining phases are believed by Hauptmann to have been worked out by this date, leading to the switch. However, some Roman ceramics and coins have been noted around mines in the Wadis Dana, Khalid and al-Abyad; when linked with the Nabataean/Roman date of the addition of a third shaft at a double-shaft Iron Age mine in the Wadi Khalid, this strongly suggests that there was some additional reworking of the DLS ore beds. However, the distinctive pollution signature of the Roman-period smelting activity indicates that the Roman mining operations overall focused predominantly on the MBS ore-beds.[31]

There is no doubt that the landscape impact of the mining activity has been considerable, as can be seen by the large deposits of mine tailings (waste) in the minor channels and the bed of the Wadi Dana and in other tributaries of the Wadi Faynan running down from the escarpment where the major exposures of the mineral-rich strata occurred.

To give some idea of the scale of the enterprise, I shall briefly describe the largest known mine chamber, which lies high in the mountains about 12 kilometers south of Khirbat Faynan. The entrance to Umm al-Amad

[31] On the pollution signatures and the ores, see Barker, Gilbertson, and Mattingly 2007, 311–12, 340–43.

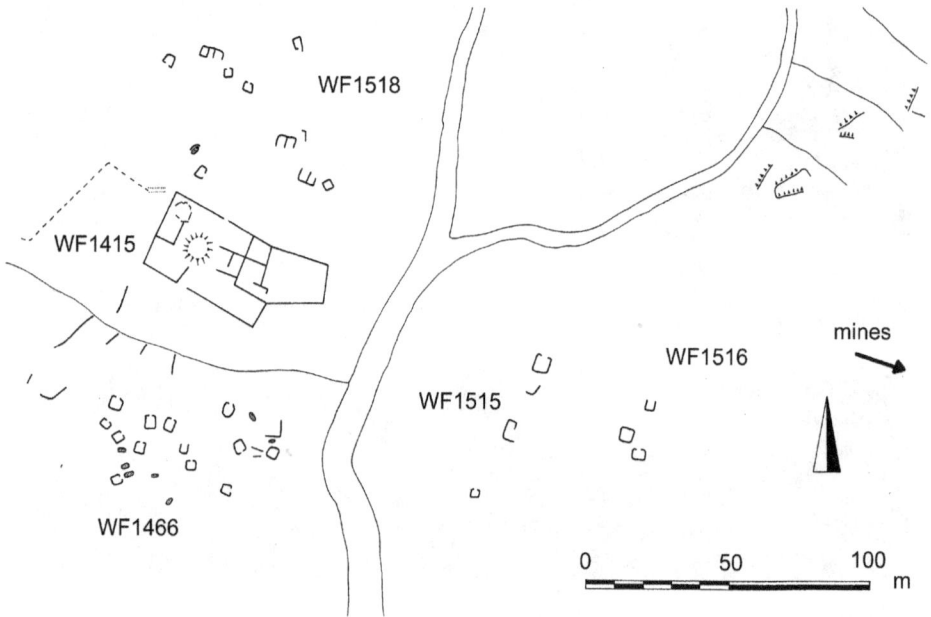

FIGURE 7.8 Plan of Khirbat Ratiye and associated structures—probably housing for the mine workforce. (From Barker, Gilbertson, and Mattingly 2007.)

(Mother of the Pillars) comprises a low slit supported on piers of un-quarried rock in a near sheer cliff face. On my first visit in 1998, enter-ing the mine involved a flat-out crawl over a dense layer of smouldering goat droppings, through acrid smoke—a truly unforgettable experience. Once inside, the chamber roof heightens, opening into a vast main gallery (120m x 55m, and up to 2.5m high) supported on rows of undug rock arches (see fig. 7.7). The impression is breathtaking.[32]

The archaeology of the Wadi Faynan focuses on Khirbat Faynan (WF1), the large settlement at the junction of the three main tributaries of the upper Wadi Faynan—the Wadis Dana, Ghuwayr, and Shayqar (see fig. 7.6)—with an impressive group of associated sites: the South Cem-etery, an aqueduct, a water pool and mill, slag heaps, and an extensive field system that extends down the Wadi Faynan to the west (WF4). This site is without doubt to be identified with ancient Phaino, the center of Roman copper mining in the Jordanian desert.[33] The preserved remains have the character of a mining town, ornamented in late antiquity with a

---

[32] Hauptmann 2000, 94–95; cf. Barker, Gilbertson, and Mattingly 2007, 311, figs. 10.3–10.4.

[33] Lagrange 1898; 1900.

series of churches—these latter reflecting the fact that it became a focus of pilgrimage following the martyrdom of Christians there during the Great Persecution.[34] At Khirbat Faynan itself, the extensive and dense settlement suggests an urban center with a fortified administrative building at its center (see fig. 7.5).[35]

The Qalb Ratiye mines were controlled by a large fortified building Khirbat Ratiye (WF1415), again suggesting the presence of some soldiers and a small bureaucracy, while the simple huts gathered around the enclosure may well have housed the miners themselves (see fig. 7.8).[36] Although major settlement concentrates on the two Khirbats, some smaller settlements are dispersed across the landscape. A number of village-like settlements are known close to the mountain face and some of these could potentially have housed miners and mining-related personnel.[37] On the other hand, some well-built farms that had existed in the landscape in the Nabataean period appear to have been abandoned—perhaps a sign of increased centralization of land and control in the valley.[38]

Smelting activity in the landscape was quite widely dispersed in the Bronze Age and Iron Age periods, but in the Roman period, smelting appears to have been almost exclusively concentrated at Khirbat Faynan, where the main visible slag heaps are of Roman date. The implications of this are important, as Roman activity is attested at a number of separate mining sites—from where the ore was evidently transported for centralized processing. The thick-walled furnaces and large tap slags of the Roman period indicate very intensive and large-scale production.[39]

The great field system WF4, covering over 100 hectares (250 acres) and extending over 5 kilometers west from the Khirbat Faynan, was already partially developed in pre-Roman times.[40] A series of "Nabataean" farms have been located in connection with discrete subareas of the overall field system. Analysis of surface pottery suggests that these sites did not continue in occupation into the Roman period. One possible interpretation of this is that the control of land was also centralized and unified under Rome, with farming henceforth carried out by people based in the main settlement at Phaino.[41] The technology of the runoff and floodwater farming systems here was designed to combat the essential background aridity and sustain a level of agriculture normally reserved for a

[34] Sartre 1993, 139–42.
[35] Barker, Gilbertson, and Mattingly 2007, 313–19.
[36] Ibid., 319–21.
[37] Ibid.,, 321–25.
[38] Ibid., 295–301, 325.
[39] Ibid., 313, 321.
[40] Ibid., 140–74, 295–301, 327–33.
[41] Ibid., 327–31.

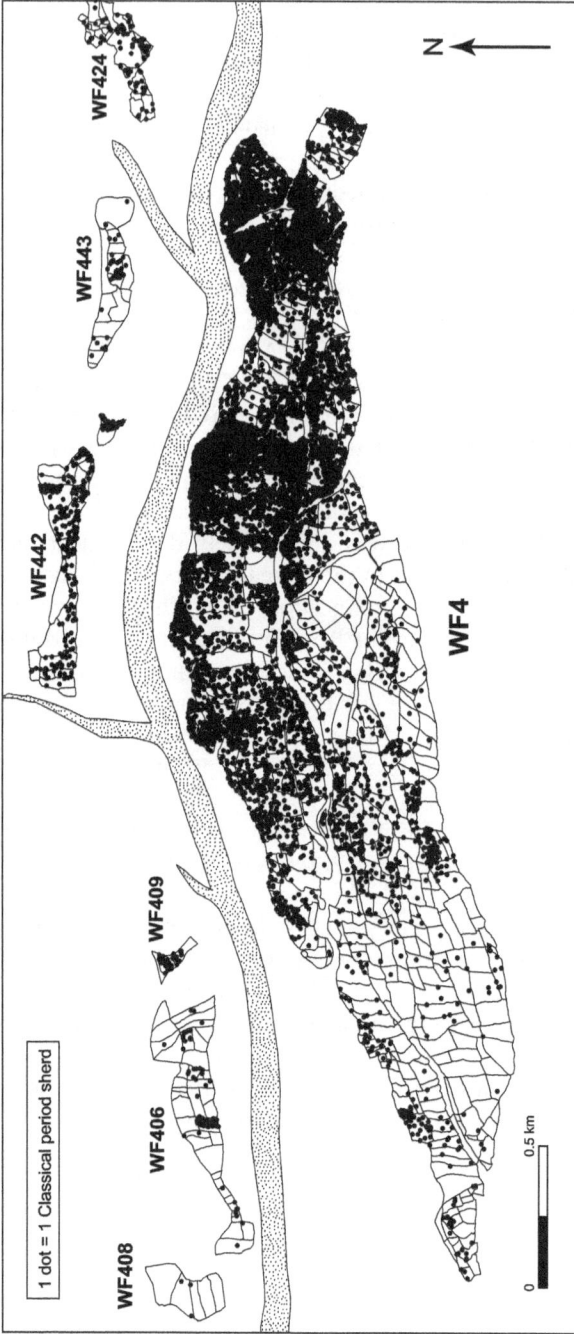

FIGURE 7.9 Shard density within the Roman/Byzantine developed field system. The high concentrations of shards, especially in the northern fields, almost certainly indicate intense manuring of the prime agricultural land to try to counteract declining productivity of the land as a result of intense industrial pollution. The southern fields are more steeply terraced and were probably exploited primarily for vines and olives. (From Barker, Gilbertson, and Mattingly 2007.)

better-watered zone. Productivity was thus artificially raised above the normal carrying capacity of such a landscape, but in so marginal a zone its long term maintenance was fragile. A peculiarity of the field system is that large parts of it are carpeted in dense ceramic scatters of broadly Roman-Byzantine date, despite the absence of substantial dwellings of this phase within the fields (see fig. 7.9).[42] The explanation for this anomalously high shard density lies in the pollution history of the Roman landscape.

The archaeological character of the Roman settlement and activity appears to have been very different to that of the Bronze Age, Iron Age, and Nabataean periods and appears to testify to a high degree of centralized control. The new evidence of this archaeological landscape can now be compared with the scant historical documentation about the area.

THE HISTORICAL CONTEXT

As has been noted already, Khirbat Faynan is almost certainly to be identified with ancient Phaino, the infamous center of Roman copper mining in the Jordanian desert and scene of horrific persecution of Christians in the fourth century AD.[43] Little is known of the site before it entered Eusebius's account of the Great Persecution, but it was clearly at that date under imperial control and being managed as part of the *res privata* of the emperor. It is plausible, though at present unprovable, that the copper mines had been taken into state ownership at the time of the Roman annexation of Nabataea in AD 106—ore deposits were one of the key resources that drove imperial expansion (and helped pay for it). The essential story of the Roman period in the Wadi Faynan region is thus that of an imperial power refashioning a landscape in order to exploit its resources. As we shall see, the nature of the Roman settlement and activity falls outside the norms of what one might expect of such a region. The operation of Rome's imperial economy can be read in the landscape that resulted.

When they annexed the Nabataean kingdom in AD 106,[44] the Romans would already have known that the exploitation of copper was well established in Faynan, and the abundance of Nabataean wares and an apparent Nabataean date for extensive parts of the large field system show that support infrastructures were in place.[45] Nonetheless, it seems clear

[42] Barker, Gilbertson, and Mattingly 2007, 166–69.

[43] Sartre 1993, 139–42.

[44] For another client kingdom taken down by Rome under suspicious circumstances, see chapter 3 of the present volume.

[45] Barker, Gilbertson, and Mattingly 2007, 293–94, figs 9.19–9.20.

that imperial incorporation led to an intensification and reorganization of metal production here that was to have profound consequences. First, let us consider the practicalities of the Roman takeover of the mines and of the settlement of Phaino. The Roman state claimed ownership of all significant mineral deposits and decorative stones,[46] though the exploitation of these was variously handled. Sometimes, the imperial monopoly was strictly maintained by the direct management of mining activities by imperial officials (military prefects or civil procurators), in other cases the rights of exploitation were leased to private companies, who contracted with the state to hand over a fixed percentage of the output.[47]

A good example of the former type of control concerns the extraordinary measures put into effect to exploit the granites and porphry of the Eastern Egyptian desert.[48] The scale, complexity and expense of the enterprise there is revealed by the establishment and maintenance of quarries, slipways and workshops, forts and fortlets, settlements for workers, animal feeding stations, wells, tracks and roads, and massive wheeled vehicles to transport 200–metric ton columns across the desert to the Nile.[49] The research has also highlighted the need to assemble and provision a very large and skilled workforce. The documentary records of the quarry sites, in the form of many *ostraca* (documents written in ink on pottery shards) on site and associated papyrological evidence, reveal a high level of organization of everything from orders for bread to the requisitioning of hundreds of draft animals (principally camels) from settlements along the Nile and in the Fayum.[50] They also demonstrate that most of the quarry workers were paid wage earners not the slaves or forced labor of popular imagination.[51] The palaeobotanical studies of Marijke van der Veen have demonstrated that the diet of many of the people at the quarries was better than had been previously imagined (when a predominantly slave labor force was envisaged) but the vast bulk of those foodstuffs were evidently produced in the Nile Valley several days journey to the west and imported.[52] Fish bones indicate that some commodities were also obtained from the Red Sea ports on the coast to the east of the mines. The pottery assemblages are also revealing of the supply mechanisms of an imperial operation.[53] What the Egyptian quarries highlight

---

[46] Suetonius, *Tiberius*, 49.2.
[47] Hirt 2004.
[48] Maxfield and Peacock 2001a, 2001b; Peacock and Maxfield 1997, 2007.
[49] See Maxfield 2001, 2003, for succinct summary accounts.
[50] Adams 2001 details the complex arrangements made for requisitioning animals.
[51] Cuvigny 1996.
[52] Van der Veen 1998, 2001; Van der Veen and Tabinor 2007.
[53] Tomber 1996.

are the lengths and expense that the Roman state was prepared to go to control the supply of both everyday necessities and of selected high-status commodities.

It is likely that the organization of the Faynan copper mines was not dissimilar in type, if not in every detail. There is certainly every indication that Phaino was one of the largest mining centers in the Roman eastern Mediterranean and was almost certainly under direct imperial control judging by late Roman references to Christians being condemned to work in the mines there. But unlike the Egyptian desert, there is no trace here of a major military camp at the heart of the mining district, though the literary sources imply the presence of some troops. The scale of the major buildings at Khirbat Faynan and Khirbat Ratiye suggest that we are dealing with fortlets manned by small groups of troops and this has implications for the nature of the workforce—commonly assumed to have primarily comprised slaves and forced labor.

The historical documentation, centered on two works of Eusebius of Caesarea, paints an horrific picture of Roman judicial savagery against the Christians sent to Phaino.[54] It is important to put the use of condemned labor in Roman mines into context, as the popular image derived from the sensational accounts of writers such as Eusebius is misleading in certain respects: "Of the martyrs in Palestine, Silvanus, bishop of the churches about Gaza, was beheaded at the copper mine at Phaino with others, in number forty save one; and Egyptians there, Peleus and Nilus, bishops, together with others endured death by fire."[55]

In AD 302, Diocletian and Maximian wrote to the proconsul of Africa instructing him to ignore customary rules of status in dealing with Manicheens—contrary to normal practice, if guilty, even rich people were to be sent to the mines of Phaino or the imperial quarries of Proconnesos. This demonstrates that Phaino was certainly under imperial control at that date, and evidently one of the larger mining centers in the east. But we should note that condemning people to the mines was conceived primarily as an extreme punishment (a deferred death sentence). In a later persecution of the mid-fourth century, the Arians in Alexandria "demanded that ... [Eutychius, a subdeacon] should be sent away to the mines; and not simply to any mine but to that of Phaino where even a condemned murderer is hardly able to live a few days."[56] Some groups of Christians were physically disabled before being shipped there, some

[54] Eusebius, *Martyrs of Palestine* (*MP*) and *Ecclesiastical History* (*EH*). See Gustafson 1994 for a discussion of the literary evidence but lacking knowledge of the archaeological correlates.

[55] Eusebius, *EH*, 8.13.5.

[56] Athanasius, *Orations against the Arians*, 60.765–66.

being lamed, others emasculated.[57] Another group of Christians sent from Egypt had the left leg tendon severed and the right eye gouged out before arriving at the mines.[58] A crucial aspect of such mutilation was that it made convict labor easier to supervise by a limited number of overseers or a small military contingent.

One could easily conclude that slaves and condemned prisoners made up the vast bulk of the workforce at Phaino and that the severe and extreme measures taken against Christians sent there in the period 303–13 were a normal pattern of brutality at the mines. The reality was almost certainly rather different.

The question is, how normal was the situation recorded by Eusebius? Fergus Millar's study of the legislation condemning people *ad metallum* is a valuable starting point for considering the true nature of such punishment.[59] The Roman state had possibly been sending people to Faynan as a form of capital sentence ever since the annexation of Nabataea in AD 106. My guess is that numbers may not have been particularly large per year, but Roman justice probably ensured a steady flow of people of generally low status and low importance. This practice continued into late antiquity, but it was only when Christians (including people of wealth, education, and status) entered this world, suffered martyrdom, and were subsequently remembered by hagiographers such as Eusebius, that the spotlight of history is turned on this issue. This applies not only to the Great Persecution of 303–12, but also to later persecutions of Catholics by Arian Christians in the AD 350s and again in the 360s and 370s, when the fate of educated Christians in the mines of Phaino again became a matter of record. It is equally clear that persecution of the Christians produced not simply high-profile individual victims but also unexpectedly large numbers of them in the justice system. Entire communities were arraigned, and to the surprise of the imperial authorities, refused en masse to yield to the threats and persuasions of the Roman judicial system. Given the chance to recant, and knowing the awful consequences of persisting, the more committed Christians refused to renounce their faith. This was an unanticipated outcome and the necessity of enforcing the threatened punishment—with the dispatch to the mines of hundreds of ordinary people (men, women, and children)—must have imposed a burden on the Roman system of supervised forced labor. There are thus grounds for doubting the typicality of the picture of treatment of Christians condemned to the mines.

[57] Eusebius, *MP*, 7.4.
[58] Ibid., 13.1–3.
[59] Millar 1984.

In this light, I think it is possible to reconstruct something of what occurred at the height of the persecutions from Eusebius's highly emotive account. From AD 306 onward, increasing numbers of Christians were transported from Egypt and Palestine and some at least of these were prejudicially maimed before being sent to "dig for copper."[60] At first small numbers may have been involved, but as the persecution grew in scale and intensity, it appears that large groups of Christians were sentenced en bloc to the mines at Phaino.[61] The majority of them were evidently housed there in communal "barracks."[62] It is difficult to come up with hard figures, but it appears that several hundred people may have been sent there over a five-year period and this may have presented unforeseen problems for the officials and soldiers stationed at the mine. With unprecedented numbers of condemned people being sent there, some even with their families, supervision and control of the workforce (and with it the security of the operation) could have been compromised. The maiming of some of the groups prior to dispatch to Phaino could be a consequence of this. It certainly does not seem to have been routine practice.

The presence of so many Christians, including several bishops, led to the growth of a Christian community with "houses for church assemblies,"[63] appointing its own bishop,[64] and, because they were denied written scriptures, listening to recitation by a blind Egyptian who knew them by heart.[65] It appears that those who became too old or infirm to work in the mines were allowed to live on, fasting and praying, in a separate settlement near the mines and this evidently became a special focus of the Christian community, led by the Bishop Silvanus and the blind "reader" John.[66] Despite a presumably high mortality rate, the community was periodically reinforced as new batches of Christians were sent there; in 306–7, most arrivals appear to have been from Palestine and Gaza; in 308–9 we hear of two groups from Egypt, one comprising 97 men, women, and children, and another of about 65 (detached from a group of 130 condemned Christians).

However, a major disaster befell the Christian community in AD 311, after the Roman governor of Palestine, Firmilianus, had visited Phaino and, observing the growing strength of the Christian community in

---

[60] Eusebius, *MP*, 13.1–3.
[61] Ibid., 5.2, 7.2.
[62] Ibid., 13.4.
[63] Ibid., 13.1–3.
[64] Ibid., 13.4.
[65] Ibid., 13.6–8.
[66] Ibid., 13.1, 13.9–10.

bondage there, wrote to the emperor Maximin to inform him about it.[67] The emperor then demanded a purge of the Christians at Phaino, which was carried out by the superintendent of the mines, supported by a military commander, or *dux* (presumably these were the two key imperial officials on the ground at Phaino). The measures taken included, first, the execution (by decapitation or burning) of people identified as the leaders of the Christian community—the Palestinian bishop Silvanus of Gaza and four Egyptians (two bishops, Peleus and Nilus, and two of the laity, Patermuthius and Elijah); second, the decapitation of all those who were "shattered by age or sickness in the mines, and those who were unable to work"; and, third, the dispersal of the remaining "able-bodied" Christians among a number of other mines and quarries in the Levant (Cyprus, Lebanon, Palestine).[68] The old and infirm group comprised Silvanus and thirty-nine other "confessors," who were evidently executed "in a single day," suggesting a brutal and sudden move against the Christian community at the mines.

The Christian martyr tradition at Phaino was not based, therefore, on the large number of deaths that probably occurred there as a result of injury, sickness, or routine ill-treatment. Rather it related to a specific set of historical events in AD 311, probably lasting a few days only, in which soldiers at the mines executed a number of the leading Christians, along with all those incapable of further physical work, and forcibly broke up the Christian community. It suggests that there was a realization on the part of the Roman authorities that the policy of sending Christians en masse to Phaino had been a mistake, in that it had created unexpected problems of control at a mine that lacked a major military garrison post. The effect of the purge was to break up the Christian community that had flourished in the absence of strong supervision and to eradicate those unfit for hard labor. The logical conclusion to be drawn from this is that—although used to dealing with some condemned prisoners—the mines in Faynan were not normally run as a large-scale penal colony with a big military garrison. This seems to fit with the archaeological evidence.

It is thus likely that at no time would condemned people have made up the entirety of the labor force and that normally they served hard labor alongside people who were paid good salaries (by ancient world standards) for doing specialized and often highly technical work. That is increasingly clear from mining and quarry sites elsewhere in the Roman world, where slaves and criminals are virtually unheard of in surviving documentation, but salaried staff are now well attested on *ostraca*,

---

[67] Ibid., 13.1–3.
[68] Ibid.,13.9–10.

inscriptions, papyri, writing tablets, and the like.[69] Problems with using slave labor include the fact that it requires constant supervision and that it is difficult to motivate other than by brutality (which reduces the working life of many of its victims). Free labor can sometimes be encouraged by differential pay scales to work more diligently and with a higher degree of technical skill. Many aspects of mining and smelting involve a high level of knowledge and technique as well as brawn. On the other hand, the Roman Empire had a tradition of disposing of some of its condemned criminals and dissidents to the mines and quarries as disposable labor in dangerous and heavy work. The logical conclusion is that, as an imperially controlled mining center, Phaino drew on a mixed pool of forced labor and free (perhaps migrant) workers. We know soldiers were present, but they appear to have been relatively few in number. If the overall labor force at the mines was suddenly increased this would have had implications not only for supervision of the mine works, but also for logistical supply. It is for these reasons that the influx of large numbers of unrepentant Christians would have presented problems for the mining authorities and created a situation that was rather abnormal.

Nonetheless, the account of the Christian sources provide several important insights into the working of the mines: we learn that some workers were housed in barracks-like accommodations; there was a community of people not directly involved in the mining and smelting operations and this was separated in some way from the main center of habitation; some forced labor was involved in work inside the mines; and there was an inspector of mines and a military officer at Phaino. A possible way to correlate this with the available archaeological data is to assume that the mining and smelting operations were administratively highly centralized at Faynan and that some of the mining workforce, along with the smelting crews, administrative personnel and military backup was accommodated in structures on the north and south banks of the Wadi Ghuwayr, close to the major Roman slag heaps (WF1 and WF11). The separate community of Christians no longer able to work must clearly have been fairly close at hand, even if physically distinct from the rest of the mining settlement. One possibility is that it was located on the east bank of the Wadi Shayqar in the area known as WF2, close to the location of a later church and Christian cemetery (perhaps reflecting a continued importance of that zone for the Byzantine Christian community).

There were clearly some significant changes in the Byzantine period when Faynan became a center of Christian pilgrimage on account of the martyrs, and a sizable Christian community lived at the site (and almost certainly continued to work as free labor in the mines). Bishops of Phaino

---

[69] Maxfield 2001, 154–55; 2003.

are mentioned in church councils and synods of 431, 449, 518, and 536, and a Bishop Theodore is attested in an inscription from WF1 in 587–88.[70]

Environmental Impacts

As we have seen, the town of Phaino served as the center for the administration of the mining district, and was the location where virtually all the smelting activity was centralized. Throughout the mountain front there were numerous mines, though the main concentration of Roman galleries were in the Ratiye Valley a few kilometers to the north of Khirbat Faynan. The major field system (WF4) was a key resource for the food supply of the mining community. All these elements (town, mines, smelting sites, and field systems) appear to have been under direct state control.

The human impact of the Roman organization of the mines at Faynan can be summarized as follows:

- There is a likelihood that the entire zone of the mines was taken into state ownership, with central authority over the district being exercised by Roman officials, perhaps backed by a few troops, based at Phaino.
- Some of the labor for the mines is believed to have been provided by slaves or convicts, but some of the mining personnel and certainly the more specialist engineering and metallurgical roles would have depended on a salaried labor force, as in other imperial mining and quarrying operations.
- Ownership of the territory around the mines allowed the state to organize food production within the runoff agriculture zone in a more unified way, possibly with an agricultural labor force also being maintained on site.
- The isolation of the mining district and the distance of many of the mines from the centralized smelting facilities at Phaino would have required a large number of draft animals and animal handlers to be based at the site on a year-round basis to transport the ore from the actual mines to the furnaces, and to bring in supplies of fuel and perhaps additional foodstuffs. All this would have greatly added to the needs of the settlement for food and water provision.
- The mine would have been a heavy net consumer of people given the dangerous and demanding nature of the work, and the intrinsic unhealthiness of smelting for everyone living in close proximity.

---

[70] Sartre 1993, 142, 145–46.

- Even if there is little evidence for a heavy military garrison in the Wadi Faynan, it is clear that this was a landscape of significant control and surveillance.[71]

An important component of the work of the Wadi Faynan project has been the investigation of the pollution signature of the ancient mining and smelting activity and an assessment of its impact on the landscape and people of the region.[72] There is now compelling evidence to demonstrate that the Roman landscape in the Faynan was severely compromised by the scale of smelting activity (see fig. 7.10). The aridity and polluted nature of the environment of the Wadi Faynan thus posed serious problems for the Roman administrators of the mines as far as

- how to sustain a large labor force in the pre-desert landscape on a year-round basis (food and water)
- how to supply the fuel requirements of large-scale metal smelting (timber and charcoal)
- how to combat the negative impacts on population and landscape of the local pollution produced by intensive metallurgy

That Roman mining activity here extended well into the Byzantine period was both a triumph and a disaster. What we have in the Wadi Faynan is a landscape that was systematically organized and comprehensively despoiled by the Romans. The well-known phrase of Tacitus, "Where they make a desert, they call it peace," has a particular resonance in the context of the evidence for the environmental degradation and pollution in Faynan.[73] It is to those aspects of the mining and smelting regime that we should now turn.

Hauptmann's estimate of Roman copper production at 2,500–7,000 metric tons should probably be seen as a minimum order of magnitude range, with a distinct possibility that actual production exceeded this level. Extrapolated on a four-hundred-year production period, the average annual copper yield of the mines based on Hauptmann's figures would have been in the order of 6.25–17.5 metric tons per year.[74]

The production of 6.25–17.5 metric tons of copper each year would have necessitated the smelting of about 60–175 metric tons of ore, consuming around 80–258 metric tons of charcoal.[75] Perhaps unsurprisingly

---

[71] This is a theme developed in an unpublished PhD thesis by my student Hannah Friedman (2008).

[72] Barker, Gilbertson, and Mattingly 2007, 334–48; Grattan et al. 2002, 2003, 2004; Grattan, Huxley, and Pyatt 2003; Pyatt et al. 1999, 2000, 2005.

[73] Tacitus, *Agricola*, 30: *ubi solitudinem faciunt, pacem appellant.*

[74] Hauptmann 2000, 97.

[75] Figures derived from Barker, Gilbertson, and Mattingly 2007, 345–46; for a slightly different set of estimates, cf. the figures in Rihll 2001.

in a pre-desert environment, there are indications of diminishing local supplies of suitable timber over time, with the possibility that large quantities of wood or charcoal were brought into the mining center on pack animals. It is clear that by the Roman period charcoal for the furnaces was brought in from the plateau above, whereas in the Iron Age a wide array of trees and scrub grew locally.[76] There are significant implications from this. The 80–258 metric tons of charcoal represents 1,200–4,000 donkey loads per year. Movement of the 60–175 metric tons of ore within the mining region from mine to smelters necessitated a further 900–2,600 donkey loads. Similarly, the copper produced at Faynan would have entailed an average of between 100 and 250 donkey loads annually for its export from the mines. The food supply needs of the mining community may have been as high as an additional 2,800 loads annually.

Added together, the import of foodstuffs and other goods not produced locally, the movement of ore from the mines to the smelters, and the import of charcoal for the furnaces and the export of copper (under suitable security arrangements) must have accounted for a considerable number of pack animals (probably mostly camels or donkeys). The fodder needs of these animals was an additional burden on the system, perhaps met by a combination of additional grain imports and by exploiting available grazing within the valley. If the landscape was extensively grazed by pack animals associated with the mines this has implications for the access to this resource of contemporary pre-desert pastoral groups. Supplying and feeding the mining operations would have become more difficult over time, with charcoal and other fuel having to be fetched from longer distances and grazing resources in the valley potentially reduced.

What about the potential for growing food within the valley? The selection of the Wadi Faynan as the Roman mining center was undoubtedly connected with the fact that there was a good water supply in the Wadi Ghuwayr and the largest expanse of potentially cultivable land in the Araba region. This could only be exploited through the use of runoff farming technology, exploiting the seasonal rainfall and flash floods of the area.[77] Progressive additions to the field system increased its integral nature, its scale, and its hydraulic sophistication. The technology of the runoff and floodwater farming systems here was designed to combat the essential background aridity and sustain a level of agriculture normally reserved for a better-watered zone. Productivity was thus being artificially raised above the normal carrying capacity of such a landscape, but in so marginal a zone its long-term maintenance was fragile.

---

[76] Barker 2002, 501; Engel 1993; Engel and Frey 1996; cf. Barker, Gilbertson, and Mattingly 2007, 344–46.

[77] Barker, Gilbertson, and Mattingly 2007, 150–74; cf. Barker et al. 1996a, 191–225.

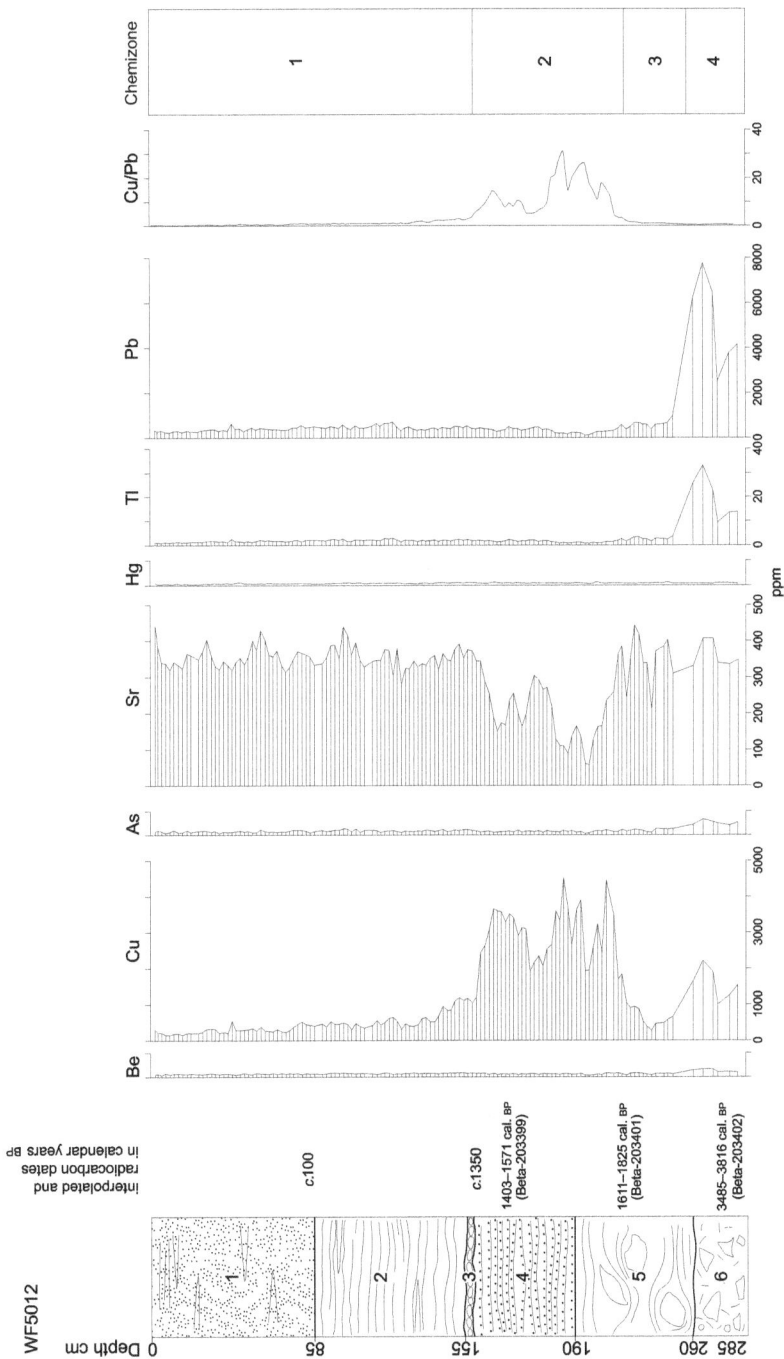

FIGURE 7.10 Graph demonstrating Roman date of pollution levels in a section excavated behind a barrage. The peak levels of a wide range of pollutants (beryllium, copper, arsenic, strontium, thallium, lead) can be equated with the more extreme pollution incidents of modern industrial metallurgical extraction and processing. (From Barker, Gilbertson, and Mattingly 2007.)

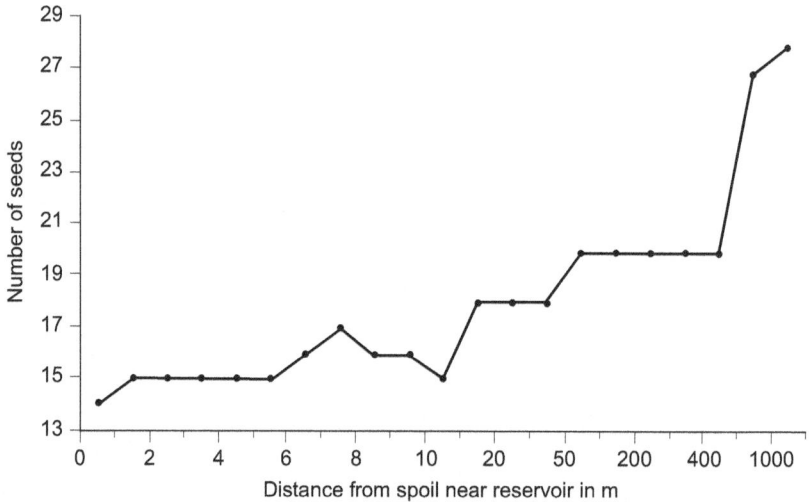

FIGURE 7.11 Declining modern plant fertility with distance from Roman slag heaps in the Wadi Faynan. (From Barker, Gilbertson, and Mattingly 2007.)

As already observed, a peculiarity of the field system is that large parts of it are carpeted in dense spreads of broken pottery of broadly Roman-Byzantine date. The geochemical analyses have demonstrated the degree to which the landscape was affected by toxic pollution from the large-scale smelting activity around the Khirbat. Brian Pyatt and John Grattan have demonstrated the continuing effects of pollution in the modern landscape of Faynan on plant fertility. The pollution reduces the yield of seed production on wild barley plants close to the major slag heaps to about 50 percent of the yield of plants 1 kilometer away. There is a demonstrable and progressive decline in plant fertility as one approaches the slag heap—an obvious pollution hot spot (see fig. 7.11).[78]

The intense smelting activity around Khirbat Faynan would have produced a dense pall of airborne pollution, from which many particles would have entered the ecosystem by falling on crops, bare fields, and the uncultivated landscape—where it would have been taken up by wild plants. The extent of Roman pollution can be guaged in part from our studies of pollution signatures in buried soil horizons close to the smelters, to the presence of toxins in samples of human bone from Byzantine cemeteries and from the continuing significant levels of heavy metals in present-day vegetation, invertebrates, and grazing animals. Radiocarbon dating of the deep sequence of deposits that built up behind a Roman barrage wall adjacent to Khirbat Faynan provides a consistent picture of

[78] Barker et al. 2000, 44–45; Barker, Gilbertson, and Mattingly 2007, 86–89.

the Roman/Byzantine period as a time of peak levels of heavy metal pollution from the smelting activity.[79]

From an area of probable Roman ore washing and intense smelting adjacent to the Khirbat Faynan, the occurrence of a broad and deadly cocktail of poisons at drastically unsafe levels is a signal demonstration of the hazards to human health that the metallurgical production posed (see fig. 7.10).[80] The revelation that high levels of the pollutants are still present even in modern vegetation and fauna living or grazing close to the major slag heaps is still more alarming. The local bedouin have for generations raised goats that are renown in Jordan for their resistance to common goat parasites. Pollution studies of samples of modern goat milk, urine, and hair now suggest that the explanation of this is that the goats have highly toxic guts that are not welcoming to parasites! Of even more concern for our research project was the demonstration that the dust particles within modern bedouin tents (where the team's daily flatbread was produced using imported flour) contaminated the finished product.[81] It is clear that the ancient mining community lived in a toxic landscape, where their food and water supplies were readily compromised by airborne pollution. Their health was further affected by their daily handling of toxic mine waste, ores, slags, and other waste materials.

It is also highly likely that ancient attempts to counter pollution in the landscape may simply have exacerbated the effects. Although perhaps not understood at the time as a consequence of pollution, problems of diminished plant or soil fertility can hardly have gone unremarked in antiquity. Study of the dense carpet of pottery within the field system is informative here. Some of the shards relate to pre-Roman sites and structures, but the vast bulk of the material dates to the later phases of use (late Roman–Byzantine) when the bioaccumulation of toxic material within the soil would have been at its worst.

Thus, the dense carpet of shards in the fields (and the relative absence of major rubbish deposits around Khirbat Faynan itself) almost certainly indicates a sustained and large-scale collection of domestic and household waste from the major settlement and the manuring of the land with it.[82] Human and animal waste has been known to improve soil and crop fertility since antiquity, and this was the obvious strategy for the ancient farmers of Faynan to adopt in response to declining yields. However, the ancient inhabitants of Faynan cannot have appreciated that the unfortunate side effect of this policy was to add the fraction of heavy metal

---

[79] Barker et al. 2000, 44–46; 2007, 335–43.
[80] Grattan et al. 2003.
[81] Grattan, Huxley, and Pyatt 2003.
[82] See Barker, Gilbertson, and Mattingly 2007, 328–32, 348 for a fuller discussion.

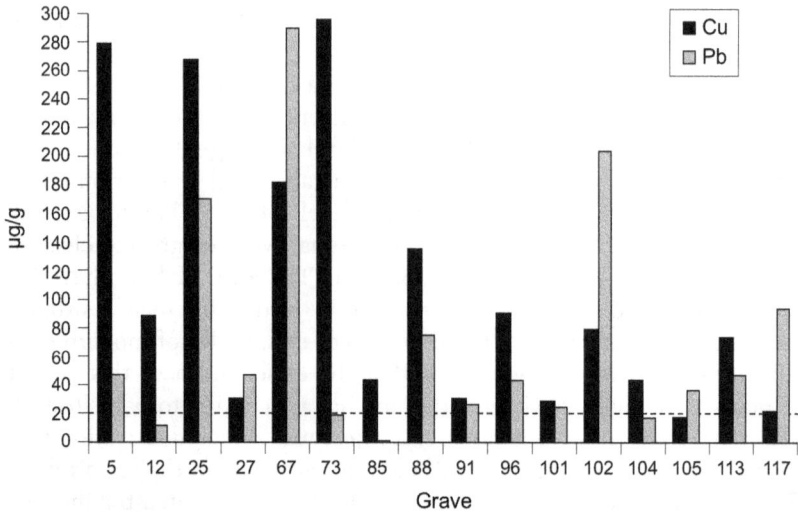

FIGURE 7.12 Pollution levels in Byzantine skeletons from the mining settlement at Khirbat Faynan, with dashed line indicating "safe" occurrence. (From Grattan et al. 2002.)

components excreted by humans and animals to the farmland. Over time this would have increased the level of heavy metals in the soil—and thus in the crops grown on the land (making them more dangerous to those who consumed them). The fertilizing effect of manuring would equally have been increasingly nullified by the higher levels of pollution. If manuring was perceived as a simple remedy to falling productivity, it was in fact almost certainly a factor in exacerbating it.

The effects on human health of exposure to the metallurgical pollution can be predicted by comparison with better-documented studies of industrialized production.[83] Copper and lead are well known poisons and both occurred at very dangerous levels in the Faynan ores. There is a large catalog of other contaminants and poisons present here—arsenic, beryllium, cadmium, mercury, thallium (see fig. 7.10). Ingestion of these toxins could lead to death from a variety of complications, but the overall cocktail is likely to have been a significant factor in reduced life expectancy for all exposed to it. The high levels of copper, lead, and other harmful contaminants would have made this population exceptionally vulnerable to any significant epidemic. This has been corroborated by studies of bioaccumulation of these same pollutants in human skeletons from the Byzantine cemetery (see fig. 7.12).[84] Two tombstones from the South

[83] Ibid., 340–43, 410–12; Grattan et al. 2002.
[84] Grattan et al. 2002.

Cemetery (WF3), evidently dating to AD 455–56, commemorated not only individual deaths but some exceptional event that had led to "the death of a third of the community."[85] The population tended to die young and needed continuous reinforcement from outside the valley, whether in the form of convict labor or free workers attracted by the higher than average wages paid by such operations. It is a terrible irony that far more Christians evidently died at Faynan after the persecutions, when they chose voluntarily to go and live and work there, than during them.

CONCLUSION

The new data from the Wadi Faynan survey provides a particularly graphic picture of the potential impacts of a Roman mining operation. The environmental and human damage inflicted by the *metalla* at Phaino are now well delineated. The infamous events of the Great Persecution there can also be more fully assessed within the context of a long-term mining operation and the extraordinary nature of the precise events of AD 303–12 understood. The story of Rome's exploitation of metals from a remote desert region represents in a microcosm key elements of the Roman imperial economy outlined in chapter 5. What we have here is an operation that defies normal rules of economic rationality in the service of a superstate. The ecological and human consequences of the rape of this landscape were profound in antiquity and are still with us to the present day.[86]

[85] Sartre 1993, nos. 107–8.
[86] Barker, Gilbertson, and Mattingly 2007, 38–57, 369–95, for discussion of the modern bedouin population of Faynan.

PART FOUR

Identity

CHAPTER EIGHT

Identity and Discrepancy

IDENTITY IN THE ROMAN EMPIRE

This chapter explores aspects of identity in the Roman provinces, with an emphasis on examples from Britain and North Africa. The first section reviews current approaches to identity and related problems (including a reprise of some of the difficulties with the Romanization paradigm). In the second part, I explain my ideas about "discrepant experience" of empire and the existence of "discrepant identities" within provincial communities. In the third and fourth sections, I illustrate this theme with reference to two provincial areas: Britannia and Tripolitana. In exploring issues like religion and the epigraphic habit, I attempt to identify distinct communities that utilized culture in very different ways one from the other. I hope to convince you of the validity of this new approach to culture change and that it offers a viable and productive alternative to the conventional notion of Romanization—a superannuated concept that I have now rejected. I also differentiate my approach from "creolization," which is most applicable to the lowest status individuals in society.[1] Jane Webster has rightly highlighted the potential for archaeologists to identify creolized slave culture in the material record of the Roman Empire, but there is a danger here that we replace an elite-centered paradigm (Romanization) with its

---

This chapter, developed from the fourth Balmuth lecture, is based around research presented and published in a number of different forums in recent years. At the core of the text lies the argument presented in my *Journal of Roman Archaeology* article on identity (Mattingly 2004a), with substantial conflations and additions. There is a necessary level of overlap and repetition with that important article, but at the same time I have endeavored to take the debate to another level. The new material provides many more concrete examples of discrepant identities than the original article, in part informed by my work on a book on Britain in the Roman Empire (Mattingly 2006c) where I tried to employ the new paradigm. I am grateful to John Humphrey for agreeing to my reworking the *JRA* paper in this manner for inclusion in this series. As well as making substantial changes to the original text, I have completely revised the notes to take account of subsequent publications. In addition, the section on ethnicity and racism has been developed from a paper delivered to RAC 7 in London (2007) and the comments on Africa from a paper in honor of Joyce Reynolds' ninetieth birthday (London, 2009).

[1] Webster 2001; cf. Ferguson 1992.

opposite.[2] We need an approach to Roman identity and material culture that combines both ends of this spectrum and the middle ground as well.

As I hope has been made clear throughout this book, orthodox approaches to Roman archaeology follow an agenda that is predisposed to emphasize the cultural achievements of the empire and the positive and benign effects of Roman rule. I am not, of course, arguing that we totally abandon the fruits of two hundred years or more of research and turn our backs on the elite culture of the Roman world—which has been the prime focus of study up to now. However, I strongly believe that we can enrich our understanding of Roman society and of the empire that they lived in if we broaden our field of vision.

What did it mean to "be Roman" in Britannia, Africa and other provinces of the Roman world?[3] At one level the question is a facile one, but it goes to the heart of current debates about the relative degrees of uniformity and diversity present in Roman society. It is self-evident that the highest degree of social conformity occurred at the upper levels of society, especially among those involved in the governance of the empire. The Roman senate and equestrian orders eventually consisted of individuals from most regions of the empire, and these people shared in a metropolitan Roman culture. Yet they were always a small elite. What of the rest of society? On the one hand there is broad acknowledgment that a Romano-Briton would have perceived considerable differences between himself or herself and Romano-Africans or Syro-Romans, and so on. The cultural mix in individual provinces differed markedly from place to place. Yet the dominant paradigm in studies of Roman provincial studies has been Romanization, a concept that emphasizes conformity, that presents cultural change as a unilateral and hierarchical process, involving the passing down of Roman culture and ideas about identity to grateful provincials (see fig. 8.1).[4] Over the years, the concept has had a considerable impact on the study of pre-Roman indigenous societies as well, though this has been less prominent in recent years in British academic circles.[5] The difficulties associated with the continued application of this paradigm are widely recognized, leading advocates to increasingly desperate measures (invoking watered-down concepts such as "vulgar Romanization" or "weak Romanization."[6]

---

[2] Webster 2005, 2008.

[3] For some initial forays, see Berry and Laurence 1998; Mattingly 2006c; Revell 2009; and Woolf 1994, 1998.

[4] For a range of publications mainly presenting the conventional understanding of Romanization, see Blagg and King 1984; Blagg and Millett 1990; MacMullen 1984; and Wood and Queiroga 1992.

[5] Haselgrove 1984; Haselgrove et al. 2001; Hill 1989.

[6] See, for example, Keay and Terrenato 2001, ix, 228–30; cf. Mattingly 2002, 2004b for contrary views.

WHAT DID THE ROMANS DO FOR US?

FIGURE 8.1 "What did the Romans do for us?" *Literary Review* cover cartoon drawing attention to review of my book *An Imperial Possession*, July 2006. (Cartoon by Chris Riddell; used with permission.)

Romanization, of course, was not a Roman concept, but it has a long pedigree in Roman studies, being traceable back to a tradition of study developed by Theodor Mommsen and Francis Haverfield in the late nineteenth and early twentieth centuries.[7] The early enthusiasm for the approach was in part at least conditioned by the involvement of European scholars at the time in their own world of colonization and empire.[8] In the circumstances, objectivity was always going to be difficult to maintain and a very close association between the scholarly view and the imperial

---

[7] For the evolution of Haverfield's ideas, see particularly Haverfield 1906, 1912, 1923, 1924. For analysis of his life and work, see Freeman 1997, 2007; Hingley 1996; 1997; 2000, 109–55; 2005; 2008, esp. 313–25.

[8] Hingley 2008; cf. Vasunia 2005.

power was the predictable result.[9] Some scholars talked of a Romanization policy akin to the (equally specious) insistence on the civilizing mission of modern white settlers.

One reaction to traditional views of Romanization has focused on a new analysis of who was responsible for promoting cultural change in the Roman provinces, with attention directed in particular to the role of provincial elites. In the model proposed by Haverfield, the native *recipients* of Roman culture were largely denied an active role, though their receptiveness to the accoutrements of civilization was noted as a key difference between the experience of the Roman Empire in Britain and the British Empire in India.[10] However, according to scholars like Martin Millett and Greg Woolf, the elite class were active agents and made significant choices about the adoption of Latin (as the language of official business); new styles of dress, architecture, and behavior (the epigraphic habit); and many items of perceived "Roman" material culture.[11] People lower down the social spectrum experienced a more diluted version of Romanization, a sort of "trickle-down" effect, through emulation of their social betters. In effect, the Millett model of Romanization is simply the flip side of the Haverfield one—both focus almost exclusively on the elite group in society, but in the former the indigenous elite are the active agents, and in the latter they are passive recipients.[12] Some scholars still emphasize the centrally directed aspect of Romanization, now increasingly linked to the reign of Augustus as a key moment of change in Roman culture.[13]

This chapter reprises the idea that identity is integrally bound up with power in society, and as such, the creation of provincial identities cannot have taken place in a vacuum, isolated from the power negotiations between the Roman Empire and its subject peoples. What is often lacking in the application of the Romanization model is consideration of how these power dynamics operated, both top-down and bottom-

---

[9] See chapter 2 of the present volume on the consequences for study of colonial Tunisia, Algeria, and Libya; cf. Munzi 2001, 2004.

[10] Haverfield 1906, 186; see also the excellent analysis of Hingley 2008, 321–25. The seven-hundred-page biography of Haverfield by Freeman (2007) incredibly does not address the Romanization debate in detail, though there are many interesting snippets buried in its lengthy footnotes.

[11] Millett 1990a, 1990b; Woolf 1992, 1997. See Millett 2004 and Woolf 2004b for recent reviews of the debate that their earlier work has sparked.

[12] On agency, see the important collection of papers in Gardner 2004a.

[13] MacMullen 2000; Torelli 1995; Wallace-Hadrill 1989; Whittaker 1997; Zanker 1988. Wallace-Hadrill 2008, a landmark study, appeared at a late stage in the preparation of this book and I have not been able to engage with it here as fully as I would have liked.

up.[14] The tensions and inconsistencies of the traditional paradigm are all too apparent in many recent provincial studies of the Roman interlude.[15]

The Romanization paradigm is a classic example of a common tendency to simplify explanation by labeling complex realities with terms that exaggerate the degree of homogeneity. This may be in terms of inventing or assuming ethnic coherence—as in the case of the "Celts," who cast a long shadow over Iron Age archaeology across Europe.[16] Classical studies have long been plagued by the two great "-izations": Hellenization and Romanization.[17] One of the most obvious impacts of the current focus on identity as a concept is that these older paradigms are becoming increasingly difficult to sustain. It could be argued that lesser "-izations"—colonization and globalization, to name just two that figure prominently in recent literature[18]—pose similar dangers of channeling argument. However, I think that what makes Romanization and Hellenization particularly unhelpful constructs is that the terms are used to describe *both* process *and* outcome, so that they have become their own explanation.[19] Self-fulfilling paradigms (that in any case were given much of their intellectual shape in the modern colonial age) provide a seriously flawed foundation for our subject in the twenty-first century.[20]

[14] Barrett 1997; Mattingly 1997b.

[15] For a wide variety of different views on Roman Germany, for example, see among others, Carroll 2001; Creighton and Wilson 1999; King 1990; Wells 1972; and Wells 2003.

[16] Collis 2003; James 1999a.

[17] Wallace-Hadrill 2007, to cite a particularly recent account, has no problem in deploying both Hellenization and Romanization in exploring identity, albeit in inverted commas—though I am not convinced by the analysis. On Hellenization more generally, see Hall 2002, 2007. On Romanization, see Hingley 2005: 14–48; James 2001a; Mattingly 2002; Terrenato 1998; and Webster 2001. Martin Millett has also moved on (2004, 169): "I now tend not to use the term Romanization partly because it has now become too loaded with contested meaning to convey conveniently any neutral idea encapsulating the process of cultural change, with which we remain concerned."

[18] On colonialism, see, among others, Given 2004; Gosden 2004; Hodos 2006; Hurst and Owen 2005; Lyons and Papadopoulos 2002; and Stein 2005. On globalization, see Hingley 2005; Hitchner 2008; Pitts 2008; and Witcher 2000.

[19] The confusion of process and outcome can be traced right back to Haverfield's delineation of the topic; see for instance, Haverfield 1923, 9–22.

[20] There remains some considerable resistance to the idea that Romanization should be abandoned by Romanists as our guiding paradigm. See the exchange provoked by my note in *British Archaeology* (Mattingly 2006d): De la Bédoyère 2007; Hingley 2007a. See also Slofstra 2002 and Schörner 2005 for works that show the perpetuation of the paradigm in Continental Europe.

Defining Identity

For an increasing number of scholars, Romanization is an obstacle to moving debate forward.[21] Here I shall outline a new framework based on the recognition of heterogeneous social and cultural behavior. *Identity* is the key word here, but it must be stressed that this is to be understood to relate to patterns of behavior, not simply to perceivable differences in material culture alone. There are encouraging indications in mainstream classics that the significance of the approach is being recognized. The monumental study of bilingualism in the Roman world by James Adams makes identity a central feature.[22] Similarly, work on Greek culture under Rome acknowledges the centrality of ideas about identity to its transmission.[23]

Identity has become a fundamental concept in archaeology in recent years,[24] and it has been particularly embraced within Roman archaeology by the British postgraduate Theoretical Roman Archaeology Conference.[25] I have also been much influenced by the important studies of the Danubian provinces by Peter Wells.[26] These works have probably not yet registered with mainstream Roman scholars as they should, but there are signs of change. The speed and scale of the uptake and the consequent decline in "Romanization studies" can be measured by comparing the program of the First Roman Archaeology Conference (RAC) held in Reading, England, in 1995 with that of the Seventh RAC (London, 2007). Figure 8.2 charts the occurrences of the words *identity* and *Romanization* in session titles, session abstracts, paper titles, and paper abstracts. The difference in emphasis between RAC 1 and RAC 7 is striking.

---

[21] Hingley 2005; James 2001a; Mattingly 2002; and Webster 2001 summarize various views. The potential confusion caused by various authors in edited volumes using the term in different ways can be seen in, for instance, Jones 1991; Keay and Terreanto 2001; Todd 2004b.

[22] Adams 2003, 351: "It is often argued in linguistic literature that language is the most important marker of identity that there is . . . This book is overwhelmingly about identity." In a similar way, Howgego, Heuchert, and Burnett 2005 uses the theme of provincial identities as a new way into the analysis of provincial coinage.

[23] Whitmarsh 2001, 26–29, 35–37.

[24] Díaz-Andreu et al. 2005; Graves-Brown, Jones, and Gamble 1996; Insoll 2007; Meskell 2001; Pitts 2007b.

[25] See, among others, the various papers in Baker et al. 1999; Bruhn, Croxford, and Grigoropoulos 2005; Carruthers et al. 2002; Cottam et al. 1995; Croxford et al. 2004, 2006; Davies, Gardner, and Lockyear 2001; Fincham et al. 2000; and Forcey, Hawthorne, and Witcher 1998. The book-length treatment of identity in urban contexts by Revell (2009) is a noteworthy attempt to move to larger-scale synthesis.

[26] Wells 1999, 2001.

RAC 1 (1995)

RAC 7 (2007)

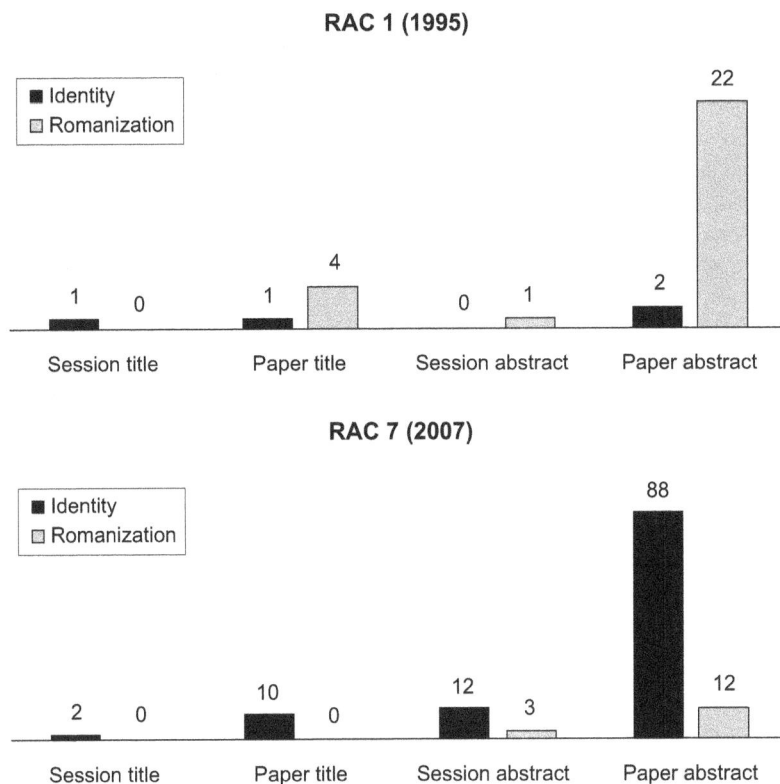

FIGURE 8.2 The relative predominance of the themes "Romanization" and "Identity" as reflected in occurrences of the terms in titles and abstracts at (a) RAC 1 (1995) and (b) RAC 7 (2007).

IDENTITY, RACE, AND ETHNICITY

The important work of Sian Jones on the archaeology of ethnicity is also highly relevant to my debate.[27] One of her key conclusions was that ethnicity is just one form of identity that societies construct. Modern conceptions of ethnicity have also been shown to be inappropriate to archaeological manifestations of early cultures.[28] Race and color in particular seem less well articulated as issues, though that is not to say that racism was absent from the Roman world.[29] Jones has emphasized the point that far from being sharply defined and uniform, expressions of identity in

[27] See Jones 1997, esp. 15–39, 106–44.
[28] Anderson 1983; James 1999a.
[29] Isaac 2004; Snowden 1983; Thompson 1989.

the past have tended to be patchy and discontinuous and ever-changing, often distorted by the application of oppositional groupings;[30] she notes that "the adoption of an analytical framework based on bounded socio-cultural units, [such as] . . . 'Roman' and 'native' . . . leads to the reification of such groups and obscures the various heterogeneous processes involved in the negotiation of power and identity."[31]

Jones's solution to the interpretational difficulties is to get away from social groups and focus instead on the locales of cultural consumption and compare groups of sites, such as rural settlements, Roman forts, and the like. In working through a case study of a group of rural sites, she demonstrates that there was considerable diversity that was obscured under the normal Romanization model, with its tendency to emphasize homogeneity and uniformity of change.[32] My own initial work on identity has drawn similar conclusions, though I prefer to work at understanding change in terms of communities and regions.

I am personally doubtful about giving ethnicity too much prominence in the debate about past identities. Nonetheless, it must be admitted that both in the Greek and Roman worlds, discourses of ethnicity played a significant role in defining insiders and outsiders, whether in the heartland territory or in relation to overseas colonies. This was a multilateral process that created not just oppositional understandings of Greek versus barbarian or Roman versus "other," but also entirely new opportunities for cultural crossover in the middle ground.[33] It is clear, for instance, that the contact situations generated by Roman imperialism produced profound and highly varied changes in behavior, material culture, and social organization at the core, in the provinces and beyond the frontiers. A fundamental issue concerns whether we are witnesses to genuine ethnogenesis or to enhanced ethnic identification, or whether the observed changes are better explained as a manifestation of other sorts of identity transformation. Moreover, if ethnicity was at some points a significant marker of identity, the archaeological evidence suggests that it was not a constant in time and space.

There are some reasons for relating this apparent ethnogenesis to colonial expansion. Writing of contacts between the Spanish and indigenous communities in South America, Neil Whitehead has coined a memorable phrase summarizing the consequential relationship between expanding states and neighboring "tribal" societies: "[I]t is in the communality of that colonial history . . . that a basic anthropological rule of

---

[30] Jones 1997, 140.

[31] Ibid., 129–30.

[32] Ibid., 132–35.

[33] Gosden 2004: 82–113; Webster 2007. On ethnicity, see Derks and Roymans 2009.

human grouping is demonstrated: *Tribes make states and states make tribes.*"[34]

What Whitehead meant by this is that the colonial contact situation works in two directions in terms of giving definition to ethnic difference. The "interdependence of enemies" tends to lead to more defined ethnic identity in the communities under attack—in part due to categories and attitudes imposed by the imperial power, in part by indigenous societies coalescing in new ways. Meanwhile, the colonial power's own sense of self-identity is reshaped through the process, reinforcing perceived core values (often of innate superiority). The idea finds a strong echo in the work of Peter Wells, who writes, "Tribes form in response to interaction between indigenous peoples and larger societies. . . . When states expand through imperial conquest or colonization, they foster the formation of discrete political and territorial units among complex, multi-lingual, culturally diverse indigenous peoples. Such 'tribal' units are easier for empires to administer than are the typical pre-imperial diverse societies. . . ."[35]

Wars of colonial expansion thus often give definition and new shape to both sides of the imperial equation, with the state building its sense of purpose and identity on its perceived distance and difference from the barbarian "other" while indigenous societies are equally reordered in opposition to the colonial aggressor. Another of the main conclusions of Whitehead's study is that the early phases of colonial contact offer a small window on precolonial autochtonous practices—if we keep in mind to look for the evidence rather than just accept the written records of the colonial power at face value. In any event, we must be extremely cautious about back-projecting the ethnic structures recorded in those sources onto the period before violent contact was established.

Race and racism have often been considered to be essentially modern constructs— that the experience of empire in the ancient world was very different from that of the nineteenth and twentieth centuries. However, there is a need now to engage with the important work of Benjamin Isaac on the possible ancient origins of racism (or protoracism, as he defines it).[36] In this magisterial survey, Isaac reviews evidence from both Greek and Roman societies, drawing broad distinctions among (proto)racism, ethnic prejudice, and xenophobia. Isaac makes a convincing case for the existence of an early form of racism, describing it as "an attitude towards individuals and groups of peoples which posits a direct and linear connection between physical and mental qualities. It therefore attributes to

---

[34] Whitehead 1992, 149; emphasis added.
[35] Wells 1999, 116.
[36] Isaac 2004.

those individuals and groups of peoples collective traits, physical, mental and moral, which are constant and unalterable by human will, because they are caused by hereditary factors or external influences, such as climate and geography."[37]

Given the complications introduced by the pseudoscientific modern application of the word, Isaac rejects the use of the term *race*, replacing it with *people*. Since racism is founded on illusory differences between peoples, race is in itself a scientific contradiction. It seems clear, however, that ancient societies dealt with perceived differences between themselves and other groups of distinctive and historically determined social identities (ethnic identities) with a degree of prejudice that merits the label *protoracism*. This went deeper than merely being a deep antipathy or fear of foreigners. Isaac provides ample evidence to back up his claim that Roman (as well as earlier Greek) writers classified humanity in ways that made a sharp divide between their own innate superiority and often drew on crude stereotypes of the inferiority of the other. Several further characteristics shared with modern racism are also relevant. These models were sometimes seen to be environmentally determined or influenced and also to be inherited and unchanging properties of the societies. Finally, the Romans in general saw migration and ethnic mixing as ultimately leading to degeneration and deterioration of the empire.[38] The importance of the ideal of purity of descent is a repeated theme in Roman literature. I shall return later to the implications of Roman racism relating to ethnic distinctions.

There is something inherently dangerous about racist attitudes when applied to perceived ethnic identities (whether the latter were real or imagined, self-adopted or imposed from the outside). In the Roman world, as in more recent colonial societies, protoracist views about the inferiority of "barbarian" peoples helped to justify war, subjugation, mass murder, enslavement, and exploitation on an unprecedented scale across vast territories. For this very reason, ethnic identities in the ancient world may have been historically contingent and of short duration. It can be suggested that they were predominantly a feature of the phases of first contact and assimilation of population groups by expanding states. Native ethnic identities became much less in evidence once people had been incorporated into the Roman Empire. Was this perhaps because the long-term interest of the empire was stability, and the protoracist overtones of Rome's ethnic categories were a strong disincentive for subject peoples

---

[37] Ibid., 23.

[38] Ibid., 225–35; Pliny, *Natural History*, 24.5.5: "By conquering, we have been conquered"; Juvenal, *Satire*, 3.60: "The Syrian Orontes has long since flowed into the Tiber."

to persist in strongly defining their own identity on ethnic lines?[39] It was on the frontiers of the empire that ethnicity tended to endure longest as a meaningful marker of difference.[40]

DISCREPANT IDENTITY: DIVERSITY AND DIFFERENT LEVELS OF CONFORMITY

Building on Edward Said's postcolonial analysis of imperial discourse as discrepant experience, a few years ago I attempted in a preliminary way to apply the same sort of approach to the Roman world.[41] The search for discrepant experience directs us to look across the social spectrum, not simply at the imperial elite, and to try and assess the impact of empire from different perspectives—including those of the colonizing power and of different elements of subject peoples. In a follow-up article in the *Journal of Roman Archaeology*,[42] I developed this into the study of discrepant identities. Here I have tried to build on the exciting current work on identity and to combine it with my earlier exploration of discrepant experience in colonial contexts.[43] I am aware that some readers of my work on this subject have been put off by the word *discrepant*.[44] What I am talking about when I use the term is the *heterogeneity* of response to Rome, to culture change and to identity (re-)formation. The meaning of *discrepant* that I am evoking above all is that of "exhibiting difference." Some recent studies of identity have employed the term *hybridization* to similar effect,[45] but I think that *discrepant* does have some added value in its secondary associations: *discordant* or *inharmonious*. The point here is that Roman provincial societies could sometimes exhibit cultural discordance as well as the broad similarities that are generally celebrated through Romanization theory.

My main contention is that individual and group identities in the Roman period were multifaceted and dynamic. What has previously been described as Romanization in effect represents the interactions of

[39] I explored these issues in a paper at the Seventh Roman Archaeology Conference in London, 2007.

[40] This is a point well-illustrated by my study of the Garamantes of the Libyan Sahara; see Mattingly 2003a, 76–90, 346–62. See also Webster 2007.

[41] Mattingly 1997a, 1997b, building on Said 1993, 35–50.

[42] Mattingly 2004a, which lies behind the present chapter.

[43] For other relevant works on identity and further bibliography, see Gardner 2002; 2007; James 1999a; James and Millett 2001; Keay and Terrenato 2001; Laurence and Berry 1998; and Pitts 2007b. On the forging of Roman identity in Italy, see Dench 2005.

[44] See, among others, Fulford 2007, 368.

[45] Hales and Hodos 2009.

multiple attempts at defining and redefining identity. A critical intellectual step here is to recognize that identity must be studied in terms of both culture and power.[46] I believe that it is possible to discern significant variability among certain important groups of people within Roman society and that the interplay among these different identities can reveal interesting things about the operation of power and reactions to it within these societies.

Western notions of ethnicity and social identity are to a large extent the product of modern nationalism and tend toward a model of singular identity affiliation, whether related to ethnicity or religion. Amartya Sen's recent critique of singular identity has struck a chord with my own developing work on multiple identities in the Roman world. A central argument of Sen's *Identity and Violence* is that much violence has been generated in human society on the basis of an illusory belief in unique ethnic or religious identities. For Sen, "singular affiliation ... takes the form of assuming that any person pre-eminently belongs, for all practical purposes, to one collectivity only—and no more and no less.... The intricacies of plural groups and multiple loyalties are obliterated by seeing each person as firmly embedded in exactly one affiliation."[47]

My point here is that the construction of ethnicities (whether in the past or by archaeologists trying to make sense of material cultures) all too often represent a compression of multiple possibilities for defining identities into a singular and potentially misleading focus.[48] Although I have highlighted the importance of native agency in cultural change, I also emphasize the colonial power networks that foreshadowed such transformations. Here again I see common ground with Sen, who has observed that there is not an equal and infinite degree of freedom for individual agency to operate in the construction of identity. Indeed, there are sometimes severe limits on our ability "to choose our identity in the eyes of others" (and especially aggressors). As Sen notes, "The constraints may be especially strict in defining the extent to which we can persuade others, in particular, to take us to be different from (or more than) what they insist on taking us to be."[49]

This highlights a crucial point about the relations between Rome and its subject peoples. While the process of conquest and assimilation into

---

[46] For similar conclusions, see also Huskinson 2002; Roymans 2004; Slofstra 2002; and Woolf 2002b.

[47] Sen 2006, 20. It is somehow no surprise to find the figure of Roma, with her name emblazoned on her shield, in the thick of the bloody action on the dust jacket of my edition. See also Anderson 1983.

[48] This is also the fundamental conclusion of Jones 1997.

[49] Sen 2006, 31.

the Roman Empire is likely to have promoted sharper delineation of ethnic identities, several factors militated against the long-term maintenance of strong ethnic identities within the imperial structure. There was scope for a significant mismatch between the self-image of ethnic identity generated within indigenous communities and the imposed ethnic stereotypes of an imperial power, the latter often explicitly protoracist. In this sense, ethnic identity was a potentially difficult and dangerous barrier to communities trying to negotiate their place in the Roman world. Isaac describes this well: "When peoples were conquered, incorporated into provinces and, in due course of time, became part of an integrated empire, this entailed a process of ethnic disintegration or decomposition. This is the essence of 'Romanization.' The Nabataeans, the Idumaeans, and the Commagemeans in the east, the Allabroges in the west, all disappeared as ethnic entities."[50]

Isaac's equation between Romanization and the decomposition of ethnic identity is clearly pertinent, though I would, of course, substitute "discrepant identity" for "Romanization." In any event, what both of us are arguing is that ethnic distinctions that became large and significant during the process of imperial expansion and assimilation were later diminished as new multiplex strategies for displaying individual and communal identity were developed.

It also follows that the Roman construction of ethnic identities served a purpose in facilitating colonial violence, while native ethnic constructions were instrumental in organizing resistance to it during the conquest phase. Much of what we learn from Roman ethnography about neighboring peoples is thus of highly dubious value since its prime purpose was to dehumanize the enemies of Rome and make their slaughter and enslavement more straightforward. The parallels with the racist underpinning of the systemic violence of modern imperialism are readily apparent.

An alternative approach is to recognize at the outset that the multiple life experiences of people will inevitably create cultural diversity and that expressing difference may be just as significant as registering similarity in the construction of identities. In the context of the Roman Empire, there are obvious implications of this view for what it meant "to become Roman" or "to be Roman."[51]

What I explore in the rest of this chapter is how discrepant experience can be developed into discrepant identity and used as an effective concept for the analysis of cultural change in the Roman world. This combines elements of postcolonial theory on discrepant experience with aspects of

[50] Isaac, 2004, 8.
[51] Hingley 2005, 91–116; cf. Woolf 1998.

TABLE 8.1

Some direct and indirect mechanisms by which imperial power structures could effect individual actions and behaviors

Intentional acts	Systemic effects	Consequential acts
Acts of conquest	Power imbalances	Resistance (armed and cultural)
Garrison deployments	Legal inequalities	Behavior modifications
Census taking	Abuses/corruption	Redefining of identities
Tax settlements	Individual exploitation	Native agency
Legal frameworks	Extortion	Cultural choices
Land confiscation and reassignment	Brutality	Emergence of greater regional
Language of government	Surveillance	and community difference
Enslavement	Opportunities	
Recruitment	Economic adaptations	
Exploitation of natural resources		
Operation of imperial economy		

creolization theory and work on identity in Iron Age societies.[52] Again, I want to stress that *discrepancy* is to be understood here not simply as a postcolonial oppositional to participation and collaboration, but as representing the full spectrum of different experiences of and reactions to the empire. Thus, I seek to incorporate traditional elite-focused approaches into my broad scheme of social analysis, not to abandon these studies in favor of an agenda that simply prioritizes resistance as a theme. My working method is to interrogate closely the archaeological record for examples of differences in the use of cultural material and to assess whether such occurrences can be attributed to distinct social practices that were being used to express notions of identity within society.

Discrepant identity has some similarities with work on *agency* and *structuration theory*.[53] I have avoided using those particular terms because I think they carry a certain amount of conceptual baggage of their own and tend to deflect attention toward issues of individual choices and away from a consideration of the constraints on choice that social power structures can impose. Imperial systems, I would argue, are more likely to impede and delimit the scope of individual agency than some other historical sociopolitical structures. In general, then, we need to balance *agency* with a more profound examination of structural influences and constraints—such as one commonly finds in imperial systems of power

[52] For new approaches to and recent work on identity in late Iron Age societies, see Bevan 1999; Creighton 2000; Cunliffe 1991; Green 1995; Gwilt and Haselgrove 1997; Haselgrove and Moore 2007; Haselgrove and Pope 2007; Haselgrove et al. 2001; and Hill and Cumberpatch 1995. Cf. Burnham 1995 on the transitions in these societies under Rome.

[53] Much recent work has developed around discussion of structuration theory (Giddens 1984); see, among others, Barrett 2001; Gardner 2002, 2004b, 2007; and Jordan 2003, 11–16.

relations. A further point to consider is that imperial structures affected local actors in several different ways. To some extent one could argue that the Roman Empire was a rather interventionist state compared to many others of the ancient world (though not all scholars would agree), but the impact was not entirely dependent on deliberate decisions by Rome to interfere in areas of its subjects' lives. In particular we might distinguish between imperial impacts on subjects through intentional acts, through systemic aspects/effects of the imperial system and consequential behaviors of imperial subjects (see table 8.1).

I have endeavored to operationalize this approach in a recent book about Britain in the Roman Empire.[54] A key issue addressed was whether I could find a degree of uniformity in diversity. In other words, could I identify broad groupings in society by slight but significant variations in the use of material culture or was there such a cultural free-for-all that no meaningful pattern could be discerned?

I have suggested that a number of factors bore particularly on individual and group identity in the Roman world:

- status (incorporating the ancient sense of class: slave, free, freed, dependent, independent, barbarian, Roman citizen, noncitizen, *humiliores*, *honestiores*, curial class, equestrian, senator, imperial household—including imperial slaves and freedmen)
- wealth (above or below subsistence, linked to market economy, derived from nonagricultural sources, and so on)
- location (urban, rural, military/civil zones, transient)
- employment (possession of craft skill, membership in guild, army)
- religion (especially exclusive sects—Mithraic devotees, mystery cults, Judaism, Christianity)
- origin (geographical or ethnic, including tribal)
- linkage by service or profession to imperial government (or not)
- whether living under civil of martial law
- language and literacy
- gender
- age

There is obviously scope for individuals to emphasize different aspects of identity at different phases of their lives or in discrete social situations.[55] Some funerary inscriptions seem to pick up on multiple identity factors, as in the case of the funerary memorial for Regina, wife of a Palmyrene merchant or soldier on the northern frontier in Britain (see

---

[54] Mattingly 2006c.
[55] Cf. the comparative study of Díaz-Andreu et al. 2005.

FIGURE 8.3 Tombstone of the freedwoman Regina from South Shields.

fig. 8.3).[56] The relief carving portrays Regina as a respectable Roman matron (with jewelery box and wool basket), though we learn from the bilingual text set up by her husband that she was his slave before she was freed and married by him. The epigraphic record of her ethnic origin with the Catuvellaunian people in southern Britain would be highly unusual in a civilian context, but is common among the military community. The act of commemoration in this form thus attached Regina very firmly to the practices and beliefs of the military community with whom she lived.

[56] *Roman Inscriptions of Britain*, 1065.

TABLE 8.2

The population of Britain in the Roman period, expressed in terms of three broad communities

		Millett 1990a	Mattingly 2006c (2nd century)	Mattingly 2006c (4th century)
MILITARY COMMUNITY	Army	10,000–20,000	45,000–55,000	20,000–25,000
	Garrison settlements	50,000–200,000	100,000	50,000
URBAN COMMUNITY	Major towns	183,971–290,057	120,000	100,000
	Small towns		25,000	50,000
RURAL COMMUNITY	Villa dwellers	1.8 ± 1.2 million - 4.6 ± 2.9 million (midpoint average = 3.3 million)	5,000	60,000
	Nonvilla settlements		1,700,000	2,215,000
TOTAL		3,665,000	2,000,000	2,500,000

BRITAIN UNDER ROMAN RULE: DISCREPANT IDENTITY AND COMMUNITIES

Estimates of the population size of Roman Britain vary widely, between one and seven million.[57] I prefer to take a quite conservative view within this range and assume an overall population of two million in the mid-second century.[58]

Table 8.2 shows the possible makeup of this figure from a number of distinct groups: the Roman governing elite, the military community, the urban community, and the rural community. Anthony Birley provides the best account of how many members of the Roman governing class (senators, equestrians, and imperial freedmen) were present in Britain at any one time as a core element of the military community.[59] The provincial governor was an imperial legate of consular status, supported by a legal expert (*iuridicus*), three legionary legates, and three military tribunes of senatorial rank. Men of equestrian rank included the provincial *procurator* (plus an uncertain number of minor *procuratores*, some probably equestrian in rank, others imperial freedmen), along with fifteen legionary tribunes and about fifty to sixty auxiliary commanders—for a total of less than eighty elite Roman officials. Even if we include legionary centurions and unknown numbers of imperial freedmen and imperial slaves,

[57] See Millett 1990a, 181–96 for a good summary.
[58] Mattingly 2006c, 356, 368.
[59] Birley 1981, 34–71; see also Birley 2005.

the core bureaucratic team in the province was very small—though its impact on our view of the culture in the province is potentially immense.

These people were the upper echelon of the military community and we can add in other groups of high visibility (archaeological and/or social): specifically, lower-rank soldiers, dwellers in the garrison settlements, the urban/rural elite (the curial class), other social groups of greater prominence such as merchants and craftspeople from overseas, and freed slaves (especially aliens). Numbers in these categories are hard to estimate. But if we lump the army (say 55,000 maximum, with 300 senior officers, approximately 4,000 *curiales*, 1,000 foreign merchants, freedmen, etc.), we still have a total of only about 60,000 (about 3 percent of our estimated population of two million). These people are responsible for the vast majority of the archaeological evidence that has traditionally been collected to illustrate life in Roman Britain.

We know very little about the remaining 97 percent of people of Britain in the Roman Empire. The enthusiasm of the bulk of the Romano-British populace for the epigraphic habit has been much debated, but even if we add in evidence of writing tablets, styli and so on to conventional inscriptional evidence, the pattern seems less impressive than for many areas of continental Europe.[60] One of the challenges facing us is to learn how to read more of the story of the 97 percent majority from the material record of the past.

Foreigners constitute an interesting category, and there is some epigraphic support for the view that they formed distinctive local communities in the towns of Britain. For instance, there are three religious inscriptions set up within a temple at Silchester by the *collegium peregrinorum*. The term *peregrini* could denote noncitizens within a settlement dominated by Roman citizens or alternatively nonlocals residing in a settlement of non-Roman citizens, where they lacked local citizen rights or were registered as domiciled. The latter explanation seems most likely at Silchester and the most recent discussion assumes that they represent foreigners temporarily resident there for reasons of trade.[61] It has become fashionable to emphasize the contribution of the native British to the development of Britain in the Roman Empire, but there are strong hints that foreigners were an influential minority at many sites in the early phases of postconquest consolidation (and probably later as well).

The military community is a good place to start trying to understand the ways in which a large social group can develop a distinctive

[60] Minimal position: Harris 1989, 269–70. Maximalist position: Hanson and Conolly 2002. See also Woolf 2002a for some reflections on the significance of literacy in the imperial project.

[61] Frere and Fulford 2002, 169–72.

identity. The Roman army in Britain, conventionally estimated to have numbered around 55,000 in the second century AD, constituted one of the most significant minority groups within the province, with its own tight-knit communities and its own distinctive vision of what it meant to be Roman.[62] Britain had one of the highest densities of military personnel in the empire, effectively 10–12 percent of the army in 4 percent of its territory—something that arguably had a profound impact on the character and development of the entire country (especially the north and west). Simon James has pointed out the extent to which the Roman army as an institution created its own sense of common identity for its diverse soldiery, drawn from all corners of the empire.[63]

The soldiery have in the past been seen as great ambassadors of Roman culture, playing a leading role in its dissemination through the provinces. What James identifies instead is the essentially self-serving use of material culture within the army, which to a large extent developed a separate version of "Roman" identity, distinguishing soldiers from civilians, rather than uniting them. He makes the important point that to talk of the Roman army as a monolithic institution is to obscure a significant degree of regional variation; we must think in terms of "Roman armies," though characteristics of the community of soldiers were widely disseminated. This military identity was far from static and was regularly refashioned and inevitably influenced by the cultural background of the soldiery—particularly noticeable with the influx of Germanic levies into the late Roman army. Recruitment into the army was at all times highly regionalized—with some areas providing a disproportionate number of recruits.[64]

What was the glue that gave the imperial army its cohesion given that there were strong regional centrifugal tendencies present? One could cite the commonality of military dress, the ideological indoctrination of the soldiery based around the routine of camp life and training, the acceptance by the recruit of a package of new identity reference points (including new Roman personal names), the common language of camp Latin (*sermo militaris*), the foundation of the army's version of the religious calendar and style of religious practice.[65] The literate modus operandi of the Roman army was a transformative force in provincial areas, but its

[62] James 1999b, 2001b.

[63] James 1999b, 16–21. Cf. Wells 1999, 229, on recruitment from beyond the frontiers of the empire.

[64] Haynes 2001, 63–64, estimates that in the Early Principate 33 percent of the known auxiliary units were raised in just two provinces (Tarraconensis and Lugdunensis). Despite an increase in local recruitment over time (drawing heavily on the military community in frontier provinces), the Roman army continued to draw on certain peoples/areas for transprovincial recruiting, such as the Batavians in the Lower Rhine; see Roymans 2004.

[65] James 1999b, 16–17.

FIGURE 8.4 The literate modus operandi of the Roman army—Roman soldiers reading at the Lunt fort.

effects were mainly in terms of creating distinctiveness for the military community and emphasizing their separation and segregation from civil society (see fig. 8.4).[66]

The main distinction here was not between provincials and nonprovincials but between the army and Britons living on either side of the frontier. The design of Hadrian's Wall does not really suggest that its purpose was to separate Romans and "barbarians," but rather that it was used to

[66] Haynes 2002; cf. Maxfield 2003 on the literate supervision of the army in the Eastern Egyptian desert.

supervise "barbarian" communities on both sides of the frontier. Did this view change over time? Development of a *civitas* of the Carvetii based on the town of Carlisle and the agricultural land in the Eden Valley is a sign of limited development, but the economic and social evolution of large areas of northern Britain seems to have been stymied.[67] Some have blamed the "backwardness" of the frontier peoples for this, but an alternative possibility is that large areas of the military zone were deliberately maintained as just that—regions to be exploited for the benefit of the garrison, with land not being released from martial law to civil law. The separation between military communities and their native neighbors was great and was expressed most clearly through the overbearing Roman identity of the former. This is perhaps an unsurprising consequence of the balance of social power in imperial frontier regions, but the implications of it have been ignored in much work to date.

I want to emphasize here that my definition of who qualified as members of the military community is very broad—including the various senior post holders, officials and military officers, the common soldiery, the veterans who chose to settle near military bases, and a large group of civilians who lived in close proximity to the forts in what are often called *vici*, but what—for want of proof that all sites carried that status— I shall refer to as garrison settlements. These were the families (official and unofficial) of the soldiery and veterans, the traders, craftspeople, and servicers of the needs and desires of the army. To varying extents the civilian elements here can be seen to behave in ways that are distinct from civilians in the civil zone of the province, but conform to the norms of the military community.

My initial approach to the archaeology of identity in Britain has been to isolate evidence in turn for the military community, the urban population, and the rural societies. Comparison between social behavior and the consumption of material culture in each group does seem to confirm the existence of major differences between the three broad groups. But there is also considerable regional and social status- and rank-based variability within each group to take into account.[68] Perhaps the clearest example I can provide of discrepant identities in practice concerns religious observances in Britain during the Roman era. Romano-British religion has tended to be presented as a monolithic amalgam of imported "Roman" and native British practices tempered by some Gallic/Germanic

[67] Higham and Jones 1985; McCarthy 2002.

[68] In relation to the urban community, different types of towns appear to have promoted varied patterns of behavior, favoring the emergence of distinctive local identities; see further Revell 2009; and also Mattingly 2008.

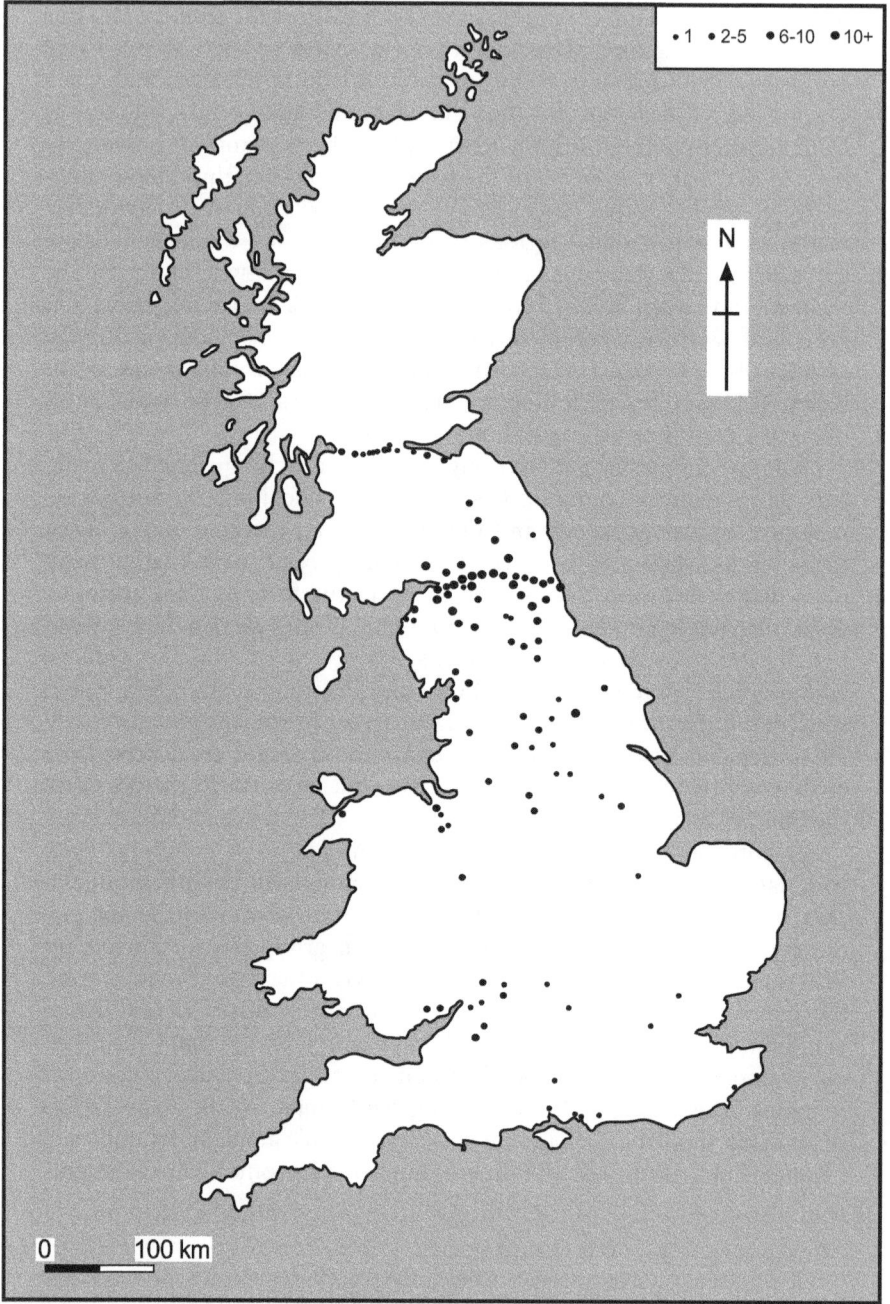

FIGURE 8.5 Distribution of Roman inscribed altars in Britain.

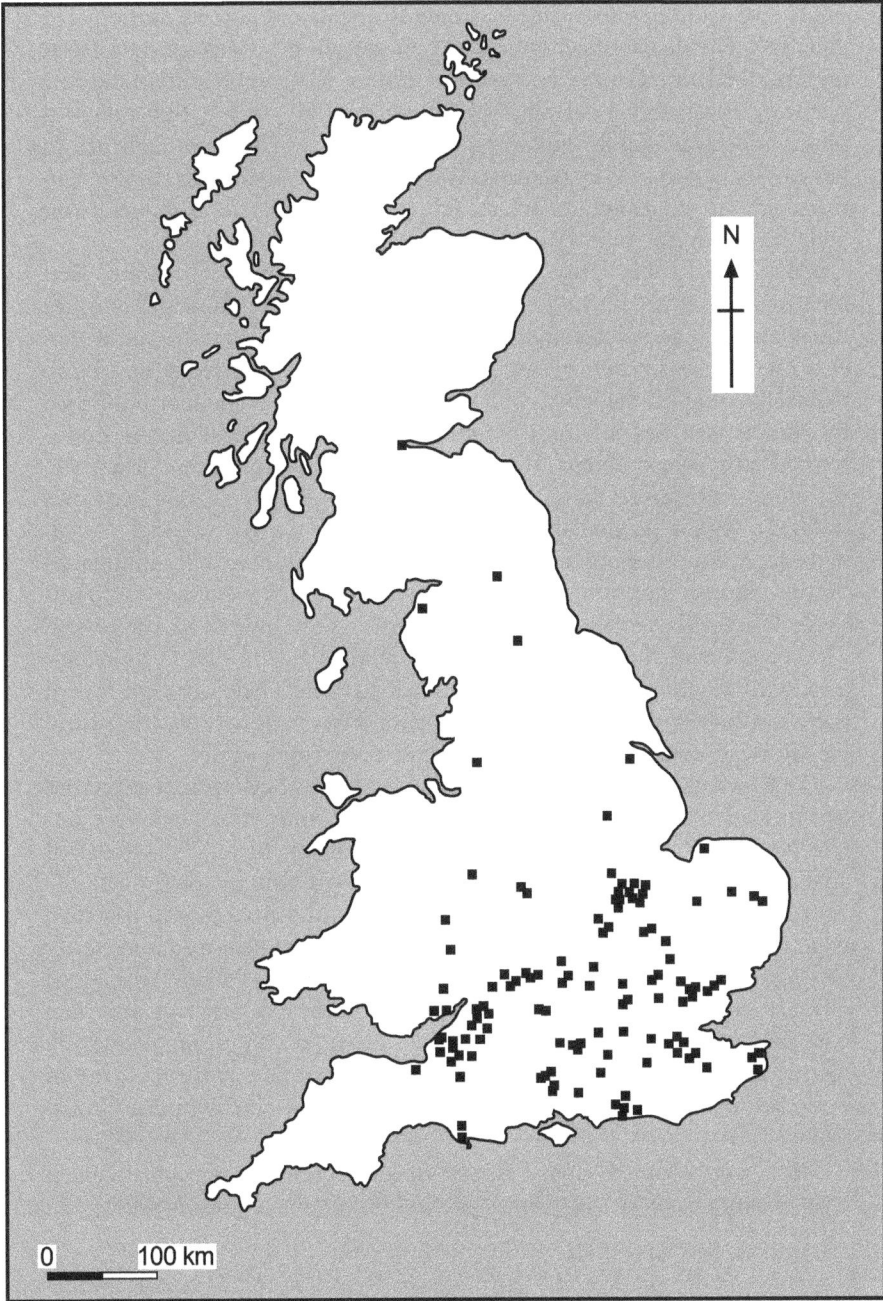

FIGURE 8.6 Distribution of Romano-Celtic temples in Britain

influences—a happy marriage in which Romans and natives participated equally.[69] The distribution of evidence of certain practices, such as erecting inscribed altars or inscribing curse tablets, worshipping in nonliterate ways, or constructing certain types of shrines, all suggest that religious observance was closely linked to social identity. The army appears to have worshipped in very different ways to civilians—though the conventional picture of Romano-British religion as a whole is disproportionately based on the military evidence.

Religion is a key area of life in which communities define their identities—at times in ways that associate them with others and at other times creating social distance between them and others.[70] Basic differences in religious practice within Romano-British society can be seen in the archaeological evidence, well illustrated by two maps first published by Millett (see figs 8.5–8.6).[71] One map shows the distribution of inscribed altars—a hallmark of conventional Roman religious practice—combining written testimony (of assistance sought, obligations and vows fulfilled), with a particular ritual practice involving the sacrifice of animals according to Roman norms. The distribution is heavily influenced by the military garrison pattern in Britain—indeed, there are comparatively few civilian examples and these are mainly limited to the towns. The second map shows the distribution of so-called Romano-Celtic temples, with an almost inverse geographical pattern. There are very few of this class of temple in the military zone and the majority are from rural locations, though examples also occur at many town sites.

The Romano-Celtic temple combines elements of classical architecture (stone walls, columns, etc.) with a distinctive concentric plan, very unlike traditional Roman temples of Mediterranean form, but typical of civil communities in Gaul. In Britain, Romano-Celtic temples are rarely associated with inscriptions linking a native and a Roman god together, which are normally found only at temples of more elaborate or overtly classical form. The general nonoccurrence of Romano-Celtic temples at military sites, where small-scale shrines of broadly classical type are more common, is strongly suggestive of basic differences in religious outlook among the soldiery and the civilian communities. The pattern is true of both Britain and Gaul/Germany, with Romano-Celtic temples almost

[69] Henig 1984; see Webster 1995a, 1997b, 1999 for excellent critique. Similar comments could be advanced about Roman art; cf. Henig 1995; Garrow, Gosden, and Hill 2007; Webster 2003.

[70] Edwards 2005; Insoll 2004.

[71] Millett 1995a, 110, 112, figs. 74–75; 1995b, 94–95, figs. 1–2. While there are geographical factors at play in some aspects of the regional presentation of markers of Roman civilization, the more likely explanation is that the variance is a cultural artifact; cf. Sargent 2002.

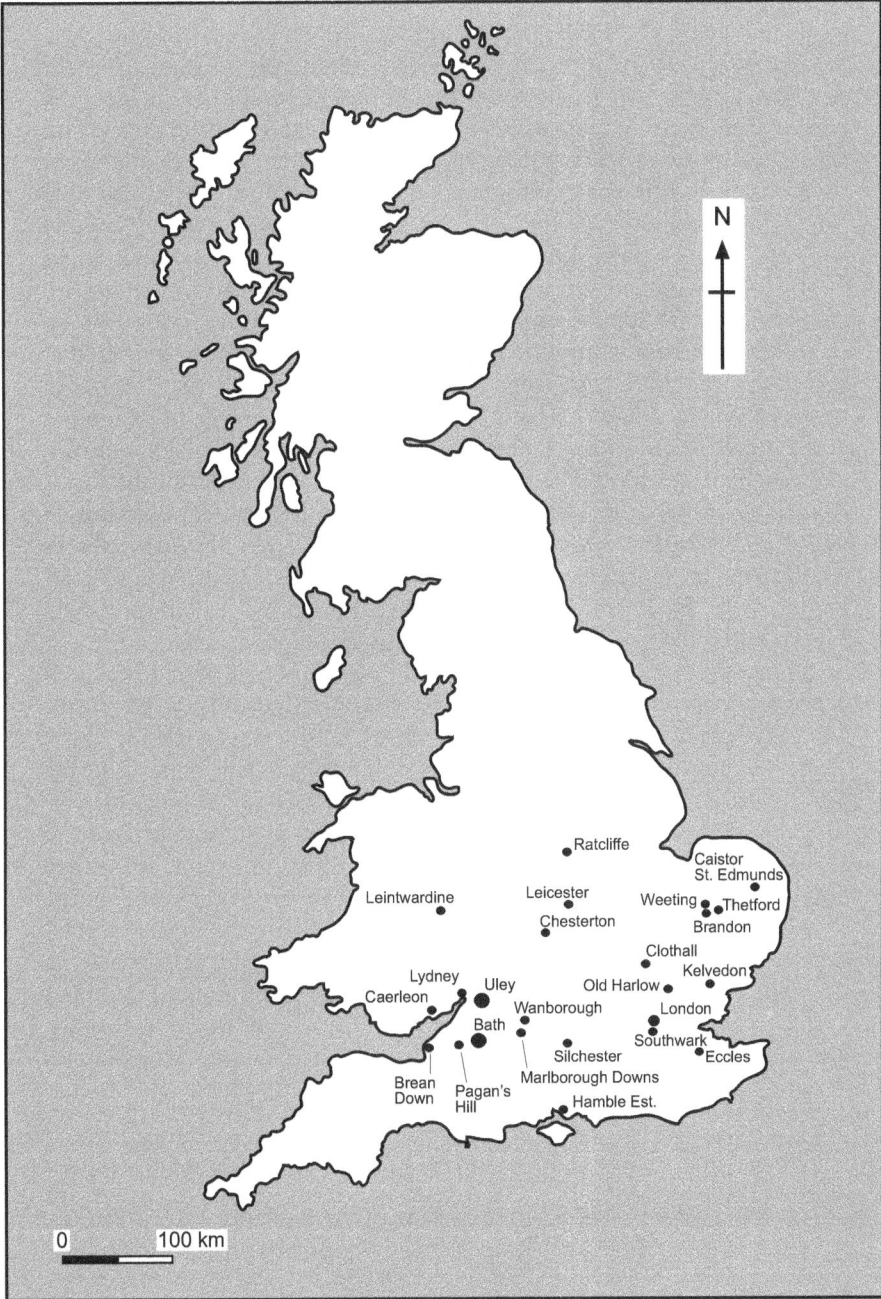

FIGURE 8.7 Distribution of curse tablets in Britain.

overwhelmingly a feature of rural shrines and small towns, and comparatively few at military sites.[72] Perhaps most interesting of all is the fact that many of the Romano-Celtic temples in rural districts have not yielded evidence of inscriptions—and, in particular, inscribed altars. This suggests that the *practice* of religion (a crucial aspect of individual identity) was very different among rural communities. Ton Derks has published data on an area of the Rhineland that has an anomalous number of "vow" related rural dedications, but this was an area notable for its strong links with military recruitment and with mercantile activity focused on military supply and cross-channel trade—both groups atypical of normal rural populations in northern Gaul, who might be expected to take on a different religious identity.[73] This is not simply a case of levels of literacy as other evidence points to the existence of literate individuals at many rural sites in Britain—identifiable from evidence of styli, seal boxes, and personal graffiti.[74] The study of seal box distribution in the lower Rhineland provides an illuminating parallel in that it again suggests a strong correlation of peaks of rural literacy with areas of prime military recruitment in the territory of the Batavians.[75] Clearly, the religious affinities of the Batavians were closer to military norms, an interpretation supported by the lack of Romano-Celtic temples in this area.[76]

In fact, southern Britain has revealed impressive and widespread evidence for a specific form of epigraphic communication between people and their gods, the so-called curse tablets or *defixiones* (see fig. 8.7). These were generally thin sheets of lead, inscribed with appeals to the gods to punish (mostly unnamed) felons who had taken items of personal property from the dedicants. An example recently discovered in Leicester illustrates the general type (see fig. 8.8).[77] In total, over three hundred curse tablets are now known, with two major caches from the temples of Bath and Uley, but other examples (many from other temples or shrines) include those from Lydney Park, Pagans Hill (Chew Stoke), Caerleon, Kelvedon, Leicester, Ratcliffe-on-Soar, Wanborough, Old Harlow, London, Leintwardine, Weeting with Broomhill, Hamble Estuary, and Marlborough Downs.[78] It is significant that there are no examples

[72] Horne and King 1980; Rodwell 1980, 557–85; Woodward 1992.

[73] Derks 1995.

[74] Hanson and Conolly 2002. See Evans 1987 for an intelligent study using the evidence of personal graffiti on pottery.

[75] For a range of studies reflecting changing perceptions, see Brandt and Slofstra 1983; Derks and Roymans 2002, 87–95; Roymans 1995, 1996, 2004; and Willems 1984.

[76] Zoll 1995b; this is contra Derks 1998. On the lack of Romano-Celtic temples, see Horne and King 1980, 494–95, fig. 17.1.

[77] Two curse tablets have recently been recovered from Roman levels in Leicester. See Tomlin 2008 for text and commentary.

[78] Tomlin 2002, 166; cf. Tomlin 1988 (Bath) and 1993 (Uley) for the major assemblages.

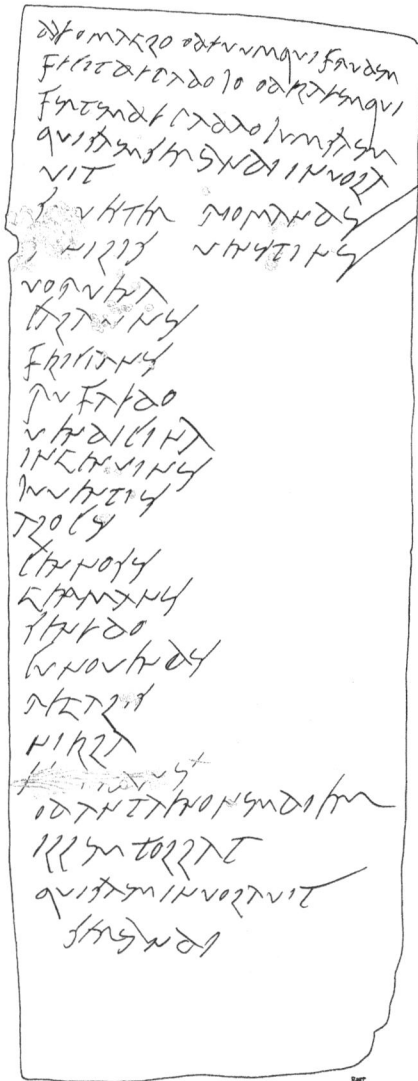

Tablet I

FIGURE 8.8 A curse tablet from Leicester. The text has been translated as follows: "I give to the god Maglus him who did wrong from the slave quarters, who stole the cloak of Servandus ... [list of 19 named suspects] ... I give (that the god Maglus) before the ninth day take away him who stole the cloak of Servandus." (Drawing by Roger Tomlin; used with permission.)

yet known from north of Nottingham (in the English Midlands) and only one example from a military site.[79]

Analysis of the names and language of the tablets suggests that they were written by native Britons. Only the examples from London certainly concerned Roman citizens (with *nomina* and *cognomina* listed) and they were the accursed, not the cursers! Of 150 personal names from Bath and 28 from the Uley material, British names outnumber Latin *cognomina* 95 to 83.[80] Tomlin contrasts this with the stone epigraphy at Bath, where of 36 individuals named, 31 were Roman citizens and many are identifiable as military personnel or outsiders visiting the spa. Was cost a factor here, or is this evidence of different sectors of the community expressing different religious preferences? Stone inscriptions were evidently more expensive than lead tablets (most of which are believed to have been inscribed by the dedicants rather than professional scribes). The items stolen from the dedicants were generally relatively minor items, too, suggesting that these were people of only moderate means. Yet comparison with other provinces would suggest that stone inscriptions were not beyond their means if they had placed particular value on them. What is most striking here is that people who had the epigraphic habit in one area of their religious practice should not also extend it to other areas of ritual in emulation of Roman norms. This strikes me as a matter of deliberate choice, with a particular aspect of Roman literate contact with the divine being ascribed value by an important sector of the rural and urban community, though they eschewed other standard elements of normative Roman religious practice.

Similar material has been recorded in other provinces (and indeed, the British material clearly followed model texts imported from elsewhere in the empire). However, there are some real peculiarities in the British corpus of curse tablets. The overwhelming emphasis in Britain on issues relating to theft is quite unlike the pattern elsewhere, where curses relating specifically to litigation, competition, commercial enterprises, and erotic or amatory adventures are also common. The almost total absence of these other types of curse in Britain suggests that we are looking at a deliberate and selective adoption of a Roman social practice that was fitted for a British need. Other regional aspects of the writing reveal Celtic transcriptions and bilingualism.[81]

Urban communities in the province reflect a more hybrid approach to religion, evident in temple architecture that includes examples of conventional classical temples alongside numerous Romano-Celtic shrines, and

---

[79] Tomlin 2002, 165–67.
[80] Ibid., 171.
[81] Ibid., 173–74.

at sites such as London and Bath, where we find both standard Roman religious inscriptions and curse tablets.

Further differences between the religious practices of the Roman soldiery and civilians in Britain can be recognized in looking at the epigraphic evidence pertaining to cults followed.[82] The army shows the fullest portfolio, ranging from traditional favorites such as Jupiter Optimus Maximus, the imperial numen, and Mars, to adopting certain eastern mystery cults, to the widespread syncretism of local cults (generally known as *interpretatio Romana*—pairing them with Roman deities), as well as incorporating the worship of local and imported divinities in unsyncretized form into the military pantheon.[83] As Webster has observed, the practice of the *interpretatio Romana* was by no means the mutual recognition of religious similarity it has sometimes rather simplistically been taken for. It was clearly often a rather unequal relationship between victorious and defeated gods, which the preponderance of syncretizing dedicants coming from the military makes appear all the more one-sided.[84] The pattern of military religious worship was both eclectic and inclusive. In Amy Zoll's important study of religious inscriptions from the Hadrian's Wall area, comprising over four hundred texts (almost half of the total known from Britain), double-named dedications are rarer than single name dedications, with a surprising number of British divinities occurring. Zoll calculates that double-named dedications comprise only 3 percent of the total in Lower Germany and 4 percent on Hadrian's Wall, suggesting that even in military zones, the incidence of name pairing was far lower than commonly believed.[85] The military "identity" of the Hadrian's Wall assemblage is clear, and Zoll notes that it "cannot be taken as representative of wider patterns of worship, either of the time or earlier."[86]

In the rural zone of the civilian province, there are plenty of iconographic representations of classical influence, though few inscriptions to help identify whether the Roman god was being worshipped in its own right, as a conflated/syncretized cult, or as an anthropomorphic representation of a local god. In one recent find from southern England, statuettes and relief plaques representing Minerva are identified without name pairing as a British goddess, Senuna.[87] The absence of epigraphic testimony to Minerva is a strong indicator that the first option is not correct. Although the choice between syncretized cult and British cult is not certain, it is surprising that no clear epigraphic attestations of double-named

[82] Jones and Mattingly 1990 [2002], 264–94; Zoll 1985a, 1995b.
[83] Jones and Mattingly 1990, 264–85.
[84] Webster 1995a.
[85] Zoll 1985b, 135–36; see also Irby-Massie 1999.
[86] Zoll 1985b, 137.
[87] Jackson and Burleigh 2007.

divinities occur at Romano-Celtic temples and these are rare in the civil zone, with many known examples being attributable to Roman soldiers or officials.[88] The more likely supposition is that many of the cults of southern Britain were worshipped in nonpaired form and possibly with different emphases in the range of human:divinity interactions.[89] In the military zone, the huge range of cults embraced by the army is the most striking feature. Roman soldiers were the most indiscriminating fishers in the polytheistic pool. The emphasis soldiers placed on literate transactions with native cults (whether identified with a Roman god or in British guise alone) also followed mainstream Roman practice.[90]

The broad differences I have delineated are summarized in table 8.3 and can be interpreted as religious manifestations of discrepant identity. I have no doubt that there is much finer detail still to be drawn out of this material to illustrate chronological, regional, and social variation.

Literacy is another key discriminator in social behavior and, in particular, the discrepancies in the application of the epigraphic habit in Britain are very marked. The military community again stands out from the urban and rural communities in many indexes. Literacy in the towns was surprisingly low-profile.[91] Combining the evidence of stone inscriptions and *instrumentum domesticum*, the strongest epigraphic signatures among the towns are, in descending order, York, London, Colchester, Cirencester, Silchester, Lincoln, Wroxeter, and Gloucester, along with several garrison settlements (Corbridge, Catterick, and Carlisle). The importance of the *coloniae*, provincial capitals, and garrison settlements in this group is clear—they were the centers with the closest links (and greatest social overlap) with the military community. The relative paucity of inscriptions in other towns is equally striking.

Funerary commemoration is an area of particularly strong military practice in comparison with the other communities. Findings from about 130 tombstones have been published from southern Britain. This figure excludes all examples from long-term military bases, like Caerleon and Chester, and serving soldiers from York. Of these 130 people, about 60 were possibly civilians, 40 related to military personnel or imperial officials, and the rest uncertain or fragmentary. For comparison, securely military tombstones from Caerleon, Chester, and York number over 100. Furthermore, over 70 of the 130 tombstones come from the five *coloniae*, the urban centers most closely linked to the military community. It is probable that some of the ostensibly "civilian" tombstones in fact related

[88] See Millett 1995b, 95, and table 1. Cf. Webster 1995a for dedicants of double-named inscriptions.

[89] Jones and Mattingly 1990, 280, fig. 8.17.

[90] Ibid., 274–80.

[91] See Mattingly 2008 for an extended discussion of this evidence.

TABLE 8.3
Religious identity in Britain defined by differences in practice

	Type	Altars	Vows	Votive feathers/ leaves	Votive letters	Curse tablets	Votive deposits in water	British cult	Syncre- tized cults	Classical cult
MILITARY AREAS	Classical	Many	Many	Some	Rare	Rare	Some	Some	Many	Many
URBAN CENTERS, INCLUDING SMALL TOWNS	Classical/ Romano-Celtic	Some	Some	Many	Some	Many	Some	Some	Some	Some
RURAL COMMUNI-TIES ("CIVIL ZONE")	Romano-Celtic	Rare	Rare	Some	Many	Many	Many	Some	Some	Rare
RURAL SITES ("MILI-TARY ZONE")	None?	None	None	None	None	None	Some	Some	None	Rare

to people with connections to the military or officialdom and at least 10 related to "foreigners"—typically, traders from Gaul who had settled in Britain. For example, a merchant (*moritix*) from Bourges, M. Verecundius Diogenes, paid for inscribed stone sarcophagi for his Sardinian wife and himself at York, where he was a *sevir* of the colony and thus possibly a freedman.

Another feature of the extant civil tombstones is the preponderance of people with Roman-style nomenclature, whether certainly Roman citizens or bearing Latinized versions of Gallic or British names. The Tammonii family at Silchester had Latinized a British name and was probably part of the curial class there. Nemmonius Verecundus from Cirencester possessed another possibly "British/Gallic" name. Almost one-third of the *civitas* centers in Britain have never yielded a civilian tombstone, a pattern that cannot be wholly explained by reference to post-Roman stone robbing or shortage of suitable stone in the first place. The gaps in the distribution map of tombstones and the general paucity of certainly British families adopting the practice are highly revealing of social attitudes and thus of different ways of demonstrating identity.

The relative low level of literate practices and the eschewing of funerary commemoration among the British elites are matched by other provincial oddities, such as the rare occurrence of statues and portrait busts. Although reconstruction drawings of British forums continue to fill them with honorific statues of prominent townsfolk, the archaeological evidence suggests that this Roman habit was as rarely adopted as the Roman toga.

I have focused thus far on traditional Roman cultural evidence—inscriptions, temples, and representations. But our enquiry into the broad characteristics of and differences among the communities in Britain can also make use of evidence for diet, where distinct patterns are apparent.[92] The same is true also for a wide range of material culture—as illustrated, for instance, by samian ware (the ubiquitous Roman fineware of the northern provinces),[93] lamps and lighting equipment,[94] general ceramic assemblages,[95] and toilet implements.[96] The different levels of uptake/

---

[92] Cool 2006. Cf. Carroll 2005; Hawkes 2002; and Meadows 1995. See also Van der Veen Livarda, and Hill 2008 for a review of the botanical evidence and Grant 2004 for a similar review of faunal data from Roman Britain. Albarella, Johnstone, and Vickers 2008 have reviewed evidence for introduction of new breeding stock (from faunal records) and detected a significant degree of variation among three sites in Essex. Grant 2004 and King 2005 have separately argued that faunal remains from Romano-British temple sites may allow us to discriminate between different sacrificial regimes and seasonality of festivals at such sites.

[93] Willis 2005.

[94] Eckardt 2002, 2005.

[95] Pitts 2005a, 2005b, 2007a, 2007b.

[96] Eckardt 2005; Eckardt and Crummy 2008.

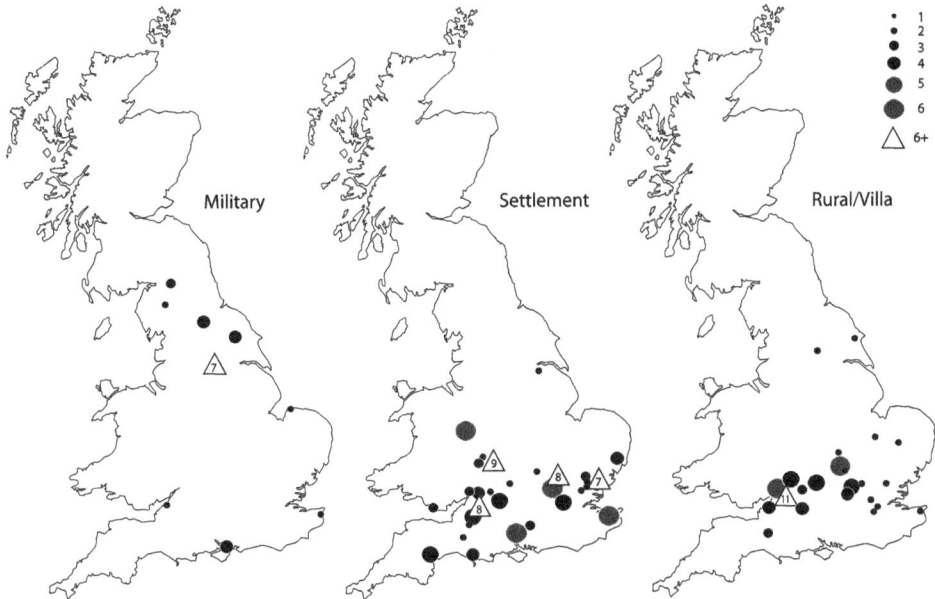

FIGURE 8.9 The social distribution of fourth-century toilet implements in Britain. (From Eckardt and Crummy 2008, 106.)

maintenance of particular aspects of material culture within the military, urban, and rural communities reflect broad differences among these groups, but also hint at a considerable degree of regional variation within the communities (see fig. 8.9). There is a growing appreciation in British archaeology that the overall character of finds assemblages at particular sites have much more to tell us about the communal identities than the traditional reporting of separate classes of artifacts has revealed.[97] There has been a good deal of interesting theoretical work on the agency of artifacts and the use of artifacts in colonial situations to express identity; it seems to me that there is considerable scope to develop this further.[98] Chris Gosden's work on the "mass power of artifacts" is particularly interesting in that he places importance on the agency of things rather than people in the process of becoming Roman.[99] It is equally clear that

[97] This was a point made long ago, in Deetz 1977. In Britain the pioneering work of Cool and Crummy is particularly significant here; see Cool 2002, 2004; Cool and Baxter 1998, 2002; Cool and Philo 2002; Crummy 1983; and Crummy, Crummy, and Crossan 1993. See also Hingley and Willis 2007; and Pitts 2005a, 2005b, 2007a.

[98] Appudurai 1986; Gell 1998; Gosden 2005; Gosden and Marshall 1999; Gosden, Petch, and Larson 2007.

[99] See Gosden 2005, esp. 93–99. His work on the power of artifacts in more recent colonial societies has revealed that "colonial relations always involved material culture"

research on the forging of Roman identities through material culture in Iron Age Europe (or elsewhere) must intersect more fully than has generally been the case hitherto with the investigation of pre-Roman art and culture.[100]

It should be apparent already that the definition of broad communities with some shared elements of material culture and social practice also throws up quite a lot of evidence of further variation within the major groups. Another stage in the project must involve the investigation of what this heterogeneity means in terms of identity. As an example, beneath the commonalities of the community of soldiers, individual units and their associated civilians might maintain elements of discrepant identity. One of the most striking instances comes from the recently published military cemetery at Brougham, in the Eden Valley in Cumbria.[101] Hilary Cool's analysis of the funerary ritual reveals some interesting identity markers. While aspects of the cremations can be readily paralleled in Roman military contexts, including the marking of some burials with tombstones of standard Roman type and the regular inclusion of standard Roman cultural items as pyre or grave goods, a number of features stand out as highly unusual. The cemetery was established on a new site in the early third century and remained in use for about a hundred years. Some aspects of the cremations are unparalleled in Britain, such as the inclusion of horses on some pyres—a practice only attested to in Free Germany, and a number of distinctive grave goods find their best parallels from the trans-Rhine or trans-Danubian areas, such as a group of large metal vessels or small bucket-shaped iron pendants. Cool concludes that there are strong reasons to suspect the presence here of cavalry *numerus* recruited in the trans-Danubian region, who expressed both their Roman military identity and their Germanic (perhaps Sarmatian) traditions in their elaborate funerary rituals.[102]

DISCREPANT IDENTITY IN AFRICA

A key question to ask is whether the peculiar insular position of Britain was a crucial determinant in making its cultural identity under Rome so multiplex, or whether other provinces could similarly reveal the existence of discrepant identities at play. My confident assertion from my initial

---

(Gosden and Knowles 2001, 16) and generated continually evolving patterns of cultural difference. See also Gosden et al. 2007.

[100] For two recent volumes where this sort of synergy is achieved between Iron Age and Roman research, see Garrow et al. 2008; Wells 2008.

[101] Cool 2004.

[102] Ibid., 437–67.

forays is that discrepant identity is by no means unique to the British situation, and that the approach will lend itself well to the reinterpretation of material from other parts of the Roman Empire.[103] Roman North Africa was a much more successful and prosperous provincial territory within the Roman Empire (see chapter 6). On the surface, it was also much more representative of our preconceptions of Roman provincial society. The region has yielded tens of thousands of Latin inscriptions (compared to the few thousand from Britain) and hundreds of towns compared to the twenty-some from Britain.[104] But in reality the territory is regionally diverse in environmental and cultural terms. To give a brief flavor of this, I offer a few reflections on just one region, Tripolitana (Libyan Tripolitania).

When I published a monograph on this region more than a decade ago,[105] the Romanization paradigm remained at the heart of my analysis, though a prime conclusion of the book was the delineation of a very different understanding of the cultural makeup of the region than had been achieved with more traditional applications of the Romanization model.[106] I specifically argued that the African evidence showed that Rome had not been "trying to enforce a complete cultural complex on their subject peoples" and that the resultant regional culture was strongly influenced by preexisting Punic and African traditions. My analysis of that cultural mix was actually broken down into separate sections on the urban community, the rural communities, and the army. Rereading this account recently, I have been struck that if the term Romanization is expurgated, how close in some respects it already came to the discrepant identity model I am now promoting.

The fourth-century *provincia* Tripolitana was constituted from a region of Africa Proconsularis, but had always been somewhat separate geographically and culturally. Although parts of the coastal zone and the chain of hill ranges to its south (the Tripolitanian Gebel) benefit from a Mediterranean climate and flora, a large proportion of the area of this map can be classified as desert or pre-desert lands. It is a region of very few perennial streams and of generally poor water resources, with great

---

[103] For instance, a recent overview of Dacia under Rome (Oltean 2007) suggests close parallels with the British case, but the attempt to shoe-horn analysis into a Romanization framework seems to me to miss some of the interpretational potential of the data.

[104] Mattingly and Hitchner 1995 provides a broad introduction in the absence of a good overall monograph in English.

[105] Mattingly 1995.

[106] Ibid., 160–70. On Romanization in an African context, see also Quinn 2003, p. 28: "[D]espite the best efforts of scholars to identify and solve problems with the traditional approach, the concept of Romanization remains fundamentally incoherent." Hodos 2006, 158–99, provides an interesting perspective on the long-term story of colonization in ancient Africa.

ingenuity being shown in the exploitation of the meagre rainfall.[107] Trip-olitania is best-known for its wealthy coastal cities, Lepcis Magna, Oea, and Sabratha, though there were also a number of other minor towns, mostly along the littoral.[108] There was little urban development in the hinterland, though many large farming estates existed there. One rea-son for this is that the major coastal cities controlled huge territories, extending up into the Gebel zone, and this was a major factor in their wealth.[109] Settled agriculture spread far beyond the modern defined limits of dry farming, representing the sedentarization of Libyan peoples, rather than, as was once claimed, the settlement of colonists from overseas.[110] The province never had a large military garrison, but there were mili-tary bases in some of the southern oases and linear barriers and small outposts controlling key transhumance routes and water sources in the desert margins.[111]

Lepcis Magna was the major and dominating urban center in the re-gion. The epithet *Magna* distinguished the town from Leptiminus on the Lesser Syrtes, but might equally have served as a comment on its distin-guished history. Even as an independent Libyphoenician civitas the town was clearly favored by Rome and the honorary promotions to *munici-pium* in AD 74–77 and to *colonia* in AD 109 were signs of great distinc-tion at a time when most *coloniae* in Africa were colonies for military veterans who were already Roman citizens. The municipal grant to Lep-cis enfranchised its nobility through membership of the town council, the appellation *colonia* conferred Roman citizenship on all the towns-people. At the times at which it achieved them, these were valuable and significant concessions. Subsequently, around AD 203, Septimius Severus granted his home town the highest honor available for a provincial town, the *ius Italicum* status, giving it the same exemption enjoyed by Italian towns from certain forms of taxation. When the province of Tripolitania was constituted at the end of the third century, Lepcis was evidently its capital.[112]

The culture and identity of the region was highly complex, and to some extent it is possible to discriminate as in Britain among broad groupings in the cities, in the countryside, and in the army that constructed their identities in discrete ways. The urban elite were Libyphoenicians—that is, families descended from Phoenician settlers intermarried with local Liby-ans. The personal nomenclature was predominantly Punic in character,

[107] Mattingly 1995; Barker et al. 1996a, 4–13.
[108] Mattingly 1995, 59–61, 116–37; cf. Di Vita et al. 1999, 18–145.
[109] Mattingly 1988b, 27–36; 1995, 138–44.
[110] Mattingly 1995, 144–52.
[111] Ibid., 68–115.
[112] See Mattingly 1995, 50–56, 116–22, 171–73 for the historical detail.

FIGURE 8.10 Dedication in Latin and Neo-Punic of the theater at Lepcis Magna on behalf of Annobal Tapapius Rufus, a member of the local Libyphoenician elite.

with a smattering of African forms. By the early first century AD many of the elite had started to Latinize their names in imitation of Roman forms. However, as the leading families gradually acquired full Roman citizenship, their selection of suitable Latin personal names often evoked memories of underlying Phoenician and African naming patterns, whether of a theophoric nature or simply in terms of phonetics.[113]

The creation of the Roman townscape at Lepcis Magna in the late first century BC and early first century AD constituted a dramatic transformation, with Lepcis boasting an impressive suite of key public buildings of Roman type by the early second century (and several instances such as the market, the theater and the imperial cult represent unusually precocious developments outside Italy). Togate statues of prominent citizens also appeared, accompanied with Latin inscriptions. Yet this was far from a complete triumph of a "Roman" identity. Through the first century AD, most of the main public inscriptions were bilingual texts, presenting information in both Latin and Neo-Punic script (see fig. 8.10). Punic was evidently still the spoken vernacular of Lepcis late in the second century AD. Even in local families with fortunes calculated as millions of sesterces, there were individuals whose lack of mastery of Latin and/or Greek was a source of embarrassment.[114]

The elite of the Tripolitanian cities seem to have made significant efforts to identify themselves strongly with the imperial project. The early

[113] Birley 1988b.
[114] This can be seen in the cases of the sister of Septimius Severus (Birley 1988a) or the adversary of Apuleius in his famous witchcraft trial (Mattingly 1995, 161).

engagement of local men, such as Annobal Tapapius Rufus (donor of the town's market and theater under Augustus), led to others later gaining access to the equestrian and senatorial orders—a clear indication of their unusual success. This is all the more interesting since the Tripolitanian cities are also atypical in revealing a very low number of immigrant families. The Libyphoenician elite thus had a much freer hand in deciding their cultural agenda than some of the other major centers in Africa Proconsularis.

Cemetery excavations at Lepcis have revealed considerable diversity of burial and commemorative practices, in part related to social status.[115] The elite practices were not simply emulating perceived Roman norms, but reflected rather different public persona for the leading citizens in life and death. For instance, many burials continued to be made in specially constructed hypogea of Libyphoenician type, designed for multiple use. After cremation, the ashes were placed in individual stone urns, often with the name of the deceased engraved in Neo-Punic characters. Over time it became customary for the wealthiest burials in the hypogea to be placed in alabaster urns engraved with Latin letters. However, there were certainly occasions when the name displayed on the outside of the tomb in Latin letters corresponded to an individual whose name was still engraved in Neo-Punic on his urn.[116] In other cases the Latin names on the urns included an indigenous cognomen, whereas public inscriptions from the town that likely relate to the same individuals tended to omit elements that were not of straightforward Latin type.[117] This is fascinating, as it suggests that many of these people retained Libyan or Pubic cognomina in the domestic context—clearly important inside the family tomb, whereas the public identity emphasized the purely Latin aspects of the assumed identity of these imperial games' players. The use of Neo-Punic script seems to have died out in the late first or early second century AD, but there was some continuity of the dualistic epigraphic tradition with a new version of the Punic vernacular using Latin letters—the so-called Latino-Punic inscriptions.[118] The earliest Latino-Punic inscription of possibly late-first-century date is argued to be a funerary text from Zliten, to

---

[115] Fontana 2001. Similarly interesting funerary variability in identity presentation is also manifested by the Garamantes of Fazzan; see Mattingly 2003a, 187–234.

[116] Fontana 2001, 166. Cf. similar observations in Carroll 2006, 258–59, about "separate public and private persona . . . individuals who had public and private names, and quite probably a public and private identity depending on the context." Stone and Stirling 2007 contains an important series of studies that show the subtle blending of Roman, Punic, and African funerary traditions in the mortuary practices of Roman Africa. See also Stone 2007.

[117] Fontana 2001, 167–68.

[118] See the important linguistic study of Kerr (2007) on the Latino-Punic inscriptions of the region.

the east of Lepcis Magna, set up by a man called Licinius Piso in honor of his parents and wife, using the local dialect, whereas he was evidently later commemorated by a Latin text dedicated by his son.[119] The incorporation of new elements into funerary rituals and linguistic and naming practices had evidently been very selective here.

Identity was thus Janus-headed in Tripolitania—serving both to bind the local elite into the power structures of the empire (much to their financial advantage), but it was also constructed so as to enshrine local traditions in a way that would have clearly differentiated the local elite from outsiders visiting or settling in the region. Here we see the inadequacy of the Romanization concept most obviously exposed. On the one hand, the top families were endeavoring to fit into the highest levels of Roman society and strongly differentiating themselves from those of lesser wealth in their hometowns. But by the same token, they had created a local sense of identity that was designed to be antipathetic to outsiders. If people failed to take the hint, things could turn nasty. One thinks of the attempt by some of the elite families in Tripoli to prosecute Apuleius—himself an African from Madauros near the modern Tuniso-Algerian border—when he had the temerity to successfully woo a local millionairess.[120] Just as similarity engenders solidarity and a sense of belonging, so difference can be used to create social exclusivity and distance.

How different were people in the countryside and in the army? It is certainly clear that the African component of the army was already extremely high by the second century AD.[121] Nonetheless, as in Britain, it seems that the army had a strong sense of its collective identity, based on shared working structures, the use of camp Latin as the language of command and records, religious behavior and so on.[122] Burial practices and funerary commemoration appear to have been very different among the military in comparison with the urban and rural communities. At the Roman fort at Bu Njem for instance, tombstones reflect military norms. Although Punic elements are not unknown in the army,[123] the predominant cultural elements are in fact Latin/Roman and Libyan.

On the other hand, the rural communities in Tripolitania demonstrate a predominant mix of Punic and Libyan culture and language, with more limited penetration of expressly Roman or Latin elements.[124] Of currently published inscriptions from the pre-desert region, 79 percent are

[119] Kerr 2007, 162–64.

[120] Mattingly 1995, 53.

[121] Le Bohec 1989a, 518–30.

[122] Adams 1994, 1999; Marichal 1992; Mattingly 1995, 168–69.

[123] The fort at Bu Njem seems to have been laid out in multiples of the Punic cubit; Mattingly 1995, 96.

[124] Mattingly 1995, 162–68.

FIG. 8.11 Latino-Punic inscription from the Libyan pre-desert.

of Latino-Punic type—that is, engraved in Latin letters but expressing the local Punic language (see fig. 8.11).[125] Personal nomenclature was dominated by Libyan onomastics, though there are some Punic, and occasional Latinized, names.[126] There are some important exceptions to the general low engagement with Roman culture, as often argued in the past for the extraordinary funerary monuments from the pre-desert center of Ghirza. However, in chapter 9, I shall show how difficult it is to interpret the iconography in terms of the conventional notions of Romanization

[125] Kerr 2007, vii–viii.
[126] See Mattingly 1995, 162–67, 202–9, emphasizing the local Libyan origin of the rural majority. Cf. Kerr 2007, which posits in-migration of Libyphoenices from the north.

TABLE 8.4
Literacy, linguistics, and religious practice in Tripolitania

	Temple type	Altars	Tombstones	Latin inscriptions	Punic inscriptions	Latino-Punic inscriptions	Libyan texts
MILITARY COMMUNITIES	Classical/ army types	Many	Many	Many	Rare	Rare	Some
URBAN COMMUNITIES	Classical/ Phoenician	Many	Many	Many	Many	Rare	Rare
RURAL COMMUNITIES	Few, most of Ammon	Rare	Rare	Rare	Some	Many	Some

TABLE 8.5
Cults and communities in Roman Tripolitania

	Phoenician or Libyan cults	Syncretized cults	Classical cults	Eastern cults
MILITARY COMMUNITIES	Vanammon	Mars Canaphar, Jupiter Hammon, Genius Gholaiae	Arae Cerei, Fortuna, Genius Gholaia, Imperial Cult, IOM, Salus	IOM Dolichenus, Sol Hieroboulos, Sol Invictus
URBAN COMMUNITIES	Milk'ashtart, Shadrapa El Qone Aras Baal-Hammon Tanit	[Caelestis, Hercules, Liber Pater, Saturn]	Amor, Apollo, Caelestis, Ceres, Concord, Di Augusti, Di Inferi et Superi, Dioscuri, Esculapius, Fortuna, Genius coloniae, Genius municipiae, Hercules, Imperial cult, Juno, Jupiter, Liber, Liber Pater, Mars, Mercury, Minerva, Nemesis, Neptune, Rome and Augustus, Silvanus, Saturn, Venus	Christianity, IOM Dolichenus, Isis, Magna Mater, Mithras, Serapis
RURAL COMMUNITIES	Abretupta Ammon ancestor cults Baal-Hammon Gurzil Mastiman? Sinifer?	[Caelestis, Hercules, Jupiter]	Mercury	Christianity

and that there were much more complex issues of power and Libyan identity bound up in these so-called classical artworks.[127] A key element of what was going on at Ghirza related to a Libyan ancestor cult and the translation of familial rituals into tribal power using an expanded iconographic repertoire.

Broad differences among urban, rural, and military sites in Tripolitania can be expressed in simplified tabular form. Table 8.4 summarizes differences in religious practice and the epigraphic habit across the broad communities. In table 8.5, the nature of divinities attested by dedications from the three broad communities are compared.[128] The rural communities (whose temples are rarely identifiable) primarily worshipped nonsyncretized Libyan gods, with a small number of dedications for the more common Roman rebrandings of Libyan/Phoenician cults (Jupiter for Hammon/Ammon; Caelestis for Tanit, Hercules for Melqart).

Some general differences of practice and cultural behavior seem to be represented here, though there was also quite a bit of internal variation within the "communities" I have defined. The exceptions to the normal pattern deserve further consideration to ascertain whether they can be explained by socioeconomic or chronological differences or by individuals constructing their identity anomalously. Discrepant identity seems to work well here in terms of differentiating between groups in society. The cultural differences were large and they do not seem to have been constructing identity in simple emulation of one another or of some assumed norm of Roman behavior. Rather, they represent deliberate reinforcement and emphasis of cultural difference between individuals and communities.

CONCLUSION

What the two case studies explored briefly in this chapter demonstrate is the potential for us to support the theory of discrepant identity from the combined archaeological and epigraphic/literary record. There is much work to be done to flesh out these provincial studies and to develop the explanatory power of this new approach. But I hope at least to have shown that the approach has merit as an alternative to the tired Romanization paradigm and to have illustrated how the current interest in identity as a research theme can be focused on the problem of hybridity and diversity within and across the Roman provinces.

---

[127] Mattingly 1999, 2003b; cf. Fontana 1998.
[128] See further Brouquier Reddé 1992a, 1992b; and Mattingly 1995, 167–68.

CHAPTER NINE

Family Values

ART AND POWER AT GHIRZA IN THE LIBYAN PRE-DESERT

ART AND IMPERIALISM

This chapter concerns the intersection of art and power in the Roman world, but it is also about how we study Roman art. A common emphasis on the *formal* qualities of so-called Romanized art has created the perception of art as symbolic of the success of Rome and of the acquiescence of indigenous peoples to its rule. From this perspective, provincial art can easily be dismissed as an often inadequate imitation of Roman style and images. In turn, this tendency has also led to greatest emphasis being placed on recording and displaying those works that attained the highest technical and stylistic affinities with examples from Rome or Italy. There is thus a strong centrist tendency in art historical studies of the Roman world and it depends to a large extent on the assumption that people in the provinces would have wished to emulate the art of the colonial power regardless of the underlying symbolism.[1] Such a view may have some truth, some of the time, in elite circles, but I suspect that the degree of direct and uncritical artistic emulation was overall rather small. Much less examined is the extent to which elements of Roman iconography or style were appropriated to serve indigenous agendas, rather than simply to mimic Roman culture.[2] If we accept this line of argument, then it is clear that while people might have amalgamated imperial imagery and elements of Roman art, the process was often critically selective and it also involved the redefinition and reinvention of native traditions of art.

There seems to me to be a further double weakness with the approach of many art historians to the Roman world; first, it is commonly

This chapter was originally published as Mattingly 2003b (in Scott and Webster 2003), having been presented as a paper at the second RAC conference in Nottingham, England, in 1997. I am grateful to the Cambridge University Press for permission to reprint a reedited and slightly emended version here and to the Department of Antiquities for permission to publish my photographs from the National Museum in Tripoli. I have made a few minor emendations to the text and some additions to the notes.

[1] Scott 2003.
[2] Webster 2003.

assumed that aesthetic values in the past were the same as those of today, and second, that this cultural "gold standard" was universally accepted throughout the empire and at all levels of society. Both of those ideas are flawed by their acceptance of a level of consensus that cannot be shown to have existed. Art and material culture are frequently hard to disentangle in past societies and the possibility that the message was frequently as important or more so than the medium should also give us pause for thought.

A specific attribute of much art is its use by different groups in society to express power relations. Recent work on "official" art of the Roman Empire has emphasized the degree to which imagery was shaped and exploited in support of the emperors.[3] Yet, similar power-based dialogues were conducted at many different levels in society through the medium of display and consumption. Much more work is certainly needed on the social significance and power connotations of imagery that was not publicly sanctioned. In addition, recent discussions of the operation of power in the Roman world have suggested that we must deconstruct the discourse of modern imperialism if we are to improve our understanding of the ancient situation.[4] Jane Webster's work on the impact of colonialism in the religious sphere is particularly pertinent in that it demonstrates perfectly the way in which iconography can become blurred, depending both on the contexts of its use and the audience.[5]

An alternative approach to the study of Roman provincial art would embrace a series of discreet perspectives and consider different underlying themes in the imperial dialogue (including resistance, imitation, and adoption). In this context, I am interested in ways in which the adoption of so-called Romanized style also facilitated the *continuation* of indigenous traditions. These then are the sorts of issues I shall explore with a case study from the Libyan pre-desert in the fourth century AD.

THE GHIRZA TOMBS

The site of Ghirza lies about 250 kilometers southeast of Tripoli (see fig. 9.1). The settlement was one of the largest in the Libyan pre-desert zone, comprising a "village" of about 40 buildings clustered together on the west side of the Wadi Ghirza, around 10 kilometers south of its junction with the Wadi ZemZem.[6] The buildings centered on several major

---

[3] Walker and Burnett 1981; Zanker 1988.
[4] Webster and Cooper 1996; Mattingly 1997a.
[5] Webster 1997a, 1997b.
[6] Brogan and Smith 1984; Mattingly 1995, 197–207; cf. Barker et al.1996b, 118–20.

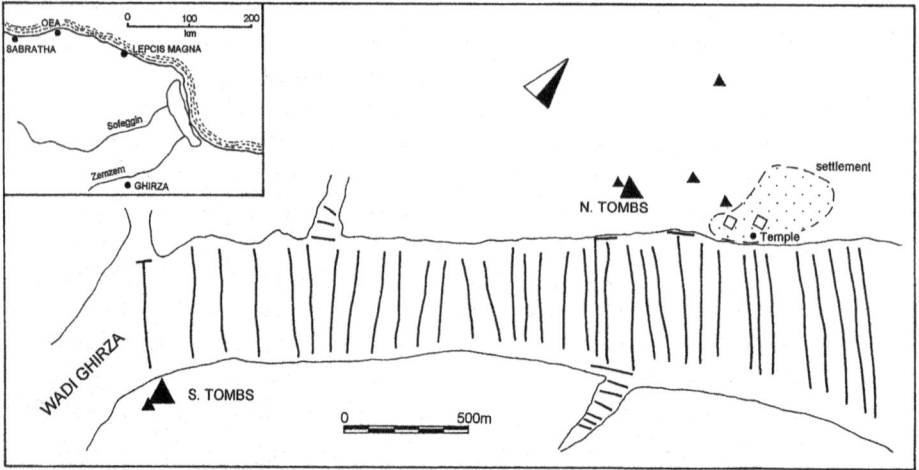

FIGURE 9.1. General plan of Ghirza, showing the relation between the settlement and its cemeteries. Inset: Map of Libya, showing location of Ghirza. (After Brogan and Smith 1984, with modifications.)

fortified structures and there was also a substantial temple, arguably of far wider significance than the village of Ghirza itself.[7] There were two cemeteries with monumental tombs at Ghirza (see figs. 9.1–9.2); the first lay a short distance south of the settlement on the west side of the wadi (the North Tombs); the second lay on the east bank about 1.5 kilometers south of the main site (the South Tombs).[8] The north group (see figs. 9.1–9.4) comprized six ashlar tombs (North A–F) and the south group another six (South A, C–G). There was an additional monument in each cemetery (North G and South B) whose function is more enigmatic. For convenience, I shall refer to the various funerary structures as NA, NB, SA, SC, and so on. The Ghirza group mostly conforms to a single architectural form, the temple type, with a series of colonnaded arcades arranged around a central masonry core, or *cella* (see figs. 9.3–9.4). In some cases the *cella* was decorated with a false doorway, with the burials normally being placed in a subterranean chamber below.[9]

The heyday of the site (and the period to which most of the tombs relate) appears to be the late third to fourth centuries AD. The mausolea constitute the single largest concentration of elite funerary monuments

[7] Brogan and Smith 1984, 40–92.

[8] Ibid., 119–226. More recent discussions of the reliefs from the tombs include Fontana 1998; and Mattingly 1999, 2003b.

[9] Barker et al. 1996a, 144–49.

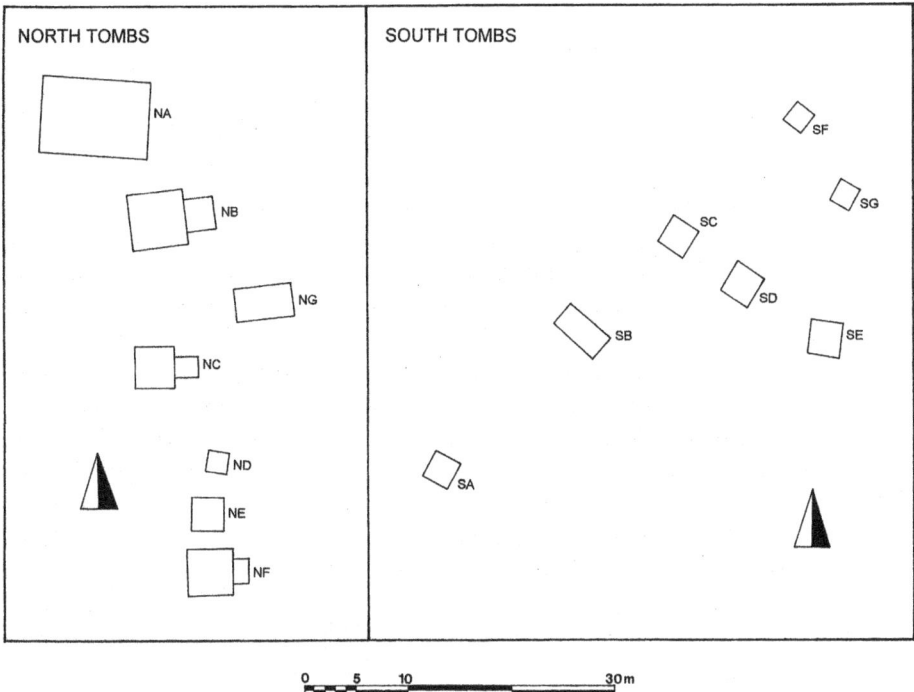

FIGURE 9.2 Plans of North and South Cemeteries. (After Brogan and Smith 1984, with modifications.)

in the region, suggesting that Ghirza had some special status within the pre-desert zone.[10] Yet reaction to these tombs and their iconography has been quite variable:

> And although I had not allowed my imagination to rise at all in proportion to the exhilarating accounts I had heard, I could not but be sorely disappointed ... I found them of a mixed style, and in very indifferent taste, ornamented with ill-proportioned columns and clumsy capitals. The regular architectural divisions of frieze and cornice being neglected, nearly the whole depth of the entablatures was loaded with absurd representations of warriors, huntsmen, camels, horses, and other animals in low relief, or rather scratched on the freestone.... The human figures and animals are miserably executed, and are generally small, though they vary in height from about three feet and a half

[10] See, for example, Brogan 1965, 47–56; Barker et al. 1996a, 144–49; and Mattingly 1995, 162–67.

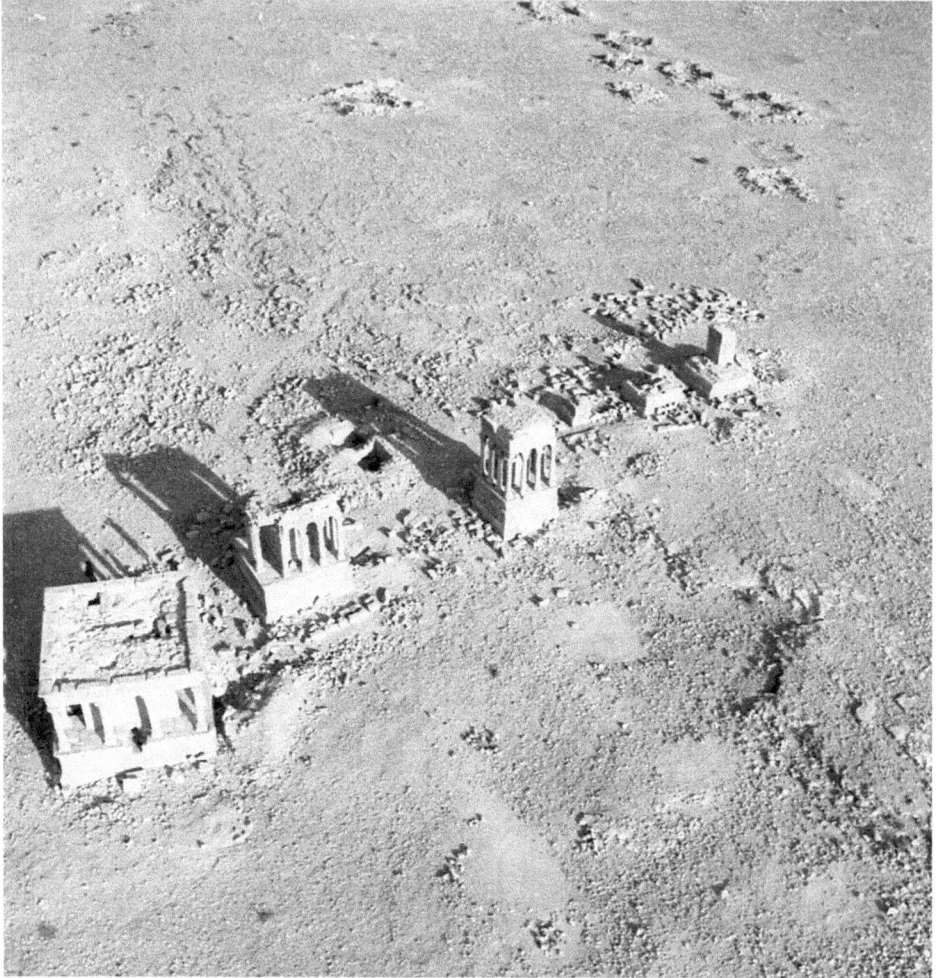

FIGURE 9.3 Aerial view of North Cemetery looking north with tomb NA on the left. (Photo: ULVS.)

a foot in height, even on the same tombs, which adds to their ridiculous effect.[11]

On me n'avait pas exageré la beauté de ces monuments. Elle a dépassé de beaucoup mon attent. Ces ruines sont les plus belles de toute la Tripolitaine . . . On ne trouve nulle part en Afrique des tombeaux comparable à ceux-ci par la richesse de la sculpture et par les proportions.

---

[11] Captain Smythe, quoted in Beechey and Beechey 1828, 504–12.

The beauty of these monuments has not been exaggerated. They sur-passed by far my expectation. These ruins are the most beautiful in the whole of Tripolitania. One cannot find anywhere in Africa tombs comparable with these for the richness of the sculpture or for their proportions.[12]

One group of scholars, then, has celebrated the art of these tombs as a sign of the "Romanization" of the pre-desert communities, a point en-hanced by the fact that several of the tombs bore Latin inscriptions. Some went so far as to claim that Italian colonists must have been responsible (though the names on the tombs are Libyan).[13] The ambivalence or dis-satisfaction of a second group of scholars is in part a product of the "oth-erness" of these tombs when judged by the highest standards of Roman decor and representation. We are dealing with a very regional style of art and symbolism. Failing to assimilate it easily with the mainstream, the tendency among some nineteenth- and early-twentieth-century scholars was to devalue it, or more insulting still, to claim that it must be Byzan-tine in date as it was so debased in style![14]

Both of the approaches described above, however, share a common per-ception that the art of the tombs was fundamentally attempting to emu-late Roman culture. The difference of opinion is essentially a question of judgment concerning the relative success achieved. We may note in pass-ing that higher standards of representational sculpture were achieved on elite estates nearer to the coast—as in the case of the well-known plowing scene from a mausoleum at Tigi.[15] Looked at from a Roman perspective the debased sculptural norms of the Ghirza reliefs are suggestive of a trickle down effect of Roman culture on the remoter fringes of empire.[16]

Yet can the tombs and their art support another type of reconstruc-tion? There is no doubt that these sculptures have some unusual char-acteristics when judged against mainstream Roman art. Key stylistic ele-ments here are the *horror vacui* and multiple horizons of many scenes, leading to some unusual and distinctly un-Roman compositional fields (see figs. 9.5–9.9).[17] These standards go back to Punic times in North Africa and find their counterpart in other areas of Romano-African art—

[12] Mathuisieulx 1912, 71–72.

[13] Goodchild 1976, 8.

[14] Merighi 1940, 177.

[15] Brogan 1965; cf. Ferchiou 1989b.

[16] The important article by Fontana (1998) appeared after the early drafts of this paper was written (and its essential shape achieved) and his analysis, though different in many respects, shares an emphasis on power and is broadly supportive of the approach adopted here.

[17] Di Vita 1964, 73–79.

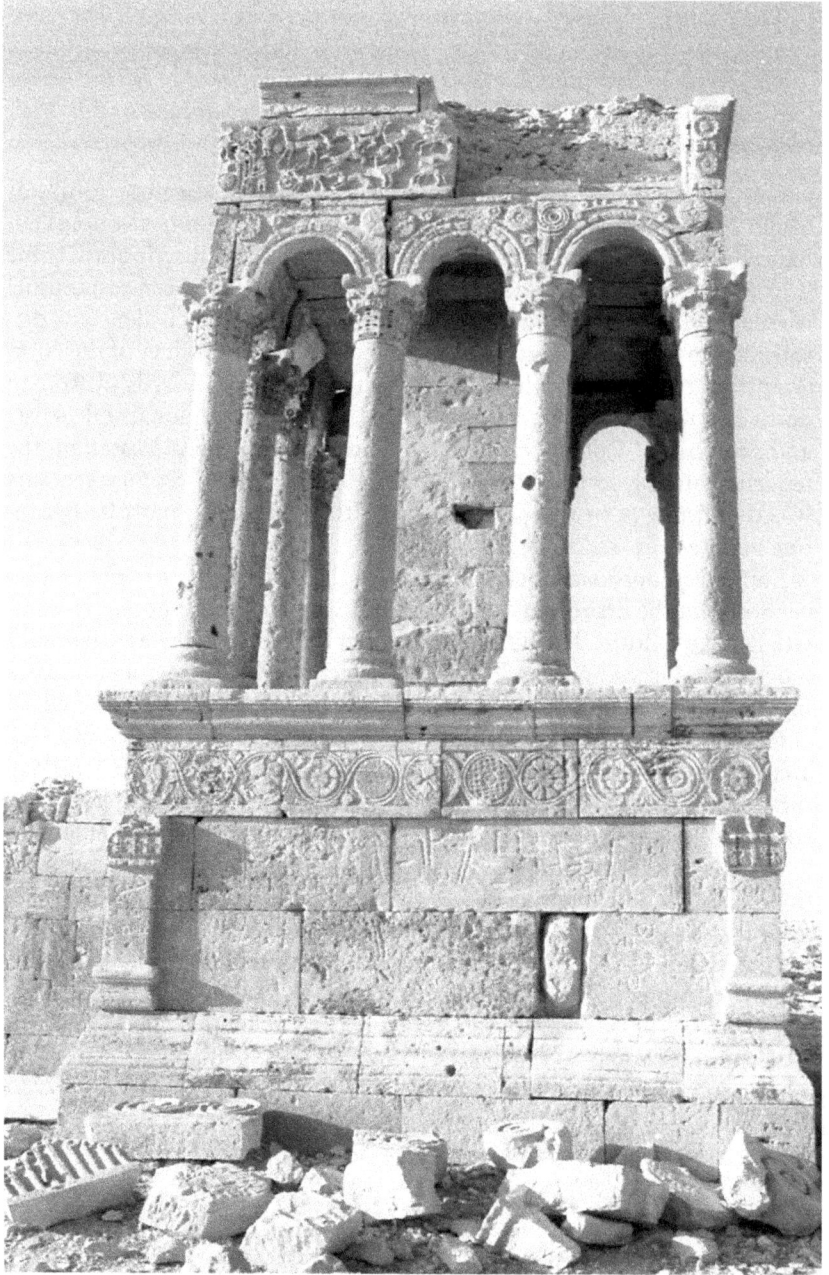

FIGURE 9.4 Detail of temple tomb NC, showing original position of reliefs on the arcade aches and on the frieze above. The surviving fragment of the frieze shows (left) the harvesting of cereals and (right) a hunting scene. (Photo: ULVS.)

perhaps most notably in mosaic composition.[18] Yet, when we explore the African context of the iconography and style, a remarkably different picture of the art emerges. In particular, the artistic themes of the Ghirza tombs have many parallels in the corpus of funerary art of other parts of Tripolitania and with Libyan and Punic sacred art.[19] I want to emphasize at the outset that these tombs must be read not simply as monuments to the dead but as structures that had a continuing religious significance for the living. The architecture of the tombs fits into a long tradition in Roman Africa, fusing Hellenistic, Punic, and Roman traditions with African ritual needs and ideology.[20] This cultural complexity—indeed, *ambiguity* is a better word—runs through art, religion, and material culture in Roman Africa.[21] We ignore at our peril the Libyan component in all this. As it happens, the closest parallel for the architectural form of the predominant temple tombs at Ghirza comes from even farther out into the desert, from the oasis center of Ghadames (see fig. 9.1 for location).[22]

THEMES IN THE ART OF THE TOMBS

In her brilliant and perceptive discussion of the tombs and their art, Olwen Brogan broadly divided the sculptures into three groups: (1) symbolic images, (2) scenes of daily life, and (3) religious scenes.[23] I have summarized these data in tables 9.1 and 9.2 and commented in another paper on some aspects of their significance.[24]

In the rest of this chapter I shall focus on imagery relating to the family and to the power networks constructed around both living and dead members of the principal families at Ghirza. The existence of two major fortified structures at the heart of the settlement and of two discreet monumental cemeteries suggests that there were two main elite families, or perhaps two branches of a single family, at Ghirza. An alternative would be to see the cemeteries as clan-based, but in Libyan society such units were in any case normally based around extended family units.[25] As a working hypothesis, then, it seems reasonable to infer the presence of two dominant families.

---

[18] See the interestingly similar ideas expressed in Fantar 1999.
[19] See Brogan 1954, 1965, 1978 for Tripolitanian funerary reliefs.
[20] See, for example, Coarelli and Thébert 1988, 761–818; see also the important collection of essays in Stone and Stirling 2007.
[21] Mattingly and Hitchner 1995, 204–9.
[22] Coro 1956; Mercier 1953.
[23] Brogan and Smith 1984, 207–12, 215–24.
[24] Mattingly 1999b.
[25] Brett and Fentress 1996, 200–270; Mattingly 1995, 17–24.

TABLE 9.1
Symbolic sculpture, fertility imagery, and mythological themes on the Ghirza tombs

Tomb No.	NA	NB	NC	ND	NE	NF	SA	SC	SD	SE	SF	SG	Other Trip, e.g.
TYPE	Te	Ar	Ar	Ar	Ar	Ar	Ob	Ar	Ar	Ar	Ar	Ar	Ar
Inscriptions	*	*	*										*
SYMBOLIC SCULPTURES													
Decorative elements													
False doors	*?	*	*		*	*	*			*			*
Star rosettes	*	*	*		*		*				*	*	*
Flower rosettes	*	*	*	*		*	*	*		*	*	*	*
Roundels	*	*	*		*					*		*	*
Segmented discs			*				*	*		*	*		
Wreaths		*					*	*		*		*?	*
Mortuary imagery													
Lions	*	*	*		*		*	*	*	*		*	*
Herbivore attacked by lion	*								*				*
Lions with bulls' heads								*				*	*
Feline masks			*					*		*	*	*	*
Winged victories		*											*
Eagles with prey	*									*		*?	*
Cockrels					*?			*					*
Peacock											*	*	*
Fish			*	*		*		*		*	*	*	*

TABLE 9.1 (cont.)

Tomb No.	NA	NB	NC	ND	NE	NF	SA	SC	SD	SE	SF	SG	Other Trip, e.g.
Symbols of fertility													
Vine scrolls	*			*								*	*
Inhabited scrolls		*	*								*		*
Cantharus	*											*	*
Two birds and cup	*												*
Bunches of grapes			*	*						*	*	*	*
Pomegranates			*								*?		*
Phallic carvings			*					*			*		*
Sacred basket (calathus)													
Date palms		*	*	*		*				*	*	*	*
Pinecones							*						*
Mythological themes													
Hercules (Melkart?)		*?							*?				
Sphinxes									*?				
Sirens			*?										

Source: Data extracted from Brogan and Smith 1984, with some additions.

Note: Tomb types are abbreviated as follows: Te = Temple type; Ar = Arcaded temple type; OB = Obelisk type.

TABLE 9.2

Scenes of daily life, hunting, ceremonial and ritual activity on the Ghirza tombs

Tomb No.	NA	NB	NC	ND	NE	NF	SA	SC	SD	SE	SF	SG	Other Trip, e.g.
SCENES OF DAILY LIFE													
Ploughing		*	*					*					*
Sowing		*	*					*					*
Clearing vegetation		*	*?					*					
Reaping		*	*					*					*
Threshing/winnowing		*	*										
Camel caravans		*	*					*					
Trading amphora?				*									
Date harvest											*		
Grape harvest											*	*	
Olive tree?									*?				
Camels		*	*		*			*					*
Cattle	*	*	*						*		*		*
Dogs		*	*		*				*	*	*		*
Goats									*	*	*		*
Horses		*	*					*	*				*
HUNTING													
Lion hunts		*	*		*?					*?			
Stag hunts		*							*				

TABLE 9.2 (*cont.*)

Tomb No.	NA	NB	NC	ND	NE	NF	SA	SC	SD	SE	SF	SG	Other Trip, e.g.
Bull fights	*	*											
Hare hunts		*			*							*?	
Ostriches and ostrich hunts	*	*	*	*	*				*	*	*		
Gazelle/antelope hunts		*	*		*							*	
Leopards/Cheetahs?		*											*
IMAGES OF THE DECEASED													
Portraits	*	*					*	*	*	*	*?	*?	*
Statues							*						*
CEREMONIAL SCENES													
Seated chieftains		*	*										*
Presentation of "gifts"?		*	*								*?		*
Punishment/executions?		*	*										
Combat scenes	*	*									*		
Armed men		*	*		*					*?	*	*	
Men on horseback		*	*		*?				*		*	*	*
SACRIFICIAL SCENES													
Bull	*												
Goat											*		
Temple with severed heads?											*		

FIGURE 9.5 Chieftain scene from Tomb NB. (Lepcis Magna Museum.)

The family links are given added emphasis on the tombs in the North Cemetery that feature detailed inscriptions (NA, NB, NC), where the importance of lineage and of the maintenance of tombs and rituals associated with them are stressed. The named individuals on these three tombs were success stories in the Roman imperial equation. They bear Roman *nomina* alongside Libyan *cognomina* and were able to pay for expensive and locally highly impressive funerary monuments. The Latin of these texts (albeit far from perfect) would at first sight appear to add credence to the view that these people were above all interested in the emulation of Roman elite behavior. However, a number of factors suggest a different conclusion, not least the fact that several others of the tombs bore texts in Punic (so-called Latino-Punic) and Libyan.[26]

IMAGERY OF POWER AND STATUS

There is abundant imagery on the tombs that speaks of individual power over others, and this may be understood to be a prime function of the tombs' iconography.[27] The so-called chieftain scenes on tombs NB and NC (and echoes of chiefly regalia also on some of the South Cemetery

[26] Brogan and Smith 1984, 181, 262–63.

[27] Ibid., 217; Camps 1989, 11–40. This is the theme that is most strongly picked up on in Fontana 1998.

FIGURE 9.6 Chieftain scene from Tomb NC.

tombs—for example, SF) are the prime evidence of this (see figs. 9.5–9.7). They appear to show the bestowal of certain items of regalia or equipment (scepter, scroll, wine cup, jug, quiver) and other gifts to an individual whose power is emphasized both by his scale in the scene and his position, seated on a folding chair.[28] The scene is paired on both NB and NC by another, more disturbing one in which two individuals appear to inflict punishment (perhaps even execute) a third man standing in submissive pose between them.[29] There are numerous other scenes showing individuals bearing arms and in several cases (tombs NA, NB, SF) these feature scenes of human combat.[30] From this we may conclude that the chieftains at Ghirza held substantial powers, and it has been plausibly suggested that these were delegated to them by Rome as part of the increasingly informal late Roman frontier arrangements.[31]

Another group of scenes depicts farming practices (see fig. 9.8). We see the entire process of the cultivation of cereals from ground clearance, to ploughing and sowing, to harvesting, threshing, and winnowing.[32] Two other scenes show camel caravans and another carving depicts an amphora being carried by a man in front of a camel bearing two further amphorae on its back and pulling a two-wheeled cart.[33] We are perhaps entitled to consider these latter scenes as illustrating the marketing of

[28] Brogan and Smith 1984, plates 63, 78.
[29] Ibid., plates 63, 79.
[30] Ibid., plates 55, 61, 123–24.
[31] Ibid., 227–32; Mattingly 1995, 194–200; cf. Rushworth 2000, 2004 on the correlation of late antique Berber kingdoms with *limes* sectors along the African frontier.
[32] See, for example, Brogan and Smith 1984, plates 64–67.
[33] Ibid., plates 67, 82, 110.

FIGURE 9.7 Scene with chieftain and regalia, tomb NC. (Jamahariyah Museum, Tripoli.)

the produce of the wadi farms (grain and liquid products such as oil and wine). These economic scenes have generally been read simply as scenes of daily life. An alternative would be to see them as symbolic of the economic power of the elite families. To take this a stage further, they could also be read as images of things requiring the protection of the ancestors honored by the tombs.

There are many depictions of men on horseback, an obvious indication of status—especially in an age when regular army units on the frontier were having their mounts withdrawn for reasons of imperial cost-cutting, and though some of these scenes show hunts, others have a more ceremonial look (for example, see fig. 9.7).[34] Sleek dogs feature not only in the thick of the action in numerous hunting scenes (see fig. 9.4, scene on frieze of tomb NC), but are also represented in other scenes.[35] Both horses and hunting dogs can be read as clear status symbols.[36]

Status is commonly denoted by subtle differences in the dress of the figures, which is in all cases very simply and schematically indicated. Most of the figures depicted in the reliefs wear very simple tunics, gathered in at the waist by belts, with heavy vertical lines presumably signifying folds in the cloth rather than texture or pattern of the weave (see fig. 9.8). The elite figures are emphasized by reason of their exaggerated size, by their central positions in ceremonial scenes, and by the fact that they are almost invariably depicted with more complex costumes (see figs. 9.5–9.7). Most commonly there are indications of outer garments worn

[34] Ibid., plates 62, 69, 70.
[35] Ibid., plates 70, 79, 82.
[36] Daumas 1968.

FIGURE 9.8 Cultivation scene, tomb SC. (Jamahariyah Museum, Tripoli.)

over the tunic. In many cases for both men and women this is indicated as a generously cut length of cloth wrapped diagonally around the body in a manner more akin to the Arab burnoose than the toga. Although in the case of portraits (see fig. 9.9) it could be argued that this represents a funeral shroud rather than an everyday garment, there are examples of full-length figures in "scenes of everyday life" who are picked out by such differentiation in costume. Indeed, diagonal lines in the depiction of dress on the Ghirza tombs can almost invariably be taken as a sign of status. In other instances (e.g., NC), men are depicted with cloaks and women with ornate dresses. In the two scenes with seated chieftain (NB and NC), the principal figure is shown wearing an ornately decorated cloak or garment with horizontal bands of ornamentation (see figs. 9.5–9.6). Other symbols of female elite status include the depictions of items of jewelry and turbanlike headresses. Overall, these costumes do not appear to emulate Roman models.[37]

IMAGERY OF THE FAMILY

Several tombs feature portraits of the deceased—this is certain for NA, SA (where a man and woman feature both as busts and statues), SC (see fig. 9.9), SD, and SE.[38] The naive style of these portraits can easily be

[37] Mathuisieulx 1912, 73.
[38] See, for example, Brogan and Smith 1984, plates 53, 99, 103.

FIGURE 9.9 Family portrait, tomb SC. (Jamahariyah Museum, Tripoli.)

mistaken for poor craftwork, but there are ample parallels for this style of representation in Roman Africa and it seems to have been deliberately maintained even at times and places when stonemasons were producing far more sophisticated work for other types of use. Typically, the style is associated with the so-called Saturn stele and with funerary monuments. Characteristic of this indigenous tradition of representation (which I shall describe as the Libyco-Punic tradition) is the frontality, the large and dominating eyes, and the differential scaling of figures in terms of importance in the scene.

As has already been noted, ancestral links are established and supported by the architectural setting and epigraphic statements of the tombs. While the Libyan notables clearly appropriate some Roman imagery, it can hardly be claimed that they aimed simply to emulate Roman culture. To summarize thus far, the Ghirza tombs are laden with power-related imagery. The question is, at whom was it aimed, and for what purpose?

THE NATURE OF THE LIBYAN ANCESTOR CULT

I have noted earlier that many images depict aspects of life requiring the protection of ancestors. That support was maintained through the observation of elaborate rites long after the death and burial of individual ancestors. The visual display of the earthly powers of ancestors could serve to remind their spirits to look to the continuance of such power in later generations. Such reverence of ancestors and their tombs was certainly an important trait of Libyan culture, and there is absolutely no need to seek explanations outside Africa for this.[39] The essential counterpart of permanent visual prompts to one's ancestors was a formal ceremony at the tomb on a regular basis. Another element of the Libyan ancestor cult was the practice of sleeping at a family tomb for the experience of visionary responses. This is attested across a broad time frame as demonstrated by the two examples below from the fifth century BC and first century AD:

> For divination they take themselves to the graves of their ancestors and, after praying, lie down to sleep upon the graves: by the dreams that come to them they guide their conduct.[40]

> The Augilae consider the spirits of their ancestors as gods, they swear by these and consult them as oracles, and, having made their requests, treat the dreams of those who sleep in their tombs as responses.[41]

The popularity of offering tables, altars, and libation spouts on tombs in the Maghreb supports the view that specific rituals were offered to the dead throughout the Roman period, and all these features are found at Ghirza. The tombs themselves evolved as sacred architecture, and the predominant adoption of the temple form at Ghirza is striking in this regard. However, the most convincing evidence of an ancient ancestor cult is provided by the two least spectacular structures in the monumental cemeteries. Both the North and South cemeteries at Ghirza contain a seventh monumental structure of near identical plan and unadorned with reliefs (NG and SB). These structures comprised a semisubterranean mortuary chamber that interconnected with a small chamber accessible from the surface and containing a bench along the back wall facing the tomb chamber (see fig. 9.10).[42] Given the lack of architectural decoration, it is possible that these structures represent some sort of vision house, where one could commune on specific occasions with the mortal remains and spiritual "vibes" of Grandad Fydel or Grandma Thesylgum. Unlike the other tombs, where there was no provision for visitors to spend time in the subterranean burial chambers, these two structures appear to be purpose-built as chapels or dream houses in which the living could pass time in close proximity to the dead.[43] The two structures

---

[39] Mattingly 1995, 207.
[40] Herodotus, *History*, 4.172.
[41] Mela, *De Situ Orbis*, 1.8.45.
[42] Brogan and Smith 1984, 178–80.
[43] Camps 1986, 151–64; Luni 1987.

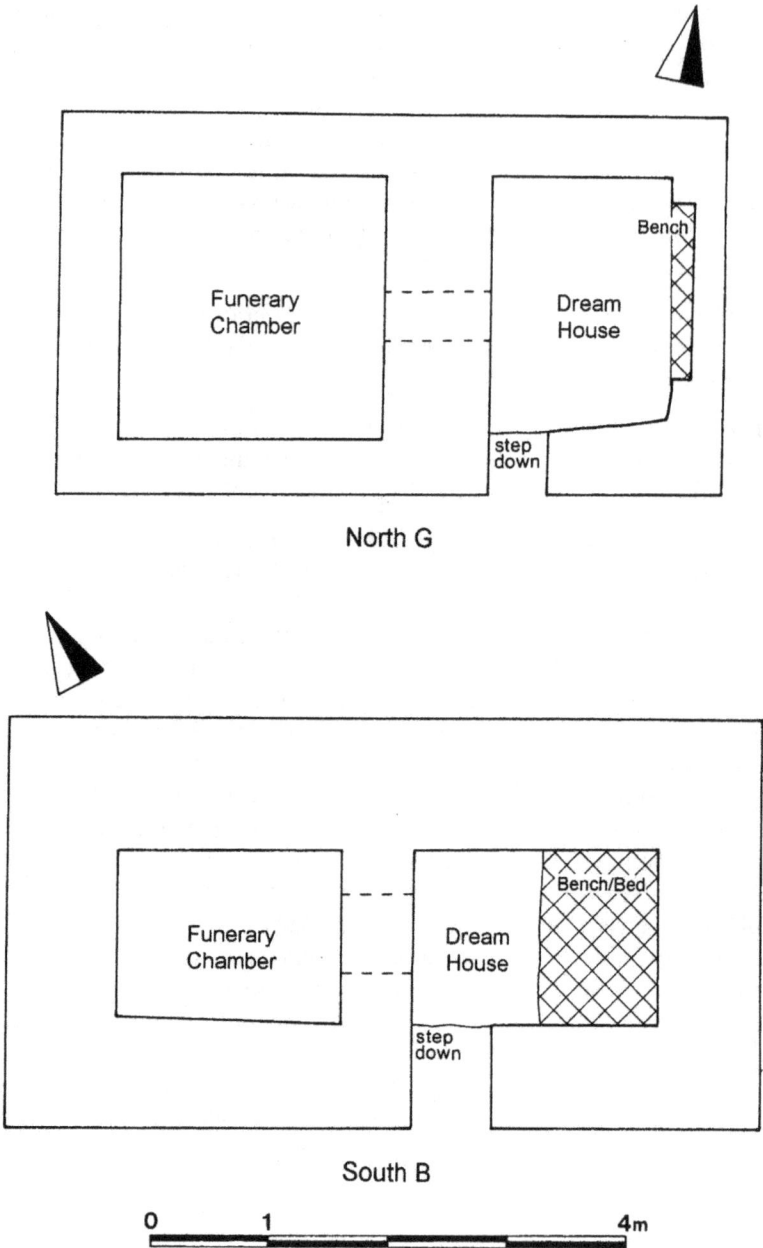

FIGURE 9.10 Comparative plans of the possible "dream houses" NG and SB. (After Brogan and Smith 1984, with modifications.)

occupy pivotal space within both cemeteries, set apart from but faced by the other tombs (see fig. 9.2). A case can be made, then, for arguing that the ancestor cult was particularly strong at Ghirza, linked in part to Ghirza's status as a regional religious center (of which more will be mentioned shortly).

The tomb inscriptions from NB and NC contain injunctions to the children and grandchildren of the deceased to continue to visit and observe rites at the tombs. Libation spouts were provided for the pouring of liquids down into the funerary chambers of the tombs, and an extraordinary Latin inscription found in close proximity to tomb NA records the celebration of an event called in the text *parentalia*, but which I doubt bore the slightest resemblance to the Italian festival of the same name.[44] The Italian ceremony was generally a commemoration of their close kinsfolk by small family groups, accompanied by simple offerings. It is likely that the Latin term is employed at Ghirza simply as the closest one to convey the concept of an ancestor cult. The Ghirza text informs us of a great sacrifice held to celebrate this *parentalia*, apparently with fifty-one bulls and thirty-eight goats being killed.[45] As family celebrations go, this was some barbecue party—there would have been enough meat here to feed several thousand people![46] Invitations to this event thus extended well beyond those actually living at Ghirza and this was probably a tribal affair, in part linked to the regional power of the settlement's leading families and in part to Ghirza's status as the probable cult center of the Libyan god Gurzil.[47] The number of animals slaughtered is ample testimony to the wealth and power of the Ghirza elite, though I suspect that in fact many of these animals were brought specially for the occasion by those attending from outside Ghirza. It is debatable whether there was enough grazing land in the immediate vicinity of Ghirza itself to support a herd of several hundred cattle, and many of these animals most probably arrived on the hoof, brought as gifts or tribute by participants in the ceremony. In this context, the imagery reflecting the personal prestige of the principal families has a clear ongoing function—after all, it would be seen at such *parentalia* celebrations by hundreds or thousands of people and would help to persuade them to continue to respect the power of the elite at Ghirza and to bestow "tribute"—gifts for the sacrifice. The scale of the sacrifice matches the impressive funerary architecture and iconography produced to honor and appease those ancestors.

[44] Brogan and Smith 1984, 135, 161, 261–62.
[45] Ibid., 162.
[46] Holloway 1975, 59–62.
[47] Mattingly 1995, 206–7.

Although the tombs may be considered to have been ostensibly Roman in influence, to a larger extent the art and iconography described above is a product of Punic and Libyan culture, and one may suggest that in part it reflects cultural resistance to Rome.[48] Much of it was of course susceptible to different or multiple readings, but the selection of images was not accidental, and virtually everything must have had significance within the cultural milieu of the Libyan pre-desert. Tombs were not simply empty memorials; they served to demonstrate the social standing of descendants and they had an important religious and sacred value in Libyan society. We may note that many standard elements of pagan Roman funerary iconography are absent or poorly represented here—scenes from classical mythology in particular. Those that are present may have been selected because they had a certain resonance in Libyan society. This role would seem to have overlapped with other areas of religious belief—a point particularly emphasized by the many parallels between the symbols on the tombs and those represented in the thousands of Saturn stelae from Tunisia and Algeria. Saturn (the Roman version of Baal Hammon) was arguably the most popular divinity in pre-Christian Africa, but his role was taken on to a considerable degree in Tripolitania by Ammon (or Jupiter Hammon), the god of the desert who seems to have shared many of Baal Hammon's attributes.[49] Many mundane decorative elements that might at first appear redolent of *Romanitas* can be shown to have special significance in Libyan religion (see figs. 9.4 and 9.7). Rosettes, roundels, vines, grapes, the date palm, pomegranates, lions, sheep, goats, livestock, peacocks, birds (especially the cockerel), and farming imagery can all be found on the Saturn stele. Lions and peacocks had associations with Tanit/Caelestis, as did fish. The grape vine, bunches of grapes, the *cantharus* can be seen as symbols of Punic Shadrapa (over time adopting much of the iconography of Liber Pater or Dionysos), and this was another cult popular among African communities (the wine jugs and cups present in the chieftain scenes on the tombs may have been for sacred rather than for profane use). We need to review much more closely these Punic and Berber cultural affiliations of the iconography of Romano-African art.[50]

In this context, the heraldic bull heads on tombs SC, SD, and SG; the bull sacrifice on NA; and the bullfights on NB and NC take on another connotation in connection with a Libyan god called Gurzil, who

---

[48] Mattingly 1996b.
[49] Brouquier Reddé 1992b, 255–66.
[50] Brett and Fentress 1996, 17–31; Camps 1980; Stone 2007.

features largely in the sixth-century poem of Corippus.[51] Gurzil was the bullheaded progeny of Ammon and clearly had a cult center in the Libyan pre-desert region. The similarity of the name with Ghirza is not of course conclusive (though we know from El-Bekri that there were tombs at a place called Gurza that were (still) worshipped in the tenth century— showing that the toponym is likely to be a very early one).[52] On the other hand, the importance of the bull iconography and the extraordinary scale of the bull sacrifice held at Ghirza, perhaps on an annual basis, are to my mind compelling arguments for the identification. So, my alternative interpretation of the Ghirza tombs links them to a distinctly Libyan cultural agenda, with a family exercising regional power in part through the close association between their own ancestor cult and a significant religious center. The artistic repertoire of the family tombs served to legitimate and enhance their power in this society.

The late Neolithic rock art of the Sahara is another possible source of inspiration for the relief art that has as yet been unexplored by classical archaeologists. Although separated from the Ghirza reliefs by at least 3,500 years, the rock engravings and paintings do detail the emergence of a hierarchical society with increasingly complex religious rituals.[53] Of particular interest in the light of the Gurzil cult is the prevalence of images of bovines in the Saharan rock, some with decorated horns, solar discs, and the like.[54] Numerous scenes show theophoric figures, with human bodies and animal heads or masks.[55] Gurzil presumably developed in part from this tradition. Future studies, then, could perhaps try to compare and contrast the image repertoire of Neolithic and Roman art in Libya.

CONCLUSION

The study of art and power merits much greater attention. Here I refer, of course, not simply to power in society (there is ample evidence from these tombs to demonstrate that function of the art), but in a broader sense to the relationship between an imperial system and the artistic production within its frontiers. Roman imperial art provided an image pool

[51] Diggle and Goodyear 1970; Mattingly 1983; cf. *Encyclopédie Berbère* 38–39, s.v. "Laguatan."

[52] El Bekri 1913, 31; Mattingly 1995, 212–13.

[53] Le Quellec 1998; Mori 1998; Muzzolini 1991; cf. Lutz and Lutz 1995; Gauthier and Gauthier 1997.

[54] Lutz and Lutz 1995, 114–28.

[55] Ibid., 145–64.

to support the legitimacy of power in provincial society. But the cultural agenda followed need not be one of simple cultural emulation (as often understood by the term Romanization). The art from Ghirza seems to borrow Roman ideas about the representation of power, but to deploy them alongside a set of family values and religious reference points that were preeminently un-Roman.[56] To that extent, Romanization seems a very inadequate and inaccurate term for the cultural process discussed in this chapter.[57]

[56] Mattingly 1995, 160–70, 202–13; see also Grahame 1998.

[57] Indeed, it seems an excellent example of discrepant identity in action on the fringes of the empire.

Empire Experienced

In exploring the experience of empire I have tried to bring together a series of new ideas about the character of Roman imperialism and colonialism, about its economic impacts, about the operation of power in colonial societies, and about the way in which people under imperial rule construct complex and overlapping identities to mediate their experience. I believe that I have offered a viable alternative to Romanization as a framework for interpretation.

At the heart of the essays that make up this volume there is a series of ideas about the nature of the Roman Empire and Roman imperialism. I shall summarize these here in the form of a series of key propositions that link across the chapters.

Proposition 1. "Roman Imperialism" Is a Valid Construct within Comparative Debates on the Nature of Imperialism and Colonialism

Is it legitimate to compare the Roman Empire with later (or earlier) manifestations of imperialism? Opinion is divided, and many differences between Roman imperialism and modern capitalist empires have been pointed out. I accept these differences are real and need to be more explicitly recognized. They also inhibit a certain type of comparative study, but I have no problem with using terms like *empire*, *imperialism*, *colonialism*, and *colonization* in relation to the Roman state as long as proper definitions are offered. To do otherwise is to deny an intrinsic quality of the Roman Empire at its height—its overwhelmingly greater scale and complexity when compared with its constituent parts or virtually all its neighbors and other states of the ancient world.[1] In the end, the structures and pathways of power in the Roman Empire (and the problems of maintaining these) have more in common with other imperial regimes across a

---

[1] Factors that set the Roman state apart include its overall territorial extent, its reach beyond its frontiers, its size of population, its armies (both for scale and organization), its communications and the infrastructure of power, its urban networks, its economic structures and the scale of interregional trade, the scale of its exploitation of natural resources, its consumption patterns, and the extraordinary opportunities of wealth, luxury, and power available to its leading elites.

broad diachronic span. I have argued in chapter 1 that we should not be afraid to explore more fully these systemic aspects of power within imperial and colonial situations. In chapter 4, I gave an illustration of how this can be achieved to shed light on transgressive use of power in sexual relations, with implications for our understanding of both the Roman experience and more recent imperial situations.[2]

Proposition 2. The Study of Roman Imperialism Is Bound Up with Subsequent Discourses on the Nature of Imperialism

As we saw in chapters 1 and 2, the study of the Roman Empire involves three separate colonial discourses—one ancient and two modern. Source criticism, of course, must take account of the distortions due to Roman representation of their own world as they saw it. The modern discourses are even trickier to disentangle. The evolution of the subject, especially in the nineteenth and early twentieth centuries, has been heavily influenced by the mental and physical engagement of generations of Western scholars in a colonial world of their own time. This has had profound repercussions in the way the discipline has been structured and the agenda that has been prioritized down to the present. There is a second intertwined discourse involving the way the Roman Empire has been consistently used in Western thought to explore and explain the experience of the late Medieval to modern reemergence of superstates, from the Spanish in South America to the British in India to Americans in Iraq. Both of these modern discourses, if unacknowledged, are obstacles to understanding the realities of the past. They distort the modern view of the Roman world in subtle and not so subtle ways. Before we even contemplate the introduction of new approaches (from postcolonial studies or elsewhere), we must recognize the need to decolonialize the discipline of classical studies.

Proposition 3. Roman Imperialism and Colonialism Were Dynamic Processes that Evolved and Were Transformed over Time

One problem with many modern attempts to model Roman imperialism is the implicit assumption that this was somehow a static and once-and-

---

[2] I also believe that until we have a better understanding of the realities of ancient imperialism, we have little chance of persuading contemporary opinion shapers and world leaders of the unforeseen consequences and impacts of neoimperialist acts. Perhaps it is time we made more compelling arguments about the experience of past empires!

for-all phenomenon, with one set of motivations and an unvarying ethos to underpin its operation. In chapter 1, comparison with broader models of imperialism and colonialism have suggested that we need to revise this view and to recognize that the nature of Roman imperialism and colonialism changed radically over time. Perhaps one of the essential characteristics of Roman colonialism was the way in which it incorporated both repressive and integrationist tendencies vis à vis conquered peoples. This was an empire that showed no compunction about shedding blood and enslaving people on an industrial scale, but that could also countenance and facilitate provincial elites joining the metropolitan inner circle of power, wealth, and influence.

PROPOSITION 4. WE HAVE MUCH TO LEARN FROM POSTCOLONIAL AND SUBALTERN STUDIES

Another key argument of chapter 1 was that we should engage more fully with the agendas being promulgated within postcolonial/subaltern studies. If we accept that Roman imperialism is a valid player in comparative studies of imperialism (proposition 1, above), then it is self-evident that the intellectual energy generated in postcolonial studies has much to offer us. If we are also to integrate our research with other current issues of international relations, such as globalization, we need to approach these topics with an awareness of how they are being discussed by postcolonial scholars. I have tried to follow this agenda in various ways in every chapter.

PROPOSITION 5. THE ROMANIZATION PARADIGM IS NO LONGER WORKABLE

Enough has been said in chapters 1 and 8 about the need to deconstruct or replace the outmoded term *Romanization*. This book represents an attempt to move the debate forward. Several of my final group of propositions relate to ways in which we might develop alternative explanatory concepts.

PROPOSITION 6. POWER IS A PARTICULARLY SIGNIFICANT CONCEPT IN THE STUDY OF ANY EMPIRE

Sometimes, it seems to me, classical scholars are more comfortable *describing* aspects of the Roman Empire than *interpreting* them. Far too much effort is still expended in delineating categories of monuments or artifacts without adequate reference to their context in terms of past perceptions or their use in social and power networks. We are also too accepting at face value of the assurances of our sources about the good intentions of Rome and its principal imperial actors. I have tried to take a more cynical and questioning view of Roman motivations in chapters 3 and 4 on power and chapters 5–7 on provincial government and exploitation of resources.

PROPOSITION 7. THERE WAS AN ECONOMIC DRIVER OF ROMAN IMPERIALISM, THOUGH LESS OVERT THAN IN SOME MORE RECENT MANIFESTATIONS OF IMPERIALISM

A major objection to comparing the Roman Empire with modern European empires has been the lack of economic drivers for the former in comparison with the capitalistic behavior of modern colonialism. The key argument of chapter 5 is that there was nonetheless an economic "bottom line" for the Roman imperial government (due to the huge cost in preindustrial terms of its army and administration) and that this influenced decisions relating both to conquest and to disposal strategies adopted with regard to conquered lands and natural resources. In this, Rome follows quite closely the behavior of other imperial powers, where short-term deflections caused by ad hoc measures and personal vainglory are counterbalanced to some extent by long-term mechanisms to exploit systematically the territory, resources, and people incorporated (exemplified by the censuses, tax systems, land survey and redistribution, monopolistic exploitation of key resources, and impressive supply systems). I have characterized these elements as the components of an "imperial economy" that operated alongside other cycles of global and local economic activity. In chapter 6, I demonstrated that the effects of imperial rule were not invariably negative for subject peoples, using rural settlement histories in Roman Africa to illustrate that "landscapes of opportunity" were created in some provinces at certain times. The counterpart of this argument, however, is that there are many provincial landscapes that reveal a very different "trajectory of development" under Rome. Much more work is needed on the regional differences (and especially those within provinces) to expand our knowledge and understanding of the economic inequalities resulting from Rome's varying political settlement imposed on subject people. This theme was expanded in chapter 7, through a case study of a Roman mining landscape that exemplifies the priority placed by the state on its monopolistic exploitation of natural resources taken over from indigenous peoples (with scant regard for the sustainability of such activity in environmental or human terms).

Proposition 8. The Concept of "Identity" Can Be Used as a Key Tool for Studying Diversity and Hybridity

A strength of my approach to culture and identity outlined in chapter 8 is that it attempts to look at society from the top down, the bottom up, and sideways on. I have outlined an approach to identity that is robust and can be replicated from region to region; it will allow us to differentiate among different broad groups in provincial societies. There are similarities here between my approach and some of the key approaches of agency and structuration theory, but I have placed considerable emphasis on analyzing agency in relation to the power structures of empire. I also emphasize the need for reinvigorated archaeological research on artifact typologies and assemblages. The theory of discrepant identity also recognizes the essential dynamism of cultural processes. It is readily apparent that, like imperialism itself, the cultural effects varied over time and space and across society. This is an ambitious and challenging new agenda, but one that I hope can advance the study of the Roman Empire into new debates suited to the twenty-first century. In chapter 9, I presented an early attempt to read an alternative transcript in the ostensibly "Roman" art from a Libyan frontier farming community of late Roman date. At the very least, the results suggest that there are limitations in much current interpretation that primarily attempts to link provincial artworks with metropolitan iconography and understanding.

Proposition 9. Traditional Strengths of Roman Archaeology/ History Are Still Core Strengths

To paraphrase: Don't throw the baby out with the bathwater. The cumulative picture I have offered is one of a complex set of relationships between the imperial state and its subject peoples. In offering a corrective to the orthodox adulatory view of the beneficence of Rome, I have focused on areas of that relationship that were more contested or difficult for provincial subjects at large. It should not be controversial to state that the Roman Empire was not a universally loved institution, but the academic agendas sustaining the study of its literature, history, art, and archaeology have tended to perpetuate an unrealistically rosy view of its operation. If nothing else, I hope to have reminded readers that experiencing empire is not always comfortable and that, for many subjects, exploitation was all they ever knew of the voracious behemoth that was Rome. However, it is not my intention to argue that we should abandon all interest in those provincials who prospered under Roman rule. The Roman Empire depended famously on its engagement of the army and regional elites in the imperial project and many of them benefited directly through participation. Their lives and identities are as critical to our understanding of the operation and experience of the Roman Empire as are the hitherto underexposed lives of slaves (for whom creolization theory is perhaps especially pertinent), the poor underclasses, and the average man or woman in the Roman street. What is required is a melding of the traditional strengths of Roman archaeology, with new theoretically informed research agendas. Roman archaeology is remarkably data-rich in comparison, say, to European prehistory. It is time to put those data to better use, not to write them off as a bad job and start completely afresh.

Proposition 10. Taking a Critical Approach to the Roman Empire Is Not a Sign of Prejudice

Some people have objected to my recent work with complaints along the lines of: "Why all the negativity? Why not simply celebrate the grandeur that was Rome and be done with it? Why translate to the past our modern discomfort with empires and imperialism?"[3] I hope the answer to those questions is clear from the content of this volume. Nor is it true that I am simply projecting my modern (postcolonial generation) view onto the ancient world. My view is critically analytical, not negatively prejudiced, but at least two reviewers of my study *Imperial Possession* have openly accused me of anti-Roman bias.[4] That grossly distorts my position, but, more seriously, the implication appears to be that

---

[3] The reviews of my 2006 book *Imperial Possession* have been illuminating in this regard, with a number of commentators clearly uncomfortable with my critical approach. Some have tried to deflect criticism of Rome by implying that things might have been just as violent or bad had the Romans never come to Britain—see, e.g., De la Bédoyère 2006, 62: "Mattingly accuses the Romans of killing 100,000–250,000 Britons ... during the conquest AD 43–83.... How many Britons died in the intertribal warfare that preceded the Roman invasion?"

[4] Selkirk 2006, 30: "The author follows the modern fashion of not liking the Romans. He does not like them at all and loses no opportunity to disparage them." Beard 2006, 55: "For Mattingly, the Romans were and are the enemy.... Mattingly is still in danger of replacing one oversimplified model with another (for 'Romans were good' read 'Romans were bad')."

pro-Roman bias, however subconsciously hidden in our academic dis-course, is not something to be concerned about. I think my agenda in *Imperial Possession* and in the present volume is clear and balanced. As one reviewer noted, "[Imperial Possession] is the portrait of a Roman Britain that was neither a Good Thing, nor necessarily, by the much cru-eller standards of the time, a Bad Thing—just different, immeasurably and unnervingly different."[5]

In trying to define and attempt to understand that difference in the Roman past, I am, of course, building on the work of past generations of scholars and enthusiasts—many of whom were well aware of the nega-tive impacts that contact with Rome sometimes entailed.[6] But I am con-sciously bringing these threads together in a new way, with an explicit focus on the breadth and diversity of experiencing life under Roman rule. In so doing I am trying to supplement the history we have previously prioritized—the elite, proempire, "winner's view"—with an alternative transcript that has always been there, lurking in the small print of the material evidence.

.   .   .

The last word belongs to a Roman, Ammianus Marcellinus, whose later fourth-century paean to the "glory that was Rome" still resonates with our preferred rose-tinted view of an exemplary and benevolent empire in its prime, despite the fact that the barbarians were already beating at the gates! This was increasingly becoming a delusional stereotype by the later fourth century, but even in relation to the High Empire we need to con-textualize such statements within a broad discourse on imperial power. Let us not belittle our subject and its explanatory potential by uncritically adopting such simplistic views as the prime basis for our understanding of ancient Rome.

> When Rome, destined to rule as long as men exist, first gave signs of worldwide brilliance, Honour and Fortune, usually at odds, agreed a permanent truce, and so the city's power continued to grow…. Boy and man, they won laurels and triumphs from every shore of the wide world. Now, in old age, their mere name is sometimes enough for vic-tory, and they live peacefully…. Our venerable city has given over to the Caesars the right to rule their patrimony, as a frugal, thoughtful

[5] Holland 2006, 41. See also Hingley 2007b for a lengthy and positive review that fully reflects the agenda I was working on.

[6] Hopefully, my intellectual debts are made clear in the abundant referencing of the pres-ent work.

and generous parent might do to her own children. Nations bask at leisure, lands are peaceful, there are no quarrels over elections, the tranquillity of Numa's time has returned. Over all the earth Rome is called mistress and queen; the authority of her grey senators is revered; the Roman people is named with honour and fear.[7]

---

[7] Ammianus Marcellinus, *Histories*, 14.6.2–6 (adapted from the translation in Dalby 2000, 13).

REFERENCES

Author Note: Some journals have progressively fallen behind their notional cover date, so will contain a different date of publication inside from what appears on the cover. In my experience these can appear in catalogs and references with either date, so I prefer to give both here—normally referencing the notional date—e.g., (1970)—but including the actual publication date in square brackets (1970) [1973] in the full reference.

Aarts, J. 2005. "Coins, money and exchange in the Roman world: A cultural-economic perspective." *Archaeological Dialogues* 12: 1–44.

Abun-Nasr, J. M. 1975. *A history of the Maghreb.* 2nd ed. Cambridge: Cambridge University Press.

Adams, C. E. P. 2001. "Who bore the burden? The organization of stone transport in Roman Egypt." In Mattingly and Salmon 2001a, 171–92.

———. 2007. *Land transport in Roman Egypt: Economics and administration in a Roman province.* Oxford: Oxford University Press.

Adams, C. E. P., and R. Laurence. 2001. *Travel and geography in the Roman world.* London: Routledge.

Adams, J. N. 1982. *The Latin sexual vocabulary.* London: Duckworth.

———. 1994. "Latin and Punic in contact? The case of the Bu Njem ostraca." *Journal of Roman Studies* 84: 87–112.

———. 1999. "The poets of Bu Njem: Language, culture and the centurionate." *Journal of Roman Studies* 89: 109–34.

———. 2003. *Bilingualism and the Latin language.* Cambridge: Cambridge University Press.

Africa et Roma. 1979. *Africa et Roma. Acta omnium gentium ac nationum conventus latiniis litteris linguaeque fovendis.* Rome: L'Erma di Bretschneider, 1979.

Akkeraz, A., and M. Lenoir. 1982. "Les huileries de Volubilis." *Bulletin d'archéologie marocaine* 14: 69–120.

Albarella, U., C. Johnstone, and K. Vickers. 2008. "The development of animal husbandry from the late Iron Age to the end of the Roman period: A case study from south-east Britain." *Journal of Archaeological Science* 35: 1828–48.

Alcock, S. E. 1993. *Graecia capta: The landscapes of Roman Greece.* Cambridge: Cambridge University Press.

———. 1997. "Imperialism and territory: Greece a landscape of resistance?" In Mattingly 1997a, 103–15.

———. 2001. "The reconfiguration of memory in the eastern Roman Empire." In Alcock et al. 2001, 323–50.

Alcock, S. E., and J. Cherry. 2004. *Side-by-side survey: Comparative regional studies in the Mediterranean world.* Oxford: Oxbow.

Alcock, S. E., and R. Osborne, eds. 2007. *Classical Archaeology*. Oxford: Blackwell.

Alcock, S. E., T. D'Altroy, K. Morrison, and C. Sinopoli, eds. 2001. *Empires: Perspectives from archaeology and history*. Cambridge: Cambridge University Press.

Aldrete, G., and D. J. Mattingly. 1999. "Feeding the city: The organization, operation and scale of the supply system for Rome." In Potter and Mattingly 1999, 171–204.

Allen, J. J. 2006. *Hostages and hostage-taking in the Roman Empire*. Cambridge: Cambridge University Press.

Alpers, M. 1995. *Das Nachrepublikanische Finanzsystem: Fiscus und Fisci in der frühen Kaiserzeit*. Berlin: De Gruyter.

Andreau. J. 2002. "Twenty years after Moses I. Finley's 'The Ancient Economy.'" In Scheidel and Reden 2002, 33–49.

Anderson, B. 1983. *Imagined communities: Reflections on the origin and spread of nationalism*. London: Verso.

Ando, C. 2000. *Imperial ideology and provincial loyalty in the Roman Empire*. Berkeley and Los Angeles: University of California Press.

Anselmino, L., M. Bouchenaki, A. Carandini, P. Leveau, D. Manacorda, C. Pavolini, G. Pucci, and P. Salama. 1989. *Il castellum di Nador. Storia di una fattoria tra Tipasa e Caesarea (I–VI sec d.C)*. Rome: L'Erma di Bretschneider.

Appudurai, A, ed. 1986. *The social life of things: Commodities in cultural perspective*. Cambridge: Cambridge University Press.

Archéologie de l'Afrique Antique. 1970. *Archéologie de l'Afrique Antique. Bibliographie des ouvrages parus en 1970 et compléments des années antérieures*. Aix-en-Provence, France: Centre National de la Recherche Scientifique.

Argoud, G., L. Marangou, V. Panayotopoulos, and C. Villain-Gandossi. 1992. *L'eau et les hommes en Méditerranée et en Mer Noire dans l'antiquité de l'époque Mycénienne au règne de Justinien*. Athens: Centre National de la Recherche Scientifique.

Arnold, W. T. 1906. *Studies of Roman imperialism*. Manchester, England: Manchester University Press.

Ashcroft, B., G. Griffiths, and H. Tiffin. 1995. *The post-colonial studies reader*. London: Routledge.

———. 1998. *Key concepts in post-colonial studies*. London: Routledge.

Axtell, J. 2001. *Natives and newcomers: The cultural origins of North America*. Oxford: Oxford University Press.

Badian, E. 1968. *Roman imperialism in the Late Republic*. Oxford: Clarendon Press.

Bagnall, R. S. 2005. "Evidence and models for the economy of Roman Egypt." In Manning and Morris 2005, 187–204.

Bailey, C. A. 1999. "The British and indigenous peoples, 1760–1860: Power, perception and identity." In Daunton and Halpern 1999, 19–41.

Baker, P., C. Forcey, S. Jundi, and R. Witcher, eds. 1999. *TRAC 98: Proceedings of the Eighth Annual Theoretical Archaeology Conference, Leicester*. Oxford: Oxbow.

Ball, W. 2000. *Rome in the East: The transformation of an empire*. London: Routledge.

Bang, P. 1997. *Antiquity between primitivism and modernism.* Workpaper 53-97. Aarhus, Denmark: Centre for Cultural Research, Uniersity of Aarhus.

———. 2002. "Romans and Mughals: Economic integration in a tributary empire." In De Blois and Rich 2002, 1–27.

———. 2006. "Imperial bazaar: Towards a comparative understanding of markets in the Roman Empire." In Bang, Ikeguchi, and Ziche 2006, 51–88.

Bang, P., M. Ikeguchi, and H. G. Ziche, eds. 2006. *Ancient economies, modern methodologies: Archaeology, comparative history, models and institutions.* Bari, Italy: Edipuglia.

Baradez, J. 1949. *Vue aérienne de l'organisation romaine dans le sud Algérienne. Fossatum Africae.* Paris: Éditions Arts et Métiers.

Barker, G. W. W. 1985. "The UNESCO Libyan Valleys Survey: Developing methodologies for investigating ancient floodwater farming." In Buck and Mattingly 1985, 291–307.

———. 2000. "Farmers, herders and miners in the Wadi Faynan, southern Jordan: A 10,000 year landscape archaeology." In *The archaeology of drylands: Living at the margin*, ed. G. Barker and D. Gilbertson, 63–85. London: Routledge.

———. 2002. "A tale of two deserts: Contrasting desertification histories on Rome's desert frontiers." *World Archaeology* 33: 488–507.

Barker, G. W. W., R. Adams, O. H. Creighton, D. Crook, D. D. Gilbertson, J. P. Grattan, C. O. Hunt, et al. 1999. "Environment and land use in the Wadi Faynan, southern Jordan: The third season of geoarchaeology and landscape archaeology (1998)." *Levant* 31: 255–92.

Barker, G. W. W., R. Adams, O. H. Creighton, P. Daly, D. D. Gilbertson, J. P. Grattan, C. O. Hunt, et al. 2000. "Archaeology and desertification in the Wadi Faynan: The fourth (1999) season of the Wadi Faynan Landscape Survey." *Levant* 32: 27–52.

Barker, G. W. W., R. Adams, O. H. Creighton, D. D. Gilbertson, J. P. Grattan, C. O. Hunt, D. J. Mattingly, et al. 1998. "Environment and land use in the Wadi Faynan, southern Jordan: The second season of geoarchaeology and landscape archaeology." *Levant* 30: 5–26.

Barker, G. W. W., O. H. Creighton, D. D. Gilbertson, C. O. Hunt, D. J. Mattingly, S. J. McLaren, and D. C. Thomas. 1997. "The Wadi Faynan Project, southern Jordan: A preliminary report on geomorphology and landscape archaeology." *Levant* 29: 19–40.

Barker, G. W. W., D. D. Gilbertson, G. D. B. Jones, and D. J. Mattingly. 1996a. *Farming the desert: The UNESCO Libyan Valleys Archaeological Survey*, vol. 1, *Synthesis.* Paris/London: UNESCO/Society for Libyan Studies.

———. 1996b. *Farming the desert: The UNESCO Libyan Valleys Archaeological Survey*, vol. 2, *Gazetteer and pottery.* Paris/London: UNESCO/Society for Libyan Studies.

Barker, G. W. W., D. D. Gilbertson, and D. J. Mattingly, eds. 2007. *Archaeology and desertification: The Wadi Faynan Landscape Survey, Jordan.* Oxford: CBRL/Oxbow.

Barker, G. W. W., and G. D. B. Jones. 1981. "The UNESCO Libyan Valleys Survey 1980." *Libyan Studies* 12: 9–48.

Barker, G. W. W., and G. D. B. Jones. 1982. The UNESCO Libyan Valleys Survey 1979–1981: Palaeoeconomy and environmental archaeology in the predesert." *Libyan Studies* 13: 1–34.

———, eds. 1984. "The UNESCO Libyan Valleys Survey VI: Investigations of a Romano-Libyan farm, part 1." *Libyan Studies* 15: 1–45.

———. 1985. "Investigating ancient agriculture on the Saharan fringe: The UNESCO Libyan Valleys Survey." In *Archaeological field survey in Britain and abroad*, ed. S. Macready and F. H. Thompson, 225–41. London: Society for Antiquaries.

Barresi, P. 1991. "Sopravvivenze dell'unità di misura punica e suoi rapporti con il piede romano nell' Africa di età imperiale." *L'Africa romana* 8: 479–502.

———. 1992. "Unità di misura nell'architettura dell'Africa tardoromana e bizantina." *L'Africa romana* 9: 831–42.

Barrett, J. C. 1989. "Afterword: Render unto Caesar." In Barrett et al. 1989, 235–41.

———. 1997. "Romanization: A critical comment." In Mattingly 1997a, 51–64.

———. 2001. "Agency, the duality of structure and the problem of the archaeological record." In *Archaeological theory today*, ed. I. Hodder, 141–64. Cambridge: Polity Press.

Barrett, J. C., A. P. Fitzpatrick, and L. Macinnes, eds. 1989. *Barbarians and Romans in north-west Europe*. BAR S471. Oxford: British Archaeological Reports.

Bartel, B. 1989. "Acculturation and ethnicity in Roman Moesia Superior." In *Centre and periphery: Comparative studies in archaeology*, ed. T. Champion, 173–85. London: Unwin Hyman.

Bartels, C., M. Ruiz del Arbol, H. van Londen, and A. Orejas. 2008. *Landmarks: Profiling Europe's historic landscapes*. Bochum, Germany: Deutschen Bergbau-Museum.

Barton, I. M. 1972. *Africa in the Roman Empire*. Accra: Ghana University Press.

Bauman, R. A. 2000. *Human rights in ancient Rome*. London: Routledge.

Bayard, D., and J.-L. Collart, eds. 1996. *De la ferme indigène à la villa romaine. La romanisation des campagnes de la Gaule*. Revue archéologique de Picardie numero special 11. Amiens, France: Revue archéologique de Picardie.

Beard, M. 2006. "Wall papers: How people lived in Roman Britain." *Times Literary Supplement* (6 October): 5–6.

———. 2007. *The Roman Triumph*. Cambridge, MA: Belknapp Press.

———. 2008. "A very modern emperor." *Guardian* (19 July): 2–3.

Beechey, F. W., and H. W. Beechey. 1828. *Proceedings of the Expedition to explore the north coast of Africa from Tripoly eastward*. London: John Murray.

Bejaoui, F. 1988. "Note préliminaire sur l'église et le baptistère de Henchir Soukrine." *Africa* 10: 98–104.

Ben Abdallah, Z. B. 1986. *Catalogue des inscriptions latines païennes du musée du Bardo*. Collection de l'École Française de Rome 92. Rome: École Française de Rome.

Ben Abdallah, Z. B., and L. Ladjimi-Sebaï. 1983. *Index onomastique des inscriptions latines de la Tunisie, suivie de index onomastique des inscriptions latines d'Afrique*. Paris: Études d'antiquités africaines.

Ben Abed, A. 1987. *Thuburbo Maius, les mosaics dans la région ouest.* Tunis, Tunisia: Institut National de l'Archéologie et d'Arts.

Ben Baaziz, S. 1985. "L'occupation humaine dans le plaine de Rohia et le Sraa Ouertane dans l'Antiquité." In *Histoire et archéologie de l'Afrique du Nord, 4e Colloque*, 289–300. Paris: 111e Congrès national des Sociétés savants.

———. 1988. "Les sites antiques de la région de Sidi el Hani." *Bulletin des Travaux de l'Institut National de l'Archéologie et d'Arts* 2: 7–15.

———. 1991a. "Les huileries de la Tunisie antique." *Cahiers du Tunisie* 43: 39–64.

———. 1991b. "Les sites archéologiques de la région de Gafsa" In *L'armée et des affaires militaires*, 535–48. Paris: 113e congrès national des sociétés savants.

———. 1993a. "La carte nationale des sites archéologiques et des monuments historiques." In *Actes du Colloque International sur l'histoire de Sétif*, 128–35. BAA supplement 7. Algiers: Bulletin d'Archéologie Algérienne.

———. 1993b. "Prospection archéologique de la région d'el Meknassi." *Bulletin des Travaux de l'Institut National de l'Archéologie et d'Arts* 4 (1989) [1993]: 29–39.

Benabou, M. 1976. *La résistance africaine à la romanisation.* Paris: F. Maspero.

———. 1977. *Tacfarinas, insurgé berbère contre la colonisation romaine.* Les Africains no 8. Paris: Les éditions du CTHS.

———. 1978a. "Quelques paradoxes sur l'Afrique romaine, son histoire et ses historiens." In *Actes du 2e Congrès Int. d'étude des cultures de la Méditerranéen Occidentale*, vol. 2, ed. M. Galley, 139–44. Algiers: Société Nationale d'Edition et de Diffusion.

———. 1978b. "Les Romains ont-ils conquis l'Afrique?" *Annales (ESC)* 33: 83–88.

———. 1980. "L'imperialisme et l'Afrique du Nord, le modele romain." In *Sciences de l'homme et conquete coloniale. Constitution et usage des sciences humaines en Afrique XIXe–XXe siècles*, ed. D. Nordman and J.-P. Raison, 15–22. Paris: Presses de l'École normale superieur.

———. 1981. "L'Afrique et la culture romaine: le problème des survivances." *Cahiers du Tunisie* 29: 9–21.

———. 1982. "Les survivances pre-romaines en Afrique romain." In Wells 1982, 13–27.

———. 1986. "Le syncrétisme religieux en Afrique romaine." *Interscambi culturali* 1: 321–32.

Benjamin, H., and R. E. L. Masters, 1966. *The prostitute in society.* London: Mayflower-Dell.

Benoit, F. 1931. *L'Afrique méditerranéene. Algérie-Tunisie-Maroc.* Paris: Wildenstein.

Benseddik, N. 1982. *Les troupes auxiliaires de l'armée romaine en Maurétanie Césarienne sous le Haut empire.* Algiers: Société Nationale d'Edition et de Diffusion.

Bernal, M. 1987/1991. *Black Athena: The Afroasiatic roots of classical civilization.* 2 vols. New Brunswick, NJ: Rutgers University Press.

Berry, J., and R. Laurence, eds. 1998. *Cultural identity in the Roman Empire.* London: Routledge

Beschaouch, A. 1974. "Découverte de trois cités en Afrique Proconsulaire." *Comptes Rendus à l'Académie des Inscriptions et Belles Lettres* 118: 219–51.

Bevan, B., ed. 1999. *Northern exposure: Interpretative devolution and the Iron Ages in Britain*. Leicester, England: School of Archaeological Studies.

Bibliographie Afrique Antique. 1973. *Bibliographie Analytique de l'Afrique Antique IV 1970*. Paris: École Française de Rome.

Birebent, J. 1962. *Aquae Romanae. Recherches d'hydraulique romaine dans l'est Algérien*. Algiers: Baconnier.

Birley, A. R. 1979. *The people of Roman Britain*. London: Batsford.

———. 1981. *The fasti of Roman Britain*. Oxford: Clarendon Press.

———. 1988a. *The African emperor: Septimius Severus*. London: Batsford.

———. 1988b. "Names at Lepcis Magna." *Libyan Studies* 19: 1–19.

———. 2003. *Garrison life at Vindolanda: A band of brothers*. Stroud, England: Tempus.

———. 2005. *The Roman government of Britain*. Oxford: Clarendon Press.

Blagg, T. F. C., and A. C. King, eds. 1984. *Military and civilian in Roman Britain: Cultural relationships in a frontier province*. BAR 136. Oxford: British Archaeological Reports.

Blagg, T. F. C., and M. Millett, eds. 1990. *The early Roman Empire in the West*. Oxford: Oxbow.

Blond, A. 1994. *A scandalous history of the Roman emperors*. New York: Quartet Books.

Boissière, G. 1883. *L'Algérie romaine*. 2nd ed. Paris: Hachette.

Bonifay, M. 2004. *Études sur la céramique romaine tardive d'Afrique*. BAR S1301. Oxford: British Archaeological Reports.

Bouchenaki, M. 1988. *Tipasa. Site du patrimonie mondial*. Algiers: Enterprise Nationale des Arts Graphiques.

Bourguet, M.-N., B. Lepetit, D. Nordman, and M. Sinarellis. 1998. *L'invention scientifique de la Méditérrannee: Egypte, Morée, Algérie*. Paris: Éditions École des Hautes Études en Science Sociales.

Bourguet, M.-N., D. Nordman, V. Panayotopoulos, and M. Sinarellis, eds. 1999. *Enquêtes en Méditerranée. Les expeditions françaises d'Egypte, de Morée et d'Algérie*. Athens: Instituts de recherché néohelléniques

Bowersock, G. W. 1987. "The mechanics of subversion in the Roman provinces." In *Opposition et résistances à l'empire d'Auguste à Trajan*, 291–317. Entretiens sur l'Antiquité Classique 33. Geneva: Fondation Hardt.

Bowman, A .K. 1994. *Life and letters on the Roman frontier: Vindolanda and its people*. London: British Museum Press.

Bowman, A. K., and J. D. Thomas. 1994. *The Vindolanda Writing Tablets (Tabulae Vindolandenses II)*. London: British Museum Press.

———. 2003. *The Vindolanda Writing Tablets (Tabulae Vindolandenses III)*. London: British Museum Press.

Brandt, R., and J. Slofstra, eds. 1983. *Roman and native in the Low Countries: Spheres of interaction*. BAR S184. Oxford: British Archaeological Reports.

Branigan, K. 1994. "The New Roman Britain—a view from the West Country." *Trans Bristol and Gloucester Archaeological Society* 112: 9–16.

Braund, D. C. 1984. *Rome and the friendly king: The character of client kingship*. London: Duckworth.

———, ed. 1988. *The administration of the Roman Empire (241 BC–AD 193)*. Exeter, England: Exeter University Press.

———. 1996. *Ruling Roman Britain*. London: Routledge.

Brenton, H. 1989. *The Romans in Britain*. In *Plays: 2: The Romans in Britain, Thirteenth Night, the Genius, Bloody Poetry, Greenland*. London: Methuen.

Brett, M., and E. W. B. Fentress. 1996. *The Berbers*. Oxford: Blackwell.

Brogan, O. 1954. "The camel in Roman Tripolitania." *Papers of the British School at Rome* 22: 126–31.

———. 1955. "When the home guard of Libya created security and fertility on the desert frontier: Ghirza in the third century A.D." *Illustrated London News* 22 (January): 138–42.

———. 1965. "Henschir el-Ausaf by Tigi (Tripolitania) and some related tombs in the Tunisian Gefara." *Libya Antiqua* 2: 47–56.

———. 1978. "Es-Senama Bir el-Uaar: a Roman tomb in Libya." In *Archaeology in the Levant: Essays for Kathleen Kenyon*, ed. R. Moorey and P. Parr, 233–37. Warminster, England: Aris and Phillips.

Brogan, O., and D. J. Smith. 1957. "The Roman frontier at Ghirza, an interim report." *Journal of Roman Studies* 47: 173–84.

———. *Ghirza: a Romano-Libyan settlement in Tripolitania*. Libyan Antiquities Series 1. Tripoli: Department of Antiquities of Libya.

Brouquier-Reddé, V. 1992a. "La place de la Tripolitaine dans la géographie religieuse de l'Afrique du nord." In *Afrique du Nord antique et Medievale. Spectacle, vie portuaire, religions*, 117–23. Paris: 115e congrès national des sociétés savants.

———. 1992b. *Temples et cultes de Tripolitaine*. Paris: Centre National de la Recherche Scientifique.

Brown, P. 1990. *The body and society: Men, women and sexual renunciation in early Christianity*. London: Faber.

Bruhn, J., B. Croxford, and D. Grigoropoulos, eds. 2005. *TRAC 2004: Proceedings of the Fourteenth Annual Theoretical Roman Archaeology Conference, Durham 2004*. Oxford: Oxbow.

Brunt, P. A. 1965. "British and Roman imperialism." *Comparative Studies in Society and History* 7: 267–88. Reprinted in Brunt 1990, 110–33.

———. 1978. "Laus Imperii." In Garnsey and Whittaker 1978, 159–91. Reprinted in Champion 2004, 163–85.

———. 1990. *Roman Imperial Themes*. Oxford: Oxford University Press.

Buck, D. J., and D. J. Mattingly, eds. 1985. *Town and country in Roman Tripolitania. Papers in honour of Olwen Hackett*. BAR S274. Oxford: British Archaeological Reports.

Burnham, B. C. 1995. "Celts and Romans: Towards a Romano-Celtic society." In Green 1995, 121–41.

Burnham, B. C., and H. B. Johnson. 1979. *Invasion and response: The case of Roman Britain*. Oxford: British Archaeological Reports.

Burns, T. S. 2003. *Rome and the barbarians 100 BC—AD 400*. Baltimore: Johns Hopkins University Press.

Butcher, K. 2004. *Roman Syria*. London: British Museum Press.

Cagnat, R. 1913. *L'armée romaine d'Afrique et l'occupation de l'Afrique sous les Empereurs*. 2nd ed. Paris: Imprimerie nationale Leroux.

Calloway, C. G. 1997. *New worlds for all: Indians, Europeans and the remaking of early America*. Baltimore: Johns Hopkins University Press.

Cameron, A., and P. Garnsey, eds. *Cambridge Ancient History*, vol. 13, *The late empire AD 337–425*. Cambridge: Cambridge University Press.

Campbell, B. 2000. *The writings of the Roman land surveyors: Introduction, text, translations and commentary*. London: Roman Society.

———. 2002. *War and society in imperial Rome 31 BC–AD 284*. London: Routledge.

Camps, G. 1980. *Berbères. Aux marges de l'histoire*. Toulouse: Les Hesperides.

———. 1986. "Funerary monuments with attached chapels from the Northern Sahara." *African Archaeological Review* 4: 151–64.

———. 1987. *Les Berbères. Mémoire et identité*. Paris: Éditions Barzakh.

———. 1989. "Les chars sahariens. Images d'une societé aristocratique." *Antiquités africaines* 25: 11–40.

———. 1993. "Liste onomastique Libyque d'après les sources latines." *Reppal* 7–8: 39–73.

Capot-Rey, R. 1953. *Le Sahara Français (L'Afrique Blanche Francaise II)*. Paris: Presses Universitaires.

Capponi, L. 2005. *Augustan Egypt: The creation of a Roman province*. London: Routledge.

Carlsen, J. 1991. "Estate management in Roman North Africa: Transformation or continuity?" *L'Africa romana* 8: 625–37.

Carlsen, J., P. Ørsted, and J. E. Skydsgard. 1994. *Landuse in the Roman Empire*. Analecta Romana Instituti Danici Supplementum XXII. Rome: L'Erma di Bretschneider.

Carlsen, J., and H. Tvarno. 1991. "The Segermes Valley Archaeological Survey (region of Zaghouan): An interim report." *L'Africa romana* 7: 803–13.

Carr, G., E. Swift, and J. Weekes, eds. 2003. *TRAC 2002: Proceedings of the Twelfth Annual Theoretical Roman Archaeology Conference, Canterbury*. Oxford: Oxbow.

Carreras Montfort, C. 2002. "The Roman military supply during the principate: Transportation and staples." In Erdkamp 2002, 70–89.

Carroll, M. 2001. "Indigenous peoples in contact with Rome." *Journal of Roman Archaeology* 14: 598–602.

———. 2005. "The preparation and consumption of food as a contributing factor towards communal identity in the Roman army." In *Limes XIX: Proceedings of the XIXth International Conference of Roman Frontier Studies*, ed. Z. Visy, 363–72. Pecs, Hungary: University of Pecs.

———. 2006. *Spirits of the dead: Roman funerary commemoration in western Europe*. Oxford: Oxford University Press.

Carruthers, M., C. van Driel-Murray, A. Gardner, J. Lucas, L. Revell, and E. Swift, eds. 2002. *TRAC 2001: Proceedings of the Eleventh Annual Theoretical Roman Archaeology Conference, Glasgow*. Oxford: Oxbow.

Chakrabarty, D. 2000. *Provincializing Europe: Postcolonial thought and historical difference*. Princeton, NJ: Princeton University Press.

Chakravarty, S. 1989. *The raj syndrome: A study in imperial perceptions*. Delhi: Rupa.

Champion, C. B. 2004. *Roman imperialism: Readings and sources*. Oxford: Blackwell.

Champion, T., and J. Collis, eds. 1996. *The Iron Age in Britain and Ireland. Recent Trends*. Sheffield, England: Collis.

Clarke, J. R. 1998. *Looking at lovemaking: Constructions of sexuality in Roman art 100 BC–AD 250*. Berkeley and Los Angeles: University of California Press.

———. 2003a. *Art in the lives of ordinary Romans: Visual representation and non-elite viewers in Italy, 100 B.C.–A.D. 315*. Berkeley and Los Angeles: University of California Press.

———. 2003b. *Roman sex 100 BC–AD 250*. New York: Harry N. Abrams.

Coarelli, F., and Y. Thébert. 1988. "Architecture funéraire et pouvoir: reflexions sur l'héllenisme numide." *Mélanges de l'École Française de Rome* 100: 761–818.

Cohen, D., and R. Saller. 1994. "Foucault on sexuality in Greco-Roman antiquity." In *Foucault and the writing of history*, ed. J. Goldstein, 35–59. Oxford: Blackwell.

Colley, L. 2002. "What is imperial history now?" In *What is history now?* ed. D. Cannadine, 132–47. Basingstoke, England: Palgrave Macmillan.

Collingwood, R. G. 1936. "Roman Britain." In Collingwood and Myres 1936, 1–323.

Collingwood, R. G., and J.N.L. Myres. 1936. *Roman Britain and the English settlements*. Oxford: Oxford University Press.

Collis, J. 2003. *The Celts: Origins, myths and inventions*. Stroud, England: Tempus.

Conrad, J. 2002. *Heart of Darkness and other tales*. With introduction by C. Watts. Oxford: Oxford University Press.

Cool, H. E. M. 2002. "An overview of the small finds from Catterick." In Wilson 2002, 24–43.

———. 2004. *The Roman cemetery at Brougham, Cumbria: Excavations 1966–1967*. London: Roman Society.

———. 2006. *Eating and drinking in Roman Britain*. Cambridge: Cambridge University Press.

Cool, H. E. M., and M. J. Baxter. 1999. "Peeling the onion: An approach to comparing vessel glass assemblages." *Journal of Roman Archaeology* 12: 72–100.

———. 2002. "Exploring Romano-British finds assemblages." *Oxford Journal of Archaeology* 21: 363–80.

Cool, H. E. M., and C. Philo, eds. 1998. *Roman Castleford: Excavations 1974–85*, vol. 1, *The small finds*. Wakefield, England: West Yorkshire Archaeological Services.

Cooley, A. E., ed. 2002. *Becoming Roman, writing Latin? Literacy and epigraphy in the Roman West*. Supplement 48. Portsmouth, RI: Journal of Roman Archaeology.

Cormack, R., and M. Vassilaki, M. 2008. *Byzantium 330–1453*. London: Royal Academy.

Cornell, T. J. 1989. "The conquest of Italy." In Walbank et al. 1989, 351–419.

———. 1995. *The beginnings of Rome: Italy and Rome from the Bronze Age to the Punic Wars (c.1000—264 BC)*. London: Routledge.

Coro, F. 1928. *Vestigia di colonie agricole Romane. Gebel Nefusa*. Rome: Sind It Arti Graf.

———. 1956. "Gadames archeologica. Storia degli studi delle esplorazioni e dei risultati su alcuni fra i piu tipici antichi monumenti dell' oasi famosa. Libia." *Rivista Trimestriale di Studi Libici* 4: 3–26.

Cottam, S., D. Dungworth, S. Scott, and J. Taylor, eds. 1995. *TRAC 1994: Proceedings of the Fourth Theoretical Roman Archaeology Conference, Durham 1994*. Oxford: Oxbow.

Cottier, M., M. H. Crawford, C. V. Crowther, J.-L. Ferrary, B. M. Levick, O. Salomen, and M. Wordle. 2009. *The customs laws of Asia*. Oxford: Oxford University Press.

Crawford, D. 1976. "Imperial estates." In *Studies in Roman property*, ed. M. I. Finley, 35–70. Cambridge: Cambridge University Press.

Crawley Quinn, J. 2003. "Roman Africa?" In "Romanization?" *Digressus Supplement* 1: 7–34. Retrieved 16 November 2009 from http://www.digressus.org/articles/romanizationpp007-034-crawleyquinn.pdf.

Creighton, J. D. 2000. *Coins and power in late Iron Age Britain*. Cambridge: Cambridge University Press.

———. 2006. *Britannia: The making of a Roman province*. London: Routledge.

Creighton, J. D., and R. Wilson. 1999. *Roman Germany: Studies in cultural interaction*. Supplement 32. Portsmouth, RI: Journal of Roman Archaeology.

Cronon, W., G. Miles, and J. Gitlin. 1992. *Under an open sky: Rethinking America's Western past*. New York: W. W. Norton.

Croxford, B., E. Eckardt, J. Meade, and J. Weekes, eds. 2004. *TRAC 2003: Proceedings of the Thirteenth Annual Theoretical Roman Archaeology Conference, Leicester*. Oxford: Oxbow.

Croxford, B., H. Goodchild, J. Lucas, and N. Ray, eds. 2006. *TRAC 2005: Proceedings of the Fifteenth Annual Theoretical Roman Archaeology Conference, Birmingham 2005*. Oxford: Oxbow.

Croxford, B., N. Ray, R. Roth, and N. White, eds. 2007. *TRAC 2006: Proceedings of the Sixteenth Annual Theoretical Roman Archaeology Conference, Durham 2004*. Oxford: Oxbow.

Crummy, N. 1983. *The Roman small finds from excavations in Colchester 1971–79*. CAR 2. Colchester, England: Colchester Archaeological Trust.

Crummy, N., Crummy, P. and Crossan, C. 1993. *Excavations of Roman and Later Cemeteries, Churches and Monastic Sites in Colchester, 1971–88*. CAR 9. Colchester, England: Colchester Archaeological Trust.

Cunliffe, B. 1978. *Rome and her empire*. London: Bodley Head.

———, ed. 1981. *Coinage and society in Britain and Gaul: Some current problems*. CBR 38. London: Council for British Archaeology.

———. 1988. *The temple of Sulis Minerva at Bath*, vol. 2, *The finds from the sacred spring*. Oxford: Oxford University Committee for Archaeology.

———. 1991. *Iron Age communities in Britain*. 3rd ed. London: Routledge.

———. 2005. *Iron Age communities in Britain*. 4th ed. London: Routledge.

Curran, J. 2005. "The long hesitation: Some reflections on the Romans in Judaea." *Greece and Rome* 52: 7–98.

Curtin, P. D., ed. 1971. *Imperialism*. London: Harper.

Curtis, J., and N. Tallis, eds. 2005. *The forgotten empire: The world of ancient Persia*. London: British Museum Press.

Cuvigny, H. 1996. "The amount of wages paid to the quarry-workers at Mons Claudianus." *Journal of Roman Studies* 86: 139–45.

Dalby, A. 2000. *Empire of the pleasures: Luxury and indulgence in the Roman world*. London: Routledge.

Dal Lago, E., and C. Katsari, eds. 2008. *Slave systems: Ancient and modern*. Cambridge: Cambridge University Press.

Daniels, C. M. 1970. *The Garamantes of southern Libya*. London: Oleander Press.

———. 1989. "Excavation and fieldwork amongst the Garamantes." *Libyan Studies* 20: 45–61.

Dark, K., and P. Dark. 1997. *The landscape of Roman Britain*. Stroud, England: Sutton.

Daumas, G. E. 1968. *The horses of the Sahara*. Trans. S. M. Ohlendorf. Austin: University of Texas Press.

Daunton, M., and R. Halpern. 1999. *Empire and others: British encounters with indigenous peoples, 1600–1850*. London: UCL Press.

Davies, G., A. Gardner, and K. Lockyear, eds. 2001. *TRAC 2000: Proceedings of the Tenth Annual Theoretical Roman Archaeology Conference, London*. Oxford: Oxbow.

Davies, O. 1935. *Roman mines in Europe*. Oxford: Oxford University Press.

De Blois, L., ed. 2001. *Administration, prosopography and appointment policies in the Roman Empire*. Amsterdam: J. C. Gieben.

De Blois, L., P. Erdkamp, O. Hekster, G. de Kleijn, and S. Mols, eds. 2003. *The representation and perception of Roman imperial power*. Amsterdam: J. C. Gieben.

De Blois, L., and J. Rich, eds. 2002. *The transformation of economic life under the Roman Empire*. Amsterdam: J. C. Gieben.

De la Bédoyère, G. 2001. *Eagles over Britannia: The Roman army in Britain*. Stroud, England: Tempus.

———. 2006. Review of D. Mattingly, "An Imperial Possession." *History Today* (August): 216.

———. 2007. Letter. *British Archaeology* (January–February): 22.

De las Casas, B. 1992. *In defense of the Indians: The defense of the Most Reverend Lord, Don Fray Bartolomi de las Casas, of the Order of Preachers, late Bishop of Chiapa, against the persecutors and slanderers of the peoples of the New World discovered across the seas / Bartolomi de Las Casas*. Trans. and ed. S. Poole. Dekalb: Northern Illinois University Press.

De Ligt, L. 1993. *Fairs and markets in the Roman Empire: Economic and social aspects of periodic trade in a pre-industrial society*. Amsterdam: J. C. Gieben.

De Romanis, F., and A. Tchernia, eds. 1997. *Crossings: Early Mediterranean contacts with India*. New Delhi: Manohar.

Deetz, J. F. 1977. *In small things forgotten: An archaeology of early American life*. New York: Anchor Books.

Dench, E. 1995. *From barbarians to new men: Greek, Roman and modern perceptions of the peoples of the central Apennines*. Oxford: Clarendon Press.

Dench, E. 2005. *Romulus' asylum: Roman identities from the age of Alexander to the age of Hadrian*. Oxford: Oxford University Press.

Derks, T. 1995. "The ritual of the vow in Gallo-Roman religion." In Metzler et al. 1995, 111–27.

———. 1998. *Gods, temples and ritual practices: The transformation of religious ideas and values in Roman Gaul*. Amsterdam: Amsterdam University Press.

Derks, T., and N. Roymans. 2002. "Seal-boxes and the spread of Latin literacy in the Rhine Delta." In Cooley 2002, 87–134.

———, eds. 2009. *Ethnic constructs in antiquity: The role of power and tradition*. Amsterdam: Amsterdam University Press.

Díaz-Andreu, M., S. Lucy, S. Babić, and D. Edwards. 2005. *The archaeology of identity: Approaches to gender, age, status, ethnicity and religion*. London: Routledge.

Dietz, S., L. Ladjimi Sebaï, and H. Ben Hassan. 1996. *Africa Proconsularis— Regional studies in the Segermes Valley of Northern Tunesia*. 2 vols. Aarhus, Denmark: Aarhus University Press.

Diggle, J., and F. R. D. Goodyear. 1970. *Flavii Cresconii Corippi Iohannidos seu de bellis Libycis Lib. VIII*. Cambridge: Cambridge University Press.

Dilke, O. A. W. 1971. *The Roman land surveyors: An introduction to the agrimensores*. Newton Abbot, England: David and Charles.

Dixon, S. 1992. *The Roman family*. Baltimore: Johns Hopkins University Press.

Domerque, C. 1990. *Les mines de la péninsula Ibérique dans l'antiquité romaine*. Collection de l'École Française de Rome 127. Rome: École Française de Rome.

———. 2008. *Les mines antiques: la production des métaux aux époques grecque et romaine*. Paris: Picard.

Dondin-Payre, M. 1988. *Un siècle d'epigraphie classique. Aspects de l'oeuvre des savants français dans les pays du bassin méditerranéen*. Paris: Centre National de la Recherche Scientifique.

———. 1991. "L'exercitus Africae inspiration de l'armée française: ense et aratro." *Antiquités africaines* 27: 141–49.

———. 2003. "L'archéologie en Algérie à partir de 1830: une politique patrimoniale." In *Pour une histoire des politiques du patrimoine*, ed. P. Poirrier and L. Vadelorge (eds), 145–70. Paris: Fondations Maison des sciences de l'homme.

Dore, J. N. 1985. "Settlement chronology in the pre-desert zone: The evidence of the fine ware." In Buck and Mattingly 1985, 107–25.

———. 1996. "Part 2. The UNESCO Libyan Valleys Archaeological Survey Pottery." In Barker et al. 1996b: 317–89.

Douglas-Home, C. 1978. *Evelyn Baring: The last proconsul*. London: Collins.

Doyle, M. W. 1986. *Empires*. Ithaca, NY: Cornell University Press.

Drinkwater, J. F. 2001. "The Gallo-Roman woollen industry and the great debate: The Igel column revisited." In Mattingly and Salmon 2001a, 297–308.

Drummond, S. K. and L. H. Nelson. 1994. *The western frontiers of imperial Rome*. Armonk, NY: M. E. Sharpe.

Duncan-Jones, R. P. 1990. *Structure and scale in the Roman economy*. Cambridge: Cambridge University Press.

———. 1994. *Money and government in the Roman Empire*. Cambridge: Cambridge University Press.

Dyson, S. L. 1975. "Native revolt patterns in the Roman Empire." *Aufstieg und Niedergang der Römischen Welt. Geschichte und Kultur Roms in Spiegel der neueren Forschung* 2: 138–75.

———. 1985. *The creation of the Roman frontier.* Princeton, NJ: Princeton University Press.

———. 1993. "From new to New Age archaeology, archaeological theory and classical archaeology: A 1990s perspective." *American Journal of Archaeology* 97: 195–206.

———. 2006. *In pursuit of ancient pasts: A history of classical archaeology in the nineteenth and twentieth centuries.* New Haven, CT: Yale University Press.

Eck, W. 2000a. "The growth of administrative posts." In Bowman et al. 2000, 238–65.

———. 2000b. "Provincial administration and finances." In Bowman et al. 2000, 266–92.

Eckardt, H. 2002. *Illuminating Roman Britain.* Montagnac, France: Éditions Monique Mergoil.

———. 2005. "The social distribution of Roman artefacts: The case of nail-cleaners and brooches in Britain." *Journal of Roman Archaeology* 18, 139–60.

Eckardt, H., and N. Crummy. 2008. *Styling the body in late Iron Age and Roman Britain: A contextual approach to toilet instruments.* Monographies instrumentum 36. Montagnac, France: Éditions Monique Mergoil.

Eckstein, A. M. 2006. *Mediterranean anarchy, interstate war and the rise of Rome.* Berkeley and Los Angeles: University of California Press.

———. 2008. *Rome enters the Greek world.* Oxford: Blackwell.

Edwards, C. 1993. *The politics of immorality in ancient Rome.* Cambridge: Cambridge University Press.

Edwards, C., and G. Woolf, eds. 2003. *Rome the cosmopolis.* Cambridge: Cambridge University Press.

Edwards, D. N. 2005. "The archaeology of religion." In Díaz-Andreu et al. 2005, 110–28.

Eich, A., and P. Eich. 2005. "War and state-building in Roman republican times." *Scripta Classica Israelica* 24: 1–33.

Engel, T. 1993. "Charcoal remains from an Iron Age copper smelting slag heap at Feinan, Wadi Arabah (Jordan)." *Vegetation History and Archaeobotany* 2: 205–11.

Engel, T., and W. Frey. 1996. "Fuel resources for copper smelting in antiquity in selected woodlands in the Edom highlands to the Wadi Araba/Jordan." *Flora* 191: 29–39.

Ennabli, A. 1992. *Pour sauver Carthage. Exploration et conservation de la cité punique, romain et byzantine.* Paris: UNESCO.

Erdkamp, P. P. M., ed. 2002. *The Roman army and the economy.* Amsterdam: J. C. Gieben.

Etherington, N. 1984. *Theories of imperialism: War, conquest and capital.* London: Croom Helm.

Euzennat, M. 1986. "La frontière d'Afrique 1976–83." In *Studien zu den Militär-grenzen Roms III. 13. internationaler Limeskongress Aalen 1983*, ed. C. Unz, 573–83. Stuttgart: Theiss.

Euzennat, M. 1992. "Grande et petite hydraulique dans l'Afrique romaine." In Argoud et al. 1992, 75–94.

———. 1984. "Les troubles de Maurétanie." *Comptes Rendus à l'Académie des Inscriptions et Belles Lettres* 128: 372–93.

Evans, J. 1987. "Graffiti and the evidence of literacy and pottery use in Roman Britain." *Archaeological Journal* 144: 191–204.

Fanon, F. 1986. *Black skins, white masks.* London: Pluto Press.

Fantar, M. 1993. *Carthage. Approche d'une civilisation.* 2 vols. Tunis, Tunisia: Alif.

———. 1999. "Rémanences et résurgences dans la mosaique romano-africaine." In *Numismatique, langues, écriture et arts du livre, spécificité des arts figures. Actes du VIIe colloque international sur l'histoire et l'archéologie de l'Afrique du nord,* ed. S. Lancel, 301–14. Paris: Éditions CTHS.

Farrington, G., ed. 1994. *The Dedalus book of Roman decadence: Emperors of debauchery.* Sawtry, England: Dedalus.

Faulkner, N. 2008. *Rome: Empire of the eagles.* Harlow, England: Pearson.

Favory, F. 1983. "Propositions pour une modélisation des cadastres ruraux antiques." In *Cadastres et espace rurales: approches et realités antique,* ed. M. Clavel-Leveque, 51–135. Paris: Centre National de la Recherche Scientifique.

Fentress, E. W. B. 1979. *Numidia and the Roman army.* BAR S53. Oxford: British Archaeological Reports.

———. 1982. "La vendetta del Moro: recenti richerche sull'Africa romana." *Dialoghi di Archeologia* 1: 107–13.

———. 1983. "Forever Berber?" *Opus* 2: 161–75.

———. 2000. "The Jerba survey: settlement in the Punic and Roman periods." *Journal of Roman Archaeology* 13: 73–85.

———. 2006. "Romanizing the Berbers." *Past and Present* 190: 3–33.

Fentress, E. W. B., A. Aït Kaci, and N. Bounssair. 1993. "Prospection dans le Belezma: rapport préliminaire." *Actes du Colloque Int. sur l'histoire de Sétif,* 107–27. BAA supplement 7. Algiers: Bulletin d'Archéologie Algérienne.

Ferchiou, N. 1989a. *Décor architectonique d'Afrique Proconsulaire (IIIe s. avant J.C.—Ier s. après J.C.* 2 vols, Tunis, Tunisia: Librairie Archéologique.

———. 1989b. "Le mausolée de Q. Apuleius Maxsimus à El Amrouni." *Papers of the British School at Rome* 57: 47–76.

———. 1990. "Habitats fortifiés pré-impériaux en Tunisie antique." *Antiquités africaines* 26: 43–86.

Ferguson, B., and N. Whitehead. 1992. *War in the tribal zone: Expanding states and indigenous warfare.* Santa Fe, NM: School for American Research.

Ferguson, L. 1992. *Uncommon ground: Archaeology and early African America 1650–1800.* Washington, DC: Smithsonian Institution Press.

Ferguson, N. 2004. *Empire: How Britain made the modern world.* London: Penguin.

Ferris, I. 1995. "Insignificant others: Images of barbarians on military art from Roman Britain." In Cottam et al. 1995, 24–31.

———. 2000. *Enemies of Rome: Barbarians through Roman eyes.* Stroud, England: Sutton.

Février, P. A. 1981. "Quelques remarques sur troubles et résistances dans le Maghreb romain." *Cahiers du Tunisie* 29: 23–40.

———. 1986. "Le monde rural du Maghreb antique (approche de l'historiographie du XIXe siècle)." In *Histoire et archéologie de l'Afrique du Nord, 3e Colloque International Montpellier*, 87–106. Paris: 111e congrès national des sociétés savants.

———. 1989/1990. *Approches du Maghreb romain*. 2 vols. Aix-en-Provence, France: Édisud.

Fincham, G. 2000. "Romanisation, status and the landscape: Extracting a discrepant perspective from survey data." In Fincham et al. 2000, 30–36.

———. 2001. "Writing colonial conflict, acknowledging colonial weakness." In Davies et al. 2001, 25–34.

———. 2002. *Landscapes of imperialism: Roman and native in the East Anglian Fenland*. BAR 338. Oxford: Archaeopress.

Fincham, G., G. Harrison, R. Holland, and L. Revell, eds. 2000. *TRAC 99: Proceedings of the Ninth Annual Theoretical Roman Archaeology Conference, Durham*. Oxford: Oxbow.

Finkel, I. L., and M. J. Seymour. 2008. *Babylon: Myth and reality*. London: British Museum Press.

Finley, M. I. 1985. *The ancient economy*. Rev. ed. London: Hogarth Press.

Fischer, D. H. 1994. *Paul Revere's ride*. Oxford: Oxford University Press.

Fitzpatrick, J. 1992. "The Middle Kingdom, the Middle Sea and the geographical pivot of history." *Review: Journal of the Fernand Brandel Center* 15: 477–521.

———. 2005. "(Not sailing) to Byzantium: Metropolis, hinterland and frontier in the transformation of the Roman Empire." *Byzantina Australiensia* 15: 101–34.

Fletcher, R. 2008. Review of B. Goff, "Classics and Colonialism." *Classical Review*, new ser., 58: 296–97.

Flower, C., and D. J. Mattingly. 1995. "ULVS XXVII: Mapping and spatial analysis of the Libyan Valleys data using GIS." *Libyan Studies* 26 (1995): 49–78.

Fontana, S. 1998. "Il predeserto tripolitano: mausolei e rappresentazione del potere." *Libya Antiqua*, new ser., 3: 149–61.

———. 2001. "Lepcis Magna: The Romanization of a major African city through burial evidence." In Keay and Terrenato 2001, 161–72.

Forcey, C., J. Hawthorne, and R. Witcher, eds. 1998. *TRAC 97: Proceedings of the Seventh Annual Theoretical Roman Archaeology Conference, Nottingham*. Oxford: Oxbow.

Foucault, M. 1963. *The birth of the clinic: An archaeology of medical perception*. Trans. A. M. Sheridan. New York: Random House.

———. 1975. *Discipline and punish: The birth of the prison*. Trans. A. M. Sheridan. New York: Random House.

———. 1979. *Power, truth and strategy*. Trans. and ed. M. Morris and P. Patton. Sydney: Feral.

———. 1980. *Power/knowledge: Selected interviews and writings 1972–1977*. Trans. and ed. C. Gordon. Brighton, England: Harvester.

———. 1981. *The history of sexuality*, vol. 1, *Introduction*. Trans R. Hurley. Harmondsworth, England: Penguin.

———. 1985. *The history of sexuality*, vol. 2, *The uses of pleasure*. Trans R. Hurley. Harmondsworth, England: Penguin.

Foucault, M. 1988. *The history of sexuality*, vol. 3, *The care of the self*. Trans R. Hurley.. Harmondsworth, England: Penguin.

Fox, F. 1929. *The British Empire*. London: A. and C. Black.

Foxhall, L. 1994. "Pandora unbound: A feminist critique of Foucault's *History of Sexuality*." In *Dislocating masculinity: Comparative ethnographies*, ed. A. Cornwall and N. Lindisfarne, 133–46. London: Routledge.

Frank, T. 1914. *Roman imperialism*. New York: Macmillan.

———. 1933. *An economic survey of ancient Rome*. Vol. 1. Baltimore: Johns Hopkins University Press.

Freeman, P. W. M. 1991. "The study of the Roman period in Britain: A comment on Hingley." *Scottish Archaeological Review* 8: 90–101.

———. 1993. "Romanization and Roman material culture." *Journal of Roman Archaeology* 6: 438–45.

———. 1996. "British imperialism and the Roman Empire." In Webster and Cooper 1996, 19–34.

———. 1997. "Mommsen through to Haverfield: The origins of Romanization studies in late nineteenth-century Britain." In Mattingly 1997a, 27–50.

———. 2001. "Roman Jordan." In MacDonald et al. 2001, 427–59.

———. 2007. *The best training-ground for archaeologists: Francis Haverfield and the invention of Romano-British archaeology*. Oxford: Oxbow.

Frémeaux, J. 1984. "Souvenirs de Rome et présence françois au Maghreb: essai d'investigation." In *Connaissances du Maghreb: science sociales et colonisation*, ed. J.-C. Vatin, 29–46. Paris: Centre National de la Recherche Scientifique.

Frere, S. S. 1974. *Britannia: A history of Roman Britain*. London: Routledge.

Frere, S. S., and M. Fulford. 2002. "The collegium peregrinorum at Silchester." *Britannia* 33: 167–75.

Frezouls, E. 1957. "Les Baquates et la province romaine de Tingitaine." *Bulletin d'archéologie marocaine* 2: 65–116.

———. 1980. "Rome et la Maurétanie Tingitane: un constat d'échec?" *Antiquités africaines_*16: 65–93.

———. 1981. "La résistance armée en Maurétanie de l'annexation à l'époque sévérienne: un essai d'appreciation." *Cahiers du Tunisie* 29: 41–69.

Friedman, H. 2008. *Industry and empire: Administration and land use in the Roman and Byzantine Faynan*. Unpublished PhD thesis, University of Leicester.

Frontières. 1993. *Frontières d'empire. Actes de la Table Ronde Internationale de Nemours 1992, Mémoires du Musée de Préhistoire d'Ile de France 5*. Nemours, France: Musée de Préhistore d'Ile de France.

Fulford, M. 1992. "Territorial expansion and the Roman Empire." *World Archaeology* 23: 294–305.

———. 2004. "Economic structures." In Todd 2004b, 309–26.

———. 2007. "An insular obsession." *Britannia* 38: 367–69.

Funari, P. P. A. 2002. "The consumption of olive oil in Roman Britain and the role of the army." In Erdkamp 2002, 246–63.

Galinsky, K. 1996. *Augustan culture: An interpretative introduction*. Princeton, NJ: Princeton University Press.

———, ed. 2005. *The Cambridge companion to the age of Augustus*. Cambridge: Cambridge University Press.

Galsterer, H. 2000. "Local and provincial institutions and government." In Bowman et al. 2000, 344–60.

Gann, L., and P. Duigan, eds. 1978. *African proconsuls: European governors in Africa*. London: Collier Macmillan.

Gardner, A. 2002. "Social identity and the duality of structure in late Roman-period Britain." *Journal of Social Archaeology* 2: 323–51.

——. 2003. "Debating the health of Roman archaeology." *Journal of Roman Archaeology* 16: 435–41.

—— , ed. 2004a. *Agency uncovered: Archaeological perspectives on social agency, power, and being human*. London: UCL Press.

——. 2004b. "Introduction: Social agency, power and being human." In Gardner 2004a, 1–18.

——. 2006. "The future of TRAC." In Croxford et al. 2006: 128–37.

——. 2007. *An archaeology of identity: Soldiers and society in later Roman Britain*. London: UCL Press.

Garnsey, P. D. A. 1968. "Why penalties became harsher: The Roman case, late Republic to fourth century empire." *Natural Law Forum* 13: 141–62.

——. 1978. "Rome's African empire under the Principate." In Garnsey and Whittaker 1978, 223–54.

——. 1988. *Famine and Food Supply in the Graeco-Roman World*. Cambridge: Cambridge University Press.

Garnsey, P. D. A., and R. Saller. 1987. *The Roman Empire: Economy, society and culture*. London: Duckworth.

Garnsey, P. D. A., and C. R. Whittaker, eds. 1978. *Imperialism in the ancient world*. Cambridge Classical Studies. Cambridge: Cambridge University Press.

——. 1998. "Trade, industry and the urban economy." In Cameron and Garnsey 1998, 312–37.

Garrard, T. F. 1982. "Myth and metrology: The early trans-Saharan gold trade." *Journal of African History* 23: 443–61.

Garrow, D., C. Gosden, and J. D. Hill. 2008. *Rethinking Celtic art*. Oxford: Oxbow.

Gauckler, P. 1897–1912. *Enquête sur les installations hydrauliques romaines en Tunisie*. Tunis, Tunisia: Direction des antiquités et belles artes.

Gauthier, Y., and C. Gaulthier. 1997. "L'art rupestre [Fezzan]." *Encyclopédie Berbère* 18: 2783–802.

Gautier, E. F. 1952. *Le passé de l'Afrique du Nord*. 2nd ed. Paris: Payot.

Gell, A. 1998. *Art and agency: An anthropological theory*. Oxford: Clarendon Press.

Geraghty, R. M. 2007. "The impact of globalization in the Roman Empire 200 BC—AD 100." *Journal of Economic History* 67: 1036–61.

Germain, R. 1955. *La politique indigène de Bugeaud*. Paris: Éditions Larose.

Gerner Hansen, C., et al. 1993. "Project Africa Proconsularis [Segermes]." *Bulletin des Travaux de l'Institut National de l'Archéologie et d'Arts* 4: 71–114.

Giardina, A., ed. 1986. *Società romana e impero tardo antico, III, Le merci, gli insediamenti*. Rome: Laterza.

Gibbon, E. 1896. *The history of the decline and fall of the Roman Empire*. Vol. 1., ed. J. Bury. London: John Murray.

Giddens, A. 1984. *The constitution of society: Outline of a theory of structuration*. Cambridge: Polity Press.

———. 1995. *Politics, sociology and social theory. Encounters with classical and contemporary social thought*. Cambridge: Polity Press.

Gilbertson, D. D., P. P. Hayes, G. W. W. Barker, and C. O. Hunt. 1984. "The UNESCO Libyan Valleys Survey VII: An interim classification and functional analysis of ancient wall technology and land use." *Libyan Studies* 15: 45–70.

Gill, A. 1995. *Ruling passions: Sex, race and empire*. London: BBC Books.

Given, M. 2004. *The archaeology of the colonized*. London: Routledge.

Goff, B., ed. 2003. *Classics and colonialism*. London: Duckworth.

Goldsmith, R. W. 1987. *Premodern financial systems: A historical comparative study*. Cambridge: Cambridge University Press.

Goldstein, J., ed. 1994. *Foucault and the writing of history*. Oxford: Blackwell.

Goldsworthy, A., and I. Haynes, eds. 1999. *The Roman army as a community*. Supplement 34. Portsmouth, RI: Journal of Roman Archaeology.

Golvin, L. 1970. *Essai sur l'architecture religieuse musulmane, I. Generalités*. Paris: Klincksieck.

Goodchild, R. G. 1949. "Where archaeology and military training go hand in hand: Roman 'home guard' outposts in Tripolitania." *Illustrated London News* 15 (October): 594–95.

———. 1950. "The 'limes Tripolitanus' II." *Journal of Roman Studies* 40: 30–38.

———. 1976. *Libyan studies: Selected papers of the late R. G. Goodchild*. Ed. J. M. Reynolds. London: Elek.

Goodman, M. 1997. *The Roman world 44 BC—AD 180*. London: Routledge.

———, ed. 1998. *Jews in a Graeco-Roman world*. Oxford: Oxford University Press.

Gosden, C. 2004. *Archaeology and colonialism: Cultural contact from 5000 BC to the present*. Cambridge: Cambridge University Press.

———. 2005. "What do objects want?" *Journal of Archaeological Method and Theory* 12: 193–211.

Gosden, C., and C. Knowles. 2001. *Collecting colonialism: Material culture and colonial change*. Oxford: Berg.

Gosden, C., and Y. Marshall. 1999. "The cultural biography of objects." *World Archaeology* 31: 169–78.

Gosden, C., A. Petch, and F. Larson. 2007. *Knowing things: Exploring the collections of the Pitt Rivers Museum 1884–1945*. Oxford: Oxford University Press.

Gourevitch, P., and E. Morris. 2008. *Standard operating procedure: A war story*. London: Picador.

Grahame, M. 1998. "Rome without Romanization: Cultural change in the pre-desert of Tripolitania (first—third centuries AD)." *Oxford Journal of Archaeology* 17: 93–111.

Gramsci, A. 1971. *Selections from the prison notebooks*. Trans. Q. Hoare and G. Nowell Smith. London: International.

Granino Cecere, M., and V. Morizio. 2007. "Nuove testimoniaze sull'administrazione dei marmi nella Roma imperiale." In Papi 2007, 127–37.

Grant, A. 2004. "Domestic animals and their uses." In Todd 2004b, 371–92.

Grant, M., and R. Kitzinger, eds. 1988. *Civilization of the ancient Mediterranean*. 3 vols. New York: Charles Scribner's Sons.

Grattan, J. P., A. Condon, S. Taylor, L. A. Karaki, F. B. Pyatt, D. D. Gilbertson, and Z. al Saad. 2003. "A legacy of empires? An exploration of the environmental and medical consequences of metal production in Wadi Faynan, Jordan." In *Geology and health: Closing the gap*, ed. H. C. W. Skinner and A. Berger, 99–105. Oxford: Oxford University Press.

Grattan, J. P., G. K. Gillmore, D. D. Gilbertson, F. B. Pyatt, C. O. Hunt, S. J. McLaren, P. Phillips, et al. 2004. "Radon and 'King Solomon's miners,' Faynan Orefield, Jordanian Desert." *Science of the Total Environment* 319: 99–113.

Grattan, J. P., S. N. Huxley, L. A. Karaki, H. Tolund, D. D. Gilbertson, F. B. Pyatt, and Z. al Saad. 2002. "Death more desirable than life? The human skeletal record and toxicological implications of ancient copper mining and smelting in Wadi Faynan, south west Jordan." *Journal of Toxicology and Industrial Health* 18: 297–307.

Grattan, J. P., S. Huxley, and F. B. Pyatt. 2003. "Modern bedouin exposures to copper contamination: An imperial legacy?" *Ecotoxicology and Environmental Safety* 55: 108–15.

Graves-Brown, P., S. Jones, and C. Gamble, eds. 1996. *Cultural identity and archaeology*. London: Routledge.

Green, M. J., ed. 1995. *The Celtic world*. London: Routledge.

———. 1986. *The gods of the Celts*. Gloucester, England: Sutton.

Greene, K. 1986. *The archaeology of the Roman economy*. London: Batsford.

Gruen, E. S. 1984a. *The Hellenistic world and the coming of Rome*. Berkeley and Los Angeles: University of California Press.

———. 1984b. "Material rewards and the drive for empire." In Harris 1984, 59–82. Reprinted in Champion 2004, 30–46.

Gsell, S. 1903. *Enquête administrative sur les hydrauliques anciens en Algérie*. Nouvelles archives des missions X. Paris: Imprimerie Nationale.

———. 1911. *Atlas archéologique de l'Agérie*. Paris: Agence nationale d'archéologie.

———. 1933. "La Tripolitaine et le Sahara au III siècle de notre ère." *Mémoires de l'Institut National de France* 43: 149–66.

Guey, J. 1939. "Note sur le 'limes' romain de Numidie et le Sahara au IVe siècle." *Melanges de l'École Française de Rome* 56: 178–248.

Guides. 1906. *Guides Pratiques Conty, Algérie—Tunisie*. Paris: Guides Conty.

Gustafson, M. 1994. "Condemnation to the mines in the later Roman Empire." *Harvard Theological Review* 87: 421–33.

Gwilt, A., and C. C. Haselgrove. 1997. *Reconstructing Iron Age societies: New approaches to the British Iron Age*. Oxford: Oxbow.

Habinek, T. and A. Schiesaro, A., eds. 1997. *The Roman cultural revolution*. Cambridge: Cambridge University Press.

Hales, S., and T. Hodos, eds. 2009. *Material culture and social identities in the ancient world*. New York: Cambridge University Press.

Hall, J. 2002. *Hellenicity: Between ethnicity and culture*. Chicago: Chicago University Press.

Hall, J. 2007. "The creation and expression of identity: The Greek World." In Alcock and Osborne 2007, 337–54.

Hallet, J. P. 1988. "Roman attitudes towards sex." In Grant and Kitzinger 1988: 1265–78.

Hallet, J. P., and M. B. Skinner, eds. 1997. *Roman sexualities*. Princeton, NJ: Princeton University Press.

Halperin, D. M. 1994. "Historicizing the subject of desire: Sexual preferences and erotic identities in the Pseudo-Lucianic Erotes." In *Foucault and the writing of History*, ed. J. Goldstein, 19–34. Oxford: Blackwell.

Hammond, N. G. L. 1967. *Epirus*. Oxford: Oxford University Press.

Hanson, W. S. 1988. "Administration, urbanisation and acculturation in the Roman west." In Braund 1988, 53–68.

———. 1989. "The nature and function of Roman frontiers." In Barrett et al. 1989, 55–63.

———. 1994. "Dealing with barbarians: The Romanization of Britain." In *Building on the past: Papers celebrating 150 years of the Royal Archaeological Institute*, ed. B. Vyner, 149–63. London: Royal Archeological Institute.

Hanson, W. S., and R. Conolly. 2002. "Language and literacy in Roman Britain: Some archaeological considerations." In Cooley 2002, 151–64.

Hanson, W. S., and I. Haynes, eds. 2004. *Roman Dacia: The making of a provincial society*. Supplement 56. Portsmouth, RI: Journal of Roman Archaeology.

Hanson, W. S., and L. J. F. Keppie, eds. 1980. *Roman frontier studies 1979. Papers presented to the Twelfth International Congress of Roman Frontier Studies*. 3 vols. BAR S71. Oxford: British Archaeological Reports.

Hardt, M., and A. Negri. 2000. *Empire*. Cambridge, MA: Harvard University Press.

Harris, R. 2006. *Imperium*. London: Hutchinson.

Harris, W. V. 1971. "On war and greed in the second century BC." *American Historical Review* 76: 1371–85. Reprinted in Champion 2004, 17–29.

———. 1978. *War and imperialism in republican Rome 327–70 B.C.* Oxford: Clarendon Press.

———, ed. 1984. *The imperialism of mid-republican Rome*. Papers and Monographs of the American Academy in Rome 29. Rome: American Academy in Rome.

———. 1989. *Ancient literacy*. Cambridge, MA: Harvard University Press.

———. 1993a. "Between archaic and modern: Some current problems in the history of the Roman economy." In Harris 1993b, 11–29.

———, ed. 1993b. *The inscribed economy*. Supplement 6. Ann Arbor, MI: Journal of Roman Archaeology.

———. 2000. "Trade." In Bowman et al. 2000, 710–40.

———, ed. 2005. *Rethinking the Mediterranean*. Oxford: Oxford University Press.

———. 2007. "The late republic." In Scheidel et al. 2007, 511–42.

Haselgrove, C. C. 1984. "Romanisation before the conquest: Gaulish precedents and British consequences." In Blagg and King 1984, 5–63.

———. 1987. *Iron Age coinage in south-east England: The archaeological context*. BAR 174. Oxford: British Archaeological Reports.

———. 1999. "The Iron Age." In *The archaeology of Britain*, ed. J. Hunter and I. Ralston, 113–34. London: Routledge.

———. 2004. "Society and polity in late Iron Age Britain." In Todd 2004b, 12–29.

Haselgrove, C. C., I. Armit, T. Champion, J. Creighton, A. Gwilt, J. D. Hill, F. Hunter, and A. Woodward. 2001. *Understanding the British Iron Age: An agenda for action*. Salisbury, England: Wessex Archaeology.

Haselgrove, C. C., and T. Moore, eds. 2007. *The late Iron Age in Britain and Beyond*. Oxford: Oxbow.

Haselgrove, C. C., and R. Pope, eds. 2007. *The early Iron Age in Britain and beyond*. Oxford: Oxbow.

Haselgrove, C. C., and D. Wigg-Wolf, eds. 2005. *Iron Age coinage and ritual practices*. Studien zu Fundmünzen der Antike 20. Mainz, Germany: Verlag Philipp von Zabern.

Hauptmann, A. 2000. *Zur frühen Metallurgie des Kupfers in Fenan/Jordanien. Der Anschnitt*, Beiheft 11. Bochum, Germany: Deutsches Bergbau-Museum.

———. 2007. *The archaeometallurgy of copper: Evidence from Faynan, Jordan*. Berlin: Springer Verlag.

Hauptmann, A., F. Begemann, E. Heitkemper, E. Pernicka, and S. Schmitt-Strecker. 1992. "Early copper produced at Feinan, Wadi Araba, Jordan: The composition of ores and copper." *Archaeomaterials* 6: 1–33.

Hauser, M. W., and D. Hicks. 2007. "Colonialism and landscape: Power, materiality and scales of analysis in Caribbean historical archaeology." In *Envisioning Landscapes: standpoints and situations in archaeology and heritage*, ed. D. Hicks, L. McAtackney, and G. Fairclough, 251–74. Walnut Creek, CA: Left Coast Press.

Haverfield, F. 1906. "The Romanization of Roman Britain." *Proceedings of the British Academy* 2: 185–217.

———. 1912. *The Romanization of Roman Britain*. 2nd ed. Oxford: Clarendon Press.

———. 1923. *The Romanization of Roman Britain*. 4th ed., revised by G. MacDonald. Oxford: Clarendon Press.

———. 1924. *The Roman occupation of Britain. Being six Ford lectures delivered by F. Haverfield*. Rev. G. MacDonald. Oxford: Clarendon Press.

Hawkes, G. 2002. "Wolves' nipples and otters' noses? Rural foodways in Roman Britain." In Carruthers et al. 2002, 45–50.

Haynes, I. 2001. "The impact of auxiliary recruitment on provincial societies from Augustus to Caracalla." In De Blois 2001, 62–83.

———. 2002. "Britain's first information revolution: The Roman army and the transformation of economic life." In Erdkamp 2002, 111–26.

Heather, P. 2005. *The fall of the Roman Empire: A new history*. London: Macmillan.

Hemelrijk, E. A. 1987. "Women's demonstrations in republican Rome." In *Sexual asymmetry: Studies in ancient society*, ed. J. Blok and P. Mason, 217–40. Amsterdam: J. C. Gieben.

Henig, M. 1984. *Religion in Roman Britain*. London: Batsford.

———. 1995. *The art of Roman Britain*. London: Batsford.

Henig, M. 2002 *The heirs of King Verica: Culture and politics in Roman Britain.* Stroud, England: Tempus.

Higham, N., and B. Jones, B. 1985. *The Carvetii.* Gloucester, England: Sutton.

Hill, J. D. 1989. "Re-thinking the Iron Age." *Scottish Archaeological Review* 6: 16–23.

Hill, J. D., and C. Cumberpatch, eds. 1995. *Different Iron Ages: Studies in the archaeology of Iron Age Europe.* BAR S 602. Oxford: British Archaeological Reports.

Hind, J.G.F. 2007. "A. Plautius' campaign in Britain: An alternative reading of the narrative in Cassius Dio (60.19.5–21.2)." *Britannia* 38: 93–106.

Hingley, R. 1991. "Past, present and future—The study of Roman Britain." *Scottish Archaeological Review* 8: 90–101.

———. 1992. "Society in Scotland from 700 BC to AD 200." *Proceedings of the Society of Antiquaries for Scotland* 122: 7–53.

———. 1993. "Attitudes to Roman imperialism." In Scott 1993b, 23–27.

———. 1995. "Britannia, origin myths and the British Empire." In Cottam et al. 1995, 11–23.

———. 1996. "The legacy of Rome: The rise, decline and fall of the theory of Romanization." In Webster and Cooper 1996, 35–48.

———. 1997. "Resistance and domination: Social change in Roman Britain." In Mattingly 1997a, 81–100.

———. 2000. *Roman officers and English gentlemen: The imperial origins of Roman archaeology.* London: Routledge.

———, ed. 2001. *Images of Rome: Perceptions of ancient Rome in Europe and the United States in the modern age.* Supplement 44. Portsmouth, RI: Journal of Roman Archaeology.

———. 2005. *Globalising Roman culture: Unity, diversity and empire.* London: Routledge.

———. 2007a. "R****ization." Letter. *British Archaeology* (July–August): 20.

———. 2007b. "Situating a post-colonial Roman Britain." *Journal of Roman Archaeology* 20: 535–40.

———. 2008. *The recovery of Roman Britain 1586–1906: A colony so fertile.* Oxford: Oxford University Press.

Hingley, R., and C. Unwin. 2005. *Boudica: Iron Age warrior queen.* London: Hambledon.

Hingley, R., and S. Willis. 2007. *Promoting Roman finds: Context and theory.* Oxford: Oxbow.

Hirt, A. M. 2004. *Mines and quarries in the Roman Empire: Organizational aspects 27 BC—AD 235.* Oxford: Unpublished DPhil thesis, University of Oxford.

Hitchner, R. B. 1988. The University of Virginia–INAA Kasserine Archaeological Survey 1982–1986. *Antiquités africaines* 24: 7–41.

———. 1989. "The organization of rural settlement in the Cillium-Thelepte region (Kasserine, central Tunisia)." *L'Africa romana* 6: 387–402.

———. 1990. "The Kasserine Archaeological Survey 1987." *Antiquités africaines* 26: 231–60.

———. 1993. "Olive production and the Roman economy: The case for intensive growth." In *La production du vin et de l'huile en Méditerranée*, ed. M. C. Amouretti and J. P. Brun, 499–508. BCH Supplement 36. Athens: École Française d'Athènes. Reprinted in Scheidel and Reden 2002, 71–83.

———. 1994. "Image and reality: Pastoralism in the Tunisian high steppe in the Roman and late antique period." In Carlsen et al. 1994, 27–43.

———. 1995. "Historical text and archaeological context in Roman North Africa: the Albertini Tablets and Kasserine Survey." In *Methods in the Mediterranean: Historical and archaeological views on texts and archaeology*, ed. D. B. Small, 124–42. Leiden, Netherlands: Brill.

———. 2005. "The advantages of wealth and luxury: The case for economic growth in the Roman Empire." In Manning and Morris 2005, 207–22.

———. 2008. "Globalization avant la letter: Globalization and the history of the Roman Empire." *New Global Studies* 2. Manuscript file received from author; available at http://www.bepress.com/ngs/vol2/iss2/art2.

Hitchner, R. B., and D. J. Mattingly. 1991. "Fruits of empire: The production of olive oil in Roman Africa." *National Geographic Research and Exploration* 7: 36–55.

Hobson, J. A. 1902. *Imperialism: A study*. London: James Nisbet.

———. 1938. *Imperialism: A study*. 2nd ed. London: Allen and Unwin.

Hodos, T. 2006. *Local responses to colonization in the Iron Age Mediterranean*. London: Routledge.

Holland, T. 2006. "Victims and/or beneficiaries." Review of D. J. Mattingly, *An Imperial Possession*. *Spectator* (8 July): 40–41.

Holloway, R. 1975. "Buccino: The early Bronze Age village of Tufariello." *Journal of Field Archaeology* 2: 11–81.

Hong, S., J.-P. Candelone, C. C. Patterson, and C. F. Boutron. 1994. "Greenland ice evidence of hemispheric lead pollution two millennia ago by Greek and Roman civilisations." *Science* 265: 1841–43.

———. 1996. "History of ancient copper smelting pollution during Roman and medieval times recorded in Greenland ice." *Science* 272: 246–49.

Hopkins, K. 1978. *Conquerors and slaves: Sociological studies in Roman history*. Cambridge: Cambridge University Press.

———. 1980. "Taxes and trade in the Roman Empire." *Journal of Roman Studies* 70: 101–25.

———. 1982. *Death and renewal*. Cambridge: Cambridge University Press.

———. 1996. "Rome, taxes, rent and trade." *Kodai* 6–7: 41–75. Reprinted in Scheidel and Reden 2002, 190–230.

Horden, P., and N. Purcell. 2000. *The corrupting sea: A study of Mediterranean history*. Oxford: Blackwell.

Horn, H. G., and C. B. Ruger. 1979. *Die Numider*. Bonn: Rhein Landesmuseum Bonn.

Horne, A. 1977. *A savage war of peace: Algeria 1954—1962*. London: Macmillan.

Horne, P. D., and A. C. King. 1980. "Romano-Celtic temples in Continental Europe: A gazetteer of those with known plans." In Rodwell 1980, 369–555.

Howe, S. 2002. *Empire: A very short introduction*. Oxford: Oxford University Press.

Howgego, C. 1992. "The supply of money in the Roman World 200 BC–AD 300." *Journal of Roman Studies* 82: 1–31.

———. 1994. "Coin circulation and the integration of the Roman economy." *Journal of Roman Archaeology* 7: 5–21.

Howgego, C., V. Heuchert, and A. Burnett, eds. 2005. *Coinage and identity in the Roman provinces*. Oxford: Oxford University Press.

Hoy, D. C., ed. 1986a. *Foucault: A critical reader*. Oxford: Blackwell.

———. 1986b. "Power, repression, progress: Foucault, Lukes and the Frankfurt school." In Hoy 1986a, 123–47.

Hunt, C. O., D. J. Mattingly, D. D. Gilbertson, J. N. Dore, G. W. W. Barker, J. R. Burns, A. M. Fleming, and M. van der Veen. 1986. "ULVS XIII: interdisciplinary approaches to ancient farming in the Wadi Mansur, Tripolitania." *Libyan Studies* 17: 7–47.

Hurst, H., and S. Owen, eds. 2005. *Ancient colonizations: Analogy, similarity and difference*. London: Duckworth.

Huskinson, J., ed. 2000. *Experiencing empire: Culture, identity and power in the Roman Empire*. London: Routledge.

———. 2002. "Culture and social relations in the Roman Province." In *The Roman era*, ed. P. Salway, 106–38. Short Oxford History of the British Isles. Oxford: Oxford University Press.

Hyam, R. 1990. *Empire and sexuality: The British experience*. Manchester, England: Manchester University Press.

IAM. 1982. *Inscriptions antiques de Maroc, 2: Inscriptions latines*. Paris: Centre National de la Recherche Scientifique.

Insoll, T. 2004. *Archaeology, ritual, religion*. London: Routledge.

———, ed. 2007. *The archaeology of identities: A reader*. London: Routledge.

Irby-Massie, G. L. 1999. *Military religion in Roman Britain*. Leiden, Netherlands: Brill.

Isaac, B. 1990. *The limits of empire: The Roman army in the East*. Oxford: Oxford University Press.

———. 1998. *The Near East under Roman rule: Selected papers*. Leiden, Netherlands: Brill.

———. 2004. *The origins of racism in classical antiquity*. Princeton, NJ: Princeton University Press.

Jacobson, D. 2001. "The Roman client kings: Herod of Judaea, Archelaus of Cappadocia and Juba of Mauretania." *Palestine Exploration Quarterly* 133: 22–38.

Jackson, R., and G. Burleigh. 2007. "The Senuna treasure and shrine at Ashwell (Herts)." In *Continuity and innovation in religion in the Roman West*, ed. R. Haussler and A. C. King, 37–54. Supplement 67. Portsmouth, RI: Journal of Roman Archaeology.

James, H. 2006. *The Roman predicament: How the rules of international order create the politics of empire*. Princeton, NJ: Princeton University Press.

James, L. 1997. *Raj: The making of British India*. London: Abacus.

James, S. 1999a. *The Atlantic Celts: Ancient people or modern invention?* Madison: University of Wisconsin Press.

———. 1999b. "The community of soldiers: A major identity and centre of power in the Roman Empire." In Baker et al. 1999, 14–25.

———. 2001a. "Romanization and the peoples of Britain." In Keay and Terrenato 2001, 187–209.

———. 2001b. "Soldiers and civilians: Identity and interaction in Roman Britain." In James and Millett 2001, 77–89.

———. 2002. "Writing the Roman legions." *Archaeological Journal* 159: 1–58.

———. 2003. "Roman archaeology: Crisis and revolution." *Antiquity* 77: 178–84.

James, S., and M. Millett. 2001. *Britons and Romans: Advancing an archaeological agenda*. CBA Research Report 125. York, England: Council for British Archaeology.

Johns, C. 1982. *Sex and symbol. Erotic imagery in the Roman world*. London: British Museum Press.

Johnson, B. 2006. *The dream of Rome*. London: HarperCollins.

Johnson, S. 1989. *Rome and its Empire*. London: Taylor and Francis.

Jones, E. L. 1988. *Growth recurring: Economic change in world history*. Ann Arbor: University of Michigan Press.

Jones, G. D. B. 1985a. "The Libyan Valleys Survey: The development of settlement survey." In Buck and Mattingly 1985, 263–89.

Jones, G. D. B., and G. W. W. Barker. 1980. "Libyan Valleys Survey." *Libyan Studies* 11: 11–36.

———. 1983. "The UNESCO Libyan Valleys Survey IV: The 1981 season." *Libyan Studies* 14: 39–68.

Jones, G. D. B., and D. J. Mattingly. 1990. *An atlas of Roman Britain*. Oxford: Blackwell. Reprint Oxford: Oxbow, 2002.

Jones, R. F. J. 1991. *Roman Britain: Recent trends*. Sheffield, England: Collis.

Jones, S. 1997. *The archaeology of ethnicity: Constructing identities in the past and present*. London: Routledge.

Jongman, W. 2002. "The Roman economy: From cities to empire." In De Blois and Rich 2002, 28–47.

Jordan, P. 2003. *Material culture and sacred landscape: The anthropology of the Siberian Khanty*. Walnut Creek, CA: Altamira Press.

Kaddache, M. 1971. *L'Algérie dans l'antiquité*. Algiers: Société Nationale d'Edition et de Diffusion.

Kallet-Marx, R. M. 1995. *Hegemony to empire: The development of the Roman imperium in the East from 148 to 62 BC*. Berkeley and Los Angeles: University of California Press.

Kampen, N., ed. 1996. *Sexuality in ancient art*. Cambridge: Cambridge University Press.

Kay, N. M. 1985. *Martial book XI: A commentary*. London: Duckworth.

Keay, S., M. Millett, L. Paroli, and K. Strutt. 2005. *Portus: An archaeological survey of the port of Rome*. London: British School at Rome.

Keay, S., and N. Terrenato, eds. 2001. *Italy and the West: Comparative issues in Romanization*. Oxford: Oxbow.

Keeley, L. H. 1996. *War before civilization: The myth of the peaceful savage*. Oxford: Oxford University Press.

Kehoe, D. P. 1984. "Private and imperial management of Roman estates in North Africa." *Law and History Review* 2: 241–63.

———. 1988. *The economics of agriculture on the Roman imperial estates in North Africa.* Hypomnemata 89. Göttingen, Germany: Vandenhoeck und Ruprecht.

———. 2007. *Law and the rural economy in the Roman Empire.* Ann Arbor: University of Michigan Press.

Kerr, R. M. 2007. *Latino-Punic and its linguistic environment.* Published PhD thesis. Gottingen, Germany: Universiteit Leiden.

Khanoussi, M. 1988. "Spectaculum pugilum et gymnasium. Compte rendu d'un spectacle de jeux athletiques et de pugilat, figuré sur une mosaique de la région de Gafsa (Tunisie)." *Comptes Rendus à l'Académie des Inscriptions et Belles Lettres* 132: 543–61.

———. 1991. "Nouveaux documents sur la présence militaire dans la colonie julienne augustéene de Simitthus (Chemtou, Tunisie)." *Comptes Rendus à l'Académie des Inscriptions et Belles Lettres* 135: 825–39.

Kiefer, O. 1934. *Sexual life in ancient Rome.* London: Routledge and Kegan Paul.

Kieran, V. G. 1995. *Imperialism and its contradictions.* London: Routledge.

King, A. 1990. *Roman Gaul and Germany.* London: British Museum Press.

———. 2005. "Animal remains from temples in Roman Britain." *Britannia* 36: 329–69.

Kolb, A. 2002. "Impact and interaction of state transport in the Roman Empire." In De Blois and Rich 2002, 67–76.

Kolendo, J. 1992. *Le colonat en Afrique sur le haut empire.* Rev. ed. Paris: Les Belles Lettres.

Kotula, T. 1976. "Les africains et la domination de Rome." *Dialogues d'Histoire Ancienne* 2: 337–58.

Krenkel, W. A. 1988. "Prostitution." In Grant and Kitzinger 1988, 1291–97.

Kunzru, H. 2003. *The impressionist.* London: Penguin.

Lacoste, C., and Y. Lacoste, eds. 1991. *L'état du Maghreb.* Paris: l'Etat du Monde.

Lamar, H., and L. Thompson, eds. 1981. *The frontier in history: North America and southern Africa compared.* New Haven, CT: Yale University Press.

Lamirande, E. 1976. "Nord-africains en quête de leur passé. Coup d'oeil sur la periode romaine et chretienne." *Revue de l'Université d'Ottawa* 46: 5–23.

Lagrange, M. J. 1898. "Phounon." *Revue Biblique* 7: 112–15

———. 1900. "Mélanges." *Revue Biblique* 9: 284–86.

Laroui, A. 1970. *L'histoire du Maghreb, un essai de synthèse.* Paris: Maspero.

Lassère, J.-M. 1977. *Ubique populus.* Paris: Centre National de la Recherche Scientifique.

Laurence, R. 1994. *Roman Pompeii: Space and society.* London: Routledge.

———. 1999. "Theoretical Roman Archaeology." Review. *Britannia* 30: 387–90.

———. 2001. "Roman narratives: The writing of archaeological discourse—a view from Britain?" *Archaeological Dialogues* 8: 90–122 (with discussants and response).

———. 2006. "Twenty-first century TRAC: Is the battery flat?" In Croxford et al. 2006, 116–27.

Lawless, R. I. 1972. "The concept of 'Tell' and 'Sahara' in the Maghreb: A reappraisal." *Transactions of the Institute of British Geographers* 57: 125–37.

———. 1978. "Romanisation et résistance berbère dans la Maurétanie Césarienne (Algérie occidentale)." In *Actes du 2e Congrès Int. d'étude des cultures de la Méditerranéen Occidentale*, ed. M. Galley, 2:161–67. Algiers: Société Nationale d'Edition et de Diffusion.

Lawson, M. 2005. "Passion play." *Guardian* (28 October): 10–14.

Le Bohec, Y. 1989a. *La IIIe légion Auguste*. Paris: Centre National de la Recherche Scientifique.

Le Bohec, Y. 1989b. *Les unites auxiliares de l'armée romaine dans les provinces d'Afrique Proconsulaire et de Numidie*. Paris: Centre National de la Recherche Scientifique.

———. 1994. *The Roman imperial army*. London: Batsford.

Leglay, M. 1961/1966. *Saturne africain, monuments*. 2 vols. Paris: Éditions Recherches Scientifique.

———. 1962. *Les Gaulois en Afrique*. Collection Latomus 61. Brussels: Collection Latomus.

———. 1966. *Saturne africain, histoire*. BEFAR 205. Paris: Bibliothèque des Écoles françaises d'Athènes et de Rome.

———. 1975. "Les syncrétismes dans l'Afrique ancienne." In *Les syncrétismes dans les religions de l'antiquité*, ed. F. Dunand and P. Lévêque, 123–51. Leiden, Netherlands: Brill.

Lemert, C. C. and G. Gillan. 1982. *Michel Foucault: Social theory and transgression*. New York: Columbia University Press.

Lendon, J. E. 1997. *Empire of honour: The art of government in the Roman world*. Oxford: Oxford University Press.

Lengrand, D. 1991. "Stephane Gsell et l'Algérie: la leçon de Rome." In *Seminaire interuniversitaire d'histoire génerale du Maghreb*, ed. A. Rey-Goldzeiguer and G. Meynier, 211–20. (Limited distribution, consulted in library of Centre Camille Jullian, Aix-en-Provence, France.)

Leone, A., and D. J. Mattingly. 2004. "Vandal, Byzantine and Arab rural landscapes in North Africa." In *Landscapes of Change: Rural Transitions, AD 300–700*, ed. N. Christie, 135–62. Aldershot, England: Scolar/Ashgate.

Lepelley, C. 1967. "Déclin ou stabilité de l'agriculture africaine au Bas Empire." *Antiquités africaines* 1: 135–44.

Le Quellec, J.-L. 1998. *Art rupestre et prehistoire du Sahara*. Paris: Payot et Rivages.

Leschi, L. 1942. "Rome et les nomades du Sahara central." *Travaux de l'Institut de Recherches Sahariennes* 1: 47–62.

Leslie, A., ed. 1999. *Theoretical Roman Archaeology and Architecture: The Third Conference Proceedings*. Glasgow: Cruithne Press.

Leveau, P. 1978. "La situation coloniale de l'Afrique romaine." *Annales ESC* 33: 89–92.

———. 1984. *Caesarea de Maurétanie: une ville romaine et ses campagnes*. Collection de l'École Française de Rome 70. Rome: École Française de Rome.

———. 1986. "Occupation du sol, geosytème et systèmes sociaux. Rome et ses ennemis des montagnes et du désert dans le Maghreb antique." *Annales ESC* 41: 1345–58.

Leveau, P. 1988. "Le pastoralisme dans l'Afrique antique." In *Pastoral econo-mies in classical antiquity*, ed. C. R. Whittaker, 177–95. Cambridge: Cambridge Philological Society.

Leveau, P., P. Sillières, and J.-P. Vallat. 1993. *Campagnes de la Méditerranée ro-maine, Occident*. Paris: Hachette.

Levick, B. 1985. *The government of the Roman Empire: A sourcebook*. London: Croom Helm.

Liberati, A. M., and F. Bourbon. 2001. *Rome. Splendours of an ancient civiliza-tion*. London: Thames and Hudson.

Lichtheim, G. 1971. *Imperialism*. London: Allen Lane.

Lieven, D. 2000. *Empire: The Russian Empire and its rivals*. London: John Mur-ray.

Lindquist, S. 1992. *"Exterminate all the brutes": One man's odyssey into the heart of darkness and the origins of European genocide*. Trans. J. Tate. London: Granta.

Lintott, A. 1972. "Imperial expansion and moral decline in the Roman Empire." *Historia* 31: 626–38.

———. 1981. "What was the 'imperium Romanum'?" *Greece and Rome* 28: 53–67.

———. 1993. *Imperium Romanum: Politics and administration*. London: Routledge.

Lo Cascio, E. 2007. "The role of the state in the Roman economy: Making use of the new institutional economics." In Bang et al. 2006, 215–34.

———, E. 2007. "The early Roman Empire: The state and the economy." In Scheidel et al. 2007, 619–50.

Love, J. R. 1991. *Antiquity and capitalism: Max Weber and the sociological foun-dations of Roman civilization*. London: Routledge.

Luni, M. 1987. "Il santuario rupestre libyco delle immagini a fronte (Cirenaica). Testimonianze della cultura libya in ambiente greci-romano: originalità e di-pendenza." *Quaderni di Archeologia della Libya* 12: 415–58.

Luttwak, E. N. 1976. *The grand strategy of the Roman Empire from the first century AD to the third*. Baltimore: Johns Hopkins University Press.

Lutz, R., and G. Lutz. 1995. *The secret of the desert. The rock art of the Messak Sattafet and Messak Mellet, Libya*. Innsbruck, Austria: Gold Verlag.

Lyons, C. L., and J. K. Papadopoulos. 2002. *The archaeology of colonialism*. Los Angeles: Getty Research Institute.

MacCormack, S. 2007. *On the wings of time: Rome, the Incas, and Peru*. Princ-eton, NJ: Princeton University Press.

MacDonald, B., R. Adams, and P. Bienkowski, eds. 2001. *The archaeology of Jordan*. Sheffield, England: Sheffield Academic Press.

Mackendrick, P. 1980. *The North African stones speak*. Chapel Hill: University of North Carolina Press.

MacMullen, R. 1966. *Enemies of the Roman order: Treason, unrest and alien-ation in the empire*. Cambridge, MA: Harvard University Press.

———. 1984. "Notes on Romanisation." *Bulletin of the American Society of Papyrologists* 21: 161–77.

———. 1988. *Corruption and the decline of Rome.* New Haven, CT: Yale University Press.

———. 1990. *Changes in the Roman Empire.* Princeton, NJ: Princeton University Press.

———. 2000. *Romanization in the time of Augustus.* New Haven, CT: Yale University Press.

Mahjoubi, A. 1978. *Recherches d'histoire et d'archéologie à Hr el-Faouar (Tunisie). La cité de Belalitani Maiores.* Tunis, Tunisia: Institut National d'Archéologie et d'Art.

Mahjub, O. 1988. "I mosaici della villa Romana di Silin." *Libya Antiqua* 15–16 (1978–79) [1988]: 69–74.

Maier, C. S. 2006. *Among empires: American ascendancy and its predecessors.* Cambridge, MA: Harvard University Press.

Malarkey, J. 1984. "The dramatic structure of scientific discovery in colonial Algeria: A critique of the journal 'Société archéologique de Constantine' (1853–1876)." In *Connaissances du Maghreb: science sociales et colonization,* ed. J.-C. Vatin, 137–60. Paris: Centre National de la Recherche Scientifique.

Manley, J., and D. Rudkin. 2005. "A pre–AD 43 ditch at Fishbourne Roman Palace, Chichester." *Britannia* 36: 55–99.

Mann, J. 1983. *Legionary recruitment and veteran settlement during the Principate.* London: UCL Press.

Manning, J. G., and I. Morris, eds. 2005. *The ancient economy: Evidence and models.* Stanford, CA: Stanford University Press.

Marichal, R. 1992. *Les ostraca du Bu Njem.* Libya Antiqua, Supplement 7. Tripoli: Department of Antiquities of Libya.

Mason, M. 1994. *The making of Victorian sexuality.* Oxford: Oxford University Press.

Mathuisieulx, H. M. de. 1912. *La Tripolitaine d'hier et de demain.* Paris: Hachette.

Mattern, S. P. 1999. *Rome and the enemy: Imperial strategy in the Principate.* Berkeley and Los Angeles: University of California.

Matthews, K. 1995. "An archaeology of homosexuality? Perspectives from the classical world." In Cottam et al. 1995, 118–32.

Mattingly, D. J. 1983. "The Laguatan: A Libyan tribal confederation in the late Roman Empire." *Libyan Studies* 14: 96–108.

———. 1987a. "Libyans and the 'limes': Culture and society in Roman Tripolitania." *Antiquités africaines* 23: 71–94.

——— 1987b. "New perspectives on the agricultural development of Gebel and pre-desert in Roman Tripolitania." *Revue de l'Occident Musulman et de la Méditerranée* 41–42: 45–65.

———. 1988a. "Oil for export: A comparative study of Roman olive oil production in Libya, Spain and Tunisia." *Journal of Roman Archaeology* 1: 33–56.

——— 1988b. "The olive boom: Oil surpluses, wealth and power in Roman Tripolitania." *Libyan Studies* 19: 21–41.

———. 1989a. "Ancient olive cultivation and the Albertini Tablets." *L'Africa romana* 6: 403–15.

Mattingly, D. J. 1989b. "Farmers and frontiers: Exploiting and defending the countryside of Roman Tripolitania." *Libyan Studies* 20: 135–53.

———. 1992. "War and peace in Roman Africa. Some observations and models of state/tribe interaction." In Ferguson and Whitehead 1992, 31–60.

———. 1994a. "The landscape of imperialism." Review of S. Alcock, "Graecia Capta." *Antiquity* 68: 162–65.

———. 1994b. "Regional variation in Roman oleoculture: Some problems of comparability." In J. Carlsen et al. 1994, 91–106.

———. 1995. *Tripolitania.* London: Batsford.

———. 1996a. "First fruit? The olive in the Roman world." In *Human landscapes in classical antiquity: Environment and culture,* ed. G. Shipley and J. Salmon, 213–53. London: Routledge.

———. 1996b. "From one colonialism to another: Imperialism and the Maghreb." In Webster and Cooper 1996, 49–69.

———, ed. 1997a. *Dialogues in Roman imperialism: Power, discourse and discrepant experience in the Roman Empire.* Supplement 23. Ann Arbor: Journal of Roman Archaeology.

———. 1997b. "Dialogues of power and experience in the Roman Empire." In Mattingly 1997a, 1–16.

———. 1997c. "Imperialism and territory: Africa, a landscape of opportunity?" In Mattingly 1997a, 115–38.

———. 1998. "Landscapes of imperialism in Roman Tripolitania." *L'Africa romana* 12: 163–79.

———. 1999. "The art of the unexpected: Ghirza in the Libyan pre-desert." In *Numismatique, langues, écriture et arts du livre, spécificité des arts figures. Actes du VIIe colloque international sur l'histoire et l'archéologie de l'Afrique du nord,* ed. S. Lancel, 383–405. Paris: Éditions CTHS.

———. 2002. "Vulgar and weak 'Romanization' or time for a paradigm shift." *Journal of Roman Archaeology* 15: 536–40.

———, ed. 2003a. *The archaeology of Fazzan,* vol. 1, *Synthesis.* London: Society for Libyan Studies.

———. 2003b. "Family values: Art and power at Ghirza in the Libyan pre-desert." In *Art and imperialism,* ed. S. Scott and J. Webster, 153–70. New York: Cambridge University Press.

———. 2004a. "Being Roman: Expressing identity in a provincial setting." *Journal of Roman Archaeology* 17: 5–25.

———. 2004b. "Nouveaux aperçus sur les Garamantes: un état saharien?" *Antiquités africaines* 37 (2001) [2004]: 45–61.

———. 2006a. "The Garamantes: The first Libyan state." In *The Libyan Desert: Natural resources and cultural heritage,* ed. D. Mattingly, S. McLaren, E. Savage, Y. Fasatwi, and K. Gadgood, 189–204. London: Society for Libyan Studies.

———. 2006b. "The imperial economy." In Potter 2006, 283–97.

———. 2006c. *An imperial possession: Britain in the Roman Empire.* London: Penguin.

———. 2006d. "Roman Britain was more than Romans in Britain." *British Archaeology* (November–December): 55.

———, ed. 2007a. *The archaeology of Fazzan*, vol. 2, *Site gazetteer, pottery and other finds*. London: Society for Libyan Studies.

———. 2007b. "Landscapes of Roman imperialism in Britain." In *Journeys through European landscapes*, ed. L. Lévêque, M. Ruiz del Arbol, L. Pop, and C. Bartels, : 149–52 . Ponferrada, Spain: COST Action A27/Azuré S.L.

———. 2008. "Urbanism, epigraphy and identity in the towns of Britain under Roman rule." In *A Roman miscellany: Essays in honour of Anthony R. Birley on his seventieth birthday*, ed. H. M. Schellenberg, V. E. Hirschmann and A. Krieckhaus (eds), 53–71. Akanthina Monograph Series 3. Gdansk, Poland: Akanthina.

Mattingly, D. J., and G. W. W. Barker. 2005. "Out of Africa: Approaches to the landscape archaeology of the North African desert." In *Territoires et paysages de l'âge du fer au moyen âge. Mélanges offerts à Ph Leveau*, ed. A. Bouet and F. Verdin, 185–96. Bordeaux, France: Ausonius Press.

Mattingly, D. J., and R. B. Hitchner. 1993. "Technical specifications of some North African olive presses of Roman date." In *La production du vin et de l'huile en Méditerranée*, ed. M.-C. Amouretti and J.-P. Brun (eds), 439–62. BCH Supplement 36. Athens: École Française d'Athènes.

———. 1995. "Roman Africa: An archaeological review." *Journal of Roman Studies* 85: 165–213.

Mattingly, D. J., and J. Salmon. 2001a. *Economies beyond agriculture in the classical world*. London: Routledge.

———. 2001b. "The productive past: Economies beyond agriculture." In Mattingly and Salmon 2001a, 3–14.

Maurin, L., and J. Peyras, J. 1991. "Romanisation et traditions africaines dans la région de Bir Mcherga." *Cahiers du Tunisie* 43 (155–56): 105–48.

Maxfield, V. A. 2001. "Stone quarrying in the eastern Egyptian desert with particular reference to Mons Claudianus and Mons Porphyrites." In Mattingly and Salmon 2001, 143–70.

———. 2003. "Ostraca and the Roman army in the Eastern desert." In *Documenting the Roman army: Essays in honour of Margaret Roxan*, ed. J. J. Wilkes (ed.), 153–74. Bulletin supplement. London: University of London Institute of Classical Studies.

Maxfield, V. A., and D. P. S. Peacock. 2001a. *The Roman imperial quarries: Survey and excavation at Mons Porphyrites*, vol. 1, *Topography and quarries*. London: Egypt Exploration Society.

———. 2001b. *Survey and Excavation at Mons Claudianus 1987–1993*, vol. 2, *Excavations Part 1*. Cairo: Institut français d'archéologie orientale.

McCarthy, M. 2002. *Roman Carlisle and the lands of the Solway*. Stroud, England: Tempus.

———. 2006. "Romano-British people and the language of sociology." *Oxford Journal of Archaeology* 25: 201–12.

M'Charek, A. 1986. *Aspects de l'évolution démographique et sociale à Mactaris au IIe et IIIe siècles après J.C.* Tunis, Tunisia: Université de Tunis.

McCormick, M. 2001. *Origins of the European economy: Communications and commerce, A.D. 300–900*. Cambridge: Cambridge University Press.

McDougall, S. 2005. *Romanitas*. London: Orion.

McGinn, T. A. J. 2002. "Pompeian brothels and social history." In *Pompeian brothels: Pompeii's ancient history, mirrors and mysteries, art and nature at Oplontis, and the Herculean Basilica*, ed. C. Stein and J. Humphrey (ed.), 7–46. Supplement 47. Portsmouth, RI: Journal of Roman Archaeology.

McNay, L. 1994. *Foucault. A critical introduction.* Cambridge: Polity Press.

Meadows, K. 1995. "You are what you eat: Diet and identity and Romanization." In Cottam et al. 1995, 133–40.

Meadows, K., C. Lemke, and J. Heron, eds. 1997. *TRAC 96: Proceedings of the Sixth Annual Theoretical Roman Archaeology Conference, Sheffield.* Oxford: Oxbow.

Mehrez, S. 1992. "Translation and the post-colonial experience: The francophone North African text." In *Rethinking translation: Discourse, subjectivity, ideology*, ed. L. Venuti, 120–38. London: Routledge.

Meikle, S. 2002. "Modernism, economics and the ancient economy." In Scheidel and Reden 2002, 233–50.

Memmi, A. 1965. *The colonizer and the colonized.* New York: Orion.

Mercier, M. 1953. "Les idoles de Ghadames." *Revue Africaine* 97, 17–47.

Merighi, A. 1940. *La Tripolitania antica.* 2 vols. Verbania, Italy: Airoldi.

Meskell, L. 2001. "Archaeologies of identity." In *Archaeological theory today*, ed. I. Hodder, 187–213. Cambridge: Polity Press.

Metty, N. 1983. "Fronton et Apulée: romains ou Africains?" *Rivista di Cultura Classica e Medioevale* 25: 37–47.

Metzler, J., M. Millet, N. Roymans, and J. Slofstra. 1995. *Integration in the early Roman West: The role of culture and ideology.* Luxembourg: Dossiers d'archéologie du musée national d'histoire.

Mignolo, W. D. 2000. *Local histories/global designs: Coloniality, subaltern knowledges and border thinking.* Princeton, NJ: Princeton University Press.

Millar, F. 1968. "Local cultures in the Roman Empire: Libyan, Punic and Latin in Roman Africa." *Journal of Roman Studies* 58: 126–34.

———. 1981. "Style abides." *Journal of Roman Studies* 71: 144–52.

———. 1984. "Condemnation to hard labour in the Roman Empire, from the Julio-Claudians to Constantine." *Papers of the British School at Rome* 52: 124–47.

———. 1993. *The Roman Near East, 31 BC–AD 337.* Cambridge, MA: Harvard University Press.

———. 2002. *The Roman republic in political thought.* Hanover, NH: New England University Press.

Miller, D., M. Rowlands, and C. Tilley, eds. 1989. *Domination and resistance.* One World Archaeology. London: Routledge.

Millett, M. 1990a. *The Romanization of Britain: An essay in archaeological interpretation.* Cambridge: Cambridge University Press.

———. 1990b. "Romanization: Historical issues and archaeological interpretations." In Blagg and Millett 1990, 35–41.

———. 1995a. *English Heritage Book of Roman Britain.* London: Batsford.

———. 1995b. "Rethinking religion in Romanization." In Metzler et al. 1995, 93–100.

———. 2004. "The Romanization of Britain. Changing perspectives." *Kodai* 13–14 (2004): 169–73.

Mitchell, D. 2004. *Cloud atlas*. London: Random House.

Mitchell, S. 2005. "The treaty between Rome and Lycia of 46 BC (MS2070)." In *Papyri Graecae Schøyen (P. Schøyen I)*, ed. R. Pintaudi, 161–259. Florence: Edizioni Gonnelli.

Modéran, Y. 1989. "Gildo, les maures et l'Afrique." *Melanges de l'École Française de Rome* 101: 821–72.

———. 2003. *Les Maures et l'Afrique romaine (Ive–VIIe siècle)*. Rome: École Française de Rome.

Mohamed, F. A., and J. M. Reynolds. 1984. "An inscribed stone from the sanctuary of Demeter and Kore in the Wadi Belgadir at Cyrene: Cult, corn and Roman revenues." *Libyan Studies* 25: 211–17.

Mohamedi, A., A. Benmansour, A. A. Amamsa, and E. Fentress. 1991. *Fouilles de Sétif 1977–1984*. Supplement BAA 5. Algiers: Bulletin d'Archéologie Algérienne.

Mommsen, T. 1968. *The provinces of the Roman Empire*. Ed. T. R. S. Broughton. Chicago: University of Chicago Press.

Moreland, J. 2001. *Archaeology and Text*. London: Duckworth.

Morgan, P. D. 1999. "Encounters between British and 'indigenous' peoples c.1500–c.1800." In Daunton and Halpern 1999, 42–78.

Mori, F. 1998. *The great civilization of the ancient Sahara: Neolithisation and the earliest evidence of anthropomorphic religion*. Trans. D. Philips. Rome: L'Erma di Bretschneider.

Morizot, P. 1991. "Economie et société en Numidie méridionale: l'exemple de l'Aures." *L'Africa romana* 8: 429–46.

———. 1993. "L'Aures et l'olivier." *Antiquités africaines* 29: 177–240.

Morley, N. 1996. *Metropolis and hinterland: The city of Rome and the Italian economy 200 BC—AD 200*. Cambridge: Cambridge University Press.

———. 2007. *Trade in classical antiquity*. Cambridge: Cambridge University Press.

Morris, J. 1979. *Pax Britannica: The climax of an empire*. Harmondsworth, England: Penguin.

Morrison, K. D. 2001. "Sources, approaches and definitions." In Alcock et al. 2001, 1–9.

Mowl, T. 2007. *Historic gardens of England: Oxfordshire*. Stroud, England: Tempus.

Munzi, M. 2001. *L'epica del ritorno. Archeologia e politica nella Tripolitania italiana*. Saggi di Storia Antica 17. Rome: L'Erma di Bretschneider.

———. 2004. *La decolonizzazione del passato. Archeologia e politica in Libia dall'ammistrazione alleata al regno di Idris*. Saggi di Storia Antica 22. Rome: L'Erma di Bretschneider.

Murray, O. 2000. "Ancient history 1872–1914." In *The history of the University of Oxford*, vol. 7, *nineteenth-century Oxford, part 2*, ed. M. G. Brock and M. C. Curthoys, 330–60. Oxford: Clarendon Press.

Muzzolini, A. 1991. "Proposals for updating the rock-drawing sequence of the Acacus (Libya)." *Libyan Studies* 22: 7–30.

Newsinger, J. 2006. *The blood never dried : A people's history of the British Empire.* London: Bookmarks.

Nicolet, C. 1976. *Tributum. Recherches sur la fiscalité directe sous la republique.* Bonn: R. Habelt Verlag.

———. 1988. *Rendre à César. Economie et societé dans la Rome antique.* Mesnil sur l'Estrée, France: Gallimand.

———. 1991. *Space, geography and politics in the early Roman Empire.* Ann Arbor: University of Michigan Press.

———. 2000. *Censeurs et publicains. Economie et fiscalité dans la Rome antique.* Paris: Fayard.

Nobles, G. H. 1997. *American frontiers: Cultural encounters and continental conquest.* New York: Hill and Wang.

North, J. 1981. "The development of Roman imperialism." *Journal of Roman Studies* 71: 1–9.

Nussbaum, F. A. 1995. *Torrid zones: Maternity, sexuality and empire in eighteeenth-century English narratives.* Baltimore: Johns Hopkins University Press.

Nutton, V. 1978. "The beneficial ideology." In Garnsey and Whittaker 1978, 209–21.

Oltean, I. 2007. *Dacia: Landscape, colonisation, Romanisation.* London: Routledge.

Opper, T. 2008. *Hadrian: Empire and conflict.* London: British Museum Press.

Orejas, A., ed. 2001. *Atlas historique des zones minières d'Europe I.* Luxembourg: Office of Official Publications of the European Communities.

———, ed. 2003. *Atlas historique des zones minières d'Europe II.* Luxembourg: Office of Official Publications of the European Communities.

Ørsted, P. 1985. *Roman imperial economy and Romanization: A study in Roman imperial administration and the public lease system in the Danubian provinces from the first to the third century AD.* Copenhagen: Museum Tusculanum Press.

Ørsted, P., J. Carlesen, L. Ladjimi Sebaï, and H. Ben Hassan. 2000. *Africa Proconsularis—Regional studies in the Segermes Valley of northern Tunisia,* vol. 3, *historical conclusions.* Aarhus, Denmark: Aarhus University Press.

Ørsted, P., L. Ladjimi Sebaï, H. Ben Hassen, H. Ben Younes, J. Zoughlami, and F. Bejaoui. 1992. "Town and countryside in Roman Tunisia." *Journal of Roman Archaeology* 5: 69–96.

Osterhammel, J., and N. P. Petersson. 2003. *Globalization: A short history.* Princeton, NJ: Princeton University Press.

Pakenham, T. 1991. *The scramble for Africa 1876–1912.* London: Weidenfeld and Nicolson.

Panella, C., and A. Tchernia. 2002. "Agricultural products transported in amphora: Oil and wine." In Scheidel and Reden 2002, 173–89.

Papi, E., ed. 2007. *Supplying Rome and the empire.* Supplement 69. Portsmouth RI: Journal of Roman Archaeology.

Parker, A., M. Russo, D. Sommer, and P. Yaeger. 1992. *Nationalisms and sexualities.* London: Routledge.

Parker, A. J. 1992. *Ancient shipwrecks of the Mediterranean and Roman provinces.* BAR S580. Oxford: British Archaeological Reports.

Parker, H. N. 1999. "The observed of all observers: Spectacle, applause, and cultural poetics in the Roman theatre audience." In *The art of ancient spectacle*, ed. B. Bergmann and C. Kondoleon , 163–79. New Haven, CT: Yale University Press.

Parker, W. H. 1988. *Priapea: Poems for a phallic god*. London: Croom Helm.

Parker Pearson, M., and I. J. N. Thorpe, eds. 2005. *Warfare, violence and slavery in prehistory*. BAR S1374. Oxford: British Archaeological Reports.

Peachin, M. 2006. "Rome the superpower: 96–235 CE." In Potter 2006, 126–52.

Peacock, D. P. S., and V. Maxfield. 1997. *Survey and excavation at Mons Claudianus 1987–1993*, vol. 1, *Topography and Quarries*. Cairo: Institut Français d'Archéologie Orientale.

———. 2007. *The Roman imperial quarries. Survey and Excavation at Mons Porphyrites 1994–1998*, vol. 2, *The excavations*. London: Egypt Exploration Society.

Peacock, D. P. S., and D. F. Williams. 1986. *Amphorae and the Roman Economy*. London: Longman.

Peddie, J. 1987. *Invasion: The Roman invasion of Britain in the year AD 43 and the events leading to the occupation of the west country*. Gloucester, England: Sutton.

Peña, J. T. 1998. "The mobilization of state olive oil in Roman Africa: The evidence of late fourth-century ostraca from Carthage." In *Carthage papers: The early colony's economy, water supply, a public bath, and the mobilization of state olive oil*, ed. J. T. Peña, J. J. Rossiter, A. I. Wilson, and C. M. Wells, 117–238. Supplement 28. Portsmouth, RI: Journal of Roman Archaeology.

Peniakoff, V. 1950. *Popski's private army*. Oxford: Oxford University Press.

Pensabene, P. 1990. "Il tempio di Saturno a Dougga e tradizioni architettoniche d'origine punica." *L'Africa romana* 7: 251–93.

Peyras, J. 1975. "Le 'fundus aufidianus': étude d'un grand domaine romain de la région de Mactar (Tunisie du nord)." *Antiquités africaines* 9: 181–22.

———. 1983. "Paysages agraires et centuriations dans le basin de l'oued Tine." *Antiquités africaines* 19: 209–53.

———. 1986. "Les campagnes de l'Afrique du nord antique d'après les anciens gromatici." In *Histoire et archéologie de l'Afrique du Nord, 3e Colloque International Montpellier*, 257–71. Paris: 111e congrès national des sociétés savants.

———. 1991. *Le Tell Nord-est Tunisien dans l'antiquité*. Paris: Centre National de la Recherche Scientifique.

Pflaum, H. G. 1973. "La romanisation de l'Afrique." *Vestigia* 17: 55–72.

Picard, G. C. 1954. *Les religions de l'Afrique romaine*. Paris: Plon.

———. 1983. "La recherche archéologique en Tunisie des origines à l'independance." *Cahiers des études anciennes* 16: 11–20.

———. 1990. *La civilisation de l'Afrique romaine*. 2nd ed. Paris: Études Augustiniennes.

Piccioli, A. 1931. *La porta magica del Sahara. Itinerario Tripoli-Ghadames*. Tripoli: Librería Editiones Minerva.

Pippidi, D. M., ed. 1976. *Assimilation et résistance à la culture gréco-romaine dans le monde ancien*. Paris: Les Belles Lettres.

Pitts, M. 2005a. "Pots and pits: Drinking and deposition in late Iron Age southeast Britain." *Oxford Journal of Archaeology* 24: 143–61.

——— 2005b. "Regional identities and the social use of ceramics." In Bruhn et al. 2005: 50–64.

———. 2007a. "Consumption, deposition and social practice: A ceramic approach to intra-site analysis in late Iron Age to Roman Britain." *Internet Archaeology 21*. Retrieved 16 November 2009 from http://intarch.ac.uk/journal/issue21/pitts_index.html.

———. 2007b. "The emperor's new clothes? The utility of identity in Roman archaeology." *American Journal of Archaeology* 111: 693–713.

———. 2008. "Globalizing the local in Roman Britain: An anthropological approach to social change." *Journal of Anthropological Archaeology* 27: 493–506.

Pleket, H. W. 1993a. "Agriculture in the Roman Empire in comparative perspective." In *De Agricultura: In memoriam Peter W. de Neeve*, ed. H. Sancisi-Weerdenburg and H. C. Teitler, 317–42. Amsterdam: J. C. Gieben.

——— 1993b. "Rome: A pre-industrial megalopolis." In *Megalopolis: The giant city in history*, ed. T. Barker and A. Sutcliffe (eds), 14–35. London: Palgrave Macmillan.

Pohl, W., I. Wood, and H. Reimitiz, eds. 2001. *The transformations of frontiers: From late antiquity to the Carolingians*. Leiden, Netherlands: Brill.

Polanyi, K., C. Arensberg, and H. W. Pearson. 1957. *Trade and market in the early empires: Economies in history and theory*. Glencoe, Illinois: Free Press.

Poncet, J. 1963. *Paysages et problèmes ruraux en Tunisie*. Paris: Presses Universitaires de France.

Portal, J., ed. 2007. *The first emperor: China's terracotta army*. London: British Museum Press.

Porter, R. 1986. Rape—Does it have a historical meaning? In *Rape: An historical and social enquiry*, ed. S Tomaseli and R. Porter, 216–36. Oxford: Blackwell.

Poster, M. 1986. Foucault and the tyranny of Greece. In Hoy 1986a, 205–20.

Potter, D. 1999. "Introduction." In Potter and Mattingly 1999, 1–16.

———, ed. 2006. *A companion to the Roman Empire*. Oxford: Blackwell.

———. 2009. *Rome in the ancient world from Romulus to Justinian*. London: Thames and Hudson.

Potter, D., and D. J. Mattingly, eds. 1999. *Life, death and entertainment in ancient Rome*. Ann Arbor: University of Michigan Press,

Pryor, F. 2003. *Britain BC: Life in Britain and Ireland before the Romans*. London: HarperCollins.

Purcell, N. 2005a. "The ancient Mediterranean: The view from the customs house." In Harris 2005, 200–32.

———. 2005b. "Colonization and Mediterranean history." In Hurst and Owen 2005, 115–39.

Purcell, N., and P. Horden. 2005. "Four years of corruption." In Harris 2005, 348–75.

Pyatt, F. B., G. W. Barker, P. Birch, D. D. Gilbertson, J. P. Grattan, and D. J. Mattingly. 1999. "King Solomon's miners—Starvation and bioaccumulation? An environmental archaeological investigation in southern Jordan." *Ecotoxicology and Environmental Safety* 43: 305–8.

Pyatt, F. B., G. Gilmore, J. P. Grattan, C. O. Hunt, and S. McLaren. 2000. "An imperial legacy? An exploration of ancient metal mining and smelting in southern Jordan." *Journal of Archaeological Science* 27: 771–78.

Pyatt, F. B., A. J. Pyatt, C. Walker, T. Sheen, and J. P. Grattan. 2005. "Environmental toxicology: Heavy metal content of skeletons from an ancient metalliferous polluted area of Southern Jordan with particular reference to bioaccumulation and human health." *Ecotoxicology and Environmental Safety* 60: 295–300.

Rabinow, P. 1984. *The Foucault reader*. Harmondsworth, England: Penguin.

Rachet, M. 1970. *Rome et les Berbères. Un probleme militaire d'Auguste à Diocletian*. Brussels: Collection Latomus.

Rathbone, D. 1991. *Economic rationalism and rural society in third-century Egypt: The Heroninos archive and the Appianus estate*. Cambridge: Cambridge University Press.

———. 2002. "The ancient economy and Graeco-Roman Egypt." In Scheidel and Reden 2002, 155–69.

———. 2003a. "The control and exploitation of ager publicus in Italy under the Roman Republic." In *Tâches publiques et enterprise privée dans le monde romain*, ed. J. J. Aubert, 135–78. Geneva: Université de Neuchâtel.

———. 2003b. "The financing of maritime commerce in the Roman Empire." In *Credito e moneta nel mondo Romano*, ed. E. Lo Cascio, 197–229. Bari, Italy: Edipuglia.

Rawson, B., ed. 1986. *The family in ancient Rome: New perspectives*. London: Croom Helm.

Rebuffat, R. 1986. "Recherches sur le bassin du Sebou." *Comptes Rendus à l'Académie des Inscriptions et Belles Lettres* 130: 633–61 (including intervention by M. Euzennat, 652–61).

———. 1988. "Les fermiers du desert." *L'Africa romana* 5: 33–68.

Rebuffat, R., M. Lenoir, and A. Akerraz. 1986. "Plaine et montagne en Tingitane méridionale." In *Histoire et archéologie de l'Afrique du Nord, 3e Colloque International Montpellier*, 219–55. Paris: 111e congrès national des sociétés savants.

Reddé, R. 1988. *Prospections des vallées du nord de la libye (1979–1980). La région de Syrte à l'époque romaine*. Paris: Armée romaine et les provinces IV.

Reece, R. 1988. *My Roman Britain*. Cirencester, England: Cotswold Studies.

Revell, L. 2009. *Roman imperialism and local identities*. Cambridge: Cambridge University Press.

Reynolds, C. 1981. *Modes of imperialism*. Oxford: Martin Robertson.

Reynolds, L. G. 1985. *Economic growth in the third world (1850–1980)*. New Haven, CT: Yale University Press.

Rich, J. 1995. "Fear, greed and glory: The causes of Roman war-making in the middle Republic." In *War and society in the Roman world*, ed. J. Rich and G. Shipley, 36–68. London: Routledge. Reprinted in Champion 2004, 46–67.

Richardson, J. S. 1991. "Imperium Romanum: Empire and the language of power." *Journal of Roman Studies* 81: 1–9.

Richlin, A. 1983. *The garden of Priapus. Sexuality and aggression in Roman humor.* New Haven, CT: Yale University Press.

———. 2006. "Sexuality in the Roman Empire." In Potter 2006, 327–53.

Rihll, T. E. 2001. "Making money in classical Athens." In Mattingly and Salmon 2001a, 115–42.

Rodwell, W., ed. 1980. *Temples, churches and religion in Roman Britain.* 2 vols. BAR 77. Oxford: British Archaeological Reports.

Rose, P. 2006. "Divorcing ideology from Marxism and Marxism from ideology: Some problems." *Arethusa* 39: 101–36.

Rosenstein, N. 2004. *Rome at war: Farms, families, and death in the middle Republic.* Chapel Hill: University of North Carolina Press.

Rostovtzeff, M. 1957. *The social and economic history of the Roman Empire.* Oxford: Oxford University Press.

Roth, J. 2002. "The army and economy in Judaea and Palestine." In Erdkamp 2002, 375–95.

Rothenberg, B. 1999a. "Archaeo-metallurgical researches in the southern Arabah 1959–1990. Part 1." *Palestine Exploration Quarterly* 131: 68–89.

———. 1999b. "Archaeo-metallurgical researches in the southern Arabah 1959–1990. Part 2." *Palestine Exploration Quarterly* 131: 149–75.

Rousselle, A. 1988. *Porneia: On desire and the body in antiquity.* Oxford: Blackwell.

Roymans, N. 1995. "Romanization, cultural identity and the ethnic discussion: The integration of the lower Rhine populations in the Roman Empire." In Metzler et al. 1995, 47–64.

———, ed. 1996. *From the sword to the plough: Three studies on the earliest Romanisation of northern Gaul.* Amsterdam: Amsterdam University Press.

———. 2004. *Ethnic identity and imperial power: The Batavians in the early Roman Empire.* Amsterdam: Amsterdam University Press.

Runciman, W. G., ed. 2004. *Hutton and Butler: Lifting the lid on the workings of power.* Oxford: Oxford University Press.

Rush, P., ed. 1995. *Theoretical Roman Archaeology: Second Conference Proceedings.* Aldershot, England: Avebury.

Rushworth, A., 2000. "From periphery to core in late antique Mauretania." In Fincham et al. 2000, 90–103.

———. 2004. "From Arzuges to Rustamids: State formation and regional identity in the pre-Saharan zone. In *Vandals, Romans and Berbers: New perspectives on late antique Africa*, ed. A. H. Merrills, 77–98. Aldershot, England: Ashgate.

Said, E. W. 1978. *Orientalism.* Harmondsworth, England: Penguin.

———. 1986. Foucault and the imagination of power. In Hoy 1986a, 149–55.

———. 1993. *Culture and imperialism.* London: Vintage.

Salama, P. 1991. "Vues nouvelles sur l'insurrection Maurétanienne dite 'de 253': le dossier numismatique." In *L'armée et des affaires militaires*, 455–70. Paris: 113e congrès national des sociétés savants.

Salgado, S. 1993. *Workers: An archaeology of the industrial age.* New York: Aperture.

Saller, R. 2002. "Framing the debate over growth in the ancient economy." In Scheidel and Reden 2002, 251–69. Reprinted in Manning and Morris 2005, 223–38.

Salway, P. 1981. *Roman Britain*. Oxford: Oxford University Press.

Sánchez-Palencia, F. J., ed. 2000. *Las Médulas (Léon). Un paisaje cultural en la Asturia Augustana*. Ponferrada, Spain: Fundación Las Médulas.

Sánchez-Palencia, F. J., M. D. Fernández-Posse, J. Fernández Manzano, and A. Orejas, A. 1996. La *zona arqueológica de Las Médulas, León. Guiá arqueológica*. León, Spain: Fundación Banesto.

Sánchez-Palencia, F. J., and J. Mangas, eds. 2000. *El edicto del Bierzo. Augusto y el noroeste de Hispania*. Ponferrada, Spain: Fundación Las Médulas.

Sargent, A. 2002. The north-south divide revisited. *Britannia* 33: 219–26.

Sartre, M. 1993. *Inscriptions de la Jordanie, vo. 4, Petra et la Nabatène méridionale, du wadi al-Hasa au golfe de'Aqaba*. Inscriptions greques et latines de la Syrie 11. Paris: P. Geuthner.

Sarup, M. 1993. *An introductory guide to post-structuralism and postmodernism*. Hemel Hempstead, England: Harvester Wheatsheaf.

Scheidel, W., I. Morris, and R. Saller. 2007. *The Cambridge economic history of the Greco-Roman world*. Cambridge: Cambridge University Press.

Scheidel, W., and S. von Reden, eds. 2002. *The ancient economy*. Edinburgh: Edinburgh University Press.

Schörner, G., ed. 2005. *Romanisierung—Romanisation. Theoretische modelle und praktische Fall beispiele*. BAR S1427. Oxford: British Archaeological Reports.

Schultz, C. E. 2006. *Women's religious activity in the Roman Republic*. Chapel Hill: University of North Carolina Press.

Schwartz, S. 2001. *Imperialism and Jewish society 200 B.C.E. to 640 C.E.* Princeton, NJ: Princeton University Press.

Schwarz, H., and S. Ray, eds. 2000. *A companion to postcolonial studies*. Oxford: Blackwell.

Scobie, A. 1986. "Slums, sanitation and mortality in the Roman world." *Klio* 68: 399–433.

Scott, E., ed. 1993a. *A gazetteer of Roman Villas in Britain*. Leicester, England: School of Archaeological Studies.

———. 1993b. *Theoretical Roman Archaeology: First Conference Proceedings*. Aldershot, England: Avebury.

———. 2006. "Fifteen years of TRAC—Reflections on a journey." In Croxford et al. 2006: 111–15.

Scott, J. C. 1990. *Domination and the arts of resistance: Hidden transcripts*. New Haven, CT: Yale University Press.

Scott, S. 2003. "Provincial art and Roman imperialism." In Scott and Webster 2003, 1–7.

Scott. S., and J. Webster. 2003. *Roman imperialism and provincial Art*. New York: Cambridge University Press.

Schumpeter, J. 1955. *Imperialism and social classes*. Cleveland, OH: Meridian.

Segrè, C. G. 1974. *Fourth shore: The Italian colonization of Libya*. Chicago: University of Chicago Press.

Selkirk, R. 2006. Review of D. J. Mattingly, "An Imperial Possession." *Current Archaeology* 205: 30.

Sen, A. 2006. *Identity and violence: The illusion of destiny*. New York: W. W. Norton.

Shaw, B. D. 1980. "Archaeology and knowledge: The history of the North African provinces of the Roman Empire." *Florilegium* 2: 28–60.

Shaw, B. D. 1982a. "Fear and loathing: The nomad menace in Roman Africa." In Wells 1982: 29–50.

———. 1982b. "Lamasba: An ancient irrigation community." *Antiquités africaines* 18: 61–103.

———. 1983a. "Eaters of flesh, drinkers of milk: The ancient ideology of the pastoral nomad." *Ancient Society* 13–14: 5–31.

———. 1983b. "Soldiers and society: The army in Numidia." *Opus* 2: 133–60.

———. 1984. "Water and society in the ancient Maghrib: Technology, property and development." *Antiquités africaines* 20: 121–73.

———. 1987. "Autonomy and tribute: Mountain and plain in Mauretania Tingitana." *Revue de l'Occident Musulman et de la Méditerranée* 41–42: 66–89.

———. 1991. "The noblest monuments and the smallest things: Wells, walls and aqueducts in the making of Roman Africa." In *Future currents in aqueduct studies*, ed. A. T. Hodge, 63–91. Leeds, Emgland: Cairns.

———. 2000. "Rebels and outsiders." In Bowman et al. 2000, 361–403.

Sheldon, R. 1982. "Romanizzazione, acculturazione e resistenza: problemi concettuali nella storia del Nordafrica." *Dialoghi di Archeologia*, new ser., 4: 102–6.

Shipley, G., J. Vanderspoel, D. Mattingly, and L. Foxhall, eds. 2006. *Cambridge Dictionary of Classical Civilisation*. Cambridge: Cambridge University Press.

Shotter, D. 2003. *Rome and her empire*. London: Longman.

Silverberg, R. 2003. *Roma eterna*. New York: Eos.

Sirks, B. 1991. *Food for Rome: The legal structure of the transportation and processing of supplies for Rome and Constantinople*. Amsterdam: J. C. Gieben.

Sirks, B. 2007. "Supplying Rome: Safeguarding the system." In Papi 2007, 173–78.

Sivanandan, A. 1997. *When memory dies*. London: Arcadia Books.

Skinner, M. B. 2005. *Sexuality in Greek and Roman culture*. Oxford: Blackwell.

Slim, H. 1983. "Recherches préliminaires sur les amphithéâtres romains en Tunisie." *L'Africa romana* 1: 129–65.

———. 1992. "Maîtrise de l'eau en Tunisie." In Argoud et al. 1992, 513–32.

Slofstra, J. 2002. "Batavians and Romans on the lower Rhine. The Romanization of a frontier area. "*Archaeological Dialogues* 9: 16–65 (including discussants and response).

Smith, R. R. R. 1987. "The imperial reliefs from the Sebasteion at Aphrodisias." *Journal of Roman Studies* 77: 88–138.

———. 2002. "The uses of images: Visual history and ancient history." In *Classics in progress: Essays on ancient Greece and Rome*, ed. T. P. Wiseman, 59–102. Oxford: Oxford University Press.

Snowden, F. M. 1983. *Before color prejudice: The ancient view of blacks*. Cambridge, MA: Harvard University Press.

Soueif, A. 1999. *The map of love*. London: Bloomsbury.

Soyer, J. 1973. "Les cadastres anciens de la région de Saint-Donat (Algérie)." *Antiquités africaines* 7: 275–92.

———. 1976. "Les centuriations romaines en Algérie orientale." *Antiquités africaines* 10: 107–80.

———. 1983. "Centuriations et cadastres antiques: études réalisées en France et en Afrique du Nord (état au 31 dec 1980)." In *Cadastres et espace rurales: approches et realités antique*, ed. M. Clavel-Leveque, 333–39. Paris: Centre National de la Recherche Scientifique.

Spivak, G. C. 1995. "Can the subaltern speak?" In Ashcroft et al. 1995, 24–28.

Stallibrass, S., and R. Thomas, eds. 2008. *Feeding the Roman army: The archaeology of production and supply in NW Europe.* Oxford: Oxbow.

Staples, A. 1998. *From good goddess to vestal virgins. Sex and category in Roman religion.* London: Routledge.

Stein, G. J., ed. 2005. *The archaeology of colonial encounters: Comparative perspectives.* Santa Fe, NM: School of American Research Press.

Stone, D. 2004. "Problems and possibilities of comparative survey: A North African perspective." In Alcock and Cherry 2004, 132–43.

Stone, D. L. 2007. "Burial: Identity and local culture in North Africa." In Van Dommelen and Terrenato 2007, 127–44.

Stone, D. L., L. Stirling, and N. Ben Lazreg. 1998. "Suburban land-use and ceramic production around Leptiminus (Tunisia): Interim report." *Journal of Roman Archaeology* 11: 304–17.

Stone, D. L., and L. M. Stirling, eds. 2007. *Mortuary landscapes of North Africa.* Toronto: University of Toronto Press.

Stucchi, S., ed. 1976. *Cirene e la Graecia. Quaderni di archeologia della Libia* 8. Rome: L'Erma di Bretschneider.

Stucchi, S. and Luni, M. eds. 1987. *Cirene e i Libyci. Quaderni di archeologia della Libia* 12. Rome: L'Erma di Bretschneider.

Swan, P.M. 2004. *The Augustan succession: An historical commentary on Cassius Dio's Roman history Books (55–56 BC–AD 14).* Oxford: Oxford University Press.

Sweetman, R. 2007. "Roman Knossos: The nature of a globalized city." *American Journal of Archaeology* 111: 61–81.

Syme, R. 1939. *The Roman revolution.* Oxford: Oxford University Press.

———. 1979. *Roman Papers* Vol. 1. Ed. E. Badian. Oxford: Oxford University Press.

———. 1988a. *Roman Papers* 4. Ed. A.R. Birley. Oxford: Oxford University Press.

———. 1988b. "Rome and the Nations." In Syme 1988a, 62–73. Originally published in *Diogenes* 124 (1983): 33–46.

Talbert, R.J.A. 2000. *Barrington atlas of the Greek and Roman world.* Princeton, NJ: Princeton University Press.

Taylor, G. R. 1953. *Sex in history.* London: Thames and Hudson.

Temin, P. 2001. "A market economy in the Roman Empire." *Journal of Roman Studies* 91: 169–81.

Terrenato, N. 1998. "The Romanization of Italy: Global acculturation or cultural bricolage." In Forcey et al. 1998, 20–27.

Terrenato, N. 2005. "The deceptive archetype: Roman colonisation in Italy and post-colonial thought." In Hurst and Owen 2005, 59–72.

Thébert, Y. 1978. "Romanisation et déromanisation. Histoire décolonisée ou histoire inversée." *Annales ESC* 33: 64–82.

Thompson, L. A. 1989. *Romans and blacks*. Norman: University of Oklahoma Press.

Thorpe, I. J. N. 2003. "Anthropology, warfare and the origin of warfare." *World Archaeology* 35: 145–65.

Thwaite, A. 1969. *The deserts of Hesperides*. London: Seker and Warburg.

Tilly, C. 1990. *Coercion, capital and European states AD 990–1992*. Oxford: Blackwell.

Todd, M. 1999. *Roman Britain*. 3rd ed. Oxford: Blackwell.

———. 2004a. "The Claudian conquest and its consequences." In Todd 2004b, 42–59.

———. 2004b. *A companion to Roman Britain*. Oxford: Blackwell.

Tomber, R. 1996. "Provisioning the desert: Pottery supply to Mons Claudianus." In *Archaeological research in Roman Egypt*, ed. D. M. Bailey, 39–49. Supplement 19. Ann Arbor, MI: Journal of Roman Archaeology.

———. 2008. *Indo-Roman trade: From pots to pepper*. London: Duckworth.

Tomlin, R.S.O. 1988. *Tabellae Sulis: Roman inscribed tablets of tin and lead from the sacred spring at Bath* Oxford: Oxford University Committee for Archaeology. Includes reprint from Cunliffe 1988, 59–277.

———. 1993. "The inscribed lead tablets: an interim report." In Woodward and Leach 1993, 113–30.

———. 2002. "Writing to the gods in Britain." In Cooley 2002, 165–79.

———. 2003. "The girl in question: A new text from Roman London." *Britannia* 34: 41–51.

———. 2008. "Paedagogium and septizonium: Two lead curse tablets from Leicester." *Zeitschrift für Papyrologie und Epigraphik* 167: 207–18.

Toner, J. P. 1995. *Leisure and ancient Rome*. Cambridge: Polity Press.

Torelli, M. 1995. *Studies in the Romanization of Italy*. Edmonton: University of Alberta Press.

Toutain, J. 1930. *The economic life of the ancient world*. London: Kegan Paul.

Treggiari, S. 1988. "Roman marriage." In Grant and Kitzinger 1988, 1343–54.

Trexler, R. C. 1995. *Sex and conquest: Gendered violence, political order and the European conquest of the Americas*. Cambridge: Polity Press.

Trousset, P. 1977. "Nouvelles observations sur la centuriation romaine à l'est d'El Jem." *Antiquités africaines* 11: 175–207.

———. 1978. "Les bornes du Bled Segui. Nouveaux aperçus sur la centuriation romaine du sud Tunisie." *Antiquités africaines* 12: 125–78.

———. 1980a. "Signification d'une frontière: nomades et sédentaires dans la zone du 'limes' d'Afrique." In Hanson and Keppie 1980, 931–43.

———. 1980b. "Villes, campagnes et nomadisme dans l'Afrique du nord antique: representations et réalités." In *Villes et campagnes Actes de la Table Ronde*, 195–203. Aix-en-Provence, France: Maison de la Méditerranée.

———. 1982. "L'image du nomade saharien dans l'historiographie antique." *Production pastorale et sociéte* 10: 97–105.

———. 1986. "Les oasis présahariennes dans l'Antiquite: partage de l'eau et division du temps." *Antiquités africaines* 22: 161–91.

———. 1987. "De la montagne au désert: limes et maîtrise de l'eau." *Revue de l'Occident Musulman et de la Méditerranée* 41–42: 90–115.

———. 1997. Les centuriations de Tunisie et l'orientation solaire. *Antiquités africaines* 33: 95–109.

Tsafrir, Y., L. di Segni, and J. Green. 1994. *Tabula Imperii Romani. Iudaea—Palaestina*. Jerusalem: Israel Academy of Sciences and Humanities.

Van Arsdell, R. D. 1989. *Celtic coinage of Britain*. London: Spink.

Van der Veen, M. 1998. "A life of luxury in the desert? The food and fodder supply to Mons Claudianus." *Journal of Roman Archaeology* 11: 101–16.

———. 2001. "The botanical evidence." In Maxfield and Peacock 2001, 174–247.

Van der Veen, M., A. Livarda, and A. Hill. 2008. "New plant foods in Roman Britain: Dispersal and social access." *Environmental Archaeology* 13: 11–36.

Van der Veen, M., and H. Tabinor. 2007. "Food, fodder and fuel at Mons Porphyrites: The botanical evidence." In Maxfield and Peacock 2007, 83–142.

Van Dommelen, P. 1997. "Colonial constructs: Colonialism and archaeology in the Mediterranean." *World Archaeology* 28: 305–23.

———. 1998. *On colonial grounds: A comparative study of colonialism and rural settlement in first millennium BC west central Sardinia*. Leiden, Netherlands: Leiden University.

———. 2002. "Ambiguous matters: Colonialism and local identities in Punic Sardina." In Lyons and Papadopoulos 2002, 121–47.

———. 2005. "Colonial interactions and hybrid practices: Phoenician and Carthaginian settlement in the ancient Mediterranean." In Stein 2005, 109–41.

Van Dommelen, P., and N. Terrenato 2007a. *Articulating local cultures: Power and identity under the expanding Roman republic*. Supplement 63. Portsmouth, RI: Journal of Roman Archaeology.

———. 2007b. "Introduction: Local cultures and the expanding Roman Republic." In Van Dommelen and Terrenato 2007, 7–12.

Vanoyeke, V. 1990. *La prostitution en Grèce et à Rome*. Paris: Les Belles Lettres.

Vasunia, P. 2003. "Hellenism and empire: Reading Edward Said." *Parallax* 9: 88–97.

———. 2005. "Greater Rome and Greater Britain." In Goff 2005, 38–64.

Vattioni, F. 1979/1980. "Per una ricerca sull'antroponima fenicio-punica." part 1. *Studi Magrebini* 11: 43–123.

Vattioni, F. 1980. "Per una ricerca sull'antroponima fenicio-punica," part 2. *Studi Magrebini* 12: 1–82.

Vera, D. 1987. "Enfiteusi, colonato e transformazioni agrarie nell'Africa Proconsulare del tardo impero." *L'Africa romana* 4: 267–93.

———. 1988. "Terra e lavoro nell'Africa romana." *Studia Storica* 29: 967–92.

Veyne, P. 1987. "The Roman Empire." In *A history of private life*, vol. 1, *From pagan Rome to Byzantium*, ed. P. Veyne (ed.), 6–233. Cambridge, MA: Belknap Press: 6–233.

———. 1988. *Roman erotic elegy: Love, poetry and the West*. Chicago: University of Chicago Press.

Vidal, G. 1989. *Empire*. London: Grafton Books.

Vita, A. di 1964. "Il 'limes' romano di Tripolitania nella sua concretezza archaeologica e nella sua realtà storica." *Libya Antiqua* 1: 65–98.

Vita, A. di, G. di Vita-Evrard, L. Bacchielli, and R. Polidori. 1999. *Libya: The lost cities of the Roman Empire.* Cologne, Germany: Könemann.

Vita-Evrard, G. di. 1979. "Quatre inscriptions du Djebel Tarhuna: le térritoire de Lepcis Magna." *Quaderni di archeologia della Libia* 10: 67–98.

Vos, M. de 2000. *Rus Africum: terra, acqua, olio, nell'Africa settentrionale. Scavo e ricognizione nei dintorni di Dougga (Alto Tell tunisino).* Trento, Italy: University of Trento.

———. 2007." Olio d'oliva per Roman e per il mercato intraregionale." In Papi 2007, 43–58.

Vout, C. 2007. *Power and eroticism in imperial Rome.* Cambridge: Cambridge University Press.

Wacher, J. S. 1987a. *The Roman Empire.* London: J. M. Dent.

———. 1987b. *The Roman World.* 2 vols. London: Routledge.

———. 1998. *Roman Britain.* 2nd ed., Stroud, England: Sutton.

Walbank, F., A. Astin, M. Frederiksen, and R. Ogilvie. 1989. *The rise of Rome to 220 BC. Cambridge ancient history*, vol. 7, part 2. Cambridge: Cambridge University Press.

Walker, S., and A. Burnett. 1981. *The image of Augustus.* London: British Museum Press.

Wallace-Hadrill, A. 1989a. *Patronage in ancient society.* London: Routledge.

Wallace-Hadrill, A. 1989b. "Rome's cultural revolution." *Journal of Roman Studies* 79: 157–64.

———. 1994. "Public honour and private shame: The urban texture of Pompeii." In *Urban society in Roman Italy*, ed. T. J. Cornell and K. Lomas, 39–62. London: UCL Press.

———. 2007. "The creation and expression of identity: The Roman World." In Alcock and Osborne 2007, 355–80.

———. 2008. *Rome's cultural revolution.* Cambridge: Cambridge University Press.

Ward-Perkins, B. 2005. *The fall of Rome and the end of civilization.* Oxford: Oxford University Press.

Waters, M. 2000. *Globalization.* London: Routledge.

Webster, G. 1986. *The British Celts and their gods under Rome.* London: Batsford.

Webster, J. 1995a. "Interpretatio: Roman word power and the Celtic gods." *Britannia* 26: 153–61.

———. 1995b. "The just war: Graeco-Roman texts as colonial discourse." In Cottam et al. 1995, 1–10.

———. 1996a. "Ethnographic barbarity: Colonial discourse and 'Celtic warrior societies,'" In Webster and Cooper 1996, 111–23.

———. 1996b. "Roman imperialism and the 'post-imperial age.'" In Webster and Cooper 1996, 1–17.

———. 1997a. "Necessary comparisons: A post-colonial approach to religious syncretism in the Roman provinces." *World Archaeology* 28: 324–38.

———. 1997b. "A negotiated syncretism: Readings on the development of Romano-Celtic religion." In Mattingly 1997a, 165–84.

———. 1999. "At the end of the world: Druidic and other revitalization movements in post-conquest Gaul and Britain." *Britannia* 30: 1–20.

———. 2001. "Creolizing the Roman Provinces." *American Journal of Archaeology* 105: 209–25.

———. 2003. "Art as resistance and negotiation." In Scott and Webster 2003, 24–51.

———. 2005. "Archaeologies of slavery and servitude: Bringing New World perspectives to Roman Britain." *Journal of Roman Archaeology* 18: 161–79.

———. 2007. "Linking with a wider world: Rome and 'barbarians.'" In Alcock and Osborne 2007, 401–24.

———. 2008. "Less beloved: Roman archaeology, slavery and the failure to compare." *Archaeological Dialogues* 15: 124–49 (with discussants' comments and response).

Webster, J., and N. Cooper, eds. 1996. *Roman imperialism: Post-colonial perspectives*. Leicester, England: School of Archaeological Studies, University of Leicester.

Weisgerber, G. 1989. "Montanarchäologie. Grundzüge einer systematischen Bergbaukunde für Vor- und Frühgeschichte und Antike." *Der Anschnitt* 7: 79–98.

———. 1996. "Montanarchäologie mehr als Technikgeschichte: Das Beispiel Fenan (Jordanien)." *Schriftenreihe Georg-Agricola-Gesellschaft* 20: 19–34.

———. 2003. "Spatial organisation of mining and smelting at Feinan, Jordan: Mining archaeology beyond the history of technology." In *Mining and metal production through the ages*, ed. P. Cradock and J. Lang, 76–89. London: British Museum Press.

Wells, C. M. 1972. *The German policy of Augustus: An examination of the archaeological evidence*. Oxford: Clarendon Press.

———, ed. 1982. *Roman Africa/L'Afrique Romaine: The 1980 Vanier lectures*, Ottowa, ON: University of Ottowa.

———. 1992. *The Roman Empire*. 2nd ed. London: Fontana.

———. 1996. "Profuit invitis te dominante capi: Social and economic considerations on the Roman frontiers." *Journal of Roman Archaeology* 9: 436–46.

Wells, P. 1999. *The barbarians speak: How the conquered peoples shaped Roman Europe*. Princeton, NJ: Princeton University Press.

———. 2001. *Beyond Celts, Germans and Scythians: Archaeology and identity in Iron Age Europe*. London: Duckworth.

———. 2003. *The battle that stopped Rome*. New York: W. W. Norton.

———. 2008. *Image and response in early Europe*. London: Duckworth.

Wesson, R. G. 1967. *The imperial order*. Berkeley and Los Angeles: University of California Press.

Wheeler, M. 1955. *Still digging: Interleaves from an antiquary's notebook*. London: Michael Joseph.

White, R. 1991. *The middle ground: Indians, empires and republics in the Great Lakes Region 1650–1815*. Cambridge: Cambridge University Press.

Whitehead, N. 1992. "Tribes make states and states make tribes: Warfare and the creation of colonial tribes and states in northeastern South America." In Ferguson and Whitehead 1992, 127–50.

Whitmarsh, T. 2001. *Greek literature and the Roman Empire: The politics of imitation*. Oxford: Oxford University Press.

Whittaker, C. R. 1978a. "Land and labour in North Africa." *Klio* 60: 331–62.

———. 1978b. "M. Benabou, 'La résistance africaine à la romanisation.'" *Journal of Roman Studies* 68: 190–92.

———. 1980. "Non-slave labour in three Roman provinces." In *Non-slave labour in the Greco-Roman world*, ed. P. Garnsey (ed.), 73–99. Cambridge: Cambridge Philological Society.

———. 1994. *Frontiers of the Roman Empire: A social and economic study*. Baltimore: Johns Hopkins University Press.

———. 1995. "Integration in the Roman west: The model of Africa." In Metzler et al. 1995, 19–32.

———. 1997. "Imperialism and culture: The Roman initiative." In Mattingly 1997a, 143–63.

———. 2002. "Supplying the army: Evidence from Vindolanda." In Erdkamp 2002, 204–34.

———. 2004a. *Rome and its frontiers: The dynamics of empire*. London: Routledge.

———. 2004b. "Sex on the frontiers." In Whittaker 2004a, 115–43.

Wickham, C. 2005. *Framing the Early Middle Ages: Europe and the Mediterranean, 400–800*. Oxford: Oxford University Press.

Wightman, E. M. 1985. *Gallia Belgica*. London: Batsford.

Wilkinson, P. 2000. *What the Romans did for us*. London: Pan Macmillan.

Willems, W. 1984. "Romans and Batavians: Regional study in the Dutch eastern river area, II." *Berichten van de Rijksdienst voor het Oudheidkundig Bodemonderzoek* 32: 39–331.

Williams, D. 1999. *Romans and barbarians: Four views from the empire's edge, first century AD*. New York: St. Martins Press.

Williams, P., and L. Chrisman, eds. 1993. *Colonial discourse and post-colonial theory: A reader*. Hemel Hempstead, England: Harvester-Wheatsheaf.

Willies, L. 1991. "Ancient copper mining at Wadi Aram, Israel: An archaeological survey." *Bull Peak District Mines Historical Society* 11: 109–38.

Willis, S. 2005. "Samian pottery, a resource for the study of Roman Britain and beyond: The results of the English Heritage funded Samian Project." *Internet Archaeology* 17. Retrieved 16 November 2009 from http://intarch.ac.uk/journal/issue17/1/1.1.html.

Wilson, A. I. 2002. "Machines, power and the ancient economy." *Journal of Roman Studies* 92: 1–32.

———. 2006. "Urban production in the Roman world: The view from North Africa." *Papers of the British School at Rome* 70: 231–73.

——— 2007. "The metal supply of the Roman Empire." In Papi 2007, 109–20.

Wilson, P. 2002. *Cataractonium: Roman Catterick and its hinterland. Excavations and research 1958–1997*. 2 vols. CBA Research Report 128–29. York, England: Council for British Archaeology.

Winkler, J. J. 1990. *The constraints of desire*. London: Routledge

Wiseman, P. 1985. *Catullus and his world: A reappraisal*. Cambridge: Cambridge University Press.

Witcher, R. 2000. "Globalisation and Roman imperialism: Perspectives on identities in Roman Italy." In *The emergence of state identities in Italy in the first millennium BC*, ed. E. Herring and K. Lomas, 213–25. London: Accordia.

Wood, M., and F. Queiroga, eds. 1992. *Current research on the Romanization of the Western Provinces*. BAR S575. Oxford: British Archaeological Reports.

Woodward, A. 1992. *Shrines and sacrifices*. London: Batsford.

Woodward, A., and Leach, P. 1993. *The Uley Shrines: Excavation of a ritual complex on West Hill, Uley, Gloucestershire: 1977–9*. London: English Heritage.

Woolf, G. 1990. "World systems analysis and the Roman Empire." *Journal of Roman Archaeology* 3: 44–58.

———. 1992a. "Imperialism, empire and the integration of the Roman economy." *World Archaeology* 23: 283–93.

———. 1992b. "The unity and diversity of Romanization." *Journal of Roman Archaeology* 5: 349–52.

———. 1994. "Becoming Roman, staying Greek: Culture, identity and the civilizing process in the Roman east." *Proceedings of the Cambridge Philological Society* 40: 116–43.

———. 1995. "Romans as civilizers: The ideological pre-conditions of Romanization." In Metzler et al. 1995, 9–18.

———. 1997. "Beyond Romans and natives." *World Archaeology* 28: 339–50.

———. 1998. *Becoming Roman: The origins of provincial administration in Gaul*. Cambridge: Cambridge University Press.

———. 2001. "Inventing empire in ancient Rome." In Alcock et al. 2001, 3311–22.

———. 2002a. "Afterword: How the Latin west was won." In Cooley 2002, 181–88.

———. 2002b. "Generations of aristocracy: Continuities and discontinuities in the societies of interior Gaul." *Archaeological Dialogues* 9: 2–16, 39–65 (including discussants' comments and response).

———, ed. 2004a. *The Cambridge illustrated history of the Roman world*. Cambridge: Cambridge University Press.

———. 2004b. "Cultural change in Roman antiquity: Observations on agency." *Kodai* 13–14: 157–67.

———. 2004c. "The present state and future scope of Roman archaeology: A comment." *American Journal of Archaeology* 108: 417–28.

Woolman, D. 1969. *The rebels in the Rif*. Stanford, CA: Stanford University Press.

Yacono, X. 1955. *La colonisation des plaines du Chelif*. Algiers: Imbert.

Ying, L. 2004. "Ruler of the treasure country: The image of the Roman Empire in Chinese society from the first to the fourth century AD." *Latomus* 63: 327–39.

York, P. 2005. *Dictators' homes: Lifestyles of the world's most colourful despots*. London: Grove Atlantic.

Young, R. J. C. 1995. *Colonial desire: Hybridity in theory, culture and race*. London: Routledge.

Zanker, P. 1988. *The power of images in the age of Augustus*. Trans. A. Shapiro. Ann Arbor: University of Michigan Press.

Zarinebaf, F., J. Bennet, and J. L. Davies. 2005. *A historical and economic geography of Ottoman Greece: The south-western Morea in the eighteenth century.* Athens: American School of Classical Studies.

Zoll, A. 1995a. "Patterns of worship in Roman Britain: Double named deities in context." In Cottam et al. 1995, 32–44.

———. 1995b. "A view through inscriptions: The epigraphic evidence for religion at Hadrian's Wall." In Metzler et al. 1995, 129–37.

INDEX

Achaia (Greece): contrasting landscapes of Roman Africa and, 146, 162–66; slow recovery from Roman conquest by, 164–66; violent passage of Roman armies in, 162–63

Acholla, 149

Adminius, 84, 85, 91, 92, 93

adultery: as colonial sexual exploitation, 104–5, 109, 114–18; Latin erotic literature on, 110; law in case of, 112; moral backlash and purity campaigns against, 113–14; Roman laws protecting married women, 109. *See also* marriages

Aelius Aristides, 26

Aeneid (Virgil), 15, 17

Africa, Roman: Africa Proconsularis, 56, 151–52; Africa Vetus, 147, 149; Benabou's cultural resistance thesis on, 20, 60–63; centuriation and land allotments in, 147, 149–51; comparing Roman Achaia and, 146, 162–66; current epigraphical studies in, 47, 237; desirability of single post-colonial perspective on, 71–72; discrepant identity in communities, xxi, 236–45; economic growth in, 146–47; emperor's estates in, 151–52; field surveys of, xxi, 66, 155–59, 160, 164, 166; French and Italian colonialism emulating, 54–57; French and Italian self-represented as inheritors of, 43, 45–53f; Garamantian people of Libyan Sahara, 63–65; impact of archaeology and history on scholarship of, 63–68; Italian restoration of monuments of, 50–53f; landscape of imperialism in, 147–66; landscape of resistance in, 159–62; Laroui's influence on postcolonial study of, 59–60; maps of, 148f, 160f, 161f; modern imperial reinforcement of inferiority of indigenous peoples of, 47–51; parallels of resistance to France and, 20, 57–59; perspectives on regaining momentum of scholarship on, 68–72; postcolonial study of Maghrebian archaeology and, 43–72; as Roman food supply resource, 152, 159; Roman hydraulic systems of, 56–57; Romanization model of, 65–68; tenurial systems used in, 153–55. *See also* North Africa; Tripolitania (province)

agency, 216–17

Agricola, 33

agriculture: imperial policy on African food exports, 159; olive oil food exports, 159; Roman Africa as source of food exports, 152; shard density indications on land productivity and pollution, 184f–85; sharecropping tenancy arrangements, 153–55

Albertini Tablets, 154, 164, 165f, 166

Alcock, Susan, xx, 164

Algeria: French army's archaeological exploration of, 55–56; French economic exploitation of, 128; French management of water resources in, 56–57; hill villages (hillforts) in, 160f; independence from French by, 44, 47; native resistance in, 58; present-day Islamic fundamentalism impacting, 67–68

"America" and Amerigo Vespucci, 100f

Ammianus Marcellinus, 275–76

Amminius (or Adminius), 84, 85, 91, 92, 93

Ammon (or Jupiter Hammon) cult, 266

anal intercourse (*pedicatio*), 107

ancestor worship, 263–67

annexation: decline of Cunobelin leading to Roman, 84–92; of Nabataean kingdom by Roman Empire, 177, 181, 183, 185; process of Roman, 84–92

Annobal Tapapius Rufus, 239f, 240

Apuleius trial (AD 158), 114, 241

archaeological field surveys: Mauretania Caesariensis, 155–56; Mauretania Tingitana, 156; Tuniso-Danish Africa

GPSR Authorized Representative: Easy Access System Europe - Mustamäe tee
50, 10621 Tallinn, Estonia, gpsr.requests@easproject.com

www.ingramcontent.com/pod-product-compliance
Lightning Source LLC
Chambersburg PA
CBHW030729280326
41926CB00086B/586